Microsoft Visual J++ Sourcebook

Jay Cross

and

Al Saganich

WILEY COMPUTER PUBLISHING

John Wiley & Sons, Inc.
New York • Chichester • Weinheim • Brisbane • Singapore • Toronto

Executive Publisher: Katherine Schowalter
Editor: Robert M. Elliott
Managing Editor: Mark Hayden
Electronic Products, Associate Editor: Michael Green
Text Design & Composition: Publishers' Design and Production Services, Inc.

Designations used by companies to distinguish their products are often claimed as trademarks. In all instances where John Wiley & Sons, Inc., is aware of a claim, the product names appear in initial capital or ALL CAPITAL LETTERS. Readers, however, should contact the appropriate companies for more complete information regarding trademarks and registration.

This text is printed on acid-free paper.

This publication is designed to provide accurate and authoritative information in regard to the subject matter covered. It is sold with the understanding that the publisher is not engaged in rendering legal, accounting, or other professional service. If legal advice or other expert assistance is required, the services of a competent professional person should be sought.

Library of Congress Cataloging-in-Publication Data:

Cross, Jay
    Microsoft Visual J++ sourcebook / Jay Cross and Al Saganich.
      p.   cm.
    Includes Index.
    ISBN 0-471-17840-3 (paper/CD-ROM : alk. paper)
    1. Java (Computer program language)   2. Microsoft Visual J++.
I. Saganich, Albert J. II. Title.
QA76.73.J38C76 1997
005.13′3—dc21   96-29888
                                              CIP

Printed in the United States of America

10 9 8 7 6 5 4 3 2 1

Contents

Introduction to *Microsoft Visual J++ Sourcebook*   ix

PART I   JAVA ESSENTIALS

Chapter 1   Object-Oriented Programming Concepts   3
Object Oriented Programming   3
What's It Good For?   7
Object-Based Programming   9
Inheritance   11
Encapsulation   12
Polymorphism   13

Chapter 2   Java and the Java Virtual Machine   14
Java Is Compiled   18
Java Is Interpreted   25
Java Verifies Code before Running It   27
Java Checks Pointers at Run-time   28
Java Picks Up after Itself   30

Chapter 3   Java Keywords and Other Tokens   32
Unicode Characters   33
Tokens   36

Chapter 4   Java Expressions and Statements   52
Primitive Types, Arrays, and References   52

	Java Expressions	55
	Java Statements	58
Chapter 5	**Java Classes, Objects, and Interfaces**	**72**
	Classes and Objects	73
	Fields	78
	Methods	80
	Interfaces	86
	Packages	87
Chapter 6	**Threads in Java**	**89**
	The Thread Class in Detail	91
	The Runnable Interface	92
	Interthread Communication	93
	Using synchronized	93
	Using wait and notify	95
	ThreadGroups	97
	POSIX Threads	97
Chapter 7	**The java.lang Package**	**99**
	Object Class	102
	String Classes	103
	Wrapper Classes	105
	Math Class	108
	System-Related Classes	109
Chapter 8	**Exceptions in Java**	**113**
	Try-Catch-Finally in Detail	115
	The Throwable Class	116
	Throw and Throws Keywords	116
	All the Standard Exceptions	118
Chapter 9	**Java Applets & the java.applet Package**	**122**
	The Difference between Java Applets and Java Applications	124
	The Applet Class	125
	The HTML APPLET Tag	127
	Constructing an Applet in an Application	128
	The AppletContext Interface	130
	The AudioClip Interface	131
Chapter 10	**The Java Abstract Window Toolkit (java.awt)**	**133**
	Graphics, Fonts, and Colors	139
	Containers, Panels, and Components	144
	Events and Observables	156
	Menus	160
	Layout Managers	163

Images   169
The java.awt.peer Package   172

Chapter 11   The java.io Package   174

Standard Input and Standard Output   176
Files and File Descriptors   177
Random Access Files   180
Byte Arrays and String Buffers   181
Pipes and Filters   183
The StreamTokenizer   184

Chapter 12   The java.uatil Package   186

Enumerations   187
Dates   189
Hash Tables   190
Vectors and Stacks   191
BitSet   192
The StringTokenizer   192
Random Numbers   193
Observables   194

Chapter 13   The java.net Package   197

InetAddresses   199
URL Utilities   200
Datagrams   202
Sockets and ServerSockets   205
Using java.net and java.io together   206

Chapter 14   Native Code   210

Native Methods   212
Better Alternatives to Native Methods   212
Java's javah Utility   216

PART II   LEARNING VISUAL J++

Chapter 15   The Visual J++ Developers Studio and the Build Process   219

A Comparison of the Windows and Java Programming Models   219
Introducing Visual J++ Workbench   224
Features of the Visual J++ Developers Studio   226

Chapter 16   Introducing the Visual J++ Developers Studio   232

Creating a Project with AppWizard   232

Chapter 17   The Java AppWizard Explained   243

What AppWizard Does for You   243
Ch17Ex1.html   244

Ch17Ex1.java   245
A Few Final Notes   255
Standalone Application Support   255

Chapter 18   Introducing the Visual J++ Resource Editors   258

The Resource Editors   258
The Graphics Editor   259
The Dialog Editor   264
The Menu Editor   265
String Tables   267
Resource Property Sheets   267
Resource Templates   268
Creating Resources   268

Chapter 19   The Visual J++ Workspace   272

The ClassView Pane   273
The FileView Pane   279
Projects and Subprojects   280

Chapter 20   Introducing the Visual J++ Debugger   289

Debugger Basics   289
The Debugger Interface   290

Chapter 21   More Debugging Technique   309

Debugging Compiler Errors   309
Debugging a Sample Application   310
Advanced Debugger Features   312
The Disassembly Window   320

Chapter 22   The Visual J++ Graphics Editor   322

The Graphics Editor Interface   322
The Graphics Toolbar   324
The Color Palette   333
The Image Menu   336
The Status Bar   338
Tips and Tricks   338

Chapter 23   The Visual J++ Dialog and Menu Editors   343

The Dialog Editor Interface   344
The Menu Editor Interface   358
Resource Templates Reviewed   362

Chapter 24   The Visual J++ Java Resource Wizard   364

The Java Resource Wizard   365
Integrating Generated Dialogs   367
Integrating Generated Menus   369
Simulating Mnemonic Keys   369

Chapter 25   **The Visual J++ Source Editor**   **378**

Basic File Operations   378
Basic Editing Operations   384
Using Multiple Source Windows   393
Tips and Tricks   395

Chapter 26   **Additional Visual J++ Tools**   **400**

Jview.exe Reference   400
JVC.exe Reference   403
Windiff.exe Reference   407
Zoomin.exe Reference   410

PART III   **ADVANCED TOPICS**

Chapter 27   **Techniques for Animation**   **415**

An Overview of Animation   415
Creating a Minimal Animation with the Applet Wizard   416
Issues Pertaining to Performance   425
Double Buffering   428
Use of the ClipRect Method   429
Eliminating Flicker   430
Arrays of Pixels   430

Chapter 28   **Java, COM and ActiveX**   **433**

Introduction   433
The Component Object Model   434
The Basics of ActiveX   435
Using ActiveX from Java   438
Exercises   451

Chapter 29   **Advanced Topics in COM and Scripting**   **452**

Introduction   452
Scripting in Depth   452
Data Access Objects   461
Trusted Versus Untrusted Classes   467
Creating Signed Cabinet Files   468
Conclusion   474
Exercises   475

Chapter 30   **The Visual J++ Database Wizard**   **476**

An Overview of the Database Wizard   476
A Sample Database   478
Creating a Database Applet with DAO   479
Understanding the Generated Code   486
Modifying the Code   489

Building an RDO Applet   489
Summary   489

Chapter 31 **Using the Java ActiveX Wizard**   **491**
Introduction   491

Appendix A **Tips of the Day**   **501**

Appendix B **Compiler Errors**   **512**

Glossary of Terms   **527**

Index   **531**

What's on the CD-ROM   **539**

Introduction to *Microsoft Visual J++ Sourcebook*

This book is a complete desk-side companion to Java and Microsoft Visual J++. It's designed to be the only book that you'll need to learn how to use Visual J++; it also provides a complete guide to Java essentials that you'll want to understand to get the most from Visual J++.

In addition to being a comprehensive tutorial on Java and Visual J++, *Microsoft Visual J++ Sourcebook* is a book you'll find useful for as long as you use Visual J++—a quick reference when you need to refresh yourself on the how-to's of both Java and J++. Whether you're a Java pro who wants to start using J++ to develop applications now, or a novice just learning about Java and Visual J++, this book's for you.

So why has Java become so quickly adopted? Among the many reasons:

- Java is easier to write and maintain than C++, but it has (very nearly) all of the capabilities of C++, and more. Thus all of the efforts to sell C++'s object-oriented benefits are applied to Java, and the world of C++ programmer are well positioned to learn it quickly.
- Java applets were for a while the only way to make animated Web pages. This reason is perhaps shallow, and not enduring, but it definitely got Java started in a big way.
- Java applications may be run without recompilation on any machine that supports Java.
- Java applications may be downloaded piecemeal from an Internet or intranet server as needed. A Java application may be enormous,

but it comes in chunks typically between one and ten kbytes in length, making for easy use on networks.

- Java has many class libraries that make it especially well-suited for use on networks and the World Wide Web in particular. As the information industry switched to this technology, java was in the right place at the right time.
- Sun Microsystems has a generally good reputation, and provided Java as a FREE easy-to-install download to anyone.
- Many university Computer Science and Engineering departments (even high schools) are now teaching Java as the first computer language for their students.

We believe that Java is fast becoming a general full-purpose programming language with which many, perhaps most, applications will be written.

WHY VISUAL J++

Visual J++ is a powerful integrated development environment for Java. It promises to become even better as time goes by—for example, with the addition of more and better wizards for creating specific kinds of applications. Among Visual J++'s features is one of the fastest Java compilers around. Also we expect new tools will be developed to better use technologies which permit objects in separate processes to communicate with each other, such as DCOM, CORBA, RMI, and JDBC. And as the new 'enterprise' packages from Sun become available, it is certain that Visual J++ will be updated to make use of them.

HOW THIS BOOK IS ORGANIZED

We have not assumed that you have done much with object-oriented programming in the past, or that you know the Java language and the standard packages of classes that come with it. So for those of you who are learning Java or who simply want a refresher course, start with Part I of this book. Part I provides a complete guide to the essential features of Java that you'll need to understand in order to get the most from Visual J++. If you're already a Java pro, you might want to skim Part I—it's loaded with tips and techniques you may not have seen elsewhere. But then, it's on to Part II—the J++ tutorial.

Part II provides a step-by-step guide to learning Visual J++. It includes lots of easy-to-follow examples and plenty of screen shots that will help keep you on the right track.

Part III of this book covers more advanced uses of both Java and Visual J++.

The CD-ROM includes a variety of resources that will help you be more productive in using Visual J++. These include lists of keyboard shortcuts (for you "mouse-aphobes"), and lists of all the methods and attributers of all of the classes and interfaces that are provided as part of the standard packages that come with Java and Visual J++. Appendix C provides a detailed listing of the contents of the CD and how to access them: But here's a quick overview:

- Source code for examples in the text.
- Solutions to the exercises at the end of each chapter.
- Handy reference material to print out and keep by your desk.
- Sun's Java 1.02 Java Developers Kit, including example code.
- Other handy tools and information gleaned from the Net.

Part I, Java Essentials

This part of the book has 14 chapters which teach the use of the Java language and its standard packages of classes, with some short hands-on examples presented from the viewpoint of a Visual J++ user. The first of these examples walks through the steps to create the example as a project, without going into the depth given in Part II of this book.

Chapter 1 presents object-oriented concepts which are used by the Java language. If you have never used an object-oriented programming language, you must read this chapter. Java is very nearly a purely object-oriented language. If the OO buzz-words have no real meaning for you, you will get lost in the rest of this book. Be of good cheer, the concepts are simple!

Chapter 2 discusses the environment that Java programs all run in, and various details of the Java Virtual Machine, including a brief overview of security.

Chapters 3, 4, and 5 teach the elements of the Java language itself, with the exception of a few slightly more advanced concepts which are reserved for later chapters. Chapter 3 covers keywords and tokens. Chapter 4 covers the expressions and statements that these keywords and tokens build. Chapter 5 deals with the definition of classes and interfaces.

Chapter 6 covers the use of threads (of execution) in Java, which in part depend on the java.lang package.

Chapter 7 covers most of the java.lang package, which is a collection of classes and interfaces which are fairly closely tied to the language itself.

Chapter 8 covers Java's exception handling capability. (This is a way to deal with errors as they occur during program execution.)

Chapters 9 through 13 cover the standard packages that come with Java. Chapter 9 covers the applet package that lets you build components to be incorporated into Web pages. Chapter 10 deals with the Abstract Window Toolkit (AWT). Chapter 11 covers input, output, and the various types of streams that may be used. Chapter 12 covers the utility package which gives us some common data structures, random numbers, dates, and other handy classes. Chapter 13 covers the network package which gives us support for sockets, URLs, and related items.

Finally Chapter 14 examines basic ways to connect Java code to libraries written in the C or C++ languages. It also includes an unsubtle effort to dissuade you from doing this!

Part II, Learning Visual J++

This major part of the book covers the use of Visual J++. Twelve chapters walk you through the use of the most important features of this great product.

Chapter 15 covers the basic building blocks of how the Studio works, and how you can build a very simple class with it.

Chapter 16 gives a more detailed look at the Studio and what its components do.

Chapter 17 explains the use of the Applet Wizard that comes with Visual J++.

Chapter 18 covers the many diverse ways that the Resource Wizard may be employed.

Chapter 19 takes a close look at the features of the Visual J++ workspace.

Chapters 20 and 21 cover the use of the Visual J++ debugger, with many examples showing good use of this facility to locate many common types of problems, including issues pertaining to multithreaded applications and applets.

Chapter 22 through 25 deal with the various editors and the Resource Wizard. Chapter 22 covers the Graphics Editor, Chapter 23 covers the Dialog and Menu Editor. Chapter 24 covers the Java Resource Wizard, and Chapter 25 covers the Source Code Editor.

Finally, Chapter 26 takes a shorter look at some additional tools provided by Visual J++.

Part III Advanced Topics

Special topics in Java are springing up all the time. It would be impossible to put them all into a single volume, and even so, it would be out of date by press time. This section covers some of the most frequently asked for or needed special topics.

Chapter 27 covers animation, especially in applets.

Chapter 28 gives an overview with some short examples of the rather complicated subject of building Java applications that connect to ActiveX components.

Chapter 29 looks at some advanced topics using Java with COM, and with the scripting languages found in most browsers—Javascript and VBScript.

Chapter 30 examines the use of the Database Wizard, with a Microsoft Access example.

Chapter 31 details the use of the ActiveX Wizard, in all it's detail, following a few examples.

TIPS, NOTES, & WARNINGS

In addition to its fine prose style code fragments, tables, and screen shots, this book has a number of boxed Tips, Notes, and Warnings. Skip these if you like, but you may find some of the most useful material is placed in these boxes—they highlight important ideas and hard-won experiences that we think you will benefit from.

ACKNOWLEDGMENTS

Thanks to all who have helped me (wittingly or otherwise) in this endeavor. Thanks to Steve Gurzler who helped hone my writing style, and Jeff Hatalsky whose stern hand guided my approach to presentation issues, and to Tricia Postle who refreshed my awareness of certain poetic virtues.

Thanks to Tod Loofbourrow who first told me to learn about Java, to Alex Newman of the Sun User Group and Java-SIGs who got me started down the path to this kind of literature, to Bob Elliott and Brian Calandra of Wiley & Sons, who helped keep a practical view of what this project should be.

Thanks to Jack Page of the Internet Academy and John Petronio of Petronio Technologies, for their insights into how to teach Java and related subjects to broad and diverse groups of people. John, in particular, was nice enough to let me use some materials I created for his courses in this book. Thanks too to the many students who have given specific suggestions as to what is missing from the various Java books in the world, especially the many brilliant people at Digital Equipment Corporation, including Dave Butenhof for his notes about POSIX threads, and others students too numerous to name.

Thanks to Aldo Castaneda et al. at Software Tool and Die for their help with commercial issues surrounding CGI, and many other considerations. Thanks to Andy Goren at TVObjects, and Adam Schwartz at Crescent Software for some lengthy discussions about ActiveX components and their place in this world. Thanks to Lisa Friendly, and many other people at Sun and JavaSoft, who have been so generous and open with their Java-related material. Many thanks to Frank Martinez et al. at Microsoft.

Thanks especially to Al Saganich, whose tireless efforts have produced a very useful tutorial, to Bob McCown whose illustrations and patience with my infrequent communications have advanced our cause immeasurably, and to Ben Sweet who created the solutions to many of the exercises on the CD-ROM.

Finally, the known world is full of people who have lent me inspiration and emotional support, and been patient with me during this effort, and first by far among them are my wife Denise, and two children, Andy and Piper. Without their constant love and occasional distractions, I would certainly not have had the will to begin.

Jay Cross, November 1996

I'd like to thank my wife Becky and my children, AJ and Jackie, for all their support during those long nights of writing, rewriting and editing.

I'd like to thank my martial Arts instructors Sifu Henrick Hamberg and Sifu Peter Stoddard who have taught me many things, not the least of which is determination.

I'd also like to thank all my special friends who helped me to retain my focus and reminded me not to be too serious all the time.

And lastly, I'd like to thank Jay Cross, without whom I would never have been involved with this book in the first place. Thanks to all!

Al Saganich, November 1996

Important Notice:

The content of this book is based on the third release candidate of Microsoft Visual J++ 1.1. There may have been changes made to the product since this release. Therefore, screen shots and examples may not be identical to the final product.

For current information about Microsoft Visual J++, you should visit http://www.microsoft.com/visualj

PART I

Java Essentials

CHAPTER 1

Object-Oriented Programming Concepts

In this chapter we cover the following topics:

- **Object-Oriented Programming**
- **What's it Good For?**
- **Object Based Programming**
- **Inheritance**
- **Encapsulation**
- **Polymorphism**

OBJECT-ORIENTED PROGRAMMING

If you have never written software before, object-oriented programming (sometimes called OOP) will be about as easy to learn as procedural programming (Figure 1.1). Since many of us regard OOP as a better way, and the way of the future, it is probably what you should learn. Since you are reading this book, you are probably committed to learning Visual J++, and so the choice is already made. This chapter won't make you an expert, but you'll know enough to quickly learn Visual J++.

Java is an object-oriented programming language. If you already use an object-oriented programming language such as Java, C++, Smalltalk, and the like, you may save yourself some time and skip ahead.

Our goal is for you to know enough about object-oriented programming so that you can comfortably use Visual J++. If you go to your local computer book store, you will find shelves upon shelves of tomes about

Figure 1.1   It's easy to connect object modules. They are self-contained, and communicate with methods and messages.

object-oriented programming, object-oriented design methodologies, object-oriented programming languages, object-based fourth generation languages, and more. We cannot possibly cover the topics in this area enough for you to be an expert after reading this book, but you'll know what you need for getting started, and maybe enough to hold up your end of a conversation at the health club.

TIP

Object-Oriented Programming Is Not Difficult

Some people are afraid of object-oriented programming and will tell you that it is difficult. They are probably talking about C++. The concepts behind object-oriented programming are quite simple and easy to implement. Many people find C++ difficult because there are many things that they have to keep track of while creating an application. It is difficult because there are many ways to express some idea in C++, and it is never clear which way is best. It is also difficult because there are many subtle errors that can be made and not be found until long after they have done their damage. None of these are because OOP is difficult. As noted in the text, OOP is easy.

Usually you can recognize OOP by the buzzwords **inheritance**, **encapsulation**, and **polymorphism**. We will discuss these in more detail below. Another sure way to know you are using object-oriented technology is when you see the keywords **class** or **object**, or the buzzwords **method** or **constructor**.

Think of a **class** as an abstract concept, and an **object** as a particular instance of that class. In large human terms, you can think of the word *chair* as being a **class** identifier for any of that group of objects that people sit on. The word *recliner* is a **class** identifier for a subset of the *chair* class. (By subset or subclass we mean that we have specified more details about what kind of chair it is, and what kinds of things it does.) The actual physical chair that you are sitting in (presuming you are sitting while you read this) is an **object**.

It is tempting to continue anthropomorphizing these computer-related concepts, but you must also see the concepts in practical terms related to Java and Visual J++.

In computer terms, you can think of an **object** as being like a data record on a disk, tape, or database with some functions available for getting or changing that data or perhaps even copying or deleting it. Imagine the **class** as the record definition, or in a database context as the Table definition, including triggers. We refer to those functions as **methods** of that **class** or **object**.

NOTE

You Don't Need an Object to Have a Class

This was one of the core disagreements between Aristotle and Plato (Figure 1.2). We are unprepared to say Plato was wrong, but with today's computers, you do not need to have an object to have a class (even a useful class), but you do need a class to have an object.

In Java, the math library functions are all methods of the Math Class, but you do not need to create a math object to use them. Using the keyword **static** in a **method** declaration says that you don't need an object created to use this method. All of the methods of the **java.lang.Math** class are **static**. These are methods such as **sin( )**, **cos( )**, **exp( )**, and the like. The exhaustive list appears in an appendix on the CD-ROM, and is also available from Visual J++'s InfoView utility.

Figure 1.2   The class *chair* does not need a universal archetype to exist.

An Example

One of the most frequently used classes in Java Language Package is a class called String. It contains a string of characters, and quite a few ways of getting information about that string. These ways are the above-mentioned **methods**. The **methods** for a **String** object are numerous and some of the following are among them:

- Seven different **constructors** (with different input parameters)
- Nine different static **valueOf** methods, which return strings representing the values of the input parameters (you don't need a String object to call these)
- A **charAt** method that returns the character at a given position

- Methods to concatenate strings
- Methods to find the length of a string
- Methods to get substrings
- Methods to find the position of a substring within a string
- Methods to compare strings and parts of strings
- Methods to trim away white space
- Methods to convert from upper to lower or vice versa

Essentially, anything you could want to do with a string of characters has been supplied as part of the class definition. If you are working with a string, you don't have to go far or load any special library to use it.

Not every class has to be as well fleshed out as the String class. It is used especially frequently and thus needs to be thorough. More special-purpose classes might have a smaller number of more complex methods.

WHAT'S IT GOOD FOR?

Object-oriented programming has been popularized for several sterling properties that it offers. The most frequently cited are reusability, high maintainability, scalability, and suitability for event-driven applications such as Graphic User Interfaces (GUIs). Let's briefly look at each of these

Reusability

When you have a working class file, particularly with Java (the language behind Visual J++), the class can be used in any Java application you build. You don't need to link it in, you simply need to invoke its constructor at run-time. If it works in one place, it'll pretty much work anywhere, anytime, without rewriting or a lot of complicated planning.

Maintainability

When non-object-oriented applications get large, they get *brittle*. Of course, software is really just information and doesn't actually develop such tactile properties as brittleness, but it does start to break badly with only minor changes. The reasons for this are manifold. Among them are that large applications have many programmers, with different ways of thinking about what is supposed to happen inside the applications no one person has a precise vision of the whole thing. Large applications also take a long time to create, and the authors will forget certain subtle details about implementation (even with good documentation). Yet another reason is that often an application's use will expand wildly outside the realm for which it was originally created. It develops a thick patchwork of new skin and skeletal structures to add new unexpected features, and no one can remember how the pieces fit. Finally, and perhaps most importantly, large applications test the very limits of both the system on which they were built and maintained and also the target system. Often there are some serious compromises made, which result in a very complicated system.

Large Java applications are pieced together from relatively small and self-contained class definitions files. Each one stands alone. They can be compiled on small systems, easily kept compatible with each other, easily documented, and do not need some convoluted architecture to operate in a moderate-sized system.

Scalability

As noted above, one reason that object-oriented applications are maintainable is that they are easily scalable. This is especially true for Java. Visual Basic is object based, but it is not all that scalable. At some point you run out of some name space resource, or something else. A Java application can almost grow without bounds (Figure 1.3). Yet even with thousands of interactive screens, it is a simple matter to change one screen and upgrade a customer's executable code. Only one fairly small new **class** file is needed. Your customers can even subscribe to a web service that automatically upgrades them any time they log in and discover they are one or more versions behind. Not only can your application keep scaling up, but it's easy to keep your customers up to date! And you don't need different versions for different platforms! Is there a catch? You do still need good people to write clean code. You do still need good version control. We have not quite arrived at software Utopia.

Suitability for Event-Driven Applications

Object-oriented languages support event-driven applications much more easily than procedural languages. This is because you do not have to write some main loop that checks for all the events. Most class definition files are event driven. You write methods that someone else calls. You write methods to handle events. You do not need to have any parts of the code that have long spaghetti-like flows of control. Everything is short, and when it's done, it is really done.

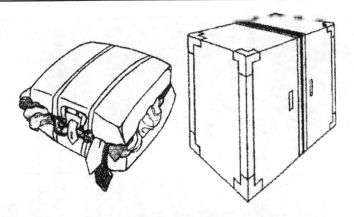

Figure 1.3   Object-oriented applications grow large more gracefully. The procedural suit case gets unmanageable when you put too much in it. It's easy to just buy another object-oriented steamer trunk to carry more.

A Recap

There are a few times in object-oriented programming when you are writing what amounts to a procedural program in an object-oriented wrapper. Our *Hello*[1] example in Chapter 2 is exactly that. We call a main method in a class. No object is created. Input is potentially taken from the command line, and it runs to completion and stops. What's the difference? On a program of this scale, it is not event driven, it is too small to bother reusing, there is very little worth scaling it up to, and there is no real difference . . . but you could scale it. You can create as many new Hello objects from another class's methods as your computer's resources will support. This means it is easily reusable as well. There is a big difference, but in applications of this size, they keep their light under a bushel.

OBJECT-BASED PROGRAMMING

Object-based programming shares some of the properties of object-oriented programming (Figure 1.4). The biggest difference is that in object-based programming, you do not create class definitions. You are

---

[1] I say *our* example, but it is nearly indistinguishable from the similar *HelloWorld* examples in practically every Java book and training course ever written.

Figure 1.4   Object-based programming is building from prefabricated parts. Object-oriented programming can do the same thing, but with OOP, you can make custom parts, too.

supplied with class libraries, and you set properties of objects that you construct from the classes in those libraries. Most drag-and-drop programming environments, such as Visual Basic and so many other so-called fourth generation languages, are object based.

When you purchase a group of **VBX**, **OCX**, or **ActiveX** components, you are buying class definitions that someone else has written in a different language (usually Visual C++). If you are a **VB** programmer, you've been working with objects all along. Does that mean you are an object-oriented programmer? *No.* On the good side, it means that you have a great idea about what you can do with graphic user interface objects, and presumably many other types as well. It means you already know about event-driven logic (see above). It also means that you have some experience with encapsulation. If you are going to Visual J++ from **VB**, or **PowerBuilder**, or **Uniface**, or anything like that, you are in for a fairly smooth ride.

INHERITANCE

Classes inherit properties from other classes. In Java, the ultimate class that all other classes descend from is **Object**. In Java, the **Object** Class is used to create objects with no data fields, but the following methods (among others):

- **equals(Object o)**   Returns a **true** if two objects have the same content.
- **getClass( )**   Returns the class of the current object.
- **hashCode( )**   Returns an **int** useful for indexing this object.
- **toString( )**   Returns a **String** somehow representing this object.
- **clone( )**   Makes a copy of this object.
- **finalize( )**   Runs this method just before the object is destroyed.

Thus every object has at least these methods—though class developers will want to override (replace with new a new version with the same name and parameters) some of these to reflect the new features that their class has.

A new **Class** inherits from its **Superclass** (sometimes referred to as its **Parent Class**). The new **Class** is called a **Subclass** (sometimes tagged with the moniker **Child Class**).

It is easy to imagine (see Figure 1.5) how, by adding many **fields** and **methods**, the *Car* and *Boat* classes (perhaps used to store data

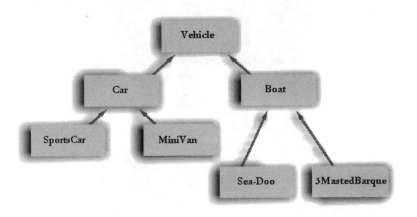

Figure 1.5   New classes add or override methods and fields from their parent classes.

about cars and boats) could extend the **Object** class. Having created a well-tested and satisfactory Car class, it would be a fairly simple matter to add a few fields and methods (perhaps dealing with a tachometer or convertible top) to create a *SportsCar* Class. Similarly, fields and methods dealing with built-in baby seats or extra passenger seating could be added to make the *Minivan* Class.

This business of extending a working class to make a new more specialized class is called (in the parlance of object-oriented programming) inheritance.

ENCAPSULATION

You can take advantage of encapsulation while programming in a procedural language, but you have to be intent on doing it, and you must be fastidious about sticking to encapsulating design rules. Proof of this is that there are some utilities available that can convert some object-oriented source languages to C, which is not an object-oriented language. You can do it, but it will be a constant struggle.

Object-oriented languages encapsulate naturally (Figure 1.6), giving developers who are maintaining or enhancing applications a number of nice features.

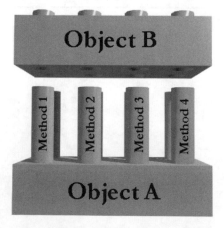

Figure 1.6   Classes keep data fields together with the methods that access or change them.

- Any code that can affect some data is usually located in the Class's source file (as methods of that class) with that data. Thus, it takes less time to understand the ramifications of a change.
- Major changes elsewhere in an application will not affect this part; thus, you do not need to rebuild every piece of an application to upgrade it.

There is more to it than just this. But for learning Visual J++, this is probably enough.

POLYMORPHISM

Polymorphism is that property of objects that allows them to be treated as other kinds of objects, and still return some meaningful results. In our above Car-Boat example, you can see that if all you wanted was to call the getLength( ) method, it shouldn't matter whether you are talking to a SailBoat object or a SportsCar object. In either case (presumably), there is such a method, and it can be called. This is especially important if your application scrolls through a collection of objects and gets data on each of them.

EXERCISES

1-1   Does a class have to be defined to create an object?

1-2   Name three buzzwords that make you think of object-oriented programming.

1-3   Can you *encapsulate* with procedural languages such as C?

Array of type fruit

Figure 1.7   Objects can act like objects from any class that supports the method you are using.

CHAPTER 2

Java and the
Java Virtual Machine

In this chapter we cover the following topics:

- **Java Is Compiled**
- **Java Is Interpreted**
- **Java Verifies Code Before Running It**
- **Java Checks Pointers At Run-time**
- **Java Picks Up After Itself**

Java is a new computer language created at Sun Microsystems by James Gosling and his team. It is almost purely object oriented; it is much simpler to learn and use well than C++. This new tool has rapidly developed into the most important language for work on the internet. It lends itself very well to distributed computing. It is well supported, and is a huge (perhaps even revolutionary) commercial success. In addition, it is fast becoming the language of choice for computer science studies in universities around the world. We have a lot to cover in these pages and so won't dally over the many colorful and oft-repeated stories of Java's origins or place in the world. If you want to know more about the history of Java, or what other people think about it, there are a number of white papers on the CD-ROM taken from numerous websites, yet more websites (start with **http://www.javasoft.com**), newsgroups (try **comp.lang.java** to start with), more magazine and newspaper articles than you can count with a short integer, and (as if you somehow got this book without looking in a bookstore or in a catalog), too many good books to name.

Our goal in this chapter is to give you enough of an idea about how Java works that the rest of the book will be erected on firmer ground than that splendid tower in Pisa.

NOTE

What Is the Java Virtual Machine?

The Java Virtual Machine is a piece of software that can either run by itself or under some other piece of software, like a browser such as Netscape (v2.0 or greater), Internet Explorer (v3.0 or greater), or HotJava. This piece of software reads Java class files, and translates those instructions to the instructions that your machine executes. It's a little more complicated than just that, and this chapter is about what else it does.

Let's start by looking at the development of a project from an idea to a block of code running on someone else's machine. Along the way, we will point out what you can do and what is being done for you. We will focus on the role that the Java Virtual Machine (*JVM*) plays in all this. In later chapters we will explain how you can express yourself using the Java language.

One Java source file can be compiled on any machine with an installed Java compiler. One Java executable can run on any platform sporting a Java Virtual Machine. The Java buzzword for this is **Platform Neutral**. It is a stated goal of the Java team that it should eventually be able to run on all platforms! (I think there is an assumption made here that a lot of systems out there today will eventually go away and not count as being in the list of "all platforms.") We will only be compiling with Visual J++ on Windows95 or NT4.0; but your Java executables can run anyplace that Netscape 2.0 runs, which includes Windows95 and NT, the Macintosh, and many systems that support X-Windows.

What gives Java the ability to run the same executable on so many different systems? You probably already know . . . Java executables are interpreted by some program that must be configured for each of those different systems. That program is called the Java Virtual Machine. Sometimes people call this the JVM, but more often it is referred to simply as Java.

> **WARNING**
>
> ### But It Doesn't Look the Same
>
> When the same Java executable is running side by side on some X-Motif box, a Macintosh, and Windows95, you can see some differences. The frames and widgets look like the window system they are running on. In systems that don't run with just-in-time compilers (JITs), the Win95 box runs noticeably slower, because of the *big-end little-end byte shuffling* (see note box that follows). In some increasingly rare cases certain Window Toolkit methods don't do exactly the same thing. An example of this last case: In Java 1.00 the Applet.setBackground(Color c) method in Solaris immediately sets the new background color on the applet and all of its added widgets, but in Win95 it only sets the background on the applet itself and requires an explicit repaint() call to effect that change. Since then (by Java 1.02), the JVMs have converged to act like the Solaris version. Java applications will always have the look and feel of the host windowing environment, but the other differences will surely fade away.

> **NOTE**
>
> ### A Clever Idea Gone Bad
>
> Back in the dawn of the microcomputer era—the early to mid 1970s—memory was at a premium. In those dark days, the clever folks at Intel followed up their 8008 microprocessor with the very popular 8080 (and its family). One clever thing that the 80 series did was save a bit of memory by storing the low byte of a multibyte integer first. This meant that if you only needed one byte, you didn't have to fetch two. You also didn't have to increment the offset to get the one you needed. Some programs saved as much as ten percent of their memory space because of this feature. For some, this was a critical difference as to whether the program could fit in what CP/M (MS-DOS's uncle) left of the 65536 bytes of memory that could be addressed. (Of course some systems didn't have nearly that much memory!)
>
> Today, Intel's Pentium processor still stores the little end first. This requires shuffling the order of all four bytes in a 32-bit integer, from 4-3-2-1 to 1-2-3-4, to make it compatible with nearly every other computer in the world. Will we ever be free from this yoke of legacy? Perhaps that's what Windows NT is all about.

Briefly then, looking at Figure 2.1, Java source code is written on any platform in a *filename*.**java** file. That code can be compiled and tested on any system with a Java compiler (Visual J++ has a fast one). That compiler produces Java byte codes in a *filename*.**class** file. Those same byte codes can be interpreted by any machine with a Java virtual machine (built into many browsers such as Netscape 2.0 and greater, HotJava, or Microsoft's Internet Explorer 3.0 or greater). Some systems have just-in-time compilers that convert the Java byte codes into native code, but for now, consider that to be just an improvement in the interpreter.

In addition to the compiler and interpreter (called **javac** and **java** respectively in Sun's Java Developers Kit [**JDK**]), most development environments also have a debugger, a documentation tool, and a tool for making files required for connecting to code written in the C language (usually referred to as native code). These and perhaps some other tools comprise the development environment. Visual J++—like Symantec

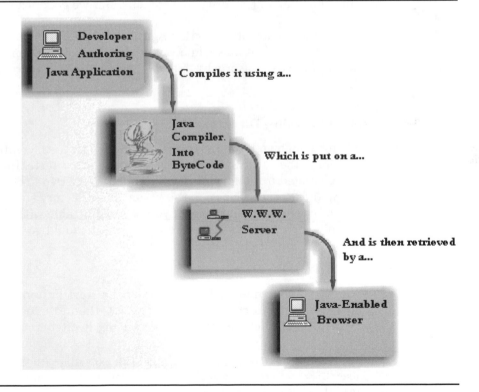

Figure 2.1   Java code from creation to distribution.

Café and others—is an Integrated Development Environment (**IDE**). If you have used Microsoft's Visual C++, Visual Basic, Borland's Delphi, or Symantec's C++ compiler, you know what an IDE is. It combines all of the tools for software development under one menu system, and unless you are writing the most trivial of programs, Java IDE's are a big improvement over the JDK.[1]

JAVA IS COMPILED

Anytime you have a project loaded in Visual J++, when you go to the **Build** dropdown menu and select any of **Compile**, **Build**, **Rebuild All**, **Batch Build**, or **Update All Dependencies**, you are instructing Visual J++ to compile one or more Java Source code files (*filename*.**java**). It does much of the same kind of compilation that a C++ compiler would do. It checks syntax, usage, types (Java is strongly typed), and external references and produces a Java executable (*filename*.**class**). This **.class** file is later run by some JVM somewhere, which interprets the byte codes into that machine's native instructions. But we get ahead of ourselves a bit . . .

Let's start by building that age old application *Hello.class*. You will do this using Visual J++ in a very simple way. If you don't understand what you are doing or why, fear not, we go into a lot more detail in Part II of this book.

Step One: Create a Working Directory

Using Windows Explorer (or MS-DOS if you want), create a directory for doing the exercises from this book and other tests. In this book we have created a top level directory called *ATestArea*. You can skip this step, and let your files go in the Visual J++ directory structure, or place them in some existing area. If you are comfortable with Windows, it is simply a matter of taste where your project should go.

Step Two: Start Visual J++

You can either do this by clicking on the start button, selecting **Programs**, then **Microsoft Visual J++ 1.1**, then **Microsoft Developer Studio**, and clicking; or if you are using it often you should have a

---

[1]In favor of the JDK are the facts that (1) It came first; (2) It is very simple to use; (3) Some early IDEs such as *Café Lite* are just front ends for the JDK; and (4) It has some great sample code.

shortcut icon on your main screen, or some toolbar (such as Microsoft Office, or Lotus Smartsuite). Click the **Close** button on the **Tip of the Day** dialog box.

TIP

No More Tip of the Day

You may find it handier to simply read all of the tips of the day in the appendices of this book, and uncheck the **Show tips at startup** box in the lower left corner of the dialog. Many busy programmers find the few seconds it takes to look at and close a tip to be a mild burden.

If you have never opened Visual J++ before, you will see the Microsoft Developer Studio looking at InfoViewer (the Online Documentation for MDS and Visual J++).

Step Three: Create a New Project

This is the last administrative task before actually doing something Java related. Click on the **File** menu item at the top, keeping the mouse depressed to see the **File** menu. Select the top item: **New**. This brings up a complex dialog box with the familiar tab motif. By default it is on the **Project** tab. (See Figure 2.2). The other tabs include **Files**, **Workspaces**, and **Other Documents**. You could create a workspace first, and then build this project in it, but we will be taking advantage of the feature that creates a new workspace for us automatically.

NOTE

What is a Workspace?

Project Workspaces, and other such terms will be explained in Part Two of this book. For now, think of it as a new Windows Folder, with some files in it that explain what files your project is made of, how they go together, and various other choices you have made, or defaults you have used.

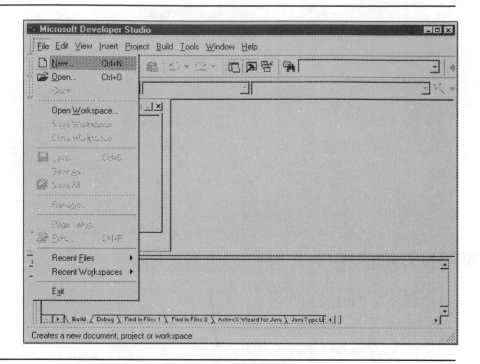

Figure 2.2   Visual Studio with the File-New drop down menu.

In the large selection field on the left: select **Java Project**. Under **Project name**: type *Hello*. Leave the radio button on **Create new workspace**. Leave Platform as the Java Virtual Machine, and under **Location:**, **Browse . . .** to the folder you want this Workspace to be in (See Figure 2.3). Note: Microsoft recommends that with the Java products, you let the **Location** stay in the default. We have not yet had a problem in our specified location, but if you are cautious, heed the word of the maker. Click **OK**.

Step Four: Create the Source File

Select **File: New** as just before. Now by default the **File** tab is selected (You already are in a project). On this dialog box, see figure 2.4, select **Java Source File** from the selections on the left. Leave the **Add to project** box checked. Make the file name match the Project name

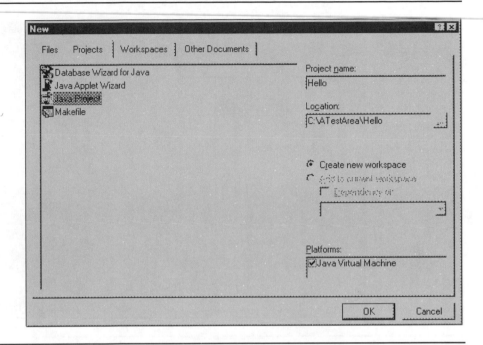

Figure 2.3   Project dialog box filled out.

(*Hello.java*), and leave the **Location** as is. This will open a blank frame, into which you can type a Java class definition. Type the following text, being sure to get the case information and punctuation correct.

```
public class Hello {
    public static void main(String[] s) {
        int k=0;
        System.out.println("Hello, I'm counting");
        for (int i=0; i<100000000; i++) {k+=2;};
        System.out.println("farewell " + k);
    }
}
```

You will notice that certain keywords are colored, and that the editor understands the meaning of curly-braces in your indenting scheme.

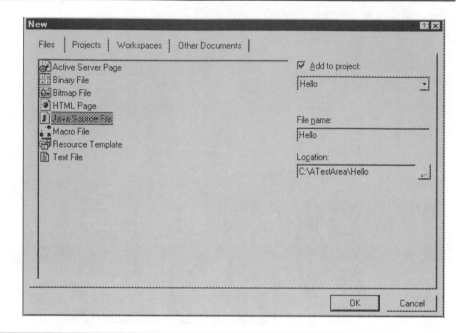

Figure 2.4   File dialog box filled out.

TIP

Indenting Schemes

Some people are very picky about how things ought to be indented. This usually comes from many lost hours of work trying to find some logical problem in a long program. The Scheme used above is good for book writers, and people with small editing screens, because it uses fewer lines of text. There is a very fervent sect that prefers to have the opening curly-braces on the line following the clause under which the block of code depends. Yet another group indents the curly-braces with the dependent code. I have seen opinions on this expressed so strongly that it reminded me of angry Bridge players. The best advice is to be fanatical about your own code, but tolerant of others.

The above is the source code for a complete Java application. You will notice that it is a Class definition. It creates one method for the class. It is the **main(String[] args)** method which must always be part of the top class in a stand-alone application. The main method in this particular app writes the text *"Hello, I'm counting"* and a new line character out to standard output. It then adds two, one hundred million times, and finally bids you *"farewell"*. (n. b. this is not an applet.)

Select **File-Save** from the menu bar at the top, this automatically saves the file as *Hello.java*, and adds it to the project as a Java Source File.

Step Five: Build the Application

On the top menu bar select **Build**, and select **Build Hello** from the drop down menu. (See figure 2.5).

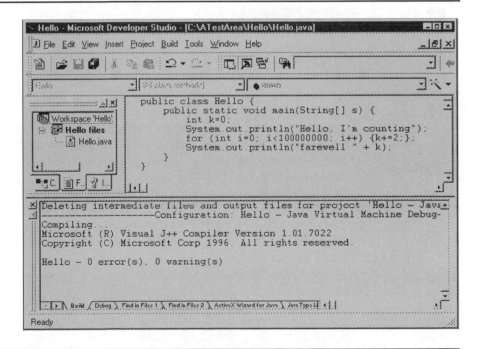

Figure 2.5   Select Build Hello

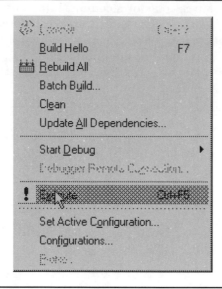

Figure 2.6   The Hello Application is Built.

In a second or so, you should have output at the bottom that looks like figure 2.6. If you look in *Hello* folder on your computer, there is now a new file called *Hello.class*. This is the Java byte code output from the compiler. It is 828 bytes long.

If instead, you have some non-zero number of errors, and you can't determine why your file is different from the example given, and the error messages seem too terse, you can load this code from the CD-ROM.

Summary

All of the steps we followed were part of using Visual J++. We have so far run the Microsoft's Java compiler, and produced Java byte codes. This 828 byte long set of byte codes will run under any Java virtual machine, and produce the same output. And like the *Tralfamadoreans* in The *Sirens of Titan*, they have done all this to say *Hello*.

JAVA IS INTERPRETED.

We just compiled some source code, and got 828 bytes not meant for human eyes to read. Java is a compiled language. On the other hand, we are now about to execute that code. To do so, we must interpret it. It is because we interpret it that there is any hope of true platform neutrality.

Byte codes are interpreted by the Java Virtual Machine. But as with many interpreters the JVM does more than just convert byte codes to equivalent native instructions. It examines it for various security considerations. At run time it makes sure that pointers are looking at valid places. If the code is running under a browser as an applet, it makes additional security checks as well: e.g. the browser may forbid reading or writing local files, or seeing the environment variables. When the application (or applet) creates new objects, the JVM looks for the appropriate *filename*.**class** files in the **CLASSPATH**, and links them in. Best of all, the Java virtual machine has an automatic low priority garbage collection thread, which prevents those unpleasant memory leaks!

> **NOTE**
>
> ### CLASSPATH? What's a CLASSPATH?
>
> There is an environment variable in most Java Development Systems called **CLASSPATH**. It is a list of the directories in which the Java Compiler, and the Java Interpreter use when looking for classes that are part of an application. These class files are not linked together at build time, but are accessed dynamically at run time, so it is essential that Java know where to look for them. **Visual J++** lets you add more directories to be searched while running in the **Microsoft Development Studio** through the **Tools-Options-Directories** dialog box.

There are several ways to run the interpreter on our new application. One is to copy the file to any machine with the JDK installed and on the command line type:

```
java Hello
```

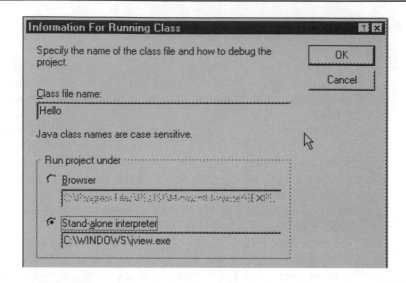

Figure 2.7   Information For Running Class dialog box.

This will write *Hello I'm counting* and after a pause, *farewell* as output, and exit back to the command prompt.

Another way is to open an MS-DOS window, and use the Microsoft JVM **jview** (in the **bin** folder under Visual J++). At the command line, type:

```
\vj\bin\jview Hello
```

Assuming Visual J++ is installed in the \vj directory, this produces the same result as above.

During program development efforts, however, the most frequent way that you will run the byte codes is by selecting Execute Hello from the Build Menu. The first time you launch this for a project, you will get yet another dialog box called **Information For Running Class**. It will ask you whether to run from the Browser, or the Stand-alone interpreter. Be certain to check the **Stand-alone interpreter**.

Execute launches an MS-DOS shell, and runs the **jview** application mentioned above. In this case however, the shell closes again as soon as **jview** is done with the **Hello** application. You will learn how

~~to set break points in the chapter in Section Two about the debugger.~~
Running with jview, this application will take a few seconds to execute.
It may take the Java interpreter a bit longer.

Now let's take a closer look at the good things that the JVM does for
you.

JAVA VERIFIES CODE BEFORE RUNNING IT

Applets are attached to web pages and automatically downloaded and
executed when anyone views that page. This allows you to add some
pretty exciting things to what used to be fairly static ways to display
and collect information. You have probably seen web pages with little
animations built in. These were probably written in Java. On the other
hand, you probably haven't seen an attractive web page with a little
program that deletes your **system.ini** file; while this world is clearly
headed in the direction of peace and harmony, you can be sure that if
it were easily done, some unenlightened, confused, or vengeful individual would already have done it. Java applets are prevented from seeing
or writing to the local file system in any but the most limited of ways,
and in some browsers, not at all.

Java forbids writing this, and many other sorts of mischievous
actions, into your applets. You cannot look at the local environment
variables (with a few limited exceptions). You can't execute programs or system calls. You can't open sockets on any machine except
the one that the host web page came from. If this sounds restrictive,
it is, but it is the kind of safety you need in an applet (Figure 2.8).
Stand-alone applications written in Java do not have these restrictions.

Another potential source of corruption that may spring to mind is
that a set of byte codes may be created by something other than a
Java compiler. For example, suppose that somehow a few bytes where
mangled in the download process that, by unfortunate coincidence,
were able to slip through http's error detection. Alternatively, suppose that one of Batman's archrivals creates a software tool that can
create byte codes without Java's usual constraints. What protection
are you offered then? The Java Virtual Machine runs code through a
byte code verifier before permitting either execution or just-in-time
compiling. At this writing there may still be a few diabolical tricks
that the byte code verifier won't notice, but as computer scientists in
the universities and elsewhere find possible problems, those clever
fellows in the *Sun Cave* are hard at work quickly plugging those
holes.

Figure 2.8   Another evil plan foiled by the Java byte-code verifier.

> **NOTE**
>
> ### There Are Other Ways to Make Byte Codes
>
> **Intermetrics** Inc. has made an **Ada95** compiler that can produce Java byte codes as output. At the other end of the spectrum, **Aimtech** has made a product called **Jamba**, which makes very decorative applets from specifications you supply through dialog boxes (no Java source code is produced). This is just the tip of the iceberg. Other such products are coming almost daily.

JAVA CHECKS POINTERS AT RUN-TIME

One of the things that Gosling and colleagues had in mind when they were first creating Java was that they wanted it to make the language much quicker to program in than C++. They succeeded admirably.

There is a white paper on the CD-ROM of this book that covers the differences between Java and C++, and it is beyond the scope of this chapter to enumerate them in detail. However, while some of these features are built into the language itself and will be covered in Chapters 3, 4, 5, and 6, some come from the support of the Java Virtual Machine.

One such feature is that the Java Virtual Machine has a built-in memory management scheme that prevents a program, at run-time, from pointing outside the bounds of an array or any other reference type variable. It also prevents using a reference that has not been initialized. When such an attempt is made, a run-time exception (error) occurs. If your method doesn't catch that kind of exception, your application stops running, with a helpful message. In C language terms, there are no **pointers** in Java that are directly available for programmer manipulation. The job of the pointers is taken care of by **references**. These constructs are covered in much more detail in the three following chapters.

WARNING

Native Code Isn't Checked at Runtime

There are numerous reasons—especially connecting to legacy code and performance issues—that might make you want to build your application with both C (or C++) and Java. This can be done, and is explained in Chapter 14, but doing so will result in an application that is (at least in part) no longer protected by the handy features of the Java Virtual Machine.

If you have never programmed in C or C++, you may not know the frustration and aggravation that come from trying to track down uninitialized pointer errors or off-the-end-of-the-array errors. These do not normally manifest themselves immediately. They alter something subtly, and the application continues for a while as though nothing was wrong, and then BANG. All pointers become suspect. You set up your debugger to tell you when your memory location is being changed, and guess what, it is being changed at an unexpected time because some other memory location has something wrong in it. The chase continues, all the while you are muttering about how certain you are that this part of the code has to be right. It is a sad story, but one that a million people can tell.

Using Java, you will not ever have to endure that indignity.

JAVA PICKS UP AFTER ITSELF

On the subject of indignity . . . another related problem that the Java Virtual Machine's memory management scheme fixes is known by the buzzword **memory leak**.

If you have only written the kind of application that executes quickly and then exits back to the system; you have had the fastidious habit of closing down all applications when you are done with them and restarting them every hour or so, just to be sure; or if you have gigabytes of memory in all your computers, you may not know of this pest, this scourge, this blight on humanity.

Put simply, a memory leak is a failure in the program logic of an application to always free up all of the memory resources it allocates. Often a large application has some flows of execution in it where the pointer to some piece of memory gets lost before that memory is returned to the system. It is probably something small or rarely used, but if the application is up long enough or used vigorously enough, eventually the system has no more memory available to allocate. In many operating systems, the result is that the computer crashes. Maybe you get a message that the application has executed an illegal instruction or that there is a General Protection Fault. Perhaps the code tests every attempt to allocate memory, and reports the problem gracefully. Either way, whoever is using the application stands to lose some work.

> **TIP**
>
> ### Memory Leaks and Commercial Success
>
> You should avoid selling a product with memory leaks. Applications developed in Java don't have memory leaks. Ergo . . .

You will not have a memory leak in an application developed in Java. The Java Virtual Machine's memory management scheme includes a background garbage collection thread. Whenever the last reference to an object or array in your application is lost, removed, or reassigned, the JVM throws that resource onto the garbage collection heap. Eventually, the garbage collection thread will free it up for future use.

What you the programmer will gain most from this is that there is one less category of programming task that you have to keep in the back of your head as you develop your applications. You no longer have to consider whether some change in your logic will permit a flow of control that creates one of the most unpleasant memory leaks.

EXERCISES

2-1   Create and run the *Hello* application above.

2-2   Change the name of the class in the *Hello* application to *Jello*. Build it. What error message do you get? Why? Better change it back.

2-3   Change the *Hello* application so that the main method takes no parameters (after all, it doesn't use any parameters). Build it. What error message do you get? Why? Change it back again.

CHAPTER 3

Java Keywords and Other Tokens

In this chapter we cover the following topics:

- **Unicode Characters**
- **Tokens**
- **Java Identifiers**
- **Literals**
- **Separators**
- **The Java Operators**
- **White Space and Comments**

Java is a computer language, and you can easily find its syntax in Visual J++'s Java Language Specification available under **InfoView**. Table 3.1 shows what the Java language is made of, from the largest of perspectives on down to the smallest. Java **applications** and **applets** are made up of **classes** and **interfaces** that the programmer writes plus classes and interfaces from other **packages**. Java packages are composed strictly of classes and interfaces. Classes and interfaces are made of statements, and so on, until we get to the bits that make up the Unicode characters (see Table 3.1 and Figure 3.1).

In this chapter we start at the smallest unit of granularity (Unicode characters), and then enumerate the various types of Java tokens. In the end you will have all the parts you need to construct any Java expression or statement (see Chapter 4).

Table 3.1 Java Language Granularity

Layer	What It's Made Of
Applications and Applets	**Classes** and **Interfaces**, both written by you, the programmer, and from the standard, commercial, and programmer created **Packages**.
Packages	**Classes** and **Interfaces**, which have access to each other's private **methods, constants,** and **fields**.
Classes and Interfaces	**Methods, Abstract Methods, Constants,** and **Fields. Interfaces** may only be made of **Abstract Methods** and **Constants** (final static variables).
Methods and Fields	**Statements** and block separators (a kind of token).
Statements	**Expressions** and **Tokens**
Expressions	**Tokens**
Tokens	**Unicode Characters**
Unicode Characters	16-bit values defined by the Unicode standard. The lowest 128 values are the same as the first 128 ASCII characters.

UNICODE CHARACTERS

If you are very new to computers, you may not have considered how character information is stored in files or memory. There are numerous ways currently in use, but the most widely used is a method known as 8-bit ASCII. In ASCII, a collection of eight bits (commonly known as a byte), which may also store numbers from 0 to 255 (2^8 minus 1), is used to store one character. That character can be any of the digits, punctuation, or upper or lower case letters on your keyboard. Another thirty or so of the represent unprintable or print control characters such as form feed, tab, bell, backspace, and electronic handshaking characters. These are the lower 128 ASCII characters. The upper 128 vary a bit. They may contain some international characters such as letters with accents, or they may contain graphics characters of various sorts. There are several standards, and some older software doesn't follow any of them.

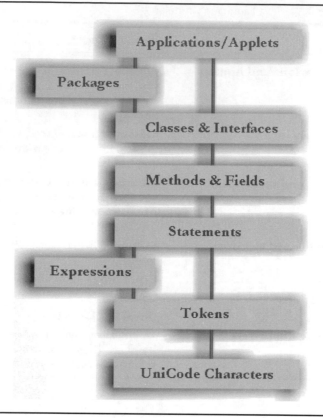

Figure 3.1   Java language granularity.

Still, unless you are using some special font such as Dingbats or Symbol, these characters are always the Latin characters, with perhaps a few embellishments.

Java uses the Unicode character set. These use sixteen bits per character. If you are from the old school, you will be shocked at the flagrant wasting of storage space by using two or more times the required storage space to hold strings, names, and other tokens.

When the high byte in a Unicode character is non-zero, it represents something outside the ASCII character set. Unicode includes characters from most of the popular known alphabets. In addition, it provides about 4,000 symbols, shapes, and dingbats. It also provides almost 21,000 Han pictograms. ISO10646, the 32-bit standard (not in use by Java) provides more complete coverage of the pictogram languages.

NOTE

Computer Archeology Today

In the really old days of this industry, when memory and storage were at a premium, characters were stored in 5-bit codes, with a shift key code to tell whether you were using upper case, lower case, numerals and punctuation, or control codes. Now with Java, we are using three times that space for each character. Yet because a computer's memory resources are so easily recycled and with Java's automatic garbage collection, it can hardly be considered wasteful. Heck, bring on the 32-bit international standard.

The Unicode standard list of supported languages is still being finalized, but at this writing the following alphabets are included (or will soon be included): Latin, Greek, Cyrillic, Armenian, Hebrew, Arabic, Ethiopic, Devanagari (for the Sanskrit-based languages), Bengali, Gurmukhi, Gujarati, Oriya, Tamil, Telugu, Kannada, Malayalam, Sinhala, Thai, Lao, Burmese, Khmer, Tibetan, Mongolian, Georgian, Hangul Jamo, and some Chinese-Japanese-Korean, including Hiragana, Katakana, Bopomofo, and many Han characters.

More information is available about Unicode at **http://www.unicode.org** or by searching on *Unicode* with any web search engine.

WARNING

It's Almost Ready

The Java Abstract Windows Toolkit does not yet support Unicode characters, so you can only make your programs display ASCII. Do not waste your precious hours trying to make an applet that writes Arabic letters on your otherwise noninternational computer. You will be disappointed.

The point of all this is that Java is ready to support internationalization, that it takes up a bit more space, and that you cannot, without a little translation, take a Java string and use it as ASCII. Note, however, that all Java compilers can read ASCII files, such as are created by Microsoft Notepad, as source code.

TOKENS

Tokens are the smallest unit of a language that conveys a meaning. In English tokens are the parts of speech and punctuation. Java has five types of tokens that make up the language. We also traditionally include comments and white space at this point (which aren't tokens to the compiler, but are to humans), so there are seven categories in this section: **keywords**, **identifiers**, **literals**, **separators**, **operators**, **white space**, and **comments**.

KEYWORDS

Java has about sixty **keywords**. Some of these are unusable relics from earlier versions of the language; some are reserved for future use. Most are essential parts of the statements that make up the language. There is one (the four-letter "g" word) that is just simply not used in polite company. Keywords are recognized by the compiler as having a special meaning, and you should not attempt to use them as identifiers (see below). The words "*true*" and "*false*" are also included here, even though technically they are not keywords, but boolean literal expressions. You still should not use them as identifiers. Also, some of the unused keywords are not keywords in some versions of Java; thus, you still shouldn't use them. These keywords and a brief account of what they are used for is given in Table 3.2 below. If the explanation of these terms seem terse, most of them will be explained in more detail in later chapters.

Table 3.2   Java Keywords (plus a few)

Unused Keywords	Meaning
byvalue	Unused (not a keyword in Visual J++)
cast	Unused (not a keyword in Visual J++)
const	Unused
future	Unused (not a keyword in Visual J++)
generic	Unused (not a keyword in Visual J++)
goto	The four-letter "g" word.
inner	Unused (not a keyword in Visual J++)
operator	Unused (not a keyword in Visual J++)
outer	Unused (not a keyword in Visual J++)
rest	Unused (not a keyword in Visual J++)
threadsafe	Unused (not a keyword in Visual J++)
var	Unused (not a keyword in Visual J++)

Table 3.2 Continued

Primitive Type Names	Meaning (more about these in the literals section)
boolean	Either has the value **true**, or the value **false**
byte	8-bit signed integer, −128 to +127
char	16-bit unsigned integer, used to store Unicode values
double	64-bit floating point number (the default floating point type)
float	32-bit floating point number
int	32-bit signed integer (the default integer type), -2,147,483,648 to +2,147,483,647
long	64-bit signed integer, plus or minus about 9.2 quintillion
short	16-bit signed integer, -32768 to +32767
void	Type of method that returns nothing

Literal Values	Meaning
false	Boolean value meaning false
null	Value of an empty reference
true	Boolean value meaning true

Modifiers	Meaning
abstract	Identifies a class or method as abstract (empty, and needing to be overridden)
final	Identifies a class as not extendable, a method you may not override, or a field as constant
native	Indicates that a method is implemented in a native library that has been loaded
private	A class, method, or field that may only be accessed by methods of this class
protected	A class, method, or field which may only be accessed by methods of this class, its subclasses, or members of this package
public	A class, method, or field that may be accessed by the methods of all classes
static	A method or field that is defined for the class, not the object of that class (no objects need to be created to use it) *(continued)*

Table 3.2 Continued

synchronized	Declares that a method may be run in only one thread at a time (it also appears in the list of statement keywords)
transient	Used to mark class fields as not persistent, such as memory mapped hardware registers
volatile	Used to mark object fields as not persistent

Special Names	*Meaning*
finalize	The reserved method name for a method that gets called when the last reference to an object is lost, but before the memory resources are made available (not actually a keyword)
super	Refers to this (see below) object, but cast as the class its class inherited from. It is used to see overridden methods and fields
this	Refers to the current object, or a constructor of the current object; useful for passing the current object as a parameter, or seeing overridden fields

Statement Keywords	*Meaning*
break	Breaks out of an iteration statement or **switch** statement
case	Labels a **case** of a **switch** statement
catch	Catches a class of **exception** in a **try** block
class	Indicates a statement is a class definition
continue	Skips to the end of an iteration statement and continues
default	Labels a **switch** block to go to if no case label matches the switch variable
do	Marks the top of the **do-while** iteration statement
else	Marks the **else** clause of an **if-else** statement
extends	In a class definition, indicates the super-class being inherited from
finally	Marks code to always be executed when exiting a **try** block
for	Indicates a statement is a **for** iteration statement
if	Beginning of an **if** or **if-else** statement

Table 3.2   Continued

implements	Part of a class definition statement that indicates which interfaces a class implements
import	Creates an abbreviation for referring to classes in a package
instanceof	Actually a **boolean** operator that returns true if an object is an instance of a particular class or its child classes, usually used in the test clause of a control flow statement, such as **if** or **while**
interface	Indicates a statement is part of an **interface** definition
new	Creates a new object or array
package	Identifies which package the current class is in (if present, must be first statement in a file).
return	A control flow statement that exits a method
switch	Marks the top of the **switch** control flow statement
synchronized	Marks a variable in a block of code for single thread use
throw	Passes control up the stack to the first method that catches (throws an **exception**) this particular exception.
throws	Indicates what exceptions might be thrown, but not caught within the method
try	Marks a **try** block in which exception may be caught (**try-catch-finally**)
while	Marks the top of the **while** loop, and bottom of the **do-while** loop; takes a **boolean** expression as an argument.

NOTE

Is instanceof a Keyword or an Operator?

There is some discrepancy as to whether **instanceof** is considered a keyword or an operator. The language specification calls it a keyword. More than half the books about Java call it an operator. It does act like an operator, but most of the operators are expressed with just a few nonalphabetic characters. In this book, we will include it in both places. (A rose by any other name . . .)

IDENTIFIERS

You choose **identifiers** as tokens to represent variables, constants, classes, objects, labels, and methods. There are a few restrictions on how an identifier can be constructed, plus a few customs that are followed throughout the software industry. A white paper by Doug Lea covers such matters and other coding conventions, is available at *http://g.oswego.edu/dl/html/javaCodingStd.html*.

Identifiers in Java are sequences of Unicode letters and digits. The length of the identifier is governed by the size of the system that is compiling your Java program. Try to keep the length of each identifier under a few megabytes if you can. Your fingertips will thank you. The first character of an identifier must be an upper- or lower-case ASCII letter that for historical reasons includes dollar sign ($) and underscore (_). So, you have 54 choices as to the first character of an identifier. After that, the Java language specification suggests you may include any Unicode letter or numeral. Java's ability to distinguish between identifiers is both case and language sensitive. The current version of Visual J++ requires that these characters be ASCII characters (the 54 previously mentioned, plus the 10 numerals).

Other than that, your identifier must not be a keyword. It may not contain any other characters than letters or numerals (or $ or _).

WARNING

You Can Do This, But Just Don't

Because identifiers are both case and language sensitive, you can create identifiers that look a lot like Java keywords. For example you could use the numeral 1, or the upper-case "i" to replace the lower case "L" in **boolean**. More extreme perhaps, in a full Unicode supporting version, you could use the Greek Omicron instead of the lower case "o", and make your program pretty confusing to read. It is easy to imagine that after a few drinks, someone might think it was funny, but the programmer who inherits your code won't be laughing.

To really drive home the point about what is legal and what isn't, we include Table 3.3 with some good and bad examples with notes about why the bad ones are bad.

Another point worth noting is that if there is an identifier with the same name in the superclass or in some other way above the current

Table 3.3   Examples of Legal and Illegal Java Identifiers

Identifier	Notes
rowLoop	Legal
$superman	Legal (dollar sign is legit)
*argv	Illegal, Java would treat "*" as an operator
76Trombones	Illegal, can't have a numeral as the first character
ioc_Queue4	Legal (underscore counts as a letter)
6.0223e-23	Illegal, this makes a better literal.
Romeo&Juliet	Illegal, Java would treat the ampersand as an operator.
WilliamShakespearesRomeoAndJuliet	Legal
whi1e	Legal (note that the fourth character is a numeral)
goto	Illegal, there is no goto, but it is still a keyword.

context in the hierarchy, the local identifier takes precedence and the more widely known identifier is hidden (or shadowed) by the local one.

LITERALS

It is often the case that you need to express some number or String value to get things started in a program. Most computer languages, including Java, have the ability to take in-line expressions and convert them to the appropriate type of constant for the computer. We call these in-line expressions **literals**.

Literals represent specific values for primitive types that are written into the source code. Literals can be divided into five types: Boolean, Character, Floating Point, Integer, and String. It may also be convenient to divide Floating Point into **float** and **double**, and to split Integer into **int** and **long**. In the following code fragment, there is a literal preceding every semicolon. Most of the different kinds of literals are represented here. Look for octal (begin with backslash-zero), hexadecimal (begin with zero-x), Unicode (enclosed in single quotes, begin with backslash-u, followed by four hexadecimal digits), and escape-type literals (enumerated in Table 3.5 below).

```
int i = 0;
long VangardLaunchAttempt = 0L;
short TetrisScore = 32767;
static String FirstName = "Werner";
final char TibetanSix = '\u1046';
protected boolean enableSelfDestruct = false;
double ProtonsInTheUniverse = 1.75e77;
transient byte FlagPortVal = 0x5a;
private float bookPrice = 39.95f;
final byte bell = \007;
public float G = 6.673e-11f;
final char FormFeed = '\f';
String r1 = "Riddle me this, Caped Crusader…\n";
```

There are some limits to what you can represent using numeric literals. These limits are the same as the limits on the primitive types they support, and are given in Table 3.4 below.

If you are familiar with C, C++, or a wealth of other programming languages, the only thing in this collection that may seem new are the Unicode literals (\uxxxx). You will notice that we mentioned escape literals above. Java supports eight of them, shown in Table 3.5.

SEPARATORS

Java has ten tokens called **separators**. Separators are found between other tokens. You will use them so fluently that you'll hardly remember that they are tokens, but here they are, loosely described, in all their understated glory in Table 3.6.

Table 3.4   Limits on Literal Values by Type

Literal Type	Minimum Value	Maximum Value
boolean	false	true
char	\u0000	\uffff
floating point	(+/-)1.40239846e-45f	(+/-)3.40282347e+38f
double	(+/-)4.94065645841246544e-324	(+/-)1.7976931348623157e+308
integer	-2147483648	+2147483647
long	-9223372036854775808L	+9223372036854775807L
String	""	<millions of characters>

Table 3.5   Java Escape Literals

Escape Literal	Unicode Value	Meaning
\b	\u0008	backspace
\t	\u0009	horizontal tab
\n	\u000a	linefeed
\f	\u000c	form feed
\r	\u000d	carriage return
\"	\u0022	double quote
\'	\u0027	single quote
\\	\u005c	backslash

Table 3.6   Java Separators

Separator	Uses
(	Used to open a parameter list for a method and to establish precedence for operations in an expression
)	Used to close a parameter list for a method and to establish precedence for operations in an expression
{	Used to begin either a block of statements or an initialization list
}	Used to close either a block of statements or an initialization list
[	Precedes an expression used as an array index
]	Follows an expression used as an array index
;	Used to end an expression statement and to separate the three clauses in the **for** statement
,	Used as a list delimiter in many situations
.	Used to separate package name from class name from method name; it is also used as a decimal point
[space]	Used to separate keywords from identifiers and other keywords

OPERATORS

Java has quite a few **operators**. Only three will surprise the C and C++ programmers who are reading this: **>>>**, **>>>=**, and **instanceof**. They might also be a bit taken aback to see **+** used as a String concatenation operator. Everything else is pretty straightforward. We include them all in Table 3.7 with some explanation as to their use.

Table 3.7   Operators in Java

Operator	Description	Number of Operands	Operand type(s)	Associativity
Unary Operators, 1st Precedence (highest)				
++	**pre-increment** (increment the operand before) evaluating the expression	1	integer, f.p.	Right
−−	**pre-decrement** (decrement the operand before evaluating the expression)	1	integer, f.p.	Right
++	**post-increment** (increment the operand after evaluating the expression)	1	integer, f.p.	Right
−−	**post-decrement** (decrement the operand after evaluating the expression)	1	integer, f.p.	Right
+	**unary plus** (does nothing)	1	integer, f.p.	Right
-	**unary minus** (multiplies by -1)	1	integer, f.p.	Right
~	**bitwise arithmetic compliment** (inverts every bit in an integer type)	1	integer	Right
!	**logical compliment** (turns true to false, and vice versa)	1	boolean	Right
(*type*)	**cast** (casts a result to a particular type)	1	all types	Right
Multiplication & Division, 2nd Precedence				
*	**multiplication**	2	integer, f.p.	Left
/	**division**	2	integer, f.p.	Left
%	**modulus** (gives remainder after division)	2	integer	Left
	Addition & Subtraction, 3rd Precedence			
+	**addition**	2	integer, f.p.	Left
+	**String concatenation**	2	String	Left
-	**subtraction**	2	integer, f.p.	Left

Table 3.7   Continued

Operator	Description	Number of Operands	Operand type(s)	Associativity
Shift, 4th Precedence				
<<	**shift left** (shifts bits in the first operand, by the number of positions specified in the second) acts like multiplying by 2 to the second operand	2	integer	Left
>>	**shift right** (same as above except to the right) acts like dividing by 2 to the 2nd operand	2	integer	Left
>>>	**shift right** with zero fill (same as above, but treats the first operand as unsigned)	2	integer	Left
Comparison, 5th Precedence				
>	**greater than** (returns boolean true if left operand is greater than the second, false otherwise)	2	integer, f.p.	Left
>=	**greater than or equal** (returns boolean true if left operand is not less than the second, false otherwise)	2	integer, f.p.	Left
<	**less than** (returns boolean true if left operand is less than the second, false otherwise)	2	integer, f.p.	Left
<=	**less than or equal** (returns boolean true if left operand is not greater than the second, false otherwise)	2	integer, f.p.	Left
instanceof	**instance of** (returns true if the first operand is of the same type or class, or subclass of the second operand; false otherwise)	2	all (first operand) a type (second)	Left
Equality Comparison, 6th Precedence				
==	**equal** (returns true for primitive types if their values are equal, and for reference types [objects and arrays] if their pointers are equal [i.e., they point to the very same object])	2	all	Left
!=	**not equal** (returns false for primitive types if their values are equal, and for reference types [objects and arrays] if their pointers are equal [i.e., they point to the very same object])	2	all	Left

(*continued*)

Table 3.7   Continued

Operator	Description	Number of Operands	Operand type(s)	Associa-tivity
Bitwise Arithmetic, 7th Precedence				
&	**arithmetic and** (each bit of the result is a one, only if the same bit was a one in both of the operands); for booleans, true if both operands are true	2	integer, boolean	Left
^	**arithmetic exclusive or** (each bit of the result is a one, only if the same bit was a one in exactly one of the operands); for booleans, true if exactly one operand is true	2	integer, boolean	Left
|	**arithmetic or** (each bit of the result is a one if the same bit was a one in either of the operands); for booleans, true if either operand is true	2	integer, boolean	Left
Logical Comparisons, 8th Precedence				
&&	**logical and** (returns true if both operands are true)	2	boolean	Left
||	**logical or** (returns true if either operand is true)	2	boolean	Left
If-Then-Else, 9th Precedence				
?:	**if-then-else** (if the first operand is true, it) returns the value of the second operand, otherwise, it returns the value of the third	3	boolean (first operand) all (second & third)	Right
Assignment, 10th Precedence (lowest)				
=	**assignment** (first operand gets the value of the second)	2	all	Right
*=	**multiply and assign** (first operand gets the product of both operands)	2	integer, f.p.	Right
/=	**divide and assign** (first operand gets the quotient of the first divided by the second)	2	integer, f.p.	Right
%=	**modulus and assign** (first operand gets the remainder of the first divided by the second)	2	integer	Right
+=	**add and assign** (first operand gets the sum of both operands)	2	integer, f.p.	Right
-=	**subtract and assign** (first operand gets difference of first minus second)	2	integer, f.p.	Right
<<=	**shift left and assign** (first operand gets the value after shifting it left the number of places named in the second operand)	2	integer	Right

Table 3.7 Continued

Operator	Description	Number of Operands	Operand type(s)	Associa-tivity
>>=	**shift right and assign** (first operand gets the value after shifting it right the number of places named in the second operand)	2	integer	Right
>>>=	**shift right with zero fill and assign** (same as above, but treats the first operand as unsigned)	2	integer	Right
&=	**arithmetic and and assign** (first operand gets the value of anding the first with the second)	2	integer, boolean	Right
^=	**arithmetic xor and assign** (first operand gets the value of xoring the first with the second)	2	integer, boolean	Right
|=	**arithmetic or and assign** (first operand gets the value of oring the first with the second); this should not be confused with !=, the much more commonly used "not equals" operator	2	integer, boolean	Right

> **NOTE**
>
> ### We Explain Casting Later
>
> In this section we assume you are familiar with the concept of casting one type of number to another. We explain casting in more detail in Chapter 4. For the time being, you can assume that it is a way of explicitly telling the compiler what type you want the result of an expression to be.

Anyone with some numerical computing experience will know to ask about how to determine the type of the result of mixed type operations, especially in light of Java being strongly typed. The rules are rather simple and based on the principle of trying to avoid losing precision.

- Two integer types (**byte, short, char, int**, or **long**) produce an **int** or a **long** (long only if one was a long, or the result requires a long)
- Two floating point types (**float** or **double**) produce a **float** if both were floats, and a **double** otherwise
- An integer type and a floating point type produce a result that matches the floating point type.

- **Booleans** aren't used in mixed mode arithmetic and can't be directly cast as anything else.

It is also worth noting that there are certain arithmetic exceptions and special conditions that may result from using these operators. Imagine the embarrassment and customer service hours if you write some numerically oriented commercial software that isn't prepared to catch and deal with these possibilities:

- Any integer divide by zero or modulo zero produces a run-time exception called **ArithmeticException**. You don't have to list these on your throw list, but you really ought to catch them. These are the only exceptions that are produced by the arithmetic operators.
- If you divide zero by zero with some kind of floating point result, you get a special value called **NaN** or Not a Number. No exception is thrown. Operations where one operand is **NaN** will produce **NaN**. You can use the **isNaN()** method of the **Float** or **Double** wrapper types (see Chapter 7 to detect this condition).
- Floating point types also support three other special values, **positive infinity**, **negative infinity**, and **negative zero**. If you perform an operation that produces a result exceeding the value-storing capabilities of the type you are using, you will get zero, or one of these three special numbers. No exceptions are thrown, so you will have to check for this if there is any possibility of them occurring. Note that in a comparison, **negative zero** will equal **zero**, but you can distinguish which is which by dividing a non-zero integer by it and seeing which infinity you get.

TIP

Bitwise Arithmetic and Shifting

Bitwise arithmetic is not complicated. It is the sort of thing that even the oldest computers could do. Bitwise arithmetic operators permit you to manipulate and test the individual bits that make up an integer type number (**byte**, **short**, **char**, **int**, or **long**). Generally, these days, you would only do this for interacting with primitive hardware devices without an API, or converting some ancient legacy database (ISAM or worse). If you are unfamiliar with it, but think you will need it for your work with Java (seems a little unlikely), consult a general computer science book.

- Operations on **long** types that make numbers that exceed plus or minus nine quintillion will wrap around without generating an exception. Similar results will occur if you explicitly cast results into integer types too small to contain them (two billion or so for **int** types, 32,768 for **short** types, and 128 for **bytes**).

We will see examples of the use of these operators everywhere.

WHITE SPACE

As noted in the overview of tokens above, aside from the single space separator character, white space is not a token in the Java language. As far as the compiler is concerned, it is some nonessential fluff to be skipped over and ignored. White space is for the benefit of humans who read and maintain the code. White space is composed of five types of characters listed in Table 3.8 below.

As a general rule, you can insert as many white space characters as you deem fit between any two tokens in a Java source code file. Normally you would do this to execute some kind of indentation scheme, and perhaps to keep individual class or method definitions on separate pages when printed out. The white space is not required. Do you recall the *Hello* application from Chapter 2? Here it is with much less white space.

```
class Hello{public static void
main(String[]s){System.out.println("Hello");}}
```

It still compiles to the same 700 bytes, but it is just a little harder to follow with the eyes, and it takes an additional second or two to figure out where to insert a new method, or a new field. In short, it has become a bit of maintenance problem. Be considerate, choose a good understandable indentation scheme, and stick to it with a religious fervor.

Table 3.8 White Space Characters

White Space Character	Escape Literal	Unicode Value
space	\<none>	\u0020
horizontal tab	\t	\u0008
line feed	\n	\u000a
carriage return	\r	\u000d
form feed	\f	\u000c

COMMENTS

Like white space, comments aren't really tokens. They are available for the human who studies the code later. Some people use program development techniques in which the comments are mostly all written first. If you don't already have a methodology, and you're in too much of a hurry to learn a formal one, try this one. It may help.

Visual J++'s Applet Wizard (soon to be a good friend of yours) lets you choose to have comments added automatically. Well, that's fine for the code it generates, but you have to comment your own code.

Java supports three types of comments: the end of line comments (C++ style), the comment block comments (old traditional C style), and a special case of the comment block, the javadoc comments. The properties of these comments are described in Table 3.9.

The first two of these are fairly simple, and can be understood pretty much completely by looking at one example. The third has some special features that will require you to read yet another appendix if you are to start using it to its best advantage. Making you an expert in javadoc is beyond the scope of this chapter.

We can see these comments at work in the following new improved *Hello* application.

```
/** Hello application
@version 1.0 @author Bruce Wayne @return void
This application says hello, and then exits.
*/
class Hello {          // begin class definition
   public static void main(String[ ] args) {
       System.out.println("Hello");
   } /* end the main method */
}     // end the Hello class definition
```

Table 3.9 Java Comment Styles

Type of comment	Opening String	Closing String	Use
End of Line	//	End of line	Short comments at the end of the line
Comment Block	/*	*/	Long comments and disabling blocks of code
Javadoc	/**	*/	Comments that will be used by the automatic documentation generator (Javadoc)

> **WARNING**
>
> ### Comment Blocks Don't Nest
>
> You can use comment blocks to hide large areas of code from the compiler. This is sometimes part of good debugging techniques. However, you should note that if you try to nest one comment block inside another, the outer one ends the first time the compiler sees the "*/" closing character string. You may be in for some unexpected results.

EXERCISES

3-1 Which of the following are not Java keywords?

The volatile private throws static and extends this double break.

3-2 Which of the following are not legal Java identifiers?

float, double, triple, 5centCigar, OneHundred%, ninetyEight#weakling, HELP, error

3-3 Which of the following are not legal Java literals?

6, +6L, 1.5e50, −1.5e50F, 12fe, 0x12fe, \007, 007, true, TRUE, True, eight, 1.5e-290

3-4 Which of the following are not legal Java operators? ·

+, -, =, ==, <<<=, #_, ^^, ^=, &, instanceof, (int), >=, >>=, ?:, \~

CHAPTER 4

Java Expressions and Statements

In this chapter we cover the following topics:

- **Primitive Types, Arrays, and References**
- **Java Expressions**
- **Java Statements**

In Chapter 3 we saw the elements that make up Java expressions and statements. In this chapter we look at how they are combined to form those expressions, and what those expressions mean. We also show how to compose these various statements, and what they mean. In Chapter 5 we show how to string these statements together to compose methods, classes, interfaces, and packages.

PRIMITIVE TYPES, ARRAYS, AND REFERENCES

One more time with the primitive types: As we have seen in the section on **keywords**, and then again in the section on **literals**, there are eight primitive types. They are the five integer types (including **char**), the two floating point types, and **booleans**. Each type's extreme values are given Table 3.4 in the section on literals. Their sizes are given in the keywords section. You might think that there couldn't be that much more to say about these things.

It is worth pointing out that in Java, copies of the primitive type variables are passed in method calls. The original cannot be changed by the calling method. **Arrays** and **objects** are passed by reference. It is a reference to these objects that is passed in a method call; thus, the one true copy can be altered by the invoked method.

It is also worth noting that there are some operators that are only meaningful for a subset of the primitive types. You cannot do the bit-wise operations on the **boolean** or floating point numbers. You cannot do the modulus operation on floating point numbers. Except for assignment to **boolean** values, you cannot do any kind of arithmetic operations on **booleans**.

Java also supports the construction of arrays. **Arrays** can be arrays of primitive types, or they can be arrays of references. This latter category permits you to construct arrays of objects, or arrays of arrays. Logically it flows that we could make arrays of arrays of objects.

Because multidimensional arrays are arrays of arrays, the subordinate arrays do not have to all be the same size (or even created). You must create the sub-array definitions in left-to-right order. Otherwise there is no reference allocated to store the sub-array.

We will see more about how to construct such arrays in the section on Java statements, but for now let's say that the three steps in creating an array of some sort are:

- Declare the reference to the array.
- Get the memory manager to create a new array (this is done using the **new** keyword), and point to it with the reference.
- Populate the array.

Some examples are given in the code fragment below

```
int lowFib[ ];                      // declare the reference
lowFib = new int[20];               // get memory management to make the array
lowFib[0] = 1;                      // first two Fibonacci numbers.
lowFib[1] = 1;
for (int j=2; j<20; j++) {          // iteration statement to populate
    lowFib[j] = lowFib[j-2] + lowFib[j-1];
}

long lowPerfects[ ] = new long[2]; // Combine the first two steps
lowPerfect[0] = 6;
lowPerfect[1] = 28;

long[ ] lowPrimes = { 2, 3, 5, 7, 11, 13, 17 };
                            // Combine all three steps.
// you can make arrays of objects, too.
Color ExtOptions[ ] = new Color[2];
```

```
// you can create multi-dimensional arrays.
byte ChessBoard[ ][ ] = new byte[8][8];

char letterArrays[12][5][ ][ ];     // Allocate 12x5 array of references to
                                    // 2 dimensional arrays.
char badError[12][ ][ ][5];         // The compiler will complain.

short[][] numbers = {{2, 3, 4}, {5, 6}, {7, 8, 9, 10, 11, 12}};
                                    // declare and fill a 2d array.
```

As seen in the examples above, Java gives you a few shortcuts so that you can combine these steps into one. We will see more of these in the section about declaration statements.

JAVA EXPRESSIONS

When we say the word "expression" in the context of a computer language, we are talking about a combination of method invocations, operators, operands, and separators that perform the computations and actions of any computer application. Aside from the expressions in expression statements, everything else is pretty much just declarations and control flow.

So now that we've had a look at all the tokens that make up expressions (well, we've had a glimpse of method invocation, but we won't lean on that too heavily just yet, so bring your towel, and don't panic), we can work out the details of how to construct an expression, and determine the order in which its parts are evaluated. We will also look at the associative rule with operators; plus we'll discuss type conversion and casting.

Constructing Expressions

You construct an expression by stringing together the component parts of the expression named just recently above (operators, operands, method invocations, and separators). Operands can be variables or constants, or they can be literals. We have just seen the list of operators, and just before that the separators. How simple can it get? So simple . . .

For starters, a single literal standing by itself is an expression. It practically evaluates itself. A single variable name standing by itself is also an expression. It has the value that the variable contains. In addition to these, you can construct an expression from any of the operators listed above, in which the operands can be either literals, variables, or other expressions, as long as they evaluate to the correct type to match what that operators need for an operand. Let's look at some examples:

```
5
x
x+5
x+5*j
(x+5)*j
18<<3
height*width*depth
k++
(-b + math.sqrt(b*b - 4.0 * a * c)) / (2.0 * a)
daylight?house.open_blinds( ): house.close_blinds( )
```

If need be, you can create very complex expressions that take millions of characters to express.

Expression Evaluation Order

You can avoid any need to know in what order expressions are evaluated, by using parentheses to override the evaluation order. You see a lot of code out there that looks like that. But code like that looks pretty amateurish. Take a few minutes and learn the simple rules of determining expression evaluation order. Figure 4.1 shows the evaluation order graphically.

- Subexpressions within the inner most nested parentheses are evaluated first.
- Parameters within a method invocation are evaluated left to right.
- Fields are selected, array indexes are evaluated, and methods parameters are evaluated before any operations are done with the field, array element, or method result.
- At the same parenthetical level, operators of the highest precedence are evaluated first (see Table 3.7).
- Once all choices from the above rules are evaluated, operators of equal precedence are evaluated in the direction of their associative

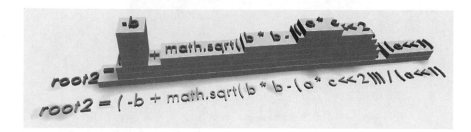

Figure 4.1   An example showing the evaluation order of a Java expression.

rule (left to right for the binary arithmetic operators; right to left for unary operations, assignments, and if-then-else).

For example, let's look at the following expression and not concern ourselves with implicit casting; simply note that *root2* is of type **double** and everything else, except the result of the square root method, is an **int**:

As an exercise, you should follow the above rules and verify that this is indeed the order in which the example expression would be evaluated by Visual J++.

Type Conversion and Casting

Java is a strongly typed language. Because of this, you, the software developer, will have to occasionally convert one type of number to another. There are a few situations where Java will do this for you without asking. These are situations in which there will be no loss of data or precision in the transfer. For example, imagine that you get a char (an unsigned 16-bit integer) as a return value from a method. You may, without explicit casting, receive this into another **char**, an **int**, or a **long**. You would have to explicitly use the casting operator to receive it into a **byte**, **short**, **float**, or **double**; and, of course, it can never go into a **boolean**.

Type coercion is done with the casting operator (the name of a type or class surrounded by parentheses). You may (with the threat of lost data) cast any numerical type into any other numerical type. You may also cast any object as any class from which that object's class inherits. You may also need to cast an object to be its own class, if you get it by a reference to one of its superclasses (as often happens when you use the polymorphism feature of an object-oriented language). Imagine, if you will, that you are a car dealer, and you have an array of *car* objects. You want to put a *sportscar* object into that array. This happens with an **ad hoc** cast (which means that you don't have to do it explicitly, Java will do it for you). Later, you pull the *car* out of the array, and, since it is from the *sportscar* subclass, to use all the *sportscar* features, you need to cast it back into a *sportscar* object.

TIP

Converting booleans to Integers and Back

Booleans can't be cast into integers (or other types), but you can convert **boolean** values to integer values and vice versa following these code examples:

```
int myInt;
boolean myBool;

. . .

// convert true to 1 and false to 0
myInt = myBool ? 1 : 0

// convert 0 to false, and everything else to true
myBool = (myInt != 0);
```

Summary Examples

In the examples in Table 4-1, assume that the following variables have been initialized with these values; also, assume that there is an object called *mnpy* with numerous methods we may invoke:

```
boolean o1 = true, o2 = false;
byte b1 = 20, b2 = -40;
short h1 = 240, h2 = 20000;
char c1 = 'A', c2 = '\uffff';
int i1 = 0, i2 = 40000;
long g1 = 2L, g2 = 50000L;
float f1 = 4.5F, f2 = 5.0e-2;
double d1 = -6.0, d2 = 39.95;
String s1 = "Zapp", s2 = "Pow";
int Array1[ ] = { 0, 10, 20, 30, 40, 50 };
```

Table 4.1   Examples of Expressions

Expression	Type	Value
h1 + i2	int	40240
s1 + " " + s2	String	"Zapp Pow"
Array1[3] * g1	long	60
g1 * f1 + b2	float	-31.0
c2 + b1	int	65555
(b1 >> (int) g1) * Array1[4]	int	200
o1?b1:b2	byte	20
d1 * b2 / h1	double	1.0
o1 & (o2 | (b1 > h2))	boolean	false
(double)(Array1[(int)g1])/b2	double	-0.5

JAVA STATEMENTS

We have built up the pieces that Java statements are made of. It is now time to take a look at how the specific statements in Java are constructed. You can think about statements in Java (or any other computer language) as being rather like the sentences in human language.

> **NOTE**
>
> ### Are Human Languages Easier than Computer Languages?
>
> Some people are intimidated by the preciseness with which you must express yourself to a computer. They feel as though this makes it much harder to deal with a computer language than, say, English. On the other hand, Java has one tense (the imperative) whereas the romance languages have about forty. Java has about sixty keywords, and maybe another thousand or so standard constant or method names. English has about half a million words (depending on what and how you count them). Keywords and method names in Java have a very small number of meanings, and you can always tell which meaning is appropriate in a given situation. English is just loaded with ambiguities, and ways that idioms change the meaning of a phrase (Did you see the old *Saturday Night Live* sketch when Ed Asner, as a retiring nuclear engineer, told his replacements, "You can't put too much water in a nuclear reactor."?)

Statement Construction

Java has quite a few different kinds of statements. It is convenient to divide them into the following categories: declarations, expressions, selection statements, iteration statements, jump statements, guarding statements, and synchronization statements. The Java Language Specification also mentions empty statements, unreachable statements, and labeled statements. These last two overlap the first seven, and the empty statements really are nothing. Still, we will cover them all.

First however, it is worth making it clear what we mean we discuss blocks of statements.

Blocks and Statements

We will often refer to **blocks** of statements. Here we will put some questions in your mouth, and answer them, in a rather dubious, but ancient rhetorical style.

- *How can you recognize a block, as opposed to any other collection of statements?*
  A block begins with an opening curly-brace, and ends with a closing curly-brace. The block of statements needs nothing else to be a block. Thus, the minimum block of statements is:

  ```
  { }          // the minimum block of statements
  ```

- *When can you use a block of statements?*
  Anywhere you can use a single statement.
- *Does this mean you can have a block of statements in the middle of a block of statements?*
  Yes.
- *Is there anything special about such a block?*
  Well, if you declare a variable inside that block, it only has a scope within that block. This could be used to hide some more widely known variable of the same name. Once the block is exited, the variable is gone.
- *Do you mean that they are crushed right out of existence?*
  Let's not get maudlin about this.

Empty Statements You may create empty statements in Java. Perhaps you would do this to create a place holder for later development, or some other trick you may learn. The empty statement does nothing, but is not illegal. You can spot one by the seemingly superfluous semicolons.

```
;;;;            // four empty statements all at once!
```

Labeled Statements Any statement in Java may sport a label. While technically we still refer to this statement by whatever type it is (e.g., iteration or selection), it is also called a labeled statement. The label has all the same rules as an identifier in terms of what characters it may contain. It is followed by a colon. There are two types of statements that take labels as parameters: the **break** statement, and the **continue** statement. We will look at these in the section about jump statements below. Since **break** and **continue** may only take iteration statement labels as their arguments, and labels are used nowhere else, a label on any other statement (while perfectly legal) is only really useful for aiding human readability.

```
loop1: while (true) { break loop1; }; // almost an empty statement
```

Unreachable Statements Just as with the labeled statements above, any type of statement can be an unreachable statement. We call a statement unreachable if there is no way for the flow of program control to get to it. Such statements are in the same block of statements with, and immediately follow, a **return**, **throw**, **break**, or **continue** statement. In such a case, control could never get to the unreachable statement.

You will never have a Java applet or application with an unreachable statement, because the compiler will give you an error if it finds one.

Declaration Statements There are five types of declaration statements: Class, Interface, Array, Object, and Primitive Type declarations. The precise form of the declaration depends on the sort of object being declared. Let's look at these five types in detail.

Class Declarations   In Chapter 1, we described object-oriented programming, of which classes are an integral part. Nearly every line of code you write in Java will be part of a Class declaration. Classes are described in much more detail in Chapter 5. Class declarations have up to six parts, which are enumerated below in Table 4.2.

The *Hello* application from Chapter 2 is a very simple example of this structure.

Interface Declarations   Interfaces (described in detail in Chapter 5) are a collection of abstract methods and constants that a class may

Table 4.2   Parts of a Class Declaration

Class Modifiers		The keywords **abstract**, **final**, or **public** (one class may not be both abstract and final).
Class	Required	The keyword **class** (It's just not a class declaration without it!)
Identifier	Required	Programmer supplied name of the class (see identifiers in Chapter 3).
Super		The keyword **extends** followed by the name of the class this class inherits from. If this part is absent, the class inherits from **Object**.
Interfaces		The keyword **implements** followed by a comma separated list of the interfaces this class implements.
Class Body	Required	Within a code block, the field and method declarations that make this class different from its parent class (e.g., **Object**).

implement, usually to make it consistent with other classes not directly in its family tree. An interface declaration has five parts, enumerated in Table 4.3.

We will be describing this construct in great detail in Chapter 5. Please look there if you need an example to make this more clear.

Table 4.3   Parts of an Interface Declaration

Interface Modifiers		The keywords **abstract** or **public**. All interfaces are **abstract**, but the compiler won't complain if you point it out.
Interface	Required	The keyword **interface** (It's just gotta be there!).
Identifier	Required	Programmer supplied name of the interface (described in Chapter 3).
Extends Interfaces		The keyword **extends** followed by a comma separated list of interface identifiers.
Interface Body	Required	Within a code block, the constants and abstract method declarations that make up this interface.

Method Declarations   In Chapter 1, we described methods, which are the action part of a class. Most of the code you write in Java will be in the bodies of methods. Methods are described in much more detail in Chapter 5. Method declarations have up to six parts, enumerated in Table 4.4.

The *Hello* application from Chapter 2 has an example of the main method being declared.

Array Declarations   There are some examples of array declarations in the beginning of this chapter. Arrays are groups of some particular type of variable. If it is an array of arrays or objects, then it is a group of references that are stored together, not the group of arrays or objects. The parts of an array declaration are given in Table 4.5.

Table 4.4   Parts of a Method Declaration

Method Modifiers		The keywords **abstract**, **final**, **native**, **private**, **protected**, **public**, **static**, or **synchronized** (several of these are mutually exclusive; for example, one method cannot be both **public** and **private**).
Return Type	Required	The name of a primitive type, class that this method returns when complete, or **void** if it returns nothing.
Identifier	Required	Programmer supplied name of the method (see identifiers in Chapter 3). There are certain methods such as **main** and **finalize** whose names are special. Also, if you are overriding a method, you must match the identifier.
Parameter List	Required	Between a pair of parentheses, a comma-separated list of type-name parameter identifier pairs. This can be an empty list: for example, **( )**.
Throws List		The Keyword **throws**, followed by a comma-separated list of all the **exceptions** that can occur in this method without being caught.
Method Body	Required	Within a code block, the fields and lines of code that make up this method. For an **abstract** or **native** method, a semicolon replaces the code block.

Table 4.5 Parts of an Array Declaration

Array Modifiers		The keywords **final, private, protected, public** or **static** (some of these are mutually exclusive; for example, one method cannot be both **public** and **private**).
Type Name	Required	The name of a primitive type or class that this array contains. If it is an array or a class, this array stores references, not values.
Identifier	Required	Programmer supplied name.
Brackets	Required	These are the open and close square brackets **[ ]**. There may not be anything inside these brackets.
Initialization		• After an equals sign, the keyword **new** followed by the same type as above, and the brackets with an integer expression.
		• After an equals sign, and within curly-braces, a comma-separated list of expressions going into the array at initialization. It can be more complicated with multidimensional arrays. See the examples at the beginning of this chapter.
		• If there is no initialization clause, the declaration only creates a reference, and a later statement will have to create the array itself.
Semicolon	Required	That's how you can tell you're done with the declaration.

Object Declarations   Like arrays, objects declarations default to creating a reference, rather than an object (see Table 4.6). You will see a good deal more about the syntax of creating objects in Chapter 5 and in many examples in later chapters.

Primitive Type Declarations   We've seen many examples already that include declarations of primitive type variables. The parts are shown in Table 4.7.

Expression Statements Expression statements are nothing more than an expression followed by a semicolon. If there is no operator in the expression, the statement will do nothing, but it is perfectly legal in

Table 4.6 Parts of an Object Declaration

Type Modifiers		The keywords **final, private, protected, public** or **static** (some of these are mutually exclusive; for example, one method cannot be both **public** and **private**).
Class Name	Required	The name of the **class** for this object.
Identifier	Required	Programmer supplied name.
Initialization		After an equals sign, the keyword **new**, and a call to one of the classes' constructor methods. If there is no initialization clause, the declaration only creates a reference, and a later statement will have to create the object itself.
Semicolon	Required	A handy end of statement indicator.

Visual J++. Expressions are described in some detail earlier in this chapter.

Selection Statements Selection statements are a branch point in the program flow. Depending on the value of some expression, the flow of control continues down one of more than one branches. There are three selection statements in Java, which we list here in increasing order of complexity: **if**, **if-else**, and **switch**. C and C++ programmers will feel very comfortable using these, and any other kinds of programmer shouldn't have much trouble either.

Table 4.7 Parts of a Primitive Type Declaration

Type Modifiers		The keywords **final, private, protected, public, static, transient**, or **volatile** (some of these are mutually exclusive; for example, one method cannot be both **final** and **transient**).
Type Name	Required	The name of a primitive type: **boolean, byte, char, double, float, int, long**, or **short**.
Identifier	Required	Programmer supplied name.
Initialization		An equals sign followed by an expression
Semicolon	Required	Yes, it's required.

if Statements   The **if** statement tests a boolean expression (supplied within a pair of parentheses). If the expression is **true**, then the following statement (or block of statements) is executed. Otherwise control goes straight to the end of the block. An example follows:

```
if (doublesCount == 3)
    monopoly.moveToken("Jail");
```

if-else Statements   Like its simple brother, the **if-else** statement tests a boolean expression in the parentheses. The difference lies in that the **if-else** statement has an **else** clause. In this case, the first statement or block of statements is executed (and the statement(s) in the **else** clause are skipped) if the expression is **true**; and the **if** block is skipped and the statement(s) in the **else** clause are executed if the expression was **false**. So, building on the above example:

```
if (doublesCount == 3)
    monopoly.moveToken("Jail");
else
    monopoly.moveToken(pipCount);
```

These examples assume that there are several methods to a class or object named *monopoly*, which may be an application dealing with counterfeit money or real estate scams in Atlantic City.

switch Statements   The last of the selection statements is the **switch** statement. The **switch** statement takes an argument that may be any expression that evaluates to an **int**, or something that may be cast to an **int** in an ad hoc way. The block of statements following the argument has zero or more case labels. These case labels must also be **ints**, and each one must be unique within that switch statement. A single label called **default** may also be present. When the switch statement is executed, control passes to the first statement after the label that matches the value of the argument. If none match, control passes to the statement after the default label. If there is no default label, it passes out of the block altogether. If a **break** statement is executed in the block, control passes out of the block.

```
switch (houseCount) {
    // Marvin Gardens
    case 0:
        rent = 24;
        break;
```

```
case 1:
    rent = 120;
    break;
default:
    rent = 0;
    System.out.println
    ("Capitalist pig! Why should you own more than one house?");
}
```

Again, switch is identical to the same named statements in C and C++.

Iteration Statements Iteration statements allow the programmer to loop through the same code over and over again, until some condition is met. Each of the three iteration statements has a **boolean** test in it, just like the **if** and **if-else** statements (above). The three statements are: the **while** statement, the **do-while** statement, and the **for** statement. Why, you may ask, do we need three when pretty clearly, we are covering the same turf with each of them? Well, they each do something a little different. Besides, they come from C and C++, and so most of Java's target audience would miss them if they were gone. In all three cases, once the condition is met, control passes to the next statement after the statement or block of statements that make up the loop.

There is one big difference between Java's iteration statements and the similarly named statements from C and C++. That difference is that the **break** and **continue** statements now permit specifying which iteration statement's block you are breaking or continuing. This is important when you have nested loops, or a **switch** within a loop, or loop within a **switch**. See the jump statements below.

while Statements   If the condition is initially **false**, the statements in the iteration block of a **while** statement are skipped altogether. If it is **true**, that block is executed, and the condition is tested again. This repeats until the condition is **false**, or until one of the jump statements (see below) moves control to somewhere outside the block.

```
while ((monopoly.cash > 150) && (houseCount < 5)) {
    MarvinGardens.buyHouse();
}
```

do-while Statements   Even if the condition is initially false, the **do-while** iteration block executes at least once. Otherwise, it is very similar to the **while** statement mentioned above. It is easy to remember this feature, because the test is at the bottom of the block.

```
doublesCount = 0;
do {
    pipCount = monopoly.rollDice( );
    monopoly.moveToken(pipCount);
} while (isDoubles && (doublesCount++ < 3));
```

for Statements   We now go from elegant simplicity to an almost Fortran-like construct called the **for** statement. If it weren't the favorite iteration statement of so many C programmers worldwide, it would surely have been jettisoned by the Java team before the alpha release. Let's get down to it.

The **for** statement starts with the keyword **for**. Within parentheses there are three clauses, separated by semicolons. The first is the initialization clause, the second is the test clause, and the final one is the increment clause. Following the closing parenthesis is the iteration block, much the same as in a **while** statement. A bit of explanation follows:

- The initialization block contains a comma-separated list of declaration and assignment statements that will be executed once, at the beginning of the iteration process. Any variable declared here have a scope only within the iteration block. (This scoping is different from C++!) This is often something like *int k = 0*.
- The test clause contains zero or one **boolean** expressions (C++ allows a comma-separated list of conditions. Java does not). No expression in this clause is the same as having the expression **true** in the clause. This is often something like *k < MAX*.
- The iteration clause is a comma-separated list of expressions that are executed at the end of each loop through the iteration block. This is usually something like *k++*, which increments the counter declared in the initialization clause.

All that being said, let's look at an example:

```
for (int j=0; j<pipCount; j++) {
    monopoly.moveToken(1);
    monopoly.tapBoard();
}
```

Jump Statements   Jump statements (break, continue, return, and throw) permit the flow of control to suddenly go to a new statement outside the more staid and controlled iteration and selection statements.

break Statements   Break statements have about the simplest syntax of any statement in Java. They have the keyword **break**, followed by an optional label as an argument. Like so many Java statements, it is terminated by a semicolon.

The **break** statement is used to exit to the bottom of the current iteration statement (**for, while,** or **do-while**) or the current **switch** statement. If a **break** statement exists outside of one of these structures, Visual J++ will give you a compile time error.

If there is no label named as the argument, the **break** statement exits out of the deepest level of nesting for iteration or **switch** statements. If one of the iteration statements is labeled, **break** exits to the bottom of the labeled loop. It is this exciting new feature (along with the labeled **continue**, and the **throw** statements) that make it possible for Java to be a serious computer language without the four-letter "g" word.

continue Statements   Like its brother the **break** statement, **continue** has a simple syntax consisting of the keyword **continue**, followed by an optional label as an argument. It, too, is terminated by a semicolon.

The **continue** statement is used to skip to the next iteration of the current iteration statement (**for, while,** or **do-while**). The continue statement has no meaning in a **switch** statement. If a **continue** statement exists outside of one of these structures, Visual J++ (and any other self-respecting Java compiler) will report the error at compile time.

If there is no label named as the argument, the **continue** statement skips to the next iteration of the deepest level of nesting for the looping statement. If one of the nested iteration statements is labeled, **continue** skips to the next iteration of the labeled loop.

return Statements   This statement returns control to whatever invoked the current method. It is a way out of the method. If the method is void, return takes no argument; otherwise, it must pass back something of the same type as the method (**int**, for example).

If the return is executed within a **try** block with a **finally** clause, the **finally** block is executed before the control is returned (see the guarding statements below).

throw Statements   The **throw** statement is part of Java's exception handling scheme (see Chapter 8). The basic idea of the **throw** statement is that **throw** takes an argument, which must be an object of a class descended from **Throwable**. These objects are exceptions. When an exception is thrown, control is passed up the levels of invocation until somewhere there is a **catch** statement for that kind of exception. Most simple programs do not explicitly throw handmade exceptions. This is because the exception handling utilities Java are not the speed-iest way to change the flow of control. But you *can* do it, and there are some situations that really call for it.

Like the **return** statement above, if the exception is thrown in a **try** block with a **finally** clause, the **finally** clause will be executed before passing control up the line.

Synchronization Statements Java is multithreaded. We will read a bit more about that in Chapter 6. If two threads each update a mem-ory location and take some action based on its contents, there is a pos-sibility that unless there is some way to lock that location, that some corruption will occur, when one thread changes the value between a test and action by the other thread. The **synchronized** statement creates such a lock.

The synchronized statement is composed of the keyword **synchro-nized**, followed by an expression that must evaluate to being a reference to an object or array, followed by a statement or block of statements. The Java Virtual Machine will attempt to lock the object or array, and will not execute that block of code until such a lock can be secured.

It is considered a good programming practice to keep such blocks of code short.

```
synchronized (monopoly.MarvinGardens) {
    if (monopoly.MarvinGardens.isAvailable( ))
        monopoly.MarvinGardens.buy( );
}
```

WARNING

Beware of Deadlock!

Any time a thread can both get a lock on one memory location and be locked out of another, it is possible for two threads to hold locks in such a way that neither can proceed. If you are developing an application where this is possible, you must safeguard yourself with some kind of timeout on at least one of the threads. Any data-base programmer can tell you how serious this issue is.

Guarding Statements There is one guarding statement. It is the **try-catch-finally** statement. There is only one **try** clause and it is used to mark a block of code as possibly generating an exception. This is followed by zero or more **catch** clauses, each of which takes a type of **exception** (class descended from **Throwable**) as an argument. If a statement in the **try** block throws an exception, it examines the catch clauses in top-down order looking for the first catch that has an exception type that the thrown exception can be cast as. If such a **catch** clause is found, the block of code in that **catch** clause is executed, and the **exception** is satisfied, and your application can proceed as normal. If no catch was found that matches the exception, control passes up to whatever invoked this method, and there is a search for an appropriate **catch** there. This process repeats until the correct **catch** is found. If all else fails, it will be found in the Java Virtual Machine, and you will see a mildly cryptic but helpful error message as your application comes screeching to a halt.

TIP

What If You Catch It, But Have to Throw It Back?

You do not need to proceed with your application as normal, just because you caught the exception. It will frequently be the case that you realize that you can only handle some of the exceptions of a certain type in the local method, but that the calling method needs to take care of the rest. In this case, at the end of the catch code dealing with the one you can't handle here, put a **throw** statement with the same exception.

If there is a **finally** clause, that clause is executed before leaving the **try-catch-finally** statement, regardless of whether an exception was thrown. You may be able to find some unexceptional ways to use the try-finally construct, but they will not make the most efficient use of the Java Virtual Machine.

The following example shows a simple use of the **try-catch-finally** construct

```
int j = 0;
try {
    // throws ArithmeticException (integer div by zero)
    j = 3/j;
}
```

```
catch (RuntimeException) {
    j = 2147483647;
}
catch (ArithmeticException) {
    j = 1;
}
finally {
    System.out.println("what did I catch? j = " + j);
}
```

In this example, the final output will show that j = 2147483647 (2^{31} −1). The reason is that, even though the exception thrown was an **ArithmeticException**—a subclass of **RuntimeException**—it is caught by the first **catch**, the second **catch** is shadowed and will never be called. Technically, this is not an unreachable statement, and so the compiler will not pick it up for you.

EXERCISES

4-1   Modify the *main* method of the *Hello* application from Chapter 2 so that it creates an array of 4096 long integers called *k*, and populates each element with the cube of the index. (e. g., *k[3] = 27;*)

4-2   Modify *Hello* again to create a 3-dimensional array called Cube. Populate each element with the sum of all three indices.

4-3   Write a Java expression that computes the velocity of an object falling in a vacuum, given its initial velocity, and assuming this is all happening near the surface of the Earth (acceleration is 9.8 meters per second).

4-4   Try adding small but syntactically correct bits of code to the main method in Hello, to be sure that you know the syntax of the control flow statements (**if, if-else, switch-case-default, while, do-while, for, break, continue, return, throw, try-catch-finally**). Build the application again with each one.

4-5   Try adding a new **static void** method to *Hello*. Call it *Goodbye*. This method should write the string "Goodbye" to standard output (like main does with "Hello"). Invoke it from **main** as the last line. Build and execute *Hello*.

4-6   Remove the **static** modifier from your *Goodbye* method declaration. Now you need to create an object to be able to invoke it. In the **main** method, create an object *h*, which is a **new** instance of the *Hello* class, and invoke its *Goodbye* method from **main**.

Java Classes, Objects, and Interfaces

In this chapter we cover the following topics:

- **Classes and Objects**
- **Fields**
- **Methods**
- **Interfaces**
- **Packages**

In this chapter we will look at classes, and interfaces, how they are defined, and some subtle nuances pertaining thereto. We also cover (briefly) packages, and what it means for a class or interface to be a member of one. Figure 5.1 shows the hierarchy in applications.

- Java applications are made of **Objects**.
- **Objects** are constructed from **Classes**.
- A **Class** is made of another **class** from which it inherits possibly some **interfaces**, plus data **Fields** and **Methods**.
- **Interfaces** are made of unchangeable data **Fields** (**constants**) and empty **methods**.
- **Fields** and **Methods** are constructed from **Blocks** of Java **Statements** (see Chapter 4).

If you are unfamiliar with the terms **Class**, **Object**, **Superclass** (or **Parent Class**), **Subclass** (or **Child Class**), **Field**, **Method**,

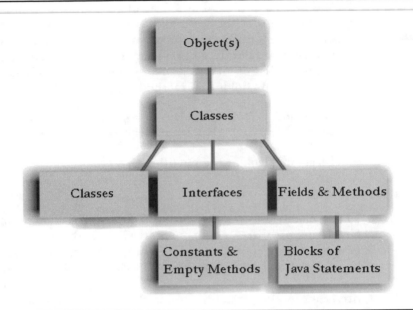

Figure 5.1   What Applications are made of.

Inheritance, Encapsulation, or Polymorphism, in a programming context, you should go back and read Chapter 1, or perhaps consult some other book or friendly expert on object-oriented programming.

CLASSES AND OBJECTS

Class and object: Someone new to object-oriented programming might tend to get these two ideas confused. They are very different, and everything we say and every example we give in the rest of this book will assume that you know the difference.

A **class** is an idea, and an **object** is more substantive. By analogy, there is, in Java, a primitive type called **byte**. This type is like a **class**. You know from the description of the type what sort of values may be stored as a **byte** (integers from –128 to 127), but the type itself is not a byte. An instance of that type—say eight bits of memory containing the number 6 (0x06)—is like an **object**. It takes up memory, it has a value, it may be changed. Similarly, we spend our time in software development defining **classes**. Our applications take these definitions and create and manipulate **objects** from them. It is that simple.

We have seen in Table 4.2 what the parts of a class declaration statement are. Briefly, we may have modifiers, we do have the word **class** and an identifier (described in previous chapters), we may have the word **extends** and a class name, and we may have the word **implements** and a list of interfaces. After this we have a block of code with definitions of the fields and methods of this class.

```
[abstract | final | public] class classname [extends
parentclassname] [implements interface1 [, interface2...]]
```

First, let's look at the modifiers.

Modifiers

Three modifiers that may be used in a **class** declaration: **abstract**, **final**, and **public**. A **class** may have both **public** and one of the other two, but it may not be both **abstract** and **final**. The reason for this will be pretty clear when you know what these modifiers mean.

abstract   A class must be declared **abstract** when one or more of its methods are **abstract**. If a class is **abstract**, no object can be created from it. The only purpose it can serve (in a Java programming context) is to be the superclass of something that is not **abstract**.

final   A class is declared **final** when the programmer does not want there to be any child classes of that class. There are various commercial and privacy reasons why you might want to do this, particularly since all someone needs to extend your class is a copy of your **.class** file(s). It may also be that you feel that the class is sufficiently fleshed out that it does everything that anyone could ever want to do with it. The **String** class that comes with Java (for example) is final.

public   If you do not declare your class **public**, it may be extended, but only other classes in the same package may access it or use its methods. C++ programmers call this "friendly". If you do declare it **public**, its public **methods** and public data **fields** may be used by any class.

> **TIP**
>
> ### All Applets Must Be Public
>
> All applets must be declared public, or they will not be available to the browser that runs them.

Extending a Class

Inheritance is one of the things that makes object-oriented programming great. The **extends** keyword is how we declare the inheriting relationship in Java. The empiricists among you are dying for an example. Imagine that we don't actually have a good package of graphics classes available, but we do have several minimal classes called *Point* (which holds public x and y integer positions and no methods) and *Line* (which holds two *Point* objects called *beginLine* and *endLine*, and has one *drawLine* method).

> **NOTE**
>
> ### Java Keeps public Classes in Separate Files
>
> Because the classes in the following examples are public, they must appear in separate files, named *Point.java* and *Line.java* respectively. If this seems like a minor burden on you file system, you will be grateful during program maintenance.

```java
public class Point {     // extends Object by default
    public int x;
    public int y;
}

public class Line {      // extends Object by default
    public Point beginLine;
    public Point endLine;
    public void Line(int bx, int by, int ex, int ey) {
        // This is a constructor which takes four ints as params.
        beginLine = new Point( );
        beginLine.x = bx;
        beginLine.y = by;
        endLine = new Point( );
        endLine.x = ex;
        endLine.y = ey;
    }

    public void drawLine(Graphics g) {
        /* ... */      // we aren't discussing the contents of
                       // this method here.
    }
}
```

You will notice that *Line* uses *Point*, without extending it. *Line* simply creates a couple of new *Point* objects, and stores them as part of the *Line* object. Suppose that we now want to create a new class that is a *Line* with new features such as a color (which we will store as an **int**) and a line width (which we will store as an **int**) in pixels.

What you need is to extend the *Line* class. Our extension will include the two new object fields—*lineColor* and *lineWidth*. It will also include a new constructor, which calls the old constructor and will override the drawLine method with one that probably calls the old *drawLine* method several times. (We won't look at the detail of this new *drawLine* method, because we haven't specified enough about the graphics system for anything we say here to be meaningful.) We could also add a methods to set the color and line width.

```
public class BetterLine extends Line {
    private int lineColor;
    private int lineWidth;
    void BetterLine (int, lc, int lw, Point b, Point e) {
        super.Line(b.x, b.y, e.x, e.y);
        setColor(lc);
        setWidth(lw);
    }
    public void setCOlor(int color) {
        lineColor = color;
    }
    public void setWidth(int width) {
        lineWidth = width;
    }

    public void drawLine(Graphics g) {
        /* ... */   // This would go into a loop and call the
                    // super.drawLine(Graphic g) method enough
                    // times, and in the right places, to make
                    // a broader line.
    }
}
```

Notice that the we have declared the two new fields as private and have restricted access to them, so that you can only update them using our two new methods. This permits us to change how these values are stored, without altering other classes that use this class. If we were being really meticulous, we would have done this with all the fields. We could also have created several new constructors to cover the different ways that you might want to pass this data.

Implementing an Interface

We will talk about the constructing of **interfaces** toward the end of this chapter. In the meantime, since **interfaces** are a key piece of **class** creation, you should know a thing or two about what they are. As we noted at the beginning of this chapter, an **interface** is a collection of **abstract methods** and constants (final static fields).

When you are creating a new **class** (by extending an old one), you may also **implement** one or more **interfaces**. You declare that you are using a particular **interface**. If you are making an **abstract class**, that may be all you need to do. However, ultimately, you will need to write the body of code that makes up the **abstract methods**. The constants are available for your use. If there are two **constants** or **methods** with the same name in the list of interfaces that you implement, Visual J++ is kind enough to point out the error at compile time, letting you know which two interfaces contain the ambiguous reference.

Methods in a class that flesh out an implemented interface have nothing to distinguish their body code from any other methods. The critical thing is that if a class (or one of its ancestor classes) has implemented a given interface, this will satisfy the **instanceof** operator, or otherwise be of use in issues pertaining to polymorphism.

A Quick Look at Threads

Another issue of some note when constructing a class is that you may create the class to run as a thread. We will look at this special feature of Java in Chapter 6, but we briefly mention it here, so that you may glimpse all the bones of classes and objects before they are fleshed out.

A class that inherits from the **Thread** class or implements the **Runnable** interface may be used to create objects that may be started as separate threads of execution. Such classes have several special methods for use in this way, in particular, the **stop** and **start** methods (you can guess what they do!) and the **run** method. The **run** method contains the body of code that the thread executes once started.

The **synchronized** keyword was created in support of this multi-threaded aspect of Java. It is used to mark certain data fields or blocks of code as something that must be locked for use by only one thread at a time, thus making it possible to write code that guarantees the integrity of the associated data.

More thread features are supported in Java, pertaining to setting a thread's priority or discovering or changing various details about its status. It is also possible to group threads for conveniently changing the status of many threads all at once.

FIELDS

Classes and objects are made of **fields** and **methods**. Briefly, fields contain data, and methods manipulate that data. You may, if you like, without fear of ridicule, refer to a field as a variable. Fields may contain any of the eight primitive types (**boolean**, **byte**, **char**, **double**, **float**, **long**, **int**, or **short**), objects of any instantiable class that can be found, or arrays of any of the above. Fields are declared outside the bodies of any of the classes' methods. Several modifiers may be used in declaring a field; they will be discussed in the following subsection.

For more information about the types that a field may be, please refer to Chapters 3 and 4.

Modifiers

The following modifiers may be used when declaring a field in a class definition: **final**, **private**, **protected**, **public**, **static**, **transient**, **or volatile**. For some added clarity, we will discuss these in two groups.

First, let's look at the three "p" modifiers that deal with the visibility of a field (**private**, **protected**, and **public**). These can probably best be understood from the following table:

Table 5.1   Visibility Modifiers for Fields in Java

Question	default	public	protected	private protected	private
Can a method of a class in the same package access this field?	Yes	Yes	Yes	No	No
Can a method of a class from a different package access this field?	No	Yes	No	No	No
Can this field be inherited by a subclass in the same package?	Yes	Yes	Yes	Yes	No
Can this field be inherited by a subclass in a different package?	No	Yes	Yes	Yes	No

You will note that private protected is less protected that private. How can you memorize this? Memorization techniques are beyond the scope of this book. But you could think of the **protected** keyword as diluting the authority of the ultimate **private** keyword when the two are used together. Also note that the default (no modifier given) gives the field a different level of visibility than any of the modifiers would. C++ programmers will recognize the default as being rather like **friendly**.

In addition to the above, the modifiers *final*, *static*, *transient*, and *volatile* may also be used. These are less related to each other, and will be treated separately:

final	A **final** field may not be changed. It is constant. Since it is constant, it is usually also marked as **static**, so as to minimize the use of system resources during execution of the application. Because it is constant, it must be declared with an initializer. (While you might think that it would simply get the default value for the field type, in fact, you get a compile time error. Visual J++ gives error J0038.)
static	**Static** fields have only one copy for an entire class of objects. You will find this useful both for constants, and for such things as keeping track of how many objects of that class have been created. You could also use it as a mailbox for some kind of inter-object communication, but for this you must be careful to not abuse good programming practices.
transient	The keyword **transient** is used to mark scratchpad type variable space. Its contents never need be saved when swapping out to disk. (Current Java implementations do not take advantage of this keyword. Visual J++ allows you to use this modifier, but does not do anything with it.)
volatile	The **volatile** modifier marks a memory location as one that can be changed from outside the Java Virtual Machine (e.g., it may be a mailbox location for some device driver). The upshot of it is that Java should not optimize this as a register variable.

> ### TIP
>
> ### More Static
>
> The **static** keyword may also be used to mark a block of code used to initialize **static** variables. This is often known as a *static initializer*. In such a case, the word **static** appears immediately before an opening curly-brace. The enclosed code is executed once for the class. You could (for example) use such a construct to load an array of zip codes and town names from an occasionally changing file at a well known URL.

METHODS

Next let's talk about methods. If you are unfamiliar with object-oriented programming, but have done some programming, you will find it easiest to think of methods as *functions, procedures, subroutines, stored procedures,* or *triggers.* Methods are a series of zero or more Java statements. They may take parameters or return values.

> ### TIP
>
> ### Methods with Zero Statements?
>
> You can think of a method with zero statements as a stub or placeholder during application development, or if it has the **abstract** modifier, it simply has unrealized potential that it will pass on to generations to come. Aside from this, there is nothing useful you can do with a zero line method.

There are a few special methods that you may include in your classes—in particular, they are the constructors, main, and finalizers. We will be talking about these immediately.

Another point about methods that may surprise non-OOP people is that you may have several methods in a single class with exactly the same name! This is what the buzzword **overloading** is all about. Such identically named methods are distinguished by their parameter lists. Each overloaded method must have a unique order of parameter types.

Methods may declare and use local variables. If one of these has a name that matches a field in the class or its parent classes, the local variable is the only one that can be seen within that method (or the block of code that contains the variable).

Constructors

Constructors are methods that are called using the **new** keyword. They create new copies of an object. Constructors have the same name as the class that they create objects for. As an odd convenience, a constructor declaration does not give a return type (We know what it returns! It returns **this**: an object of the class it constructs). Constructors also should not contain a **return** statement (Visual J++ treats constructors as though they are **void** [return nothing] and gives a compile time error [J0084] if a return is found).

It probably goes without saying, but a constructor must be **public** if classes outside of the current package should be able to use the object being defined.

Constructors are used to initialize the fields in a new object, and to create the sub-objects (called other constructors), which are fields of the new object.

Constructors may be overloaded. Often, one constructor has all the program logic for construction, and the other constructors ferret out the information from the parameter list, set a few defaults, and then call the one true constructor. The following incomplete code fragment shows a few constructors for a Rectangle class.

```
// assumes a class called point, with two fields, x & y.
public class Rectangle {
    Point topLeft;
    Point lowRight;

    public Rectangle (int x1, int y1, int x2, int y2) {
        topLeft = new Point(x1, y1);
        lowRight = new Point(x2, y2);
    }
    public Rectangle (Point p1, Point p2) {
        this (p1.x, p1.y, p2.x, p2.y);
    }
    public Rectangle (Rectangle r) { // similar to the clone method.
        this (r.topLeft.x, r.topLeft.y, r.lowRight.x,
            r.lowRight.y);
    }
}
```

The three constructors give users of this class the ability to create new rectangle objects in three convenient ways. Note that there is now logic in place to make certain that the points really are top left and lower right. Because we are invoking the one true constructor from the others (using the **this** keyword), we need only add that logic to one of the constructors (thus removing some maintenance headaches later). We leave that logic as an exercise to the reader.

Main

We have seen the **main** method in Chapter 2's *Hello* example. It turns a class into an application, and it is the method that is called first when a class is loaded by the Java interpreter. To be recognized as the real **main** method, it must be both **static** and **void**, and it must take an array of **Strings** as its only parameter. You may overload the main method, but only the one matching the criteria in the previous sentence will ever be called to launch your application.

The **Strings** that get passed to it are the space delimited parameters from the command line. The first parameter is in *args*[0].[1] C and C++ programmers will recall that their very similar *argv*[ ] array contains the first parameter in *argv*[1].

TIP

Applets Can Have <u>main</u> Methods

Applets don't need **main** methods, because they are classes loaded by something that is already running (your browser). You can, however, add a **main** method to an **applet**, so as to permit standalone operation of the **applet** without the browser. Such a **main** method creates a **frame** and adds the **applet** to the **frame**. If run as an **applet** under a browser (such as *Netscape Navigator*, *Hot Java*, or *Internet Explorer*), the **main** method is never invoked, but its potential to be a standalone application is there.

Finalize

The last of the special methods that we are looking at here is **finalize( )**. **Finalize** is called by the **Garbage Collection** thread just before an object's resources are returned to your digital compost heap. It is unpre-

---

[1]We have called the array *args* for no better reason than that is what many other Java programmers use to name this same array in their **main** methods. Within the constraints of identifier naming (see Chapter 3) you may call yours whatever you like.

dictable when this will occur, as the Java interpreter normally keeps **Garbage Collection** running at a very low priority until the resources start getting scarce.

If you are a good and thorough programmer, you won't need to rely on **finalize( )**. Memory resources are taken care of automatically. Other system resources, such as *file locks*, *tcp/ip sockets*, *database connections*, and the like ought to be freed up in a more explicit and timely fashion. Still, if you are creating a class that uses these resources, and you are afraid that you might have some exceptional paths of execution that do not free these resources, you may test for each one of them explicitly in your finalize method, and free them.

Modifiers

Eight modifiers may be applied to a method in a class definition: **abstract**, **final**, **native**, **private**, **protected**, **public**, **static**, and **synchronized**. The three visibility modifiers (**private**, **protected**, and **public**) have the same properties as they do for fields (see Table 5.1 above). **final** and **static** also appear with the fields, but these we will list below with the others:

abstract	An **abstract** method has no body code and must be overridden in a subclass that may be used to create an object. You may have empty methods that are not **abstract**. Such stubs do not cause a class to be **abstract**; you may only have **abstract methods** in a **class** that has been declared **abstract**.
final	A **final** method may not be overridden. Any subclasses must accept the **final** method as it is. Note that it can still be overloaded.
native	The **native** modifier creates a stub in the class definition that, when invoked, passes control to a function or procedure some loaded library. (A method of the **System** class loads libraries.) We will see more of this in Chapter 14.

static	A **static** method has one copy for the entire class. It does not need to have an object created to be invoked. It is invoked using the *class name*, not the *object identifier*. The *java.lang.math* class has quite a few handy **static** methods. Methods of that class can invoke static methods by just the method name.
synchronized	A **synchronized** method may only be executed by one object at a time. Since Java supports many simultaneously running threads of execution (see Chapter 6), it is sometimes the case that data integrity can only be preserved if certain bits of code are single threaded. The **synchronized** modifier guarantees that for a method. If a second object tries to invoke such a method while the first object is still in it, the second thread is blocked until the first one completes. As noted in Chapter 4 above, **synchronized** may also be used to lock a field or variable for a block of code.

There are some limitations on what combination these modifiers can be used in. You cannot, for example, make an **abstract** method either **final** or **native**. There is no point in making an abstract method synchronized, since for the new method to be **synchronized**, you must declare the overriding method **synchronized** in the subclass that fleshes out the code for the formerly **abstract** method.

Return Values

Methods of Java classes may be **void** (in which case they execute, but return no value to the calling method), or they may return a value. Those values may be any of the eight primitive types (**boolean**, **byte**, **char**, **double**, **float**, **int**, **long**, **short**), an object of any class that is available in the **CLASSPATH**, or an **array** of any of the above. If the return value is a primitive type, the actual value is returned. If it is an object or an array, a reference (a pointer) to it is returned.

> **NOTE**
>
> ### A void Method
>
> The **main** method that we saw in Chapter 2 is a **void** method. It runs, but returns nothing,

With non-void methods, some care must be taken that all nonexceptional paths of execution end with a **return** statement that returns the correct type of value. (Even better if it returns the correct value, but correct value is not required to avoid a compile time error.)

If an uncaught **exception** (see Chapter 8) occurs during execution of the method, you cannot pass a return value, and you shouldn't worry about it. You should consider where the exception is going to be caught, and whether or how the application is going to recover.

A method's return type is declared after any modifiers and before the method's identifier.

Parameters

Methods may have parameters. These are placed between the parentheses that identify (to the compiler) a token as a method. If there are no parameters, this parenthetical pair must still be there, but they are empty.

A method may have as many parameters as definitions that will fit in the Java Virtual Machine (potentially millions, but for sake of the humans who will maintain the application, try to keep it under ten whenever possible). These parameters are defined for each method, and you may have several methods with the same name, but different parameter lists (this is called *overloading*). Parameters may be any of the eight primitive types (**boolean**, **byte**, **char**, **double**, **float**, **int**, **long**, **short**), an object of any class which is available in the **CLASSPATH**, or an **array** of any of the above.

In our method declaration, we must, for each parameter, give the type of the parameter, and give the identifier by which that parameter will be known in the body code of the method. If there is more than one parameter, these pairs come in a comma-separated list. For an example, look back at the rectangle constructors a few pages back.

INTERFACES

Let's assume for the moment that you would like a group of classes (user input screens, for example) to all have certain properties in common, but each one needs to inherit its primary properties from classes describing the database tables that each screen is built for. Java does not permit multiple inheritance, but you can still accomplish the above goal in a straightforward manner.

Java has a construction called an **interface**. You can think of it as a class definition that is so stripped down and abstract that it is acceptable to use in multiple inheritance.

We saw in Table 4.3 the parts of an interface declaration. In practice, such a declaration looks like the following:

```
[abstract | public] interface interfacename [extends
interface1 [, interface2...]] { constants and method names }
```

An **interface** may contain only **final** fields (constants) and **abstract** methods. An interface may, on the other hand, inherit fields and method names from as many other interfaces as you can type. The compiler will give you an error if you inherit two identical constants or method names.

> **TIP**
>
> ### Names of Interfaces
>
> You may use any Java legal identifier for the name of your interface, but in some circles there is a convention that interface names begin with an uppercase character, and end with *able* (e.g., **Throwable**, **Runnable**). Thus, the interface name is a verb made into an adjective describing some property of the class that implements it. This is good for English language maintainers of your code.

As we have noted above, interfaces are a simple way to answer the needs of multiple inheritance. (Java does not allow one class to inherit from two different classes. This has resulted in making Java code significantly easier to work with than C++, which does allow it.)

> **TIP**
>
> ### Avoid Redundant Code
>
> If you are an experienced programmer, you know that you do not want to make the same change in many bodies of code. The chance for forgetting one or making a typo in one is too great and jeopardizes the integrity of your application.
>
> If a significant number of lines of code will be repeated every time a class implements the methods in an interface, you should consider redesigning your application so that the interface is inherited and implemented by one partially abstract class. Let the subclasses inherit from this middle class.

PACKAGES

Classes and interfaces may be collected to form a package. Methods of classes in a package may access the protected methods and fields of objects created from other classes (and interfaces) in the same package. There is really not much more to say about it than that, except that:

- The package name must reflect the directory structure relative to the CLASSPATH, in which the **.class** files will be stored. Just as with the import statement, a period replaces the slashes or backslashes in the path name.
- The package statement must be the first meaningful (comments and white space exempted) line of the file.

Java 1.02 (the Java version of Visual J++) comes with eight standard packages to aid and abet writing useful applications in Java. These are **java.applet**, **java.awt**, **java.awt.image**, **java.awt.peer**, **java.io**, **java.lang**, **java.net**, and **java.util**. These and some packages that are coming in the near future are described in the chapters ahead, beginning with the **java.lang** package in Chapter 7.

EXERCISES

5-1   What must be the name of the source file that holds the definition of the *Hello* **class**?

5-2   What must be the name of the byte code file that holds the *Hello* **class**?

5-3   What is the relative directory structure from the CLASSPATH to the byte-code file holding *java.lang.Object*?

5-4   What does the statement *import java.lang.*;* do?

5-5   If your file system supports a maximum of 255 characters in a
file name, what is your maximum length of a **class** name? (You
wouldn't normally make a name that long, but you could create
an automated naming system that would.)

5-6   Can you make a class in a new package that inherits a **private
protected** field from a class in another package?

5-7   Declare a *temperature* class that stores the temperature as
double, and the scale as a **char**. Give it methods to get and set
the values, as well as methods to print its value in Fahrenheit
and Celsius.

5-8   Extend this class to also handle Kelvin. (Extra points for additional obscure temperature scales).

CHAPTER 6

Threads in Java

In this chapter we cover the following topics:

- **The Thread Class in Detail**
- **The Runnable Interface**
- **Interthread Communication**
- **Using Synchronized**
- **Using Wait and Notify**
- **ThreadGroups**
- **Posix Threads**

When we use the term thread in a computer context, we are usually speaking of threads of execution. Simply, there is a pointer stored somewhere that tells us which instruction will be executed next. One thing that each instruction does is update that pointer. Traditional programming languages are single threaded. A multithreaded capability was possible by running more than one program at the same time.

When we say that Java is multithreaded, we mean that the Java Virtual Machine supports multiple threads of execution, and that the language has some built-in features that help overcome some of the biggest difficulties of having several simultaneous threads dealing with the same data.

NOTE

Your Application Has at Least One Thread

Java applications start with one thread (not counting the background Garbage Collection thread). An application begins with the **main(String[ ] args)** method. In an applet, first the **init( )** method is called, then the **start( )** method, then whatever event handling or repaint operations are needed. Either way, you start with one thread and may launch more as you see the need.

You may well ask, "Why would you want to have multiple threads of execution?" The answer is that it enables you to do things a bit more asynchronously, such as reading keyboard or mouse input while waiting for an image to download from the net, while rendering the next frame of an animation, and while opening a socket to a database engine. Multiple threads means that you do not need to construct some big polling loop as your main program (see Figure 6.1).

Figure 6.1   Threads are sequences of program instructions, and one thread can launch or communicate with others. They have methods to send messages to other threads, just like motorists.

Some of the issues to which Java supports solutions are:

- How do you create a new thread?
- How do you set a threads priority?
- How do you guarantee that only one thread may access a particular data item during critical times?
- How do you guarantee that some piece of code may only be executed by one thread at a time?
- How do you get a thread to wait for an event to occur?
- How do you tell a waiting thread that the event has occurred?
- How do you get two threads to communicate with each other?

We will discuss these solutions in this chapter.

NOTE

Multithreaded not Multiprocessor

As of this writing, there is no Java that takes advantage of multiple processors. You would think that this would be a natural benefit of being multithreaded. Perhaps some day it will be. Java does have (and will soon have more) capabilities for distributed processing, but this is not the same as automatic optimization for multiple CPUs. All of Java's threads run within one Java Virtual Machine, and there is no Java Virtual Machine that has been written to seamlessly use this complicated technology.

There are two ways to create a class that makes thread objects in Java. The first is to extend the **Thread** class in the **java.lang** package. The second is to implement the **Runnable** interface from that same package.

THE THREAD CLASS IN DETAIL

The **Thread** class implements the **Runnable** interface (see below). The details of the methods supported here are listed in the appendices with all of the other classes that are part of the standard packages.

- The **Thread** class has seven constructors, which distinguish between whether you are providing it with a Runnable object, whether you are giving it an initial name, and whether you are making it part of some pre-existing group of Threads.

- It has three constants that tell us the maximum, normal, and minimum priorities that the threads are run at.
- It has two class (static) methods that provide information about the active threads:
  - **activeCount( )** tells how many threads from this ThreadGroup are currently active.
  - **enumerate( )** tells how many threads from this ThreadGroup are active, and populates an array with references to each of them.
- It has several class (static) methods that provide information and control to the current thread, such as the ability to wait, or yield, or dump the stack to standard error.
- It has many instance methods that permit the thread (or others) to:
  - get and set the thread's name
  - get and set the thread's priority
  - determine whether the thread is still alive
  - get and set whether the thread is a daemon (background) thread.
  - wait till a thread dies (**join( )**)
  - start, stop, suspend, and resume
  - There is a method that contains the thread's executable code.

There is not much more to the basic construction than that. You may take any object of a class that implements Runnable, and pass it to a thread constructor. You may then, using a reference to the new thread object, call the start method, and get it running.

Alternatively, you may simply define a class that extends **Thread**, and create an instance of it. You may put the call to the start method right into the constructor.

Either way, once a thread is running, you may call its public methods, including both the ones you have written, and the ones that are a standard part of the **Thread** class. You may raise or reduce its priority; you may start or stop it.

THE RUNNABLE INTERFACE

We noted above that the **Thread** class implements the **Runnable** interface. This interface is very simple. There is one method, called **run( )**. Any class that implements this interface, and fleshes out the **run( )** method can be used to create a **Thread** object. All of the features mentioned above will be available to that object. When the thread's **start** method is invoked, the object's **run** method gets started.

INTERTHREAD COMMUNICATION

You can write your threads so that once launched, they owe no allegiance to the mother thread, and that they are islands unto themselves. This is fine for trivial examples and threads that do not live a long time, providing output, but no useful information, to the application. For any other kind of thread, you will need to keep the lines of communication open. The simplest way to do this is to build into your Runnable class task-specific methods that enable this sort of dialog.

Imagine, for example, that you have an application running on some small primitive rotating spacecraft. There is a Thread that keeps track of the direction of some reference star, and another thread that collects image data from a very simple camera and puts in some very limited memory space. Perhaps there is a third thread that handles communications from Earth. You need to assemble an image of a temporarily nearby planet. If the camera thread *cam* has a method called *setCollect(***Boolean** *collecting)*, the rotational reference thread can call this method to turn collection on and off.

```
Boolean collecting = false;
// Some code to initialize minWin and maxWin to look at the planet.
// note: cam is the name of another thread known to this one.
while (true) {
    // some code to increment reftime, or set it to zero when
    // the reference star is observed.
    if (!collecting && (refTime > minWin) && (refTime < maxWin)) {
        collecting = true;
        cam.setCollect(true);
    }
    if (collecting && ((refTime < minWin) || (refTime > maxWin))) {
        collecting = false;
        cam.setCollecting(false);
    }
}
```

Threads with a lot of continuous data can communicate by opening streams between each other. We will see an example of this in a later chapter.

USING SYNCHRONIZED

When two threads are accessing and changing the same data, unless precautions are taken, there is the possibility that one thread will corrupt the efforts of the other. Database programmers are well aware of the putrefying effects that this can have on referential integrity. Well,

Java is multithreaded, and so precautions must be taken. Luckily, Java allows you to declare that a method is single threaded (i.e., that only one thread at a time may be executing it). It also allows you to declare that while executing a certain block of code, some data locations are only available to one thread (This is like a database row lock). See the section on Synchronization statements in Chapter 4.

This can be used to guarantee referential integrity, but if used unwisely, it can also cause a condition known to practitioners of the trade as *deadlock*. Deadlock occurs when one thread has locked a particular field and cannot proceed with its execution until the lock on another field is relinquished, yet that second field is locked by a method waiting for the first field to be available (see Figure 6.2). Needless to say, more complicated deadlocks can occur, but generally they resolve down to this.

TIP

Avoiding Deadlock

To avoid deadlock, you must either not use **synchronized** (a bad idea), or build in timeouts and plans for backing out gracefully for any place where deadlock is a possibility.

Figure 6.2   Deadlock happens when two threads are waiting for each other to lift a lock. When four cars stop at an intersection, who has right of way?

USING wait AND notify

A thread calls the **wait( )** method when it has nothing better to do, and trusts that it will be notified when something important comes up. This lets the thread put itself to sleep. Another thread can call the first thread's **notify( )** method when that important thing comes up. This will wake up that thread. Usually that important thing is that the worker thread is finished and needs to be put on the garbage collection heap.

> ### NOTE
>
> #### Notify( ) **Must Be Called from a Synchronized Method**
>
> Since **notify( )** tells the mother thread that the child thread is has changed state (usually from active to inactive), it probably only takes a moment of pondering to verify that you really need the method that calls **notify** to complete before the notified thread resumes.

When would you use such a construct? Perhaps in a situation where you have a main thread that is assigning tasks to a limited number of task-oriented threads, such as calculating the usefulness of a particular move in a chess game. The main thread would hand out the assignments from a stack, and then go to sleep. The worker threads, when done, would store their result and wake up the main thread, which would destroy the worker thread, create a new one with a new assignment, and then go back to sleep.

An Example

I created the following example for the Petronio Technology Group, a technical education company, for whom I occasionally teach Java classes. With their kind permission, I now present it to you.

We have misplaced our copy of the CRC Math Tables, and we want a list of all the prime numbers below a certain number. Well, of course, if that number is under a thousand, we already have that list memorized, but still, it helps make a good example.

Here, we are going to create two classes—one is the main program, which starts a collection of worker threads. The resulting list of primes is printed to standard output. The other is the worker class, which calculates whether a particular number is prime or not.

```
/* primes.java v.8-26-96 JAC
    This is a demonstration of how multiple threads may
    be used in an application. It is not an efficient
    way to do this particular task, but it shows some
    easy features of using threads in Java.
*/

public class primes extends Object {
    static int maxPrime;
    public static void main(String args[]) {
        System.out.println("Here come the primes below value indicated");
        System.out.println(" this is not an ordered list.");
        // this try-catch set up is used to handle bad input from users.
        if (args.length == 0) maxPrime = 100;
        else
        try {
            // Double is a wrapper class which we will see in
            // Chapter seven.
            if (Double.valueOf(args[0]).intValue() > 100) {
                System.out.println(" ** number too high, using 100");
                maxPrime = 100;
            }
            else if (Double.valueOf(args[0]).intValue() < 10) {
                System.out.println(" ** number too low, using 10");
                maxPrime = 10;
            }
            else maxPrime = Double.valueOf(args[0]).intValue();
        }
        catch (NumberFormatException e3) {
            System.out.println(" ** Non-numeric parameter, using 50");
            maxPrime = 50;
        } // End of try-catch handling.
        System.out.println("The max number tested for being prime is "
            + String.valueOf(maxPrime));
        new print_prime(2);
        for (int i=3; i<=maxPrime; i+=2) {
            new print_prime(i);
        }
    }
}

class print_prime extends Thread {
    int check_num;

    print_prime(int check) {
        check_num = check;
        this.start();
    }
```

```
public void run() {
    boolean isPrime = true;
    for (int i = 2; i<(Math.floor(Math.sqrt(check_num))+1); i++) {
        if (check_num%i == 0) {
            if (check_num == 2) break; // Special case
            isPrime = false;
            // System.out.println(" — " + check_num + " " + i);
            break;
        }
    }
    if (isPrime) {
        System.out.println(String.valueOf(check_num));
    }
}
}
```

Note that in this example, no effort is made to end the lives of the threads, and some Java implementations continue running until a control-C is hit. You can fix this and other features in the examples below!

THREADGROUPS

Along with Threads in the Java standard packages is the **ThreadGroup** class. This class permits the collecting of several threads into one group for ease of dealing with many threads simultaneously. Using **Thread Groups**, a method can **stop**, **suspend**, or **resume** many threads at once. It also provides a built-in way to get an enumerated list of all the threads in a group.

This is not the sort of thing that you will add to small applications, but it is a nice feature to have around when you are constructing large applications that will come close to using all of a system's resources.

POSIX THREADS

As of sometime in 1995, the POSIX committee added a threads definition to their standard. These threads are supported by a set of library calls that access an operating system's kernel thread capabilities. There is a good bit of similarity between the POSIX threads and the threads that Java supports. Both kinds of synchronization (single-threaded code, and record locking) are supported. What this means for the present in Java is nothing. Current versions of Java won't be taking advantage of this feature. In the near future, POSIX threads will be used when porting Java to new systems, and presumably for creating new versions of Java on already Java-enabled systems.

EXERCISES

6-1   Modify the *Primes* example so that the results are sorted into an array. Do this by making a new method in the *Primes* class that the *print_prime* threads call instead of writing to **System.out**.

6-2   Modify your results from exercise 6-1 above to have the Main method print the sorted list of primes in the end. Do this by keeping a list of all the *print_prime* threads launched, and printing the list when they are all complete.

6-3   Modify your result from exercise 6-2 above to have the main method only keep a limited number (4) of *print_prime* threads running. Do this by adding a static getNext method to the Primes class that returns the next number needed and updates the list. Also change the *print_primes* run method to call that getNext method when done the previous number.

6-4   How will you recognize the end of the list? What should happen then?

6-5   Redesign the Primes application to use **wait( )** and **notify( )**. Which code looks simpler?

The java.lang Package

In this chapter we cover the following topics:

- **Object Class**
- **String Classes**
- **Wrapper Classes**
- **Math Class**
- **System-related Classes**

The Java language is extended by the **packages** (libraries of classes) that programmers have available to them. Java comes with several of these as a standard part of the language. With Java 1.02 (the version supported by the initial release of Visual J++) there are eight standard packages, which include support for input and output, network connections, images, a windowing toolkit, some data structures, and applet support.

In this chapter we will look at one of these eight standard packages, the **java.lang** package. This package is closely tied to the language, and has the special property that you do not need the **import** statement to use the shorthand notation to reach any of its constituent members. It is also (with **java.awt**, the abstract window toolkit) one of the two largest and most complex of the standard packages.

This package includes the **Threads** which we discussed in Chapter 6, and it also includes the **Exceptions**, which we will discuss in Chapter 8. The rest of its contents will be discussed here.

java.lang package

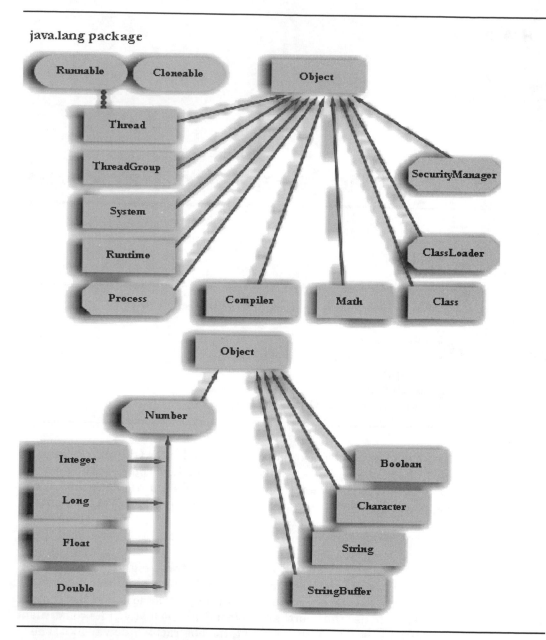

Figure 7.1   The java.lang package.

java.lang package (cont'd)

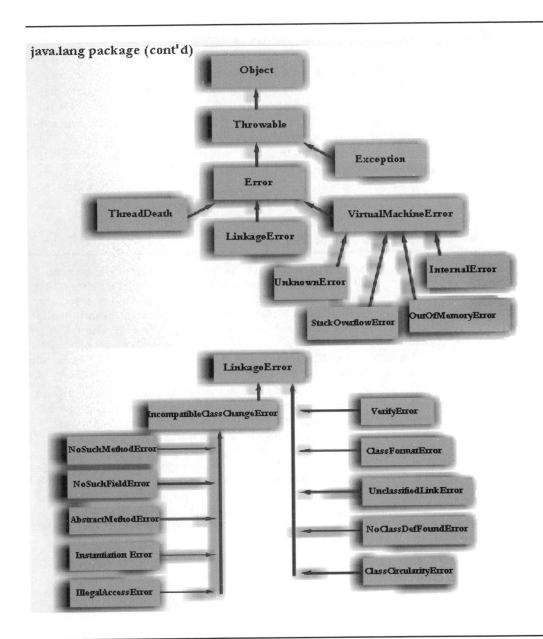

Figure 7.1   Continued

OBJECT CLASS

All objects in Java descend from the **Object** class. You have had a few glimpses of the **Object** class in previous chapters. Because all classes descend from **Object**, all classes may access **Object's** protected methods (**clone( )** and **finalize( )**), and all objects can be cast as an **Object**. This last feature is useful for storing arrays of objects, or building functions that may return a variety of types.

There are five methods that you may need to override in children of the **Object** class. These are enumerated in Table 7.1.

Table 7.1   Methods of Object That May Be Overridden

equals(Object o)	This method returns a **boolean.** Normally, it is intended to return **true** only if the object passed to it is the same class as the current object (**this**), and all of the fields of the two objects contain the same values. If you are overriding this method, it is considered prudent to call the **equals** method of any object that is a field of the current object. (They will in turn do the same to objects they contain.) If you are going to store objects of a particular class in a **Hashtable** (part of the **java.util** package), this method must be implemented.
hashcode( )	This method returns an **int.** How you choose to create an int from this an object of your class is up to you. If you are going to have a small number of entries, you should choose an algorithm that produces small values, such as bytes. In any case, choose something that distributes values relatively evenly over your chosen range. It is not critical that different objects produce different values. If you are going to store objects of a particular class in a **Hashtable** (part of the **java.util** package), this method must be implemented.
toString( )	This returns a **String.** Normally that string includes the class name and field names and values of all the important fields in the object.
clone( )	This returns an object that is a copy of the current (**this**) object. If the **clone** method is available, the subclass must implement the **Clonable** interface. This interface has no methods, but its presence is tested by the Java Virtual Machine. An implementation of the **clone( )** method should duplicate the values in any fields in the object, calling the clone methods for any objects that themselves are fields in the object.
finalize( )	Does this class allocate any non-memory resources? If so, you should make sure that the finalize method closes them. This method is normally called by the Garbage Collection thread just before an objects memory resources are returned to the system.

In addition to these, there are the **notify( )**, **notifyAll( )**, and **wait( )** methods, which we have seen in Chapter 6. Well, all right, we didn't actually see the **notifyAll** method in Chapter 6, but it is just like **notify**, except that it wakes up all waiting threads (not just one).

Class Class

This sounds silly or perhaps obscenely self-referential, but you will find this critical to large complex and distributed applications. Read on.

The last public (or protected) method of **Object** is the **getClass( )** method. This returns an object of the class **Class** (also in **java.lang**). The Class class is final, and so nothing inherits from it. There is one object of type Class for each class that is currently loaded in your application.

The methods of the **Class** object permit you to:

- (**forName**)   Get the Class object for a given class name, or if not yet present load a given class.
- (**getInterfaces**)   Get the list of interfaces that this class implements.
- (**getName**)   Get the name of this class
- (**getSuperclass**)   Get the Class object for the superclass of this class.
- (**isInterface**)   Determine whether this class is an interface.
- (**newInstance**)   Create a new instance of a class without using the **new** keyword.
- (**toString**)   There is also a **toString** method (see above).

Compiler Class

The compiler class is another class that nothing inherits from (**final**). It permits an application to compile a class on the fly, or potentially do some other compiler operations. This can prove especially useful when creating classes dynamically. Its **compileClass** and **compileClasses** methods are the ones that you are most apt to use. These are not the sorts of methods that you will be invoking lightly, but if you are going to create an application that permits users to design their own classes on the fly, this (and a few Class methods listed above) is something you will need.

STRING CLASSES

Strings are objects that contain an arbitrary number of Unicode characters. In spite of what *The Microsoft Word Thesaurus Tool* says, **Strings** and **Threads** are quite different in this context (see Chapter 6).

Two classes support strings: the **String** class and the **StringBuffer** class. What distinguishes the two is that **Strings** don't change, but the contents of one **StringBuffer** can change. On closer inspection, the differences are more detailed than that. The **StringBuffer** methods really only support inserting into, appending to, modifying, and determining the size and capacity of **StringBuffers**. The String methods support conversions from numeric types to strings, making comparisons, indexing, finding substrings, changing cases, or trimming white space.

Those familiar with C and C++ will find that just about anything they normally used from *<string.h>* is available in the methods of **String**.

The methods of these two classes are listed in the appendices, and what they do is fairly self-evident (and easy to verify). We list a few handy methods that will help with your first Java efforts, and the exercises below.

String Methods

String(String s)	A constructor, usually used with a literal string
String(char[ ] c)	Creates a String from an array of char values
valueOf(boolean b)	Returns either the string "true" or "false"
valueOf(int i)	Returns a string of numerals representing the value of i
valueOf(double d)	Similar to above, except for a double (floating point number)
compareTo(String s)	Like the C function *strcmp*; returns zero if they match
concat(String s)	Returns a string that is a concatenation of the current string and the string passed as a parameter
length( )	Returns the length of the current string
substring(int begin, int end)	Returns a substring from one index to the other
toCharArray( )	Returns a char array with the same string contents; this may be handy for hashing algorithms

toLowerCase( )	Returns the current string converted to lower case
toUpperCase( )	Guess what this does (see above)
trim( )	Removes white space characters from the end of the String

StringBuffer Methods

StringBuffer(int length)	A constructor, makes a buffer of a given size
StringBuffer(String s)	A constructor, makes a buffer just big enough for the given String
append(String s)	Appends a string to the end of the string in the buffer
capacity( )	Returns the current total size of the buffer
insert(int Offset, String s)	Inserts a string at the given offset
setCharAt(int index, char c)	Changes the character at the given offset into the string
setLength(int length)	Changes the length of the buffer; if the new size is smaller, this could lose data

You may not use any class as often as **String**. Since so much information is textual, the methods in **String** and **StringBuffer** will be constantly used. It will pay you well to review the appendix with the list of these methods and learn them.

WRAPPER CLASSES

Java supports several wrapper classes for the primitive types. Specifically they are **Boolean**, **Character**, **Double**, **Float**, **Integer**, and **Long**. You will notice that these names all have initial caps. Notice also that Integer and Character are spelled out. Lastly you should observe that Byte and Short are not present (they are supported under the Integer wrapper).

Wrapper classes have a number of handy methods for converting or testing properties of instances of the various primitive types. In addition to this, objects of the wrapper classes store one instance of that type. My ten-year-old son describes it as having a nice clean number wrapped with lots of object junk. He's not too far from the mark, but he is undervaluing the object junk.

It is worth going to the appendix and checking out all of the methods that these classes have.

Boolean

The Boolean class is a wrapper for the **boolean** primitive type. It has two constants, **TRUE** and **FALSE** whose values are **true** and **false** respectively. It also has a **valueOf( )** method that returns a **boolean** (note the lower case *b*, indicating the primitive type, not the wrapper class) based on **String** input. It has a method **booleanValue( )** that returns the value of the variable being wrapped (either **true** or **false**).

```
Boolean BWrapper;
boolean b
BWrapper = Boolean.getBoolean("true");
b = BWrapper.booleanValue();
```

Notice that in the above code fragment, **getBoolean** is a method of the class, and doesn't need an object to be created to use it. It is referenced by naming the class. The **booleanValue** method, on the other hand, gives the value of the contained boolean. It is referenced by naming the object.

Character

The character class is a wrapper for the **char** primitive type. It is a little more complicated than the Boolean wrapper class, but not by much. It has two integer constants, **MAX_RADIX** and **MIN_RADIX**, which are useful when checking to see if a character is a digit (A radix tells what base the number system in use is. Java supports small number of different radices, including 2, 8, 10, and 16).

The Character class has a few class methods for testing whether a given character (passed as a parameter) is a digit, or white space, upper case, lower case (**digit**, **isDigit**, **isLowerCase**, **isSpace**, **isUpper Case**). It also has a method to guaranty that the returned character is upper case, and a similar one for lower case (**toUpperCase**, **toLower Case**).

Aside from these, there is a constructor and an object method **charValue( )**, which returns the value of the char that is wrapped by this object.

```
Character CWrapper;
char c;
int digVal;
CWrapper = new Character('M');
if (Character.isDigit('5')
    CWrapper = new Character(' ');
if (Character.isSpace(CWrapper.charValue()))
    System.out.println("Since when is 5 not a digit?");
```

Notice in the above code fragment that we are using some class methods, accessed by naming the class (**isDigit**, and **isSpace**). We also use the **charValue** object method inside the parameter list of the **isSpace** method. To a newcomer to object-oriented programming, this may look a bit awkward, but you will get comfortable with this kind of construction via endless repetition. Notice also that we call the constructor twice for the same reference. When the second one is created, the first is thrown on the collection heap.

Double and Float

The **Double** and **Float** wrapper classes are very similar. The main differences deal with the **MAX_VALUE** and **MIN_VALUE** constants, which are about 10^{308} and 10^{38} respectively for the maximums, and somewhere near the reciprocal of that for the minimums. In addition to these there are constants for **POSITIVE_INFINITY**, **NEGATIVE_INFINITY**, and for **NaN** (Not a Number). There are class methods for testing for the infinite (**isInfinite, isNaN**). (Eschatology in a broader sense is currently outside the scope of Java, but there may eventually be a package that covers it.) There are methods for converting **longs** to **doubles**, and vice versa; also **floats** to **ints** and back again. There are methods for converting **Strings** to numbers.

```
Double DWrapper;
Float FWrapper;
double d;
float f;
long g;
DWrapper = new Double("6.0223e23");
FWrapper = new Float(DWrapper.floatValue( ));
d = DWrapper.doubleValue()
g = Double.doubleToLongBits(d);    // note overflow, but no error.
f = 1.0e30 * FWrapper.floatValue(); // max float exceeded.
if (Float.isInfinite(f))
    System.out.println("Some infinities are bigger than others");
```

In the above code fragment, we have shown the use of a few handy methods of the **Double** and **Float** wrapper classes.

Integer and Long

The **Integer** and **Long** wrapper classes are similar to each other as well. The biggest difference is the **MAX_VALUE** and **MIN_VALUE** constants (plus or minus about two billion for **Integer**, and plus or minus about nine quintillion for **Long**). Integers and Longs have no equivalent to infinity, but are blessed with parseInt methods that permit converting Strings to integers of any supported radix. There are also methods for creating **ints**, **longs**, **floats** or **doubles** from the value wrapped by the object.

```
Integer IWrapper;
Long LWrapper;
int i;
long g;
double d;
IWrapper = new Integer(5);
LWrapper = new Long(6);
d = IWrapper.doubleValue( );
i = Integer.parseInt("0377", 8); // An octal number.
g = Long.parseLong("3000000000");
```

Again, we are using some class methods, and some object methods. You can tell which is which by whether they are referenced by the class (**Long** or **Integer**) or by the object identifier (*IWrapper* or *LWrapper*).

MATH CLASS

Java is nearly a pure object-oriented language, thus, there are no libraries of math functions. What we have instead (supplied in **java.lang**) is a **Math** Class. The **Math** class has no constructors and no fields. It is purely a collection of methods, all of which are static (class methods).

There are double precision constants for the base of natural logarithms and the ratio of the diameter and circumference of a circle called **E** and **PI** respectively.

Aside from these, there are quite a few handy methods, including trig functions such as **acos**, **asin**, **atan**, **atan2**, **cos**, **sin**, and **tan**. There are some additional transcendental functions such as **exp**, **log**, **pow**, and **sqrt**. There are also some absolute value functions, rounding

functions, truncating functions, maximum and minimum comparison
functions (handy for sorting), and a random number generator.

```
double radius, circumference, angle, chord;
radius = 7910.0;
circumference = radius * Math.PI;
angle = (2.5/360.0) * (2.0 * Math.PI); // 2.5 degrees
chord = 2.0 * Math.sin(angle/2.0);
```

In the above code fragment, we see that we need to mention the
Math class with each invocation of a Math method. We also see that the
trig functions work in radians, not degrees.

SYSTEM-RELATED CLASSES

Additionally, there are four classes in the **java.lang** package that support the system (aside from the Compiler class, which we have already
discussed). These are **Process**, **Runtime**, **SecurityManager**, and
System. These classes deal with some system-dependent features. The
methods themselves are the same across all Java supporting platforms,
but some of the parameters used in the invocations will need to be tailored to a particular environment.

Process

A process is a separate process going on (potentially) outside the Java
Virtual Machine. It is not a Java Thread. It is a separate application or
system call.

    Process is an abstract class. You cannot make a new process object.
Instead, when you invoke **Runtime.exec( )** (see below) a system dependent subclass of process is created for you. This class has methods for
destroying the process and getting the Input, Output, and Error
streams from the process. (**getErrorStream( )**, **getInputStream( )**,
and **getOutputStream( )**).

    There is not much more to it than that. To sum up, when a process
is created for you, you get one of these to help handle that process.

Runtime

Runtime has a class method called **getRuntime( )**. If you invoke this,
you get a Runtime object for the current platform. It allows you to handle some system-dependent tasks in a platform-independent way. It is
worth looking at the appendix to make a mental note of what methods
Runtime provides.

Runtime's most popular method is the one that allows an application to launch a new process by running commands on the operating system. This method is called **exec( )**. There are several versions of this with varying parameter lists.

Runtime has an **exit** method that enables your application to cause the entire Java interpreter to stop running. It has methods (**free Memory( )** and **totalMemory( )**) that let you find out how much memory is available in the system. It has methods for getting IO streams that convert between Unicode and whatever the local character encoding is (almost always ASCII so far) (**getLocalizedInputStream( )**, **getLocalizedOutputStream( )**). There are methods that speed up the process of Garbage Collection (**gc( )**, **runFinalization( )**). There are methods for loading dynamic libraries (**load( )** and **loadLibrary( )**). There are also methods to enable the tracing of instructions and method calls (**traceInstructions( )**, **traceMethodCalls( )**).

Some of the above methods can be performed using the similar calls in the **System** Class (see below).

SecurityManager

If you are not creating a browser, you probably won't need to implement this abstract class. It sets the various security lockouts on Java applets. It is beyond the scope of this Java primer to tell you much more about this class. Still, if you are planning to build a large distributed system, you may want to play with this a bit. Check the appendix.

System

The **System** class provides handy methods to access information from the system in a platform-independent manner. The **System** class is final, and has nothing but static methods. You will never need to create a **System** object. Simply call directly the many handy class methods that are provided.

> **NOTE**
>
> ### Now You Know
>
> Do you recall all of those uses of **System.out.println**("*Hello*"); ? Now you know what they are. **println** is a method of the **PrintStream** class. **System.out** is an instance of that stream.

Aside from providing the three standard IO streams (**in**, **out**, and **err**) provides the following:

- **arraycopy**   A method for copying arrays
- **currentTimeMillis** A method for getting the current time in milliseconds
- **exit**   Same as the Runtime method, causes the Java interpreter to stop running
- **gc**   Same as the Runtime method, steps up garbage collection (by making it synchronized)
- **getProperties**, **getProperty**, **setProperty**   Provide control on environment variables
- **load**, **loadLibrary**   Same as the Runtime methods, load dynamic libraries
- **setSecurityManager** Implements a security manager (see above)

WARNING

Security May Be an Issue

If you are building large applications in Java, the system class will become a good friend of yours.

Still, one of Java's big selling points is that it is more secure than most languages against the slings and arrows of outrageous hackers. Java will continue to be secure, but you may, by invoking other programs, open yourself to other kinds of attacks. Bear in mind such homilies as "A chain is only as strong as its weakest link." If security is an issue for you, you should only exec very trusted applications at your site.

EXERCISES

7-1   Create a class called *myColor*, which extends Object by having three long fields, *redVal*, *greenVal*, and *blueVal*. Also, make it clonable, and write **equals** and **hashCode** methods.

7-2   Write a main method for your *myColor* class. Make that method call the *Class.forName("myColor")* method. Write the names of the interfaces that make up this class to **System.out**.

7-3   Create the **toString** method for your class. Construct the string by putting all of the information Class will tell you about your class into a StringBuffer, and add the information in your data fields.

7-4   Make getColor and setColor methods that show the user a logarithmic scale of color intensity. (Hide the linear numbers from the user.) Use the Math methods to convert them, and wrapper methods to convert doubles to longs.

7-5   Make a new private field that stores the time of last change. Use the **System.currentTimeMillis** method to keep track of it. Make a method that tells how long it has been since the last change. Modify *setColor* to zero that field.

7-6   Make a method that reports the free and total memory available in the system.

CHAPTER 8

Exceptions in Java

In this chapter we cover the following topics:

- **Try-Catch-Finally in Detail**
- **The Throwable Class**
- **Throw and Throws Keywords**
- **All the Standard Exceptions**

As the name implies, exceptions are a way to deal with the unexpected. In a lot of programming environments, these tend to be called errors. For example, if your application is going to open a disk file for reading, in normal operation, that file would be open. Certain exceptions are possible, however, such as:

1. The file may have permissions set that prevent reading it.
2. The file's directory information may be corrupt.
3. The file may not exist where the application is looking.
4. The hardware supporting the file i/o may not be available.
5. The operating system's file handling functions may be corrupt.
6. There may not be enough memory available to construct the file buffers.

How do you handle these things? In other languages, they may be handled by getting some kind return value back from the function that opens the file. Then the application must handle the situation with a collection of if-then type statements.

The **java.lang** package supplies a class called **Throwable** that helps to implement Java's exception-handling mechanism. (Those familiar with C++ 4.0 will recognize this as being very similar to their own familiar exception handling.) Briefly, when an exception occurs, the method recognizing the exception creates an **exception** object and **throws** it. It is up to the hierarchy of methods that called the exceptional one to catch that exception and handle it.

The mechanism for catching such exceptions is the **try** block, followed by **catch** clauses (Figure 8.1). If an exception occurs within a **try** block, the following **catch** clauses get first dibs on it. If none of them can handle it, control passes back to the method that called the current

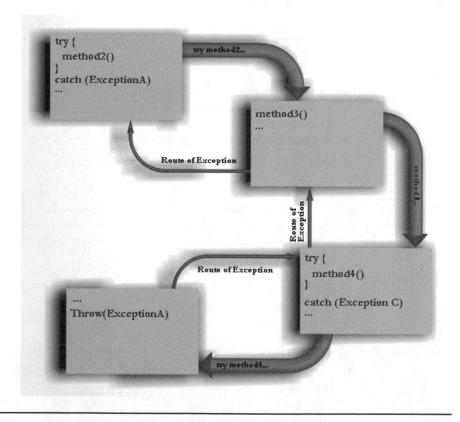

Figure 8.1   If a method can't catch an exception, the method that called it gets a chance, and so on.

one. If that call was in a **try** block, its **catch** statements get a shot at it. Ultimately an uncaught exception goes up to the Java interpreter, which reports the exception and exits.

As part of truth in advertising, methods are required to report what exceptions they may throw in their declarations. This does not include such runtime exceptions as integer divide by zero, but it does cover most of the exceptions supplied by the standard packages.

TRY-CATCH-FINALLY IN DETAIL

In Chapter 4 we saw a brief explanation of the try-catch-finally block. It is really very simple, and may not need much more explanation than that, but let's review it and look at an example.

You may mark a block of code (enclosed within curly-braces) with the **try** keyword. If an exception occurs while the interpreter is executing that block of code, it unhesitatingly goes to the collection of **catch** statements that immediately follow the **try** block.

These **catch** statements take an exception as a parameter. If the **exception** thrown is the same class as the **catch** statement's parameter (or a subclass of the parameter), the **catch** statement is invoked, and the **exception** is cleared. If the block of code in the **catch** statement can't handle this particular **exception**, you may throw it again in the **catch** block, and let a higher level method handle it.

If there is a **finally** clause, it will be executed regardless of whether there was an exception. This is a good place to deallocate system resources that might get skipped with the path of execution being suddenly changed. Some Java applications use a **try** block with a **finally** clause, and have no **catch** statements in between. This is a perfectly reasonable construction.

Perhaps the simplest example that you will run into of this try-catch business is sleep. It is almost ubiquitous.

```
try {
    Thread.sleep(1000); // waits 1000 milliseconds
}
catch (InterruptedException e) { // no big deal, do nothing.
}
```

In this example, the **try** block contains one statement: a method call to the **Thread** class method **sleep**. If you look at that method in the appendix, you can see that it declares that it throws the **Interrupted Exception**. We are therefore obliged, when we use this method, either to catch that exception or report in our method declaration that it too throws the **InterruptedException**. So rather than let some interrupt kick us out of our flow of control and leave us in who knows what state, we catch it.

In this case, the catch method calls the particular exception object *e*. We do nothing with this exception, but as exceptions go, it is a pretty harmless one.

THE THROWABLE CLASS

Exceptions (and errors) are descended from the **Throwable** class (part of the **java.lang** package). This class has two constructors: in one you supply a String with a hopefully useful message; in the other you don't. The other methods supplied by the **Throwable** class include:

- **fillInStackTrace**, which extends the stack trace if an exception is partially handled, and then rethrown.
- **getMessage**, which returns the message associated with this exception (or error).
- **printStackTrace**, which sends the stack trace to standard error (by default), or to whatever PrintStream you send it to.
- **toString**, which you may override as you see fit.

Normally, there is not a lot of logic that needs to be part of the exception itself. It is merely a token to be passed from method to method, until the event that triggered it is resolved to the taste of the application developer. You may create your own application or package specific exceptions simply by extending the **Throwable** class (well, actually extending its subclass **Exception**). The following example shows how you might to this.

```
public class OxygenFuelCellAboutToExplodeException extends Exception {
    public String toString( ) {
        return { "Houston, we've had a problem"};
    }
}
```

As you can see there is very little left for you to do, except create the class.

THROW AND THROWS KEYWORDS

These two keywords look very similar, and both participate in the exception handling mechanism of Java. They are very different in their usage, however, and if you are new to Java you should be careful to learn the difference. (Rest assured that the compiler will always tell you if get them confused.)

Throws

You may remember Table 4.4 in which we described the parts of a method declaration—the last item before the body code block was the **throws** list. This is a list of exceptions that this method could potentially throw, which any good program calling it should be prepared to catch. It is really that simple. If you look at the definition of the Thread class in the appendix, you will see the sleep method as:

```
public static void sleep(long millis) throws InterruptedException;
```

It is because of this declaration that we must put any calls to **Thread.sleep** in a **try-catch** block. Failure to do so will result in a compile time error, unless it is part of a method that already declares that it throws that same exception.

Throw

Now you know how to create a class of exceptions, how to catch them, and what happens when you don't. There is another exception-related keyword in Java, and that is Throw. You saw some discussion of this in Chapter 4, under the Jump statements.

To aid in your understanding of this topic, we return to that venerable rhetorical style, the dialog:

*When can you execute a **throw** statement?*

Anytime.

Where does the flow of control go then?

In the hierarchy of method calls, somewhere, perhaps back in the Java interpreter, there is something that catches that exception. After executing every **finally** clause along the way, execution goes to that **catch** statement.

If the exception was not caught, can the flow of control somehow get back to the same place?

Not without starting all over.

If my method catches an exception, and then determines that it is not fully handled, what do I do?

You already have the **exception** object. Just **throw** it again.

Is this really simpler than handling errors in a procedural language?

Yes, and the more complex your application, the more you will realize it.

WARNING

Throw Objects Not Classes

Some new Java programmers are inclined to try to use **throw** with a **class** as the parameter. You should note that the **throw** statement takes an exception **object** as an argument, not an exception **class**, so it is up to the application to create that object before the throw is called.

Let's look at a short example that throws an exception:

```
if (LiquidOxygenFuelCell.getPressure( ) > LiquidOxygenFuelCell.MAX_PRESSURE) {
    e = new OxygenFuelCellAboutToExplodeException( );
    throw e;
}
```

Naturally, there is a great deal left to the imagination about the class *LiquidOxygenFuelCell*, but hopefully the example demonstrates the simple mechanism of throwing an exception—in this case the object *e*, which is an instance of the *OxygenFuelCellAboutToExplodeException* class.

ALL THE STANDARD EXCEPTIONS

Many exceptions are supported under Java; every new package will have more. We can see the exceptions in Figure 8.2.

Similarly, Java has a number of throwable errors. You can catch these if you want, but generally, if it is an error that is generated, you are probably in bigger trouble than can normally be handled in software. If it is an **OutOfMemoryError**, you might try killing a few processes; if it is an **IllegalAccessError**, you may want to inform the user, and give him or her more legal options. Generally, with an error, however, you should just let the application die, and then you should figure out why it happened using the debugger or some system maintenance tool. These errors are seen in Figure 8.3.

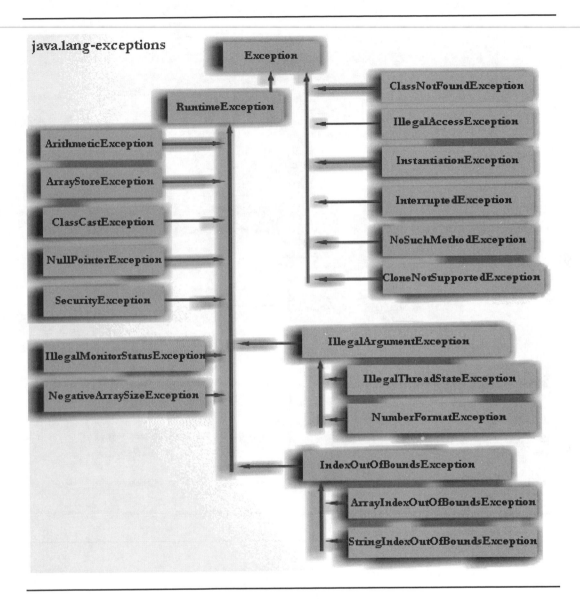

Figure 8.2 Exception classes in Java.

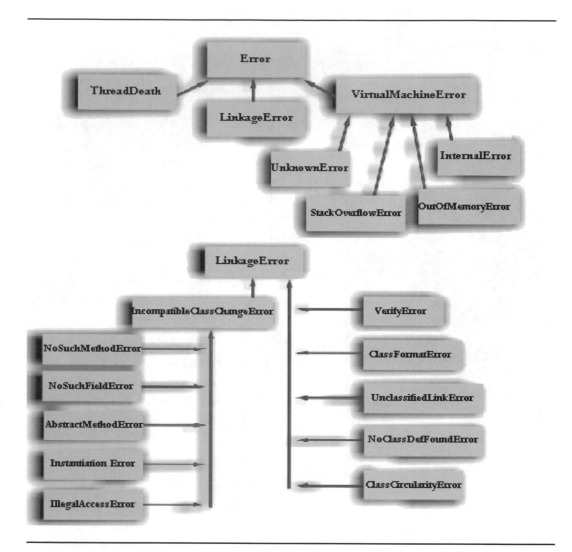

Figure 8.3   Error classes in Java.

EXERCISES

8-1   Create an application called *power* that takes up to two numbers on the command line (the **args[ ]** array in main), and converts them from **String** to doubles. The application should then print the value of the first one, raised to the second one as a power (e.g., *java power 3.0 2.0* would yield a result of 9.0).

8-2   Build in **try-catch** blocks that catch the **NumberFormat Exception**.

8-3   Find out what exception to catch if there is fewer than two numbers on the command line. Catch it, and do something useful as a default.

8-4   Create your own exception to throw if the result is infinite, zero, or not-a-number. Catch it.

CHAPTER 9

Java Applets & the java.applet Package

In this chapter we cover the following topics:

- **The Difference Between Java Applets and Java Applications**
- **The Applet Class**
- **The HTML APPLET Tag**
- **Constructing an Applet in an Application**
- **The AppletContext Interface**
- **The AudioClip Interface**

If it weren't for applets, you probably wouldn't have heard of Java yet. Applets are colorful and animated little toys on web pages. They are included in an HTML page by using the <APPLET...> tag. However, they have now become more than that. With connections to applications on the server side, potentially including database engines, applets have expanded to include what we in the business call thin clients.

Applets depend on the Java-enabled browser that is viewing the web page to provide the applet context, and to call the **init**, **start**, and **repaint** methods of the applet.

Applications, on the other hand, may stand alone. They can do anything that a full-fledged application in any other language may do (maybe more).

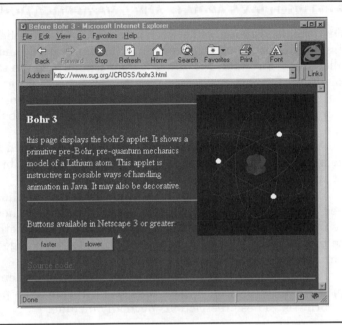

Figure 9.1   An eye-catching web page with an applet in the upper right corner.

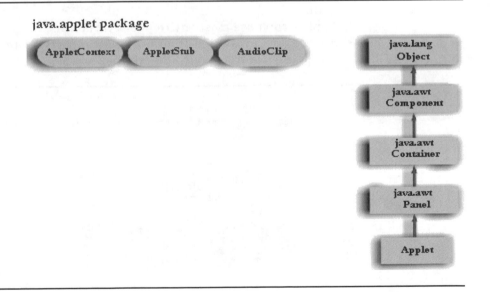

Figure 9.2   The java.applet package.

THE DIFFERENCE BETWEEN JAVA APPLETS AND JAVA APPLICATIONS

What are the differences between an applet and an application in Java? First, with an applet, the browser is the application, and the applet is called by the browser, according to instructions given in the HTML document. Applets come with many built-in features. They are an extension of a graphics panel, so there is an assumption of graphics capabilities. There is an assumption that there is a source for the web page, and such context features as a status line.

A nontrivial applet must have either its **init** method fleshed out, or the **start** method (or both). These are hooks that the browser uses to get the applet initialized and started.

It must also have either its **update** or **paint** method filled in (or, once again, both). The browser calls the **repaint** method, which calls the **update** method. If you don't override the **update** method, it will call the **paint** method. This happens every time the web page is redrawn on your screen.

Another (perhaps the biggest) difference between applets and applications is that an applet has certain restrictions placed on it by the browser. These restrictions normally include:

- The browser prevents most or all disk input and output on the client system. (Netscape prevents all disk I/O, some other browsers permit writing to a particular temp directory in the browser's folder [path].)
- Applets can't see most environment variables.
- Applets are prevented from opening connections to any system except the one from which the web page came.

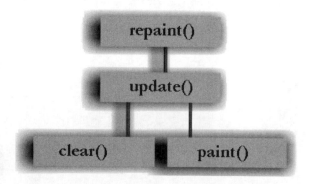

Figure 9.3   Browser calls repaint and chain begins.

- They cannot allocate most system resources (except memory and client sockets).
- Applets cannot start processes on the local system.

An application has no more restrictions than an application written in any other language.

- The only way into an application is through the main method.
- They are not restricted as to which URLs they can open.
- They have the same file access permission as any other application on your system.
- They can see all of the environment variables in the current shell.
- They can invoke any command or application on the local system (except when blocked by system permissions).
- They can listen to server sockets.

Summing up, an applet is a special class that has been created for use by browsers, and is therefore subject to enormous security restrictions. An application is trusted and needs not be so constrained.

NOTE

Security Gets in the Way!

Stop whining. Applets get loaded and execute automatically. You can do many useful things with applets as thin clients. All the file I/O and network connections can be done on the server side. If applets could do file I/O, they could be used to do all sorts of malicious things, and you wouldn't know until it was too late. Someday, when no one is ill-tempered and all code is bug free, these restrictions can be dropped; but until then these precautions are here for your own safety.

THE APPLET CLASS

The **Applet** class is the mother of all applets. That is not to say it is a great one by itself; it is really rather plain. It will usually appear as a featureless gray box that does nothing. It is the superclass from which all other applets have extended.

Applet comes with about twenty methods, which will each come in handy in some situation or another. These methods are:

Applet( )	The default constructor.
destroy( )	Destroys the applet, and cleans up its resources.
getAppletContext( )	Returns an **AppletContext** object for this applet (see below).
getAppletInfo( )	Programmers should use this to supply author and version info.
getAudioClip(URL url)	Returns an audio clip from a given URL.
getCodeBase( )	Returns the URL of the applet.
getDocumentBase( )	Returns the URL of the HTML document in which the applet is embedded.
getImage(URL url)	Returns an image from the given URL. Note this method returns almost immediately, and the image gets filled in as it arrives. This may result in some quirky behavior on some systems.
getParameter (String name)	Returns a String with the value of any parameter from the APPLET tag in the HTML document with the given name.
getParameterInfo( )	Returns an array of Strings with the name, type, and description of each parameter known to the applet.
init( )	Programmer-supplied method. This is the first method called by the browser.
isActive( )	Returns a boolean telling whether the applet is active. (An applet becomes active just before its start method is called.)
play(URL url)	Plays an audio clip.
resize(int width, int height)	Called to tell the applet to resize itself. The effect this has depends quite a bit on the browser.
setStub (AppletStub stub)	Don't worry about this, this is the interface between the applet and the browser, but normally you shouldn't be using it explicitly.

showStatus (String msg)	Write a message to the browser's status line.
start( )	Start the applet. You, the programmer, supply the body code for this method.
stop( )	You may flesh this one out too. This is called just before **destroy( )**.

Some of the above methods are overloaded and have optional calling parameters. Check the appendix for more information.

The traditional first applet can be written as follows:

```
import java.applet.Applet; // create naming short cuts for Applet & awt
import java.awt.*;         // you'll see more on the awt later.
public class Hello extends Applet {
    public void paint(Graphics g) {
        g.drawString("Hello", 30, 50);
    }
}
```

This new class Hello extends the applet class, and overrides the paint method, which used to do nothing, and now draws the one line of text—"Hello"—at the location 30 pixels from the left boarder and 50 pixels down from the top boarder.

You may recall from earlier chapters that the **import** statement doesn't load anything, it merely makes it so that we may refer to **java.applet.Applet** simply as **Applet**. We may also now refer to any of the **java.awt** classes by name without the **java.awt** prefix. This instead of saying *public void paint(**java.awt.Graphics** g)*, we have made an easier to read line of code.

THE HTML APPLET TAG

Having an ideally prepared applet is fine, but if you do not have an appropriate **APPLET** tag in your HTML (HyperText Markup Language) document, no one will ever see it. The nature of an HTML APPLET tag varies a bit from HTML version to HTML version.

If you are unfamiliar with HTML, you should either take the examples on faith, or you should learn about it from another source. There are many adequate books on the subject, and it should only take you an hour or so to get comfy with it.

HTML supports an APPLET tag, which like the IMAGE tag permits placing and defining the size and source for an image that is part of the document. Minimally, an applet tag looks like this:

```
<APPLET CODE=Hello.class WIDTH=300 HEIGHT=200>
<P>This is a message for people who's browsers are not Java enabled.
</APPLET>
```

This minimal use of the tag would create a place on the web page that was 300 pixels wide and 200 pixels long, in which an applet called Hello.class would go. On the server, that applet would have to be saved in the same directory as the HTML page on which it appears.

There are optional parts to the APPLET tag. We list the parts as following parts (items inside square brackets are optional):

```
<APPLET
    [CODEBASE=url for the applet]
    CODE=filename for the applet
    WIDTH=width in pixels
    HEIGHT=height in pixels
    [ALT=text that appears instead of the applet on non-Java browsers]
    [NAME=name of the applet object]
    [ALIGN=alignment such as top, middle, bottom]
    [VSPACE=pixels of vertical margin around the applet]
    [HSPACE=pixels of horizontal margin around the applet]
>
[<PARAM NAME=parameter name VALUE=parameter value>]
[<PARAM NAME=parameter name VALUE=parameter value>]
...
[HTML replacing applet in non-Java browsers]
</APPLET>
```

Standards are still developing that will enable scripting languages to interact with applets via the NAME feature of the applet. Such features are in place, but they are changing very rapidly. We will discuss some of these in Part III of this book.

It is also worth noting that the EMBED tag should soon also be able to handle applets.

CONSTRUCTING AN APPLET IN AN APPLICATION

You may build a class that can be used as an applet, but which, when run directly by the interpreter, will also run by itself. Intellectually, it is not difficult, and Visual J++'s Applet wizard does most of the work for you The hand-waving explanation is that you must create a main method that creates a **frame** (see Chapter 10), onto which you add the applet. You then must call the applet's **init** and **start** methods. All in all, not that complicated.

```java
/* Jay Cross, copyright 1996
 *
 *  The goal here is to create a minimal applet which
 *  may run as a stand alone application.
 *  Note that if there is any use of the applet
 *  context, such as showStatus, these methods must
 *  be provided by the calling Frame.

import java.awt.*;
import java.applet.*;

public class StandAlone extends Applet {

    Font theFont = new Font ("TimesRoman",Font.Bold,24);

    public static void main (String s[]) {
        Frame f = new Frame ("My Window");
        StandAlone hi = new StandAlone();
        hi.init();
        hi.start();

        f.add("Center", hi);
        f.resize(300,200);
        f.show();
    }

    public void paint (Graphics g) {
      g.setFont(theFont);
      g.setColor(Color.cyan);
      g.drawRect (5, 5, this.size().width-10, this.size().height-10);
      g.drawString("On my own two feet", 30, 30);
    }
}
```

Thus, we see that while there are differences between applets and applications, you can have both in one place. In this case, when invoked as an applet, the application code stands unused. When coming up as an application, the main method and frame simulate the context provided by a browser.

THE APPLETCONTEXT INTERFACE

In addition to the **Applet** class, the **java.applet** package provides an interface called **AppletContext**. This interface is fleshed out and used to create an object that is passed to the applet. That object has the following methods:

getApplet(String name)	Returns an applet, given its name. (Doesn't work on all browsers.)
getApplets( )	Returns an enumeration list of all the applets in this context. (May not work consistently on all browsers.)
getAudioClip(URL url)	Returns an AudioClip from a given URL.
getImage(URL url)	Returns an Image from a given URL.
showDocument(URL url)	Shows the document at a given URL. Note: an optional parameter lets you establish where it will be shown.
showStatus(String msg)	Write a message to the browser's status bar.

It is possible using the **getApplet** or **getApplets** methods to establish communication between two applets on the same page. This is accomplished by getting a reference to the other applet, and invoking its public methods.

```
import java.applet.*;
import java.awt.*;
import java.util.*;
public class Talker extends Applet {
    Enumeration en;
    Listener Recv;

    public void init() {
        // Now try to get some Applet contexts.
        en = this.getAppletContext().getApplets();
        while (en.hasMoreElements()) {
            Object o = en.nextElement();
            String name = o.getClass().getName();

            if (name.equals("Listener")) {
                if (Recv != null)
```

```
                              // do nothing, we found a second one.
                    else
                        Recv = (Listener) o;
                }
            }
        }

        public boolean mouseDown(Event e, int x, int y) {
            Recv.getMsg("I got a mouse event", x, y);
            return true;
        }
    }
```

The above code fragment assumes that there is another applet on the same web page called *Listener*. The *Talker* applet finds that applet, and (whenever it gets a mouseDown event) invokes its *getMsg* method, which we presume is able to get a **String** and two **ints** and do something with them.

You will learn much more about events in the next few chapters.

THE AUDIOCLIP INTERFACE

Java's applet package has a class supporting audio clips. This is called the AudioClip interface. Whenever you get an audioClip, the following three methods have been supplied:

loop( )　　Continuously plays the audio clip (it had better be a tasteful clip).

play( )　　Plays the audio clip once.

stop( )　　Stops playing the audio clip.

You may well ask, why is the audio clip control here? The answer is that it had to go somewhere. Do not be surprised if sometime in the next year or so a much more comprehensive audio package becomes available. Until then, here it is.

EXERCISES

Note all applets need corresponding pieces of HTML. You will need to create them, too.

9-1　　Name five nasty ways you could use applets if they didn't restrict file access or local process invocation.

9-2 Write an applet that gets all of the **AppletContext** information it can and uses the **java.awt.Graphics.drawString** method repeatedly to put it on the screen.

9-3 Write an applet that uses the **getParameter** method to get the code name that the applet will use for future communication. Build that parameter into your HTML document.

9-4 Modify the previous example to also write that code word on the status bar of the browser.

9-5 Write the Listener applet mentioned in the above example so that it has the getMsg method, make it take the data it gets from that method, and write it out to the status line.

CHAPTER 10

The Java Abstract Window Toolkit (java.awt)

In this chapter we cover the following topics:

- **Graphics, Fonts, and Colors**
- **Containers, Panels, and Components**
- **Events and Observables**
- **Menus**
- **Layout Managers**
- **Images**
- **The java.awt.peer Package**

Are you the sort who checks out how long each chapter is before starting to read it? Don't look, and keep a bookmark handy. This is a long one. Why is it long? It is long for two reasons. First, because there are a lot of classes and methods in the Abstract Windows Toolkit; and second, because we finally know enough Java that we can start showing more riveting examples (Figure 10.1).

If you are the type to skip around a lot, you may also know that Visual J++ provides some resource editors that take away a bit of the need to know the AWT intimately. Be assured that it is still important for you to be familiar with how this all works. So read on, intrepid student, and learn the AWT.

A friend described the AWT as supporting the lowest common denominator of all the target windows systems it is supposed to support. Still there is a lot there. The AWT supports Windows95, Windows

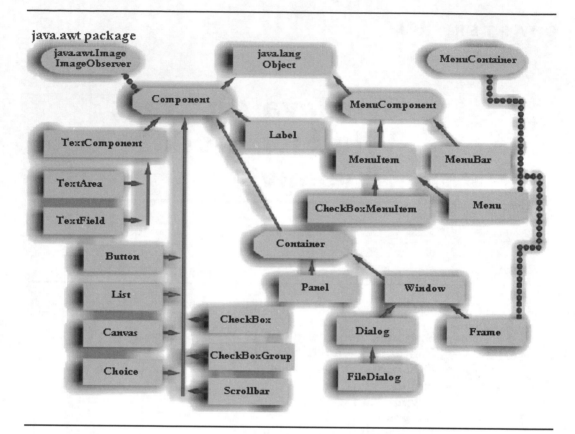

Figure 10.1   The java.awt package.

NT, the Macintosh, and several flavors of X-Windows supporting UNIX, such as Solaris and IRIX. If you have been creating applications in C++ for any of these environments, Java's AWT will seem familiar (Figure 10.2). You may be used to some features that are not supported under Java. Bear with it, this is the price of platform independence.

It is convenient to divide the AWT into eight groups of classes. These make up our subheadings, and include: graphics, containers, events, menus, layout managers, dialogs, images, and the peer package. Of these, images and the peer package are actually separate packages. The image package is a natural extension of the AWT, but the peer package contains the connections to the native window system. You, the application developer, should never have to use this one.

java.awt package

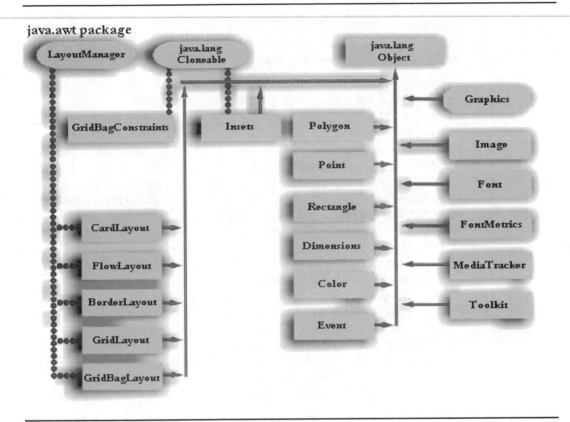

Figure 10.1   Continued

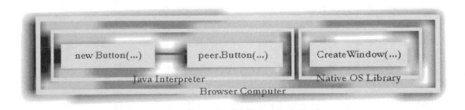

Figure 10.2   When Java is ported to a new environment, the AWT stubs are built to make use of the native window toolkit. As a result, a Java application has qualities that are particular to the system on which it is running.

To follow all of the examples in this section, you will need to create a stripped-down applet, which we will add to. To do this in Visual J++, follow these steps. (Refer to Chapter 2 for details. If you have more detailed questions, see Part II of this book.)

1. Start **Visual J++** (double click the icon).
2. From the **File** menu (top left) select **New.**
3. On the **Project** page of the dialog, make sure **Create new workspace** is checked.
4. From the **Type** menu (left side of dialog), select **Java Applet Wizard**. In the **Name** box call it *awtTest*. Make sure your location is someplace reasonable. In these exercises it will be in a default created in Chapter two (*C:\ATestArea\awtTest*). Click **Create...** .
5. On **Step 1 of 5**, select **As an applet only**. Our examples will not have the optional source file comments, but you may include them if you like.
6. On **Step 2 of 5**, you would **like a sample HTML file. Width** of *320* and **Height** of *240* will be fine.
7. On **Step 3 of 5**, you do not want **your applet to be multi-threaded**, you don't **want support for animation**, and you don't want any **mouse event handlers added**.
8. On **Step 4 of 5**, you do not need any parameters, so just go to **next**.
9. On **Step 5 of 5**, replace line two **Author: Unknown**, with *Author:* and *your name*. Click **Finish**.
10. Review the **New Project Information** Page, and Click **OK** (assuming no glaring errors).

If you look at the **FileView** page, and open the *awtTest files* folder, you will see an **html** file, and a **java** file. The html file is the minimal web page supporting the applet. It has the applet between a pair of horizontal rules (lines), and it has a hyperlink (href) to the source file (not required, but a nice feature). The .html file looks like this:

```
<html>
<head>
<title>awtTest</title>
</head>
<body>
<hr>
<applet
    code=awtTest.class
    id=awtTest
    width=320
    height=240 >
</applet>
```

```
<hr>
<a href="awtTest.java">The source.</a>
</body>
</html>
```

The java file is the source code for the applet itself. We will be modifying this in this chapter. Before we modify it at all, it looks like this:

```java
import java.applet.*;
import java.awt.*;

public class awtTest extends Applet
{

    public awtTest()
    {
    }

    public String getAppletInfo()
    {
        return "Name: awtTest\r\n" +
            "Author: Cross & Saganich\r\n" +
            "Created with Microsoft Visual J++ Version 1.0";
    }

    public void init()
    {
        // If you use a ResourceWizard-generated "control creator" class to
        // arrange controls in your applet, you may want to call its
        // CreateControls() method from within this method. Remove the
        // following
        // call to resize() before adding the call to CreateControls();
        // CreateControls() does its own resizing.
        // -------------------------------------------------------------
        resize(320, 240);
    }

    public void destroy()
    {
    }

    public void paint(Graphics g)
    {
    }

    public void start()
    {
    }
```

```
public void stop()
{
}

}
```

We will remove the constructor (*awtTest( )*), and the **getAppletInfo**, **init**, **destroy**, **start**, and **stop** methods, and a few blank lines. The result looks like this:

```
import java.applet.*;
import java.awt.*;

public class awtTest extends Applet
{
    public void paint(Graphics g)
    {
    }
}
```

NOTE

A Quick Review of What This Applet Does

- This applet will not appear to do anything.
- The two import statements provide shorthand ways to say **Applet** instead of **java.applet.Applet**, and **Graphics** instead of **java.awt.Graphics**.
- A new class is defined (called awtTest), which is a subclass of the Applet class.
- It's one method is the paint method, which takes a **Graphics** object as a parameter (see below), returns no value (**void**), and does nothing when executed (no body code).
- Both the class, and its **paint** method are **public**ly available.

The **init** and **start** methods are called by the browser. In this case, we didn't override them, and so the default applet methods (which do nothing) are invoked.

The **paint** method for this applet is called by the **update (Graphics g)** method (which you may also override), which itself is called by the **repaint( )** method, which is final. **repaint( )** is called by the browser at appropriate times.

This bit of Visual J++ behind us, let's proceed to learning about the AWT.

GRAPHICS, FONTS, AND COLORS

Simplest of all windows features are the graphics elements, including the colors and fonts. They are static and therefore have few mysterious properties. These features are supported by several of the classes in the Abstract Window Toolkit (AWT). In particular, these are the **Color**, **Font**, **FontMetrics**, **Graphics**, **Point**, **Polygon**, and **Rectangle** classes. These classes are described in detail in the appendices, but let's look at how they are used.

Color

Colors in Java have 16,777,216 (2^{24}) possible values, because there are three component colors (red, green, and blue, usually referred to as r, g, and b respectively), which each may have values of 0 to 255. How Java stores these is unimportant.

AWT's Color class has three constructors, permitting the use of separate rgb values, a single int with values 0 to 16777215, or the use of floats. The class also provides eleven built in colors, namely **black**, **blue**, **cyan**, **darkGray**, **gray**, **green**, **lightGray**, **magenta**, **orange**, **pink**, **red**, **white**, and **yellow**. Additionally, there are methods that permit conversion from rgb to hue, saturation, and brightness (hsb) values, and methods for getting and setting the component values of a color object.

The following code fragment shows how you may create a **Color** object. Actually using one will be demonstrated in the section on the Graphics class.

```
Color c1, c2, c3;
int rval;
c1 = new Color(127, 0, 0); // a dark red
c2 = Color.blue;           // c2 is now a reference to a class constant.
c3 = c2.brighter( );       // c3 is a brighter blue than blue.
rval = c1.getRed( );       // rval gets 127.
```

Font

Java supports fonts through the **Font** class. A font object stores the information required to keep track of what font is being used. This includes the name, size, and style of the font. In Java 1.02 (the version used in the first release of Visual J++) there are three font names available (**TimesRoman**, **Helvetica**, and **Courier**). Three styles are built in (**PLAIN**, **BOLD**, and **ITALIC**). The sizes are said to be in points, and while no concrete physical dimension can really be appropriate, it is not a bad approximation. Font objects also include several handy methods for manipulating these values, such as **getName**, **getSize**, **getStyle**.

The following code fragment shows how you may create a **Font** object. Actually using one will be demonstrated in the section on the Graphics class.

```
Font f1, f2;
f1 = new Font("Helvetica", Font.BOLD, 72); // Create Banner Headlines.
f2 = new Font("TimesRoman", Font.PLAIN, 6); // for legal contracts.
if (f2.equals(f1))
    System.out.println("Something is rotten in the state of Denmark");
```

FontMetrics

You can create fonts all you like, but there are times when you need to know more about your text before you use it. For this reason, Java also provides a **FontMetrics** class. The methods of this class can be used to tell you the length (in pixels) of a character or **String** in a particular font. It can also be used to find the size of ascenders (the upper tail on the *d*, for example) and descenders (e.g., the lower tail on a *p*). Such measurements are needed when you are laying out or moving text in an animation.

The following code shows how you might create a **FontMetrics** object and use it.

```
FontMetrics fm1;
Font f1 = new Font("Courier", Font.ITALIC, 16);
String s1 = "Holy Hannah, Batman! She's a mermaid!";
int horiz, vert;
fm1 = new FontMetrics(f1); // create the FontMetric for this Font.
horiz = fm1.stringWidth(s1);
vert = fm1.getHeight( );   // don't need String to get the Height.
```

There are several other things you can do with **FontMetrics**, but it will probably be rare that you'll need to. Check the appendix for more details.

Point

You can already guess what a Point object is. It holds an x and y value (integers), representing Cartesian coordinates. This class is used by several other classes in the AWT, and also provides the handy method translate(int x, int y), which adds x and y to their counterpart fields within the Point. Unusually, these fields may be accessed directly.

```
Point p = new Point( 100, 100);
p.translate(-50, 100);              // p now is (50, 200)
```

Polygon

Another handy class for Graphics object methods in Java is the **Polygon** class. **Polygons** contain two arrays of integers, one for x values and one for y values. It also has another integer telling how many points are in the polygon object. Oddly, polygons do not use arrays of Points (see above); perhaps they will in version 1.1, or in the forthcoming 2D and 3D graphics packages.

Polygons also have handy methods to tell if a point is inside the polygon (**inside(int x, int y)**), to add a new Point (**addPoint(int x, int y)**), and to get the smallest rectangle that includes all of the Polygon (**get BoundingBox( )**).

The following code fragment shows two ways to construct a **Polygon**.

```
Polygon p1, p2;
int[ ] xvals = {100, 50, 150};
int[ ] yvals = {50, 150, 150}; // values for an isosceles triangle
int npoints = 3;
p1 = new Polygon(xvals, yvals, npoints); // create the isosceles
triangle.
p2 = new Polygon( );
p2.addPoint(100, 50);
p2.addPoint(50, 150);
p2.addPoint(150, 150);          // identical to the polygon above.
```

Rectangle

Rectangles store four **ints**. These are the **x** and **y** values for the upper left corner, and the **width** and **height** of the rectangle. Rectangle objects also have several methods that hasten the answers to certain frequently asked questions, such as whether a particular Point is contained within, or what Rectangle is the intersection of two others. There are many constructors for Rectangle objects, and you should check the appendix to learn them. Here we will show you one:

```
Rectangle r1 = new Rectangle(30, 50, 200, 100);
```

This creates a horizontal rectangle that extends from 30 to 230, and down from 50 to 150.

Graphics

All of the above (**Color**, **Font**, **FontMetrics**, **Point**, **Polygon**, and **Rectangle**) are items used in the Graphics methods. You may not create a new Graphics object. You must get one using the **getGraphics( )** method of either a Component or an Image. You may also invoke the **create( )** method of a Graphics object to copy an existing one. If you do make one with **create( )**, you must be sure to free up the Windows resources it uses by calling its **dispose( )** method when you are done with it.

There are many handy methods that Graphics gives you. Many of their names are self-explanatory. Here is a representative sample, (see the appendix for a complete list):

- **clearRect(x, y, width, height)** — Creates a rectangle filled with the current background color.
- **clipRect(x, y, width, height)** — Shrinks the current clipping region.
- **copyArea(x, y, width, height, dx, dy)** — Copies an area to the offset dx, dy.
- **draw3DRect(x, y, width, height, raised)** — Makes a rather disappointing raised or lowered button.
- **drawArc(x, y, width, height, startAngle, arcAngle)** — Draw part of an elipse.
- **drawLine(x1, y1, x2, y2)** — Draw a line.
- **drawOval(x, y, width, height)** — Draw an ellipse.
- **drawPolygon(p)** — Draw a polygon object.
- **drawRect(x, y, width, height)** — Draw a rectangle.
- **drawString(s, x, y)** — Write a string in the current font and color starting at x, y.
- **fillArc(x, y, width, height, startAngle, arcAngle)** — Useful for Pie charts.
- **fillOval(x, y, width, height)** — Polka dots anyone?

• **fillPolygon(p)**	It is interesting when one boarder crosses another.
• **fillRect(x, y, width, height)**	You know what this does.
• **setColor(c)**	All new objects drawn on this Graphics will be this color, until the next **setColor** is called.
• **setFont(f)**	All new Strings will be in this Font, until the next **setFont** is called.

Let's look at an example that uses the Graphics class methods. Do you recall our awtTest example? It is time to modify it (by hand). Figure 10.3 shows the results.

Let's add a few Graphics methods to the paint method, so that we have:

```
import java.applet.*;
import java.awt.*;

public class awtTest extends Applet
{

public void paint(Graphics g)
{
    int sWidth;
    int sHeight;
    Font f1 = new Font("Helvetica", Font.BOLD, 24);
    FontMetrics fm1 = g.getFontMetrics(f1);
    s1 = "Java Man";
    sWidth = fm1.stringWidth(s1);
    sHeight = fm1.getHeight( );

    int maxX = this.size().width; // applet dimension x
    int maxY = this.size().height; // applet dimension y
    g.setColor(Color.blue);
    g.fillRect(0, 0, maxX, maxY); // make whole applet blue.
    g.setFont(f1);
    g.setColor(Color.white);
    // draw the string centered in the applet.
    g.drawString(s1, (maxX-sWidth)/2, (maxY+sHeight)/2);
    g.drawOval(0, 0, maxX, maxY);
    g.drawOval(1, 1, maxX-2, maxY-2);
    g.drawOval(2,2, maxX-4, maxY-4);
    }

}
```

Figure 10.3   The result of our graphics Java Man example.

CONTAINERS, PANELS, AND COMPONENTS

Component is the superclass of all Windows GUI objects except menus. Because this class is **abstract**, there are no component objects—don't even look for them. Even some of the subclasses of component are abstract. Classes that inherit from **Component** are: **Button, Canvas, CheckBox, Choice, Container, Label, List, Scrollbar,** and **TextComponent**. **TextField** and **TextArea** both extend **TextComponent**. **Window** and **Panel** both extend **Container**; **Frame** extends **Window**; and **Applet** (remember **Applet**?) extends **Panel**. In addition to all this, there is a second parallel path of inheritance for **MenuComponents**, shown in Figure 10.4.

We will take only a brief look at these components. Expertise with Java will require some experience with using these features, but Visual J++ has resource editors that you will probably use to implement these objects.

Component

Component gives its children many handy methods. These include mouse (and other) events such as **mouseDown, mouseUp, mouse Drag,** or **lostFocus**. Also included are methods that enable us to hide

java.awt.Component

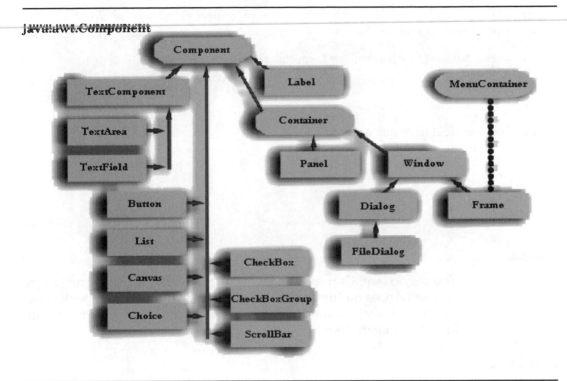

Figure 10.4 The Component family tree.

or reveal the component in the container it is part of (**hide, show**). There are methods that permit setting the **Font** or **Color**, getting the current **Graphics** object, or dealing with **Images**. Since all of the following objects are descended from Component, they all get these wonderful properties.

Button

A **Button** is a simple GUI object that generates an ACTION_EVENT with the **Button** label (a **String**) as the argument. When added to a container and drawn, it appears to be a 3D rectangle that is depressed while being clicked.

In the code fragment below, we show creation of the button, adding it to a flow layout panel (see below), and catching an action on this button. We will see more about component actions later in this chapter.

```
Button b1;                          // create a reference as an object field
public void init( ) {
    ...
    b1 = new Button("Riddler");   // create the button itself
    this.add(b1);                 // add the button to the panel
                                  // (or Applet, Frame, or Window)
    ...
}
public boolean action(Event e, Object arg) {
    if (e.target == b1) {
        ...                           // button b1 was clicked. do something.
        return true;
    }
    return false;
}
```

Canvas

You may extend **Canvas** to add a paint method or to include an image.
By itself it does nothing more than supply a featureless area with event
handling. We will show an example of using a canvas in the section on
layout managers below.

Checkbox

Checkboxes stare a **boolean** state variable. The also maintain a
label, and a graphical checkbox in a container. They may be collected
together using another AWT class called **CheckBoxGroup**, which lets
you create a set of *Radio Buttons* (in which at most one may be checked
at any time).

```
Checkbox cb1;                       // create a reference as an object field
public void init( ) {
    ...
    cb1 = new Checkbox("Bat Signal");   // create the checkbox itself
    this.add(cb1);                      // add the checkbox to the panel
                                        // (or Applet, Frame, or Window)
    ...
}
public boolean action(Event e, Object arg) {
    if (e.target == cb1) {
        ...                               // change the state of the bat signal.
        return true;
    }
    return false;
}
```

Or if you would like to see a Checkbox Group . . .

```
CheckboxGroup cbg1;                    // create a reference as an object field
public void init( ) {
    ...
    Checkbox penguin, riddler, joker; // make three cb refs.
    cbg1 = new CheckboxGroup( ); // create the checkbox group object.
    penguin = new Checkbox("Penguin", cbg1, true);
    riddler = new Checkbox("Riddler", cbg1, false);
    joker = new Checkbox("Joker", cbg1, false);
    this.add(cbg1);
    ...
}
public boolean action(Event e, Object arg) {
    if (e.target instanceof Checkbox) {
        if (e.target.getLabel( ).equals("Penguin") {
            ...                        // special handling for Penguin.
            return true;
        }
        else if (e.target == cbg1.getCurrent( )) {
            ...                        // handle the arch foe
            return true;
        }
    }
    return false;
}
```

In the above example, the references to the **checkboxes** have a scope only within the **init** method, and so cannot be accessed directly. We used Java's **instanceof** operator to ferret out the cause of the action. We show the special handling of the *Penguin* event, so as to demonstrate how you may determine if a particular component has been selected without having a reference to it available. Note that the **CheckBoxGroup** does not inherit from **Component**, and so does not generate action events by itself (see Events and Observables below).

Choice

Choice objects are used to support a dropdown menu. The end user may select one of the choices, and the String contained in that choice becomes the value of the Choice object. The choice class has several useful methods, including **addItem( )**, which adds a new item to the choice menu; **countItems( )**, which reports the number of items already on the list; **getSelectedItem( )**, which returns the String of the selected choice, and several others for dealing with indices, and hard-coded choices.

```
Choice ch1;          // create a reference as an object field
public void init( ) {
    ...
    ch1 = new Choice( ); // create the choice object itself
    ch1.addItem("Bat-arang");
    ch1.addItem("Bat-mobile");
    ch1.addItem("Bat-tub");
    ch1.addItem("Bat-robe");
    this.add(ch1);      // add the choice to the panel
                        // (or Applet, Frame, or Window)
    ...
}
public boolean action(Event e, Object arg) {
    String s1;
    if (e.target == ch1) {
        s1 = ch1.getSelectedItem( );
        ...             // do something with s1
        return true;
    }
    return false;
}
```

Label

Can there be any more complex and subtle object than the **Label**? Yes, mostly they all are. Still, **Label** objects provide more features than you might guess. **Labels** can have their text (and the alignment of that text) changed at runtime. They can also be polled to find the current value of that text (**getText( )**). In addition, they have the **Component** abilities to **hide( )** or **show( )** themselves, or have their colors or fonts changed, for example. If you need to, you may extend the **Label** class and add code to the normal mouse events. Yes, they look simple and can act simple, but they are so much more. Will you ever use the really exotic special features? Hopefully not.

```
public void init( ) {
    Label l1 = new Label("Danger High Voltage");
    Label l2 = new Label("Bat Reactor", Label.CENTER);
    ...
    this.add(l1);
    this.add(l2);
}
```

Note that the second label has used the constructor with an alignment parameter. These may have values of **Label.LEFT**, **Label.**

CENTER, and **Label.RIGHT**. These are three integer constants, which are publicly available as part of the Label class.

List

List objects store lists of Strings which appear on the screen; if there are enough strings, this may be a scrollable list. One field of this object determines whether multiple items on this list may be selected at once. Another field determines the number of items which may be visible at once.

When an end user double clicks on an item in the list, it generates an action event. If it selects the item, it is a **LIST_SELECT** event. If the item was previously selected, it is a **LIST_DESELCT** event. Most components don't have their own built in event type (see Events and Observables below).

```
List list1;                          // create a reference as an object field
public void init( ) {
    ...
    list1 = new List(3, true);       // list has 3 rows, and mult. selection
    list1.addItem("Bat-phone");
    list1.addItem("Bat-belt");
    list1.addItem("Bat-boat");
    list1.addItem("Bat-masterson");
    this.add(list1);                 // add the list to the panel
                                     // (or Applet, Frame, or Window)
    ...
}
public boolean action(Event e, Object arg) {
    if (e.id == Event.LIST_SELECT) {
        ...                          // scroll through list to act on
                                     // the selected items.
        return true;
    }
    return false;
}
```

Note that the usual methods of handling these events will also apply. We show the **e.id ==** approach, because in this case, we can, and to support the software equivalent of biodiversity.

Panel

Panel objects are subclasses of **Containers**. They themselves do not do much. They may be placed as objects added to some layout or another. Components may be added to the **Panel**. When this is done, the **Flow** layout manager is the default inside the **Panel** (see Layout Managers below). Generally, you will find that **Panels** are handy when you are putting multiple items onto one side of a **Border** layout, or in some unified section of another layout. We will see code examples with **Panels** in the section on Layout Managers below.

Applets are a subclass of **Panel**.

Scrollbar

You know what a scroll bar is. It may be horizontal, or vertical. When you create it, you may assign:

- Its orientation (Scrollbar.HORIZONTAL or Scrollbar.VERTICAL)
- Its initial value
- How far it moves when you click on the end points (called page size)
- Its minimum value
- Its maximum value

> **NOTE**
>
> ### Floating Scrollbars Come in One Size
>
> If you add a **Scrollbar** to a flow layout, resizing it has no obvious effect. It will be a small almost useless item on your **Panel**. **Scrollbars** work best in some layout that defines the size of the object in it, such as **Border** layout, or **Grid** Layout (see Layout Managers below).

Scrollbars are another type of component that have some built-in event types in the Event objects. These are **Event.SCROLL_LINE_UP**, **Event.SCROLL_LINE_DOWN**, **Event.SCROLL_PAGE_UP**, **Event.SCROLL_PAGE_DOWN**, and **Event.SCROLL_ABSOLUTE**. We use these in pretty much the same way we used the Events in **Choice** above. In any case, when you receive such an event, you should probably get the scrollbar value. It is contained in an **Integer** wrapper and is passed as the **arg** field of the Event. Alternatively, use the **getValue( )** method to determine what the **Scrollbar's** current value is.

```
Scrollbar sb1;               // create a reference as an object field
public void init( ) {
```

```
        ...
        sb1 = new Scrollbar(Scrollbar.VERTICAL,
            50, 10, 0, 100);   // create the scrollbar object
        this.add(sb1);         // add the scrollbar to the panel
                               // (or Applet, Frame, or Window)
        ...
    }
    public boolean action(Event e, Object arg) {
        int ival;
        if (e.target == sb1) {
            switch (e.id) {
            case Event.SCROLL_LINE_UP:
            case Event.SCROLL_PAGE_UP:
            case Event.SCROLL_ABSOLUTE:
            case Event.SCROLL_PAGE_DOWN:
            case Event.SCROLL_LINE_DOWN:
                ival = ((Integer)e.arg).intValue( );
                ...              // Do something with this info.
            }
            return true;
        }
        return false;
    }
```

TextArea

TextAreas are GUI components that can store many lines of scrollable text. When you create one of these items, you can specify the number of rows and columns, whether it is editable by the end user, what the textual content is, and many other things (see Figure 10.5). You can mark a part of the text as selected. Because it is a **Component**, you may also use the component methods, and set the **Color** or **Font**.

Put this **init** method into your minimal **Applet** and see what happens:

```
    public void init() {
        TextArea ta;
        String s1 = "Riddle me this\nWhen is a door not a door?";
        Font f1 = new Font("Helvetica", Font.ITALIC, 18);
        ta = new TextArea(s1, 8, 30);
        ta.setFont(f1);
        ta.setForeground(Color.blue);
        this.add(ta);
    }
```

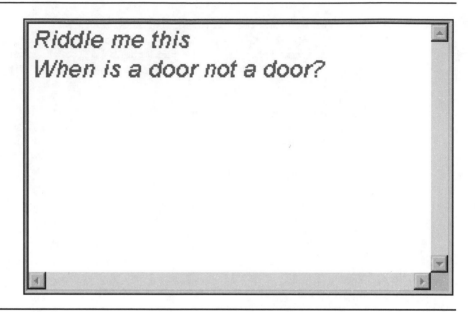

Figure 10.5   A TextArea object.

TextField

TextFields are to **TextAreas** as one-liners are to shaggy dog stories. They have one line and a number of convenient properties, including the ability to set the echo character for concealing passwords from prying eyes.

Window

Generally, you will use the children of Window (**Dialog**, **FileDialog**, and **Frame**). You could use it by itself. It makes a rectangle on the screen. It has no border or menu bar. (Is this an opportunity? Can you make a better border and menu bar? It's up to you, but it sounds like a lot of work to me.)

You will notice, if you try to add a window to an applet, that the only constructor requires the parent Frame. The same is true for Dialog and FileDialog. You must get the parent of your applet, as is shown in the code fragment below.

```
public void init() {
    Window w;
    w = new Window((Frame)this.getParent( ));
    w.resize(200,150);              // Give it a size.
    w.setBackground(Color.red);     // We want to notice it
    w.show( );                      // Windows are hidden by default.
}
```

If you put this init method into your applet (see above), you will notice that the red box appears somewhere, usually near the upper left corner of your screen. If you move and resize Internet Explorer, you will find that the Window you have created does not move. It disappears when you exit IE3.

If you do create a **Window** object, be sure to call its **dispose( )** method when you are done with it, so that the Windows resources it uses are freed up.

Dialog Like its superclass, **Window**, **Dialog** requires a **Frame** to be created. It also must be declared modal or not (If it is modal, nothing else can be done until the box goes away). Like **Window**, you can simply add it to your **Applet**, **Panel**, or what have you, but if you are not adding it to a Frame, you must find the Frame object that is the parent of the **Dialog**. You may also give it a title at creation time.

Also like **Window**, you should dispose of it when you are done with it. This will free up those precious Windows resources. Figure 10.6 illustrates a minimal **Dialog** box.

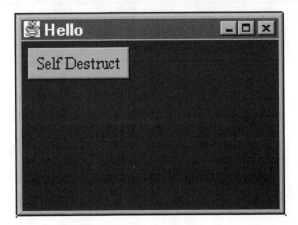

Figure 10.6   A minimal **Dialog** box (with a hopefully unimplemented button).

> ### TIP
>
> ### A Good Programming Practice
>
> Many Java programmers like to make dialog boxes that are sub-classes of **Dialog**. This permits customizing the action events and keeping them better encapsulated. In this modern day, you probably won't worry about this much, since this kind of thing will be handled by Visual J++'s resource wizards.

```
public void init() {
    Dialog d;
    d = new Dialog((Frame)this.getParent( ), "Hello", true);
    d.setLayout (new FlowLayout (FlowLayout.LEFT);
    d.resize(200,150);    // Give it a size.
    d.setBackground(Color.red);  // We want to notice it
    d.add(new Button("Self Destruct");
    d.show( );
}
```

FileDialog Java provides another very handy Dialog box, the **File Dialog** (see Figure 10.7). While the code to create one of these looks a

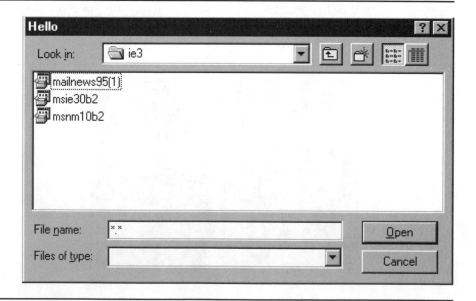

Figure 10.7   A FileDialog box (almost no code required).

great deal like the code for any dialog box, it includes several handy methods for getting and setting the directory, the filename filter, the filename, or setting whether it is an *open file* or *save as* dialog box.

It is up to the programmer to catch the events that the **FileDialog's Buttons** generate to get the information from the box.

```
public void init() {
    FileDialog fd;
    fd = new FileDialog((Frame)this.getParent( ), "Hello", FileDialog.LOAD);
    d.show( );
}
```

Frame Frames are windows used for the top level of applications. They are constructed in more or less the same way as a Dialog box, but they do not need to know the parent frame. Among the properties that a frame has are:

- An associated icon image (you can set it)
- A cursor type (crosshair, default, hand, move, text, wait, and eight resize cursors)
- A menu bar (see Menus below)
- The special events it inherits from **Window** (**WINDOW_ DESTROY**, **WINDOW_ICONIFY**, **WINDOW_DEICONIFY**, **WINDOW_MOVED**)

As with the **Dialog** class, **Frames** are typically subclassed for ease of better encapsulation of events. Also, like **Dialog FileDialog** and **Window**, if your application creates one of these things, it should also call its **dispose( )** method when it is done, so as to free up the Windows resources that it holds.

As noted above, **Frames** support menus. We will not go into these now, but bear it in mind. In a few pages we will discuss programming with menus in Java.

Components You Create

It is not difficult to create a new **Component**. You start by creating a class that extends **Component**. You need to supply a few other things:

- You need to create the fields that store the state of your component. For a button, this may include the text on the button, and whether it is currently depressed.
- You need to write one or more constructors.

- You need to provide methods for getting and setting your state fields.
- You need to write a paint method, which draws the Component.
- You need to override the **preferredSize** and **minimumSize** methods, so that the layout managers can tell how big the component should or must be.

It doesn't take a whole lot, but if you are going to use a lot of these, you should make sure that they work exactly right.

EVENTS AND OBSERVABLES

Many of our examples have included a bit of event handling. You may even be starting to feel like an expert! Expert or not, you probably would like a bit more of an overview (and some more details, too) of how events work in Java. Figure 10.8 shows Java's event handling hierarchy.

When an event is generated (by the native Windows environment), it is delivered to the lowest level component associated with the event. That component's **postEvent** method receives it, and (unless you override it to do otherwise) it first calls **handleEvent**. If that returns **false**, it calls the appropriate (if any) special event handler (such as **mouseDown**). If all of these return **false**, the **postEvent** method of

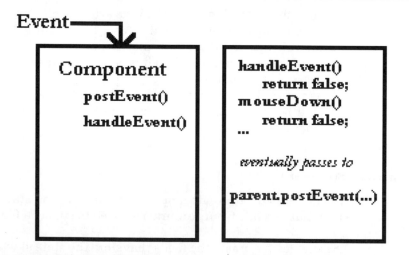

Figure 10.8   The event handling hierarchy.

the immediately enclosing **Container** object is called. This repeats until an event handler method returns a **true**, or until all **Container** objects are exhausted.

Quite a few methods are available to you that allow you to act on events. When you write code for the bodies of these methods (all of which return a **boolean** value), in every case, you should return a **true** if you are done with the event, and a **false** if you are not. A **false** return will direct the event handling to continue on to objects higher in the who-owns-what hierarchy. These event handling methods of **Component** are covered in the following sections.

Mouse Events

- **mouseDown(Event e, int x, int y)**
- **mouseDrag(Event e, int x, int y)**
- **mouseEnter(Event e, int x, int y)**
- **mouseExit(Event e, int x, int y)**
- **mouseMove(Event e, int x, int y)**
- **mouseUp(Event e, int x, int y)**

The mouse events are generated when the mouse moves, or is clicked. If it is a mouse click event (**mouseUp** or **mouseDown**), you may use the Event methods **e.controlDown( )**, **e.metaDown( )**, and **e.shiftDown( )** to determine which mouse button was depressed. You could otherwise determine which special keys were depressed by using the flags field of the event, and the **SHIFT_MASK**, **CTRL_MASK**, **META_MASK**, and **ALT_MASK**. This latter method is the only way to determine if the **Alt** key was depressed.

The other two parameters give the mouse coordinates at the time of the Event.

TIP

Mouse Move Events Are Numerous

Be sure that you do not often handle mouse move events with complex code. These events happen very often in a GUI environment, and if too many components are looking at mouse move events at once, you may find performance is impacted.

Key Events

- **keyDown(Event e, int key)**
- **keyUp(Event e, int key)**

As with the mouse click events, you may determine which special keys were depressed with the flags field and the masks or by calling the special methods. The Event object has some other information of value. The key parameter tells which character was generated by the keyboard.

Focus Events

- **gotFocus(Event e, Object what)**
- **lostFocus(Event e, Object what)**

Focus events occur when a particular **Component** either becomes or stops being the active **Component** on the screen. These events are best used for catching things where a change in content might not trigger any other kind of event, such as when focus leaves a **TextField** without a carriage return being struck. The what parameter tells *what* object got or lost focus.

Other Events

- **action(Event e, Object what)**
- **handleEvent(Event e)**

Use the **action** method to handle component actions, such as **Button** clicks or carriage return, in a **TextField**. The *what* parameter is the component that generated the action **Event**.

The **handleEvent** method receives all **Events** (mouse, focus, action, or otherwise) that come to a specific component (such as your applet). Some components, such as **Scrollbars**, generate events that may only be handled with **handleEvent( )**. Be sure this method returns **true** exclusively for events it handles.

Special Event Methods

- **deliverEvent(Event e)**
- **postEvent(Event e)**

The **deliverEvent** method is used to pass an **Event** object to a **Component**. This can be done completely under program control with an Event generated by your code. Why would you do this? There will be times when this might reduce the redundant code in your application or otherwise simplify your design. One such case might be when you have some representation of your keyboard on the screen, and you are performing the same actions on both mouse and key events. With judicious use of **deliverEvent**, you can maintain only one body of action code. (You could otherwise solve this with a private method that both handlers call.) If you do a lot of program design, you'll find other reasons to use this.

You normally wouldn't change the **postEvent** method, described above. It determines the order in which the various event handlers get a shot at the delivered **Event**. You might want to change it to streamline operations if you knew that only a very few types of events were to be handled by a specific **Component**. This might be part of your strategy for speeding up a sluggish application.

The Event Class

What does an **Event** look like? We've been discussing how to handle them for quite a while now, so perhaps it is best if we had a better idea of what it is. An **Event** is an object of class **Event**. This class is described in the appendix, but here is a quick summary of what it has:

- Three handy constructors
- Many constants for identifying **Event** types
- Four masks for identifying the depressed special keys on the modifiers field
- Twenty constants for identifying special keys
- An **arg** field of type Object, whose actual type depends on the **Event** type
- An **evt** field, which is a reference to the next **Event** (can be handy in sophisticated **Event** handling applications)
- An **int**, which stores the **Event** type (see first group of constants above)
- A **key** field, which contains the key pressed on the keyboard (for key events)
- The **modifiers** field, which stores information about which special keys are depressed
- The **target** object, which is a reference to the **Component** generating the **Event**
- The **when** field is a **long** integer with the system time that the **Event** was generated
- The **x** and **y** fields give the mouse position at the time of the **Event**

- There are some handy methods for determining the state of the special keys (Control, Shift, and Meta)

All of the fields mentioned above are public and may be accessed directly, without any encapsulating methods. To create an event object call the constructor (using the **new** keyword) and then fill in the instance fields as desired.

Observables

Outside the AWT, in the **java.util** package, there is a class called **Observable** and an interface called **Observer**, which can be used for creating event like occurrences. We will be treating these in the chapter on the java.util package.

In the meantime, keep in mind that they do not generate **Event** objects. Subclasses of **Observable**, when their contents change, notify objects, which implement the **Observer** of this occurrence. We will see an example of this in another chapter.

MENUS

Menus in the AWT are attached to **Frames**. Several classes and interfaces support these menu systems, including the **abstract** class **MenuComponent**, the interface **MenuContainer**, and the classes **Menu**, **MenuBar**, **MenuItem**, and **CheckBoxMenuItem**. We will briefly review the features of these classes and interfaces, and show or examples of their use.

MenuComponent

Any class extending the **MenuComponent** class may override the few methods contained in the class. These methods permit getting and setting the **Font** used for text in the menu system, getting the parent **MenuContainer** object, and posting events.

MenuContainer

Classes may contain a menu if they implement this interface; **Frame**, **Menu**, and **MenuBar** do this. You could create one yourself if it seemed useful. The methods you need to create are:

- **getFont( )**, which gets the font in use by the contained menu.
- **postEvent(Event e)**, which handles the direction of events coming to this container (usually passed up from the contained menu).

- **remove(MenuComponent c)**, which removes a menu component (such as a **MenuItem** object) from the contained **Menu**.

MenuBar

This is the top structure in a menu system. It has the following methods which you will find useful: a constructor, which has no parameters.

- **add(Menu m)**, which adds a new pulldown menu to the menu bar.
- **remove(MenuComponent m)**, which removes a menu from the menu bar.
- **setHelpMenu(Menu m)**, which adds a menu to a position reserved for help menus.

When you are constructing a menu system, create a **MenuBar** object, and add it to the Frame using the Frame object's **setMenuBar (MenuBar m)** method.

Menu

Pulldown menus are held as **Menu** objects. These objects have methods that permit adding **MenuItems**, removing **MenuItems**, adding separators into the menu, establishing whether a menu will stay up when the mouse button is released (**isTearOff( )**, the default for Win95), or changing that state, and, of course, a constructor or two. Create these object using the **new** keyword, and **add** them to your **MenuBar**.

MenuItem

MenuItems are created and added to a **Menu** object. These objects have methods to disable them (make them nonselectable and gray them out), to enable them, to determine their enable/disable state, and to change the label they have on the menu. Note that a **Menu** object is a **MenuItem**, and so may be added as an item to the **Menu** list.

When a **MenuItem** is selected, it generates an **ACTION_EVENT**, providing the label of the **MenuItem** as the argument for the event.

CheckboxMenuItem

This is a menu item that maintains the state of whether it has been checked. It has **getState( )** and **setState( )** methods, which enable this to be utilized within the application.

An Example

Well, that was easy. Let's look at a trivial example. Let's add this **init** method to your minimal applet. Figure 10.9 illustrates a frame with a **MenuBar** object attached.

```
public void init() {
    Frame f;
    MenuBar mb1;
    Menu m1, m2, help1;
    CheckboxMenuItem cmi1, cmi2;
    MenuItem mia1, mia2, mia3, mia4;
    MenuItem mib1, mib2, mib3;
    MenuItem hi1, hi2, hi3, hi4;

    f = new Frame("Menu Test");
    f.resize(300,200);
    mb1 = new MenuBar( );
    f.setMenuBar(mb1);
    m1 = new Menu("TearOff", true);
    m2 = new Menu("Not TearOff", false);
    help1 = new Menu("Help", true);
    mb1.add(m1);
    mb1.add(m2);
    mb1.setHelpMenu(help1);
    mia1 = new MenuItem("Solve Riddle");
    mia2 = new MenuItem("Undisguised Voice");
    mia3 = new MenuItem("Sort Crime Clues");
    mia4 = new MenuItem("Create Peace in Our Time");
    mib1 = new MenuItem("Initiate self destruct sequence");
    mib2 = new MenuItem("Abort Self Destruct Sequence");
    mib3 = new MenuItem("Self Destruct Without Delay");
    hi1 = new MenuItem("About the Bat-puter");
    hi2 = new MenuItem("About Self Destruct");
    hi3 = new MenuItem("About Help");

    m1.add(mia1);
    m1.add(mia2);
    m1.add(mia3);
    m1.add(mia4);
    m2.add(mib1);
    m2.add(mib2);
    m2.add(mib3);
    help1.add(hi1);
    help1.add(hi2);
    help1.addSeparator();
    help1.add(hi3);
```

```
      f.show( );
   }
```

In the above example, we did not include an event handler to do anything with these events, but it is simply a matter of looking for action events with the given label string as the **arg** object, and invoking some appropriate method when you find it.

LAYOUT MANAGERS

Java has five standard layout managers built in to the AWT. You can build others, and most vendors of Java development tools do. The standard Java layout managers work on a principle that you should provide guidelines for where components should go, but you should not fix them exactly. Most people from the Windows environment prefer to know exactly where things are going. Now you can choose either one, but the standard layout managers use the sliding component model.

Generally, it is doubtful that you will need to know a great deal about these layout managers, because the Resource Wizards will take care of most of this for you. Still, it is useful to have an idea what it is that those wizards need to do.

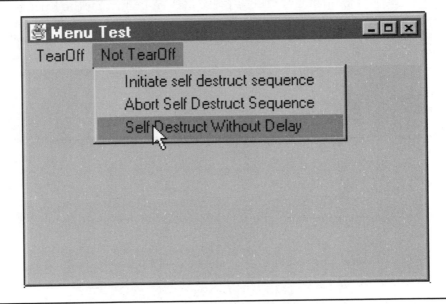

Figure 10.9   A frame with a MenuBar object attached.

Any **Container** must have a layout manager. As we have noted before, **Applets** have **FlowLayout** as their default. You create a layout manager object, like anything else, with the **new** keyword. You add it to your Container object using the **setLayout( )** method. This method takes a **LayoutManager** object as a parameter. Once that has been done, you must use the methods of that Layout manager to add **Components** to your **Container**.

The five layout managers are:

- **BorderLayout**, which has 5 positions—north east, south, west, and center.
- **CardLayout**, shows one component at a time, usually a container.
- **FlowLayout** (the default on any panel, including applets), left to right, then top to bottom.
- **GridBagLayout** (the most complex of the lot), which gives great control as to where components should go, but requires a lot of code to do it.
- **GridLayout**, which creates an ordered array of components.

BorderLayout

This layout manager has five position into which it may place Components. These positions are known by the Strings **North**, **East**, **South**, **West**, and **Center**. Border layout is very handy for putting scroll bars onto a canvas to make some kind of scrollable drawing pallet. It can also be used for placing status bars, icon repositories, and anything else that is normally kept off to one side, or at the top or bottom.

TIP

Put a Container on a Border

If you need to have more than one component on the side of your applet, try putting a panel, with Grid or Flow layout attached, as the component on your east border.

The following **init** method creates buttons on the sides of an applet and puts a panel into the center. Figure 10.10 illustrates this process.

```
public void init( ) {
    Panel p = new Panel( );
    p.add(new Label("All Around the Town", Label.LEFT));
```

```
        this.setLayout(new BorderLayout( ));
        add("East", new Button("East Side"));
        add("West", new Button("West Side"));
        add("North", new Button("North Side"));
        add("South", new Button("South Side"));
        add("Center",p);
    }
```

CardLayout

CardLayout has a lot in common with a linked list. Only one of the **Components** that have been added to this **Container** may be visible at one time. You may progress through the various components by calling the **first**, **last**, **next**, or **previous** methods of this layout manager. You may also elect to **show** a named **Component**.

A frequent use for **CardLayout** is to place a card layout **Panel** inside some construct that presents the allegory of flipping through pages or tabbed folders. These events cause the swapping of attached **Panels**, which themselves are loaded with other **Components**, used to convey the information your application presents.

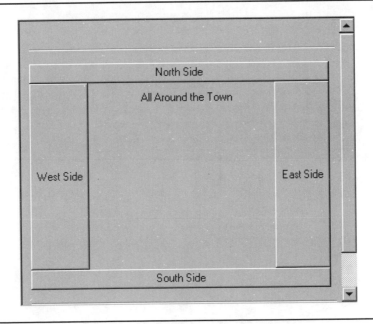

Figure 10.10   An illustrative use of BorderLayout.

You will make your own **CardLayout Panel** in the exercises below.

FlowLayout

What is the default layout manager for your applet? If you have been reading along, you know it is **FlowLayout**. **FlowLayout** simply lays out the **Components** from right to left in the order that they are added to the **Panel**. If they exceed the width of the **Panel**, they go on to the next line.

This is convenient because it requires the least thought. It is inconvenient, because you cannot organize where a **Component** will be placed. This is especially useless for placing a **CheckboxGroup**, as you can well imagine.

The following **init** method shows how you might use **FlowLayout** to place several buttons on a screen. Figure 10.11 illustrates an instructional use of **FlowLayout**.

```
public void init( ) {
    this.setLayout(new FlowLayout( )); // Included for completeness.
    for (int i = 0; i < 20; i++) {
        add(new Button("Button "+Integer.toString(i)));
    }
}
```

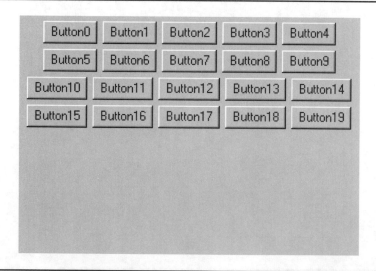

Figure 10.11   An example of FlowLayout with an unmanageable number of buttons.

GridBagLayout

GridBagLayout requires attaching a **GridBagConstraint** object to each **Component** that is placed in the Container object. **GridBagConstraints** allow you to specify details about how many and which grid elements the component will take up, and where within that/those cell(s) the component lies.

Unlike **GridLayout**, **GridBagLayout** lets you specify rows and columns of varying sizes within the array, though the programmer should note that **Components** will expand the grid if not given their minimum size (e.g. a Button needs enough room for its label.)

You may find it fun, or perhaps therapeutic to try altering the various **GridBagConstraint** attributes, to see how these things behave. We have given you a start down that road with the following example. If you do not find the meaning of the constraint attributes obvious, try changing them, and look at the result. Try altering the relative position and weighting factors.

Figure 10.12 Your applet with twenty grid cells, and sixteen Buttons. Notice that the insets have given a little margin around each button, which otherwise fill the cells, and that some buttons are taking up two cells.

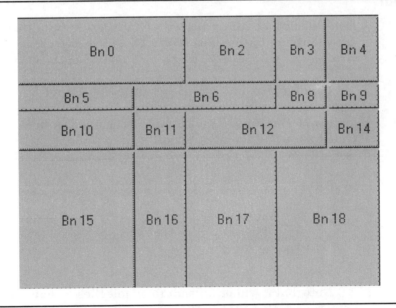

Figure 10.12   Your applet with twenty GridBagLayout Buttons on it. Notice that our failure to anchor the leftmost buttons has resulted in unexpected behavior.

```
public void init() {
    int cw[ ] = {105, 45, 80, 45, 45};
    int rh[ ] = {60, 20, 35, 123 };
    GridBagLayout gbl = new GridBagLayout( );
    gbl.columnWidths=cw;
    gbl.rowHeights=rh;
    GridBagConstraints gbc[] = new GridBagConstraints[20];
    Button b[ ] = new Button[20];
    this.setLayout(gbl);
    for (int i=0; i<20; i++) {
        b[i] = new Button("Bn "+Integer.toString(i));
        gbc[i] = new GridBagConstraints( );
        gbc[i].gridx = i%5; gbc[i].gridy = i/5;
        gbc[i].fill = GridBagConstraints.BOTH;
        gbc[i].insets = new Insets(1, 1, 1, 1);
        if (i%6 == 0) gbc[i].gridwidth = 2;
        gbl.setConstraints(b[i], gbc[i]);
        add(b[i]);
        if (i%6 == 0) i++;
    }
}
```

GridLayout

Don't confuse **GridLayout** with **GridBagLayout**. They are both layout managers in the Java AWT. The similarity dries up about there. GridLayout uses a very orderly grid and all of the elements fit rather neatly.

GridLayout is often used within one **Panel** of a more complex screen. It is useful for making things like calculator keypads or other arrays of **Buttons**. The example below shows how you might use **GridLayout** and a lot of **Scrollbars** to simulate a graphic equalizer (see Figure 10.13).

```
public void init( ) {
    this.setLayout(new GridLayout(1, 18));
    for (int i = 0; i < 18; i++) {
        add(new Scrollbar(Scrollbar.VERTICAL, 5, 1, 0, 11));
    }
}
```

Note that it will be difficult to handle these events without building an array of references to these **Scrollbars**. You could go without, but it would require capturing the mouse coordinates from the event, and calculating which Scrollbar must have moved.

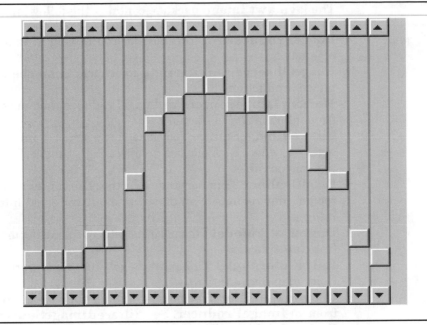

Figure 10.13   A graphic equalizer? Not without event handling.

IMAGES

There is an **Image** class in the AWT. You can't create one—you must receive it from **Applet.getImage( )** method, or the **Component. createImage( )** method. This class provides methods to determine the actual height and width of an image, as well as a way to query the **ImageObserver** object to get values for various properties of the Image.

Most of the clever image facilities in Java 1.02 (the version used by the first release of Visual J++) are in the sub package, **java.awt.image** (not to be confused with the class **java.awt.Image** [note the capital *I*]). These do not give you new ways to get images, but they give you a lot of help in manipulating them.

One point worth noting is that images are transferred asynchronously. This means that the **getImage** call returns immediately, but the image itself will arrive when it gets there. A method is provided to permit checking on the status of this transfer. The Resource Wizard will usually take care of this for you, but you ought to know why the code looks so convoluted.

The **java.awt.image** package contains the following classes:

- **ImageProducer** An interface for connecting to image consumer objects.
- **ImageObserver** An interface for checking on the status of the image production.
- **MemoryImageSource** An ImageProducer that makes an image from information in memory.
- **FilteredImageSource** You can string a series of **ImageProducers** together, where each one has an effect on the image. This makes that pipeline possible.
- **PixelGrabber** This permits collecting the contents of pixels from rectangular regions of an image, and putting them into an array of integers.
- **DirectColorModel** This permits getting color information directly from the pixels.
- **IndexColorModel** This permits getting color information from a Color map array.
- **CropImageFilter** This permits taking only a portion of an image from an **ImageProducer**. See **FilteredImageSource** above.
- **RGBImageFilter** This is an abstract class that you can extend to make color shifts to an image.

You can load and draw an image from a **.gif** file at a URL. This is fairly straightforward and only uses the methods from applet and from the AWT, as can be seen in this code fragment:

```
Image im1;

public void init() {
    im1 = getImage(getDocumentBase(),"BluBall1.gif");
}
public void paint(Graphics g) {
    int imWidth = 20; // known to be the width of this image
    int imHeight = 21; // known to be the height of this image
    g.drawImage(im1, 0, 0, imWidth, imHeight, this);
```

You can also create an image the hard way as we do here. If you build this applet, you will notice that it takes a little while to execute on a Pentium. This is because of the excessive bit-shuffling that is going on. Depending on your Java implementation, you may also notice that the colors come from a small pallet, even though more colors are theoretically available to you. This should improve with future graphics packages.

```java
import java.awt.*;
import java.awt.image.*;
import java.applet.*;

public class imgPlay extends Applet {
    int[] light = new int[256];
    int[] dark = new int[256];
    int[] backImage = new int[4096];
    Image diamond;

    public void init() {
        Color lightColor = new Color(0, 0, 0);
        Color darkColor = new Color(0, 0, 0);

        for (int i=0; i<192; i++) {
            lightColor = new Color(64, i+64, i+64);
            light[i] = lightColor.getRGB();
            darkColor = new Color(32, i+32, i+32);
            dark[i] = darkColor.getRGB();
        }
        for (int i=0, j=0, n=0; i<64; j++, n++) {
            if (j==64) {
                j = 0;
                i++;
                // showStatus(" new i = " + i);
            }
            if (i==64) break;
            if (i<32) {
                if (i>j) backImage[n] = light[j];
                else if (i>64-j) backImage[n] = dark[64-j];
                else backImage[n] = light[i];
            }
            else {
                if (64-i>j) backImage[n] = light[j];
                else if (i<j) backImage[n] = dark[64-j];
                else backImage[n] = dark[64-i];
            }
        }

        diamond = createImage(new
            MemoryImageSource(64, 64, backImage, 0, 64));
    }   // end of init()

    public void paint(Graphics g) {
        g.drawImage(diamond, 0, 0, 64, 64, this);
    }
}  // end of applet.
```

We will see more about images when we look at animation in Part III.

THE java.awt.peer PACKAGE

When the Java AWT is ported to a new operating environment, classes must be created to fill in all of the methods declared in the interfaces in **java.awt.peer**. This is done by connecting to the native GUI components. There are quite a number of these interfaces (completely abstract classes). You will probably never have to do this yourself, and if you do, you will need more help from Sun Microsystems than this book can give you. Luckily, Java is already supported under Win95 and WinNT.

There is a close correlation between these interfaces and the classes in the AWT. For example, the **java.awt.Button** class is an implementation of the **java.awt.peer.ButtonPeer** interface. If you feel the need to port Java to **OpenVMS**, the **Amiga**, or perhaps even **CP/M**, you will find yourself learning more about Java and Graphics User Interfaces than anyone you ever heard of. Sometimes its best to avoid such anachronisms.

EXERCISES

10-1   Follow the directions above, and make the minimal applet.

10-2   Using the **Graphics** object that comes with your applet's **paint** method, experiment with the **Color** and **Font** objects, and make it write your name in gold 36 point letters centered on a navy background.

10-3   Put a **Rectangle** around your name, so that it is midway between the letters and the edge of the applet.

10-4   Add a four-pointed white star (using a filled **Polygon**) to your applet.

10-5   Add a **Button** called "star" to your applet.

10-6   Add a **boolean** field called *displayStar* to your applet. Make the **paint** method only draw the star if *displayStar* is **true**.

10-7   Add a **handleEvents** method that catches the **Button** click event, changes the state of *displayStar*, and calls the **repaint( )** method of the applet.

10-8   Use the **BorderLayout** manager for your applet. Put the Button on the side.

10-9   Create a **Panel** in the **Center** of the **BorderLayout**. Add the **Graphics** (including the star) to the **Panel**.

10-10   Create a **CardLayout** for your **Center Panel**. Put **Buttons** on the left and right that scroll through the **Panels** in the center.

10-11   Add the various **Components** to your Panels on the **Card Layout**.

CHAPTER 11

The java.io Package

In this chapter we cover the following topics:

- **Standard Input and Standard Output**
- **Files and File Descriptors**
- **Random Access Files**
- **Byte Arrays and String Buffers**
- **Pipes and Filters**
- **The StreamTokenizer**

Without some kind of input and output, no Java project could be anything but a decoration or a bauble. Java has a standard package called **java.io**, which provides input and output streams, as well as the ability to handle files.

When you first look at the collection of stream classes defined in this package, it may be bewildering (Figure 11-1), but on closer inspection, you will notice that they are mostly just specialized Stream types, all descended from the two basic types, **InputStream** and **Output Stream**. In addition to these, we see the File related classes, and a useful **StreamTokenizer** class.

Of the **InputStream** child classes, there are the **ByteArray InputStream**, the **FileInputStream**, the **FilterInputStream**, the **PipedInputStream**, the **SequenceInputStream**, and the **String BufferInputStream**. Several children of the **FilterInputStream** are already provided. These include the **BufferedInputStream**, the

java.io package

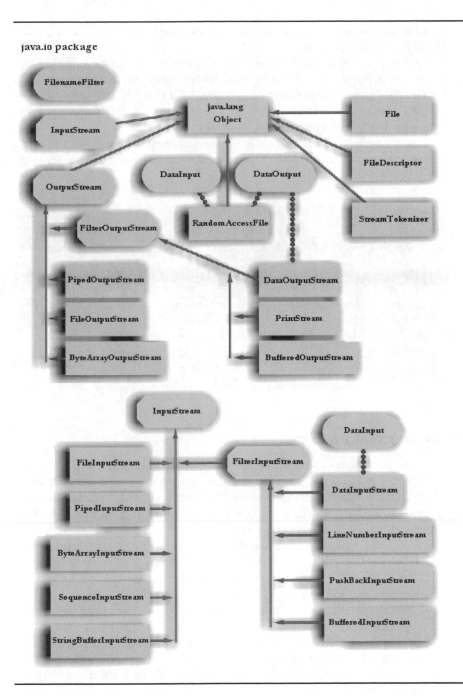

Figure 11.1   The java.io package.

DataInputStream,   the   **LineNumberInputStream**,   and   the **PushbackInputStream**.

Within the **OutputStream** family, there are fewer classes, but there are still quite a few, including: **ByteArrayOutputStream**, **File OutputStream**, **FilterOutputStream**, and **PipedOutputStream**— the **FilterOutputStream** being the parent of **BufferedOutput Stream**, **DataOutputStream**, and **PrintStream**.

To some degree, the names of these classes tell almost all you need to know about them, but we will describe them more fully in the sections below.

> **NOTE**
>
> ### Applets Can't Do File I/O, but They Still Need Streams
>
> Many browsers forbid applets from doing any kind of file I/O on the client system. This is good, because it prevents you from unknowingly picking or executing something that will fill up your hard disk (or worse). But an applet can still make use of streams. Applets may open connections to the computer that served the web page they are contained in. We will see in the next chapter that you may send a stream through a socket between the client and the server.

STANDARD INPUT AND STANDARD OUTPUT

We have seen several examples of the **System.out** stream in the early chapters. Technically, this stream is part of the **java.lang.System** class. It is defined as an instance of the **java.io.PrintStream** class (as is **System.err**). This class supports **print** and **println** methods (the difference being that **println** appends a new line character).

The **java.lang.System.in** stream is a generic **InputStream**, which supports a **read** method in several forms. Most simply, you may use it to read one byte at a time from the standard input stream, much the way you would have used the C function *getchar*.

You should really only use these methods with nongraphics applications. The AWT (see Chapter 10) provides other facilities for capturing keyboard and mouse input and delivering screen output. Most browsers have a panel you may select that displays output from Java applets, but since this is normally hidden, it is usually used only for debugging purposes.

We can construct an instructive application that accepts keyboard input, echoes consonants to standard output, and vowels to standard error (perhaps this can be expanded to be useful on *Wheel of Fortune*). Under normal circumstances, standard out and standard error go to the same place (your screen), though they may have different priorities doing so. At the operating system command prompt, you can usually redirect one or the other to a file.

```
import java.io.*;
public class XVowels {
    public static void main(String args[ ]) {
        int testchar;
        System.err.prinln("Enter a letter");
        while (true) {
            testchar = System.in.read();
            if (testchar < 'A') break;
            if (testchar > 'z') break;
            if ((testchar > 'Z') && (testchar < 'a')) break;
            switch (testchar) {
            case 'A': case 'E': case 'I': case 'O': case 'U':
            case 'a': case 'e': case 'i': case 'o': case 'u':
                System.err.println("Vowel found: " + testchar);
                break;
            default:
                System.out.println("Consonant: " + testchar);
                System.err.println(testchar);
            }
        }
        System.out.println("Non character found: exiting");
    }
}
```

This application is not so clever as to determine whether Y or W are being used as vowels. We present it so that the reader may see a simple use of standard input and output. You may invoke it from your DOS window so that it sends consonants to a file (consonants.txt) and vowels to your screen by typing the following:

```
java XVowels > consonants.txt
```

FILES AND FILE DESCRIPTORS

Java's **File** class is a lot more than just a reference to a file. It provides class fields to store the separator characters for your path and filename (usually '\' or '/'). It also has many methods that can be used to determine various details about the file in question, such as:

- **canRead( )**, which tells whether this application has read permission on the file.
- **canWrite( )**, which tells whether this application has write permission.
- **delete( )**, which deletes the current file (if permitted).
- **exists( )**, which tells whether a given file already exists.
- **getAbsolutePath( )**, which returns the full path of the file.
- **getName( )**, which returns the name of the file.
- **getParent( )**, which returns the name of the parent directory.
- **getPath( )**, which returns the path portion of the file.
- **isAbsolute( )**, which tells whether the path is from root or relative.
- **isDirectory( )**, which tells whether the file is actually a directory.
- **isFile( )**, which tells whether the file is a file.
- **lastModified( )**, which returns the last modified date of the file.
- **length( )**, which returns the length of the file.
- **list(FilenameFilter ff)**, which returns a list of all the files in the directory matching the Filename Filter.
- **mkdir( )**, which creates a directory.
- **mkdirs( )**, which creates all nonexistent directories in the current path.
- **renameTo(File dest)**, which changes the name of the current file.

There is no create file method. To create a file, we construct a **FileOutputStream** object with a **File** object for a nonexistent file. Most of the above methods return a **false** if they fail. The **FileOutputStream** constructor will throw an **IOException** if it fails. Be prepared.

The following example shows how we may employ Files in Java. It is a simple application that reads a file and writes a file with the same content, but the carriage returns have been removed. This is a pretty worthwhile application if you do a lot of moving files from DOS to UNIX.

```
/* File win2unix.java
*
* this program reads a file and writes a new copy of the file
* with all of the line feeds removed.
*
* Parameters:
*     first parameter is the Windows file name.
*     second [optional] parameter is the unix file name.
*         if there is no second parameter the file is
*         written to win2unix.txt.
*
* This file is a classroom demonstration. A commercial
```

```
 * program of this sort would have more features and error checking.
 */

import java.io.*;

public class win2unix extends Object {
    public static void main(String args[ ])
    throws IOException {
        String WinFileName;
        String UnixFileName = "win2unix.txt"; // default file name

        switch (args.length) {
        case 2:
            UnixFileName = args[1];
        case 1:
            WinFileName = args[0];
            striplf(WinFileName, UnixFileName);
            break;
        default:
            System.out.println("Usage: java win2unix <winFile> |<unixFile>|");
        }
    }
    // do the work of the application.
    public static void striplf(String WFileName, String UFileName)
    throws IOException {
        byte[ ] inBuf = new byte[512];
        byte[ ] outBuf = new byte[512];
        int byteCount;
        FileInputStream W;
        FileOutputStream U;
        File WFile = new File(WFileName);        // declare files..
        File UFile = new File(UFileName);
        W = new FileInputStream(WFile);          // open files
        U = new FileOutputStream(UFile);
        try {
            while (true) {
                int outCount = 0;
                byteCount = W.read(inBuf);        // read original record.
                if (byteCount == -1) return;      // EOF, finally clause will
                                                  // close files.
                for (int i = 0; i < byteCount; i++) {
                    if (inBuf[i] != '\r') {
                        outBuf[outCount++] = inBuf[i];
                    }
                }
                U.write(outBuf, 0, outCount);     // write stripped record.
            }
```

```
        }
    catch (IOException e) {
        System.err.println("striplf: "+e.getMessage());
        throw e;    // detected the error, but don't want to continue.
    }
     finally {                                  // close the files on any exit.
        if (W != null) {
            try W.close(); catch(IOException e);
        }
        if (U != null) {
            try U.close(); catch(IOException e);
        }
    }
  }
}
```

Of course, this example doesn't test the file names given to be sure that they aren't directories, or that the input file already exists, nor does it get confirmation that we are allowed to write all over the output file. Since these are simply done and are similar in all computer languages, we leave such tasks as an exercise for the reader.

RANDOM ACCESS FILES

RandomAccessFile objects in Java are a separate family of objects from the rest of the stream-oriented classes. They provide the ability to open and close files for random access. You may seek any position within the file, and you many read or write in a variety of formats, including all of the primitive types.

The constructor has a parameter called **mode**. This is a string that tells what you may do with a file. The possible values for the **mode** parameter are:

- **"r"** for read only
- **"rw"** for read and write access

The following code fragment show how you may create a **RandomAccessFile** object and do something with it. In a real example, you would want to do a little more in the catch clause.

```
RandomAccessFile raf;
int ival;
// open a new file for read and write
```

```
try {
    raf = new RandomAccessFile("test.tmp", "rw");
    raf.writeChars("This is a test");
    raf.seek(4);                    // point at the blank between 'This' and 'is'
    ival = readUnsignedByte;        // gets 32 (the ASCII value of blank).
}
catch (IOException e) {
    System.err.println("Error with Random access file IO ");
}
finally {
    raf.close( );
}
```

Check the appendix for more about the methods of random access files. Play with them if you like. There is nothing mysterious about them.

BYTE ARRAYS AND STRING BUFFERS

Among the several types of streams provided by the java.io package are: **ByteArrayInputStream**, **StringBufferInputStream**, and **ByteArrayOutputStream**. There is no *StringBufferOutputStream*, but if you think about it for a moment, you'll see that you don't really need it.

These classes provide the ability to treat data in memory as though it were coming from some stream from a file, pipe, or socket. They each have a few simple methods, some of which we describe here. Look in the appendix for a complete list.

ByteArrayInputStream

constructor	Takes a byte array reference as a parameter, with optional length and offset.
read( )	Reads the next byte.
read(byte[ ] b, int off, int len)	Reads a specified part of the array into an array.
skip(long n)	Skips the next n positions. Note since we are using a long, we are limited to byte arrays of less than eighteen quintillion bytes.

StringBufferInputStream

Constructor	Takes a String reference as an input parameter. Why not a **StringBuffer**? Who knows, but it is a **String**, not a **String Buffer**, and Visual J++ will flag the error if you try to make it a **StringBuffer**.
read( )	Reads the next byte.
read(byte[ ] b, int off, int len)	Reads a specified part of the array into an array.
skip(long n)	Skips the next n positions. Note since we are using a long, we are limited to byte arrays of less than eighteen quintillion bytes.

ByteArrayOutputStream

constructor	Takes an optional size parameter.
reset size	Throws out current data, and starts writing from the beginning again.
write(int b)	Writes a single byte to the Stream.
write(byte[] b, int off, int len)	Writes a specified part of the array parameter to the stream.

TIP

A Good Use of ByteArrayStreams

Ultimately, your application is apt to use data from streams directly, and perhaps pass it back into another stream. These ByteArray constructs are a little awkward compared to storing data directly into fields and variables as needed.

These three classes (**ByteArrayInputStream**, **ByteArray OutputStream**, and **StringBufferInputStream**) are especially useful in debugging or building test classes for partially completed applications. It will often be the case while you are developing a class with streaming methods that you would like to test them with known, easily controlled data. This is what these classes are for.

PIPES AND FILTERS

Pipes are very simple. Output pipes from your object send data to input pipes of another object (especially threads), and vice versa. The methods available for this sort of communication are few, and so you may want to use one of the Filter input streams to give you more flexibility of expression. Figure 11.2 illustrates pipes, filters, sinks, and sources. The Pipe stream classes are: **PipedInputStream** and **PipedOutput Stream**. Aside from the simple Filter streams (**FilterInputStream** and **FilterOutputStream**), some special subclasses of these are available:

- **BufferedInputStream**, which is used to make faster use of system I/O facilities.
- **DataInputStream**, which is used to provide methods to handle direct storage of the primitive types.
- **LineNumberInputStream**, which keeps track of the number of lines passed through the stream.
- **PushbackInputStream**, which is useful if you'd like to peek at the next byte in the stream, but shove it back if you decide it is a command that a different method (or object) should handle.
- **BufferedOutputStream**, which is used in tandem with Buffered InputStream.

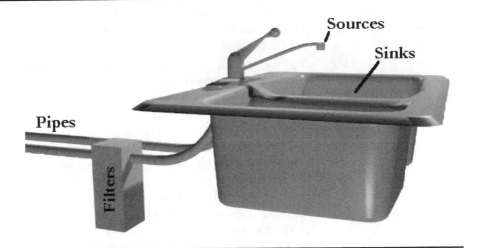

Figure 11.2   Pipes, filters, sinks, and sources.

- **DataOutputStream**, which is used in tandem with DataInput Stream.
- **PrintStream**, which has methods to convert the primitive types to character strings (used by **System.out**).

We see above that it is a simple matter to find a stream's output and connect it to another stream's input. Further, it is a simple thing to take that stream and pass it to a filter stream or a file stream. We leave it to the reader to create an example that does something a bit more useful with these constructs. It is essential that you learn how these things work, since you will have many utilizations for these constructs in your larger applications.

THE STREAMTOKENIZER

Java provides a helpful **StreamTokenizer** class. This class provides many of the methods that we will see a bit later in the **java.util. StringTokenizer** class, with the addition of a few more that improve its ability to be used to make a simple parser. These are the methods for testing for End Of Line (EOL), keeping track of line number, and for avoiding passing any Java type comments through the Stream Tokenizer.

EXERCISES

11-1   Write an application that gets user input from **System.in**, and in one mode, converts from inches to centimeters, and in another mode converts centimeters to inches (2.54 centimeters per inch), writing the results to **System.out**.

11-2   Modify the application so that **System.in** is passed to a **DataInputStream**, for ease of converting numeric input to double precision numbers.

11-3   Write an application that reads a file and converts it using the ROT13 filter. This filter was used in the ancient days of the internet to protect people from having to read tasteless dirty or otherwise non-PC jokes. It maintains case, but rotates letters thirteen places in the alphabet, thus converting A to N, and N to A, likewise, B to O, and M to Z.

11-4   Write a joke or opinion that is marginal, whether it requires ROT13 or not, and use exercise 3.

11-5   Create a class with a method that receives information in a **PipedInputStream** that it uses to create Color objects.

11-6   Write a class with a method that transmits information required to make Color objects.

11-7   Write a class that creates threads of exercises 5 and 6 above and sets up communication between them. (This will be more important later when you are writing distributed applications or stringing together stream filters.)

CHAPTER 12

The java.util Package

In this chapter we cover the following topics:

- **Enumerations**
- **Dates**
- **Hash Tables**
- **Vectors and Stacks**
- **BitSet**
- **The StringTokenizer**
- **Random Numbers**
- **Observables**

Dates, data structures, and random numbers . . . What do they have in common? They are utilities that didn't easily fit into the other packages. On the other hand, connected or not, these are valuable utilities, and it is good that Java provides them. Figure 12.1 provides an overview of the **java.util**.

Specifically, the **java.util** package has utilities for:

- **BitSet** Handling large arrays of individual bits.
- **Date** Handling calendar and clock arithmetic.
- **Enumeration** An interface for keeping a list of objects.
- **Hashtable** A data structure that you may come to like.
- **Observable** A class of objects that, when its contents change, notifies a list of Observers.

java.util package

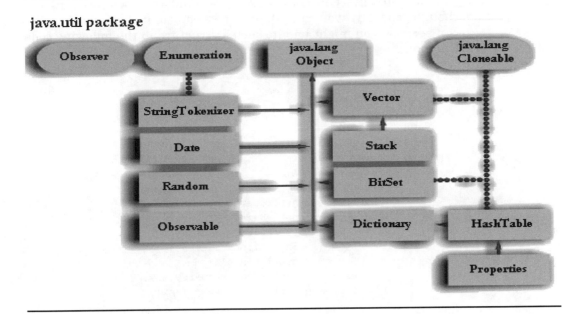

Figure 12.1   The java.util package.

- **Properties** A special hash table, used, among other things, for conveying environment variables to an application.
- **Random** A class used for generating pseudo-random numbers.
- **Stack** A special extendible array with push and pop methods.
- **StringTokenizer** A utility to help parse strings into substrings.
- **Vector** An indexed array that may grow as needed.

Let's take a closer look at how you might use these utilitarian classes.

ENUMERATIONS

There is an interface called **java.util.Enumeration**. Quite a few methods in the Java packages return objects that implement the enumeration interface. This interface demands two methods:

- **hasMoreElements( )**, which tells whether there are more elements in the enumeration.
- **nextElement( )**, which returns the next element in an enumerated list.

You only get one chance to go through an enumeration list, though generally, you can ask for a new copy of it if you need to. We can see how you might handle such a structure in the following code fragment.

```java
import java.util.*;
import java.awt.*;

public class Hello {
    public static void main(String[ ] args) {
        Enumeration en1;
        Properties pr1;
        String s1, s2;
        pr1 = System.getProperties( );
        en1 = pr1.propertyNames( );
        while (en1.hasMoreElements( )) {
            s1 = (String)en1.nextElement( );
            System.out.println(s1);
            s2 = (String)pr1.getProperty(s1);
            System.out.println(" >> " + s2);
        }
    }
}
```

This application shows the use of the **Enumeration** type, along with a revisit to our old friend the **System** class. In this case, we are getting the environment variables that our application is allowed to see. We are also getting a glimpse at another **java.util** class called **Properties**. **Properties** are a subclass of **HashTable**, which we will see later. **HashTables** and **Vectors** also have methods that produce **Enumeration** objects. The above construct is the standard way of handling them.

WARNING

Ordering Is Not Guaranteed

Enumeration lists are fairly common in Java. Your programs should not assume that the lists will be created in any particular order. You may initially see a tendency for the first objects added to the list being the first objects out, but don't count on it.

DATES

Dates are stored as the number of milliseconds since midnight GMT, January 1, 1970. Date objects provide many useful methods for getting or setting the date and time in a particular date object.

NOTE

Why Not Have a Better Date?

Java's **Date** class is very useful for the sorts of things that computers are mostly used for today. The class reports the year as the number of years since 1900. Can you guess whether it handles the calendar reform that shifted George Washington's birthday from the February 11 to 22? (It doesn't.) It also doesn't handle time units smaller than milliseconds very well. Also, we are, by now, all aware of the dilemma that we are facing with the year 2000 conversion . . .

Why not create a new date object; one that won't soon be obsolete; one that will satisfy every imaginable use for a date. Let's use two longs, one to store the number of seconds since some date well before the big bang (let's say 30 billion years ago). This number would have to wrap around in six hundred billion years (the universe should be pretty much entropied out by then). We can use a second long to store atto-seconds (an atto-second is 10^{-18} seconds). We can complete the unit by storing a third long that can be used for keeping the track of trillionths of jiffys (a jiffy is 10^{-23} seconds. It is approximately the time it takes something moving at the speed of light to cross the radius of a proton).

All this would require 24 bytes, plus a little object overhead. Is this too much to ask?

Date objects are created with one of several constructors, which permit creating the current date or dates specified with a **long**, a **String**, or some or all of the following: *year, month, dayOfMonth, hour, minute, second*. They also provide methods for getting or setting these values, including such methods as **setHours(int hours)** and **getSeconds(int seconds)**. For a complete list, see the appendix.

We can see a bit of how you might use **Date** objects in the following code fragment:

```
Date d1, d2;
long g1;
d1 = new Date( );                      // current date & time
g1 = d1.getTime( );                    // expressed as a long
d2 = new Date(g1+86400000);            // One days worth of
milliseconds.
while (d2.before(new Date( ))) {
    // ... some long loop that runs for one day.
}
```

In the above fragment, we saw the use of a few of the critical date methods. The other methods should be almost self-explanatory. Try them out.

HASH TABLES

Dictionary is a class in the **java.util** package. It is abstract, but it is used as the parent of the **HashTable** class. You will probably never use the **Dictionary** class directly.

You will use **HashTable** objects. Hash tables are a way of storing two parallel arrays of objects (which the **HashTable** object treats as one), one of which being pointers (keys) to the other (the values). Typically, the index array would contain some easily hashed object such as a **String**, a primitive type wrapper, or a **Date**. The other array would contain something a bit more complicated, such as a weather report, a library record, a D&B credit record, a digitized photograph . . . that sort of thing.

HashTables have several methods that you will use frequently. These include:

- **clear( ):** Clears all elements from the table.
- **contains(Object value):** Reports whether a particular object is in the table.
- **containsKey(Object key):** Reports whether a particular key is in the table.
- **get(Object key):** Gets the value object associated with a particular key.
- **elements( ):** Returns an enumeration list of the values in the table.
- **isEmpty( ):** Reports whether the table is empty.
- **keys( ):** Returns an enumeration list of the keys in the table.
- **put(Object key, Object value):** Adds a new item to the table.
- **remove(Object key):** Removes the elements associated with a particular key.

Perhaps it is easiest to see how this works in a small application. The following code fragment creates a list of **Colors** (values), which are associated with particular **Dates** (keys).

```
HashTable colorDate( );
colorDate = new HashTable( );
colorDate.put(new Date(1997,5,30), new Color(Color.red));
colorDate.put(new Date(1997, 6, 14), new Color(Color.white));
colorDate.put(new Date(1997, 7, 4), new Color(Color.blue));
```

In the above example, we have created a **HashTable** object, and populated it.

Java provides a subclass of **HashTable** called **Properties**. This class is used by the **java.lang.System.getProperties( )** method to return the environment variables that are available to your application. The **Properties** class may be used for loading hash tables from a stream.

VECTORS AND STACKS

What does the word **Vector** mean to you? Is it a one-dimensional matrix? Is it an arrow pointing the way in some Cartesian coordinate system? Is it an animal that transmits some disease-bearing organism? Is it a course followed by an aircraft? Now it has a new meaning. A **Vector** is a class of expandable arrays in Java.

Java **Vectors** have a certain initial size and expand as needed. This can be very handy when you are creating objects (such as purchase orders) for what will be a large database. Most purchase orders have one or a very few items in them. How do you decide what is the maximum number of spaces you want to reserve for these items on one purchase order object? With **Vectors**, you don't have to make millions of empty String spaces in your database. You can allocate only what is needed.

Vector objects have a number of elements, each of which is an object. These elements are indexed. When inserting a new element, you either call the **addElement(Object obj)** method, which puts the new element at the end of the **Vector**, or you insert the element at a particular point in the **Vector** (with the **insertElementAt(Object obj, int index)** method), and all higher elements move up one. There is never an empty slot in a **Vector**. **Vectors** also supply methods for removing elements, changing the contents of an element, and getting an enumeration list of all the objects in a particular **Vector**.

You will write a short program using a **Vector** object as one of your exercises.

There is a subclass of the **Vector** called the **Stack**. In addition to the usual **Vector** methods (which you shouldn't have to use with a **Stack**), there are the methods **empty( )**, **peek( )**, **pop( )**, and **push( )**. Can you guess what these do? They implement a *First In Last Out* stack. If you have spent much time in computer science, you know how handy this structure can be. Stacks are best used in situations where newer situations must be handled before old ones, but ultimately, they must all be handled.

BITSET

Memory is generally getting cheaper. Still, there are some situations in which it is useful to store information in individual bits. The **java.util.BitSet** class makes this a little easier.

> **NOTE**
>
> ### Denser Isn't Necessarily Faster
>
> An array of booleans takes up eight times as much space as a **BitSet** object with the same information. As an exercise, use the **Date** class and write an application to determine which is faster: setting every other element of an array of booleans, or every other element of a **BitSet**.

BitSet objects have methods that let you set or clear individual bits. There are also methods that let you **and**, **or**, or **xor** one **BitSet** with another.

Because the index into the **BitSet** is an **int**, the largest size **BitSet** that you may create, even on a muscle machine, is a quarter gigabyte. Hopefully this won't impair your big bit-oriented project.

THE STRINGTOKENIZER

Another small but useful utility in the **java.util** package is the **StringTokenizer**. Objects of this class have methods for converting a string to a list of strings. You may collect these tokens using the enumeration methods described above, or you may get them with parallel methods named for tokens instead of elements.

Optional constructor parameters allow you to choose what the delimiter is. The default is the blank space. Another optional constructor parameter dictates whether you will get these delimiter characters as tokens.

The following simple example shows the use of this facility in a little application.

```java
import java.util.*;
import java.io.*;

public class StringTokenizerTest {
    public static void main(String args[ ]) throws IOException {
        String command, p;
        char[] dummy;
        DataInputStream user = new DataInputStream(System.in);

        while (true) {
            System.out.println("Enter a String to Tokenize: ");
            command = user.readLine();     // get user input
            if (command.length() == 0) break;
            StringTokenizer st;
            st = new StringTokenizer(command);
            System.out.println("command has "+st.countTokens()+" tokens");
            while (st.hasMoreTokens()) {
                System.out.println(" ->"+st.nextToken());
            }
        } // end while (true)
    }
}
```

What could be simpler? Learn the **StringTokenizer**, and use it where ever you need to parse strings. It is helpful to use the same methods as everyone else.

RANDOM NUMBERS

Some people love games. Other people like a certain random quality to lend that certain artistic verisimilitude. Still others are stuck doing Monte Carlo calculations for their nuclear physics work. Regardless of why you need them, it is reassuring to know that Java provides a fairly nice random number generator.

The **java.util.Random** class allows you to set the seed value (when you need to repeat a sequence), as well as get **floats** or **doubles** with values between 0.0 and 1.0. Similar methods permit getting **ints** or **longs** anywhere in the range that those values cover. A special method is provided that gives you doubles in a Gaussian distribution, centered on 0.0 with the standard deviation at 1.0.

> ### NOTE
>
> ### Random vs. Pseudorandom
>
> Like most random number generators, the one in **java.util** is actually pseudo-random. To be truly random, you would need some kind of hardware device, such as a high-speed clock connected to an alpha particle detector near an alpha source. It would probably be cheap enough to construct, but that level of randomness is seldom needed.

How would you use this class? See the simple example below.

```
import java.util.*;
import java.io.*;

public class RandomTest {
    public static void main(String args[ ]) throws IOException {
        Random r1 = new Random( );
        int j;
        double d;
        for int i=0; i < 10; i++) {
            j = r1.nextInt( );
            d = r1.nextDouble( );
            System.out.println("Randoms: "+ j + " " + d);
        }
    }
}
```

OBSERVABLES

Back in the days of structured programming, we used to joke about the *conditional come-from* as being a missing element in our application description language. Here it is. You may create a class of objects that notify all interested parties when the objects have changed.

Essentially, you must encapsulate the data that may be changed, and build into the **setXXXX** method (whatever **XXXX** is) something that tests to see if the new value is different from the old, then calls its own **setChanged** method, and then the **notifyObservers** method.

Objects implementing the Observer interface may call the **add Observer(this)** method of the observable object and get themselves put on the list to be notified (there is also a **deleteObserver(this)** method).

Objects that implement the Observer interface must flesh out a method called **update(Observable obs, Object arg)**, in which *obs* is the Object that changed, and *arg* is the parameter passed by the **notifyObservers** method (which can be **null**). It is up to the Observer's **update** method to determine what object changed and what to do with the new value. Figure 12.2 shows an illustration of using the **Observer** class.

This sort of thing is especially useful in GUI environments, where things may be changed in any number of ways, but you would like things to stay synchronized with each other.

In the above example, we see an **Observer** thread watching an **Observable StringBuffer**. When that StringBuffer changes, the **Observer's** update method is called. You can imagine what sorts of useful things can be put into that update method.

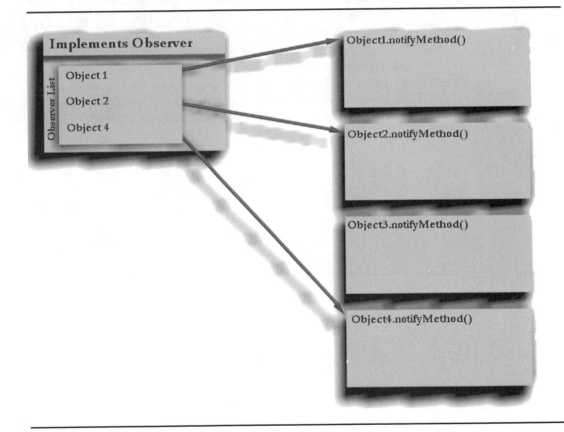

Figure 12.2   Using the Observer class.

EXERCISES

12-1   Write an application that computes the difference in years, days, hours, minutes, and seconds between the current time and a time given as a runtime parameter.

12-2   Write an application that takes names and phone numbers and pairs them in a **HashTable**.

12-3   Extend exercise 2 with an **Enumeration** list to pull them out again. Find a way to alphabetize the list.

12-4   Make a new application that stores names and phone numbers in a **rolodexCard** object of your own creation. Store these cards in a **Vector** object.

12-5   Update exercise 4 so that the list is stored alphabetically.

12-6   Name three situations in which it might be useful to use the **BitSet** objects.

12-7   Write an application that lets you guess a random number between 0 and 1024. Make it chastise the user severely if it takes eleven or more guesses.

12-8   Write an application in which you launch two threads, one of which awaits keyboard input, while the other awaits notification from the first that the letter Z has been entered.

CHAPTER 13

The java.net Package

In this chapter we cover the following topics:

- **InetAddresses**
- **URL Utilities**
- **Datagrams**
- **Sockets and ServerSockets**
- **Using java.net and java.io Together**

As with the **java.io** package, Java would not have come to the forefront of media attention were it not for the **java.net** package. **java.net** provides the classes that create and handle the network connection for Java applications (and applets). Those familiar with network programming will find this package rather simple and elegant, supplying all your needs in convenient well-thought-out ways.

You will find **java.net** small and tasteful: You can count the classes you will use in this package on the fingers of both hands (with thumbs to spare). Figure 13.1 shows the structure of the **java.net** package. Of special note are:

- **DatagramPacket:** These are the packets sent and received by **DatagramSockets** (see below).
- **DatagramSocket:** These sockets are used for the simple (non-TCP) **Datagram** protocol.
- **InetAddress:** This stores an internet address.

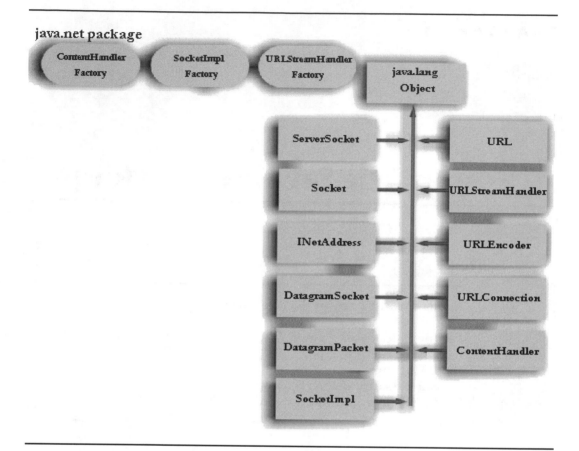

Figure 13.1   The java.net package.

- **ServerSocket:** These listen for client applications to request connections.
- **Socket:** This is the object wrapper around a TCP socket on the host system.
- **URL** (Uniform Resource Locators): These have many properties. This lets you get and set them.
- **URLConnection:** This provides manual control of a URL connection.
- **URLEncoder:** This is used to convert your Strings to Strings containing only the standard URL characters.

Two of the classes mentioned above are the **DatagramPacket** and **DatagramSocket**. These provide a low-level service that doesn't provide confirmation of receipt, or guarantee sequential or even timely reception. On the other hand, they are quicker and require a lot less overhead. These are useful in situations such as sending one-time messages such as e-mail, or quick interactive situations in which losing one packet from a stream is not critical. For most practical applications where TCP resources are not reaching the limit, the TCP sockets (**Socket** and **ServerSocket**) are recommended.

Some of the examples in this section may be difficult for you to get running on standalone Win95 or WinNT environments. They depend on correct configuration of TCP on your machine. If the only TCP you have done is with your browser, you may have trouble. It is beyond the scope of this book to troubleshoot your system in this way. If you have this kind of problem, seek professional help.

INETADDRESSES

InetAddress objects are optionally used when creating **Datagram Packets** (see below) and opening TCP **Sockets**; they are returned by the **getInetAddress** method of the **ServerSocket**.

An **InetAddress** object contains an internet address. This address can be retrieved from this object either as a name, in the form of a String (e.g., *microsoft.com*), or as an array of bytes, representing the familiar old *127.0.0 1* format.

> **NOTE**
>
> ### Internet Addresses and Unsigned Bytes
>
> Java does not support unsigned **bytes**. As a result, when you get this array, you may find yourself looking at some negative numbers. Don't be alarmed . . . they will work fine the way they are, but if you want to look at them, just convert them to **shorts** or **ints** and mask off all but the last eight bits, as follows:
>
> ```
> byte ba[ ];
> int addr = new int[8]; // some extra for Miss Manners
> InetAddress ia = getByName(microsoft.com); // create the
> InetAddress object
> ba = ia.getAddress( ); // load the byte array
> for (int i=0; i< ba.length; i++)
> addr[i] = ba[i] & 0x000000ff; // mask off the high bytes.
> ```

The **InetAddress** class has three static methods that generate **InetAddress** objects. Aside from these, there are no constructors.

URL UTILITIES

We will discuss three classes that support **URLs**. These are **URL**, **URLConnection**, and **URLEncoder**.

URL Objects

URL objects hold URLs (Uniform Resource Locators). These are pointers to some file (or other resource) on the internet (or within your computer). URLs are composed of several parts, including:

- A **protocol** (such as http, ftp, file, or several others)
- A **host** (such as microsoft.com)
- An optional **port** (such as 80 for httpd, or 21 for ftpd)
- A **path** and **file name** (including optional **parameters** for a CGI executable)

URL objects can be created with one of several constructors supplying the above components. They also have methods that permit getting the information about the contained **URL** (such as **getFile**, **getHost**, **getProtocol**, and **getPort**), plus methods to open the connection, open a stream from the URL, determine whether one URL points to the same location as another, and a few other methods that you might use once in a while (see the appendix).

Calling the **openConnection( )** method of a **URL** object returns a **URLConnection** object (see below).

URLConnection Objects

If you are not content to trust that a particular **URL** is going to always be there and give you the input stream you really want, you may get a **URLConnection** object and do some additional manipulations. Among the things that these objects provide are:

- Opening the connection.
- The ability to guess the content type from the name of the file.
- Setting which content handler to use when getting the file.
- Getting information about the length, type, and date of the content.
- Getting header information.
- Determining whether input or output stream are available.

* Opening input or output streams
* And many more.

The following code sample opens a URL connection, and grabs a file.

```
import java.applet.*;
import java.awt.*;
import java.io.*;
import java.net.*;

public class Errata extends Applet implements Runnable {
    Thread myThread;
    TextArea a = new TextArea(20, 60);
    URL myUrl;

    public void init() {
        String sug = "http://www.sug.org/BOOKS/vjppSourcebook/errata.txt";
        try {
            this.myUrl = new URL(sug);
        }
        catch (Exception e) {
            showStatus("error trying to get errata");
        }
        add(a);
    }

    public void start() {
        if myThread == null) {
            myThread = new Thread(this);
            myThread.start();
        }
    }

    public void stop() {
        if (myThread != null) {
            myThread.stop();
            myThread = null;
        }
    }

    public void run() {
        InputStream conx;
        DataInputStream text;
        String line;
        StringBuffer b = new StringBuffer();
```

```
try {
    conx = this.myUrl.openStream();
    text = new DataInputStream(new BufferedInputStream(conx));
    while ((line = text.readLine()) != null) {
        b.append(line + "\n");
    }
    a.setText(buf.toString());
}
catch (Exception e) {
    showStatus("Error reading file: " + e.getMessage());
}
    }
}
```

If you want to get the feeling that you are programming for the internet, this is the class to start playing with. For further excitement, you should try experimenting with Content Handlers.

URLEncoder Objects

Not all strings are appropriate for use in **URLs**. For example, you may not have an embedded space. Certain other punctuation (or control) characters must be represented in their hex format. Only a subset of the ASCII character set may be used. All of the higher Unicode characters are ruled out.

There is a **URLEncoder** class, which has one class method (you don't need to create an object of this type). Its one true method is to take a given string, replace all of the embedded blanks with plus signs (+), and replace all of the special characters with a percent sign followed by a two hex digits (e.g., %07 for the **Bell** character).

DATAGRAMS

DatagramPackets are sent, one at a time, to and from **Datagram Sockets** (Figure 13.2). Once sent, each one is forgotten. There is no built-in confirmation of reception. But with the very little that they do for you, they take very little overhead, and have their uses in situations where system resources or performance are at a premium.

DatagramPacket

DatagramPackets meant for transmission are created with a constructor that specifies the array of bytes to be sent, its length, and the **InetAddress** (see above) and port to which it will be sent. A packet

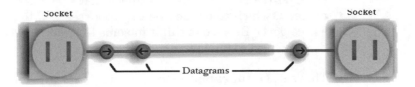

Figure 13.2   DatagramPackets are sent over the internet from one DatagramSocket to another.

meant for reception is created only with a pointer to the array of bytes and its length. The other methods available let you get:

- **getAddress( ):** The InetAddress of a packet.
- **getData( ):** Its contents.
- **getLength( ):** Its length.
- **getPort( ):** The port to which it is assigned.

How could it be simpler? We will see a code fragment supporting this structure after the **DatagramSocket** has been described.

DatagramSocket

It probably goes without saying, but **DatagramSockets** are the sockets through which the **DatagramPackets** pass. You may, when constructing a **DatagramSocket** object, specify what port is to be used. If you do not, one will be assigned for you.

When to Specify a Port

If you are planning to receive a **DatagramPacket,** you should either assign the port, or otherwise get its number and publish it. How else will anyone know what socket to send things to?

In addition to the constructors, **DatagramSockets** have several useful methods including:

- **send(DatagramPacket p),** which sends a given datagram packet.
- **receive(Datagram Packet p),** which fills the byte array and sets the length of a given **DatagramPacket** object.

- **getLocalPort( )**, which gets this socket's port address.
- **close( )**, which frees the system resources tied to the socket (such as the port). Be sure to call it in some finalize method to guarantee that the port is made free.

That's it. **Datagrams** are very straightforward (and therefore their use is discouraged). When you do use them, there are a few things that you must build up to send a packet:

- Create the packet's message (a byte array), usually from a Unicode string.
- Create the **InetAddress** object indicating where the message will be sent.
- Create the **DatagramPacket** object.
- Create the sending **DatagramSocket** object.
- Send the packet(s).
- Close the **DatagramSocket** object to free the system resources.

Datagrams have their place, as we can see in the following fanciful example:

```
import java.net.*;

public class SendDatagram
    public static void main (String args[ ]) throws Exception {
        byte[ ] b1 = new byte[1024];     // enough for most practical purposes
        String s1 = "Launch Jovian Atmospheric Probe";
        int len = s1.length;             // 31 in this case.
        int port = 32767;                // Galileo command port (hypothetical)
        InetAddress ia1 = InetAddress.getByName("Galileo.org");
        s1.getBytes(0, 31, b1, 0);       // convert Unicode to bytes.
        DatagramPacket dp1 = new Datagram (b1, len, ia1, port);
        DatagramSocket soc1 = new DatagramSocket( );
        soc1.send(dp1);                  // send the first packet.
        soc1.close( );                   // we could have sent more before
                                         // closing.
    }
}
```

Our example shows that **Datagrams** are useful when the time delay between source and destination is significant. At the receiving end, you may could use something equally simple, such as:

- Create a buffer (byte array) for the received message.
- Create the **DatagramPacket** object using that buffer.

- Create a **DatagramSocket** object on the listening port.
- Wait for reception (a strong argument for the use of threads!).
- Convert the byte array to a more manageable String object.
- Repeat the last two steps as needed.
- Close the **DatagramSocket** object to free the system resources.

```
import java.net.*;

public class ReceiveDatagram
    public static void main(String args[ ]) throws exception {

        String command;
        byte[ ] b2 = new byte[1024];
        DatagramPacket dp2 = new DatagramPacket(b1, b1.length);
        DatagramSocket soc2 = new DatagramSocket(32767);
        soc2.receive(dp2); // wait until a packet comes.
        command = new String(b2, 0, 0, dp2.getLength());
        // parse and act on the command instructions omitted
        System.out.println(command);
        soc2.close( );
    }
}
```

You may have noticed the discrete use of the **throws exception** clause in the main method declarations above. That and the failure to employ threads were part of a concerted effort to show just the use of the **Datagrams** at their most basic. You would, of course, want to catch the **UnknownHostException** that constructing an **InetAddress** object could create, or the **SocketException** that constructing the sockets could create, or the **IOException** that you could catch while sending or receiving the packets.

You could also be clever and launch the receive method in a thread that you could monitor, and perhaps shut down if too much time goes without getting a packet. The above examples aren't fail-safe, but they are comprehensible.

SOCKETS AND SERVERSOCKETS

You will also want sockets that support some kind of handshaking for interprocess communication or other direct communication purposes. The java.net package supports this kind of socket with the **Socket** and **ServerSocket** classes (Figure 13.3). With sockets from these classes, you get streams—you do not get packets.

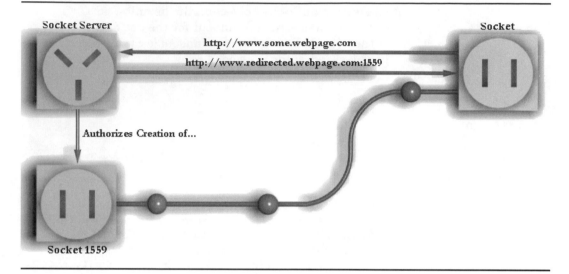

Figure 13.3   Sockets and ServerSockets from the java.net package.

ServerSocket objects sit looking at a port, waiting for a connection. When it comes, the **accept** method returns a **Socket** object for maintaining the communication link between the client and the server. Socket objects handle input and output streams between the two nodes.

In addition to these primary functions, **Sockets** and **Server Sockets** have methods that enable the user to determine their important qualities, such as the port number, the **InetAddress**, and a few other important details.

USING java.net AND java.io TOGETHER

When you are using the **Socket** and **ServerSocket** objects from **java.net**, the flow of data goes through streams. It is essential, therefore, to also use the methods of the **java.io** package. These streams permit the transmission of several kinds of data. Some of the things you can do with such streams include:

- Sending text files from one file filter object to another.
- Sending data field content to create clone objects at the remote site.
- Sending a series of command packets that can be interpreted by the receiving object and used for local method calls.
- Queuing transactions.

> **TIP**
>
> ### You Can Even Send Classes
>
> In the **java.lang.System** class and **java.lang.Compiler** class are sufficient tools to enable you to write an application that receives the source code for a new class, compiles it, downloads data with which to create objects of this class, and perhaps even invokes its methods (if it implements a known interface).
>
> Can you think of some interesting ways to use this technology?

In the following examples, we illustrate how you can open such sockets and connect their I/O to streams. In the first example, we do no more than create a **ServerSocket** that reports what gets sent to it by a **telnet** session. This is the traditional first **Socket** application:

```
import java.io*;
import java.net.*;

class TServer {
    public final static int PORT = 9999;
    int port;
    ServerSocket listen;
    Socket talk;
    byte b[] = new byte [4096];
    int count;

    public static void main (String s[]) {
        port = PORT;
        try {
            listen = new ServerSocket (port);
        }
        catch (Exception e) {
            System.out.println ("trouble");
        }
        talk = listen.accept();     // wait here until someone calls
        InputStream is = talk.getInputStream();
        while (true)  {
            count = is.read(b);
            if (count == -1) exit (0);
            System.out.println(b);
        }
    }
}
```

Notice that the application echoes the **telnet** stream out to the **System.out** stream. It also sends confirming data to the **telnet** application that talks to it. It ends the application when it gets a *self-destruct* command.

In the second example, we create a client application that does the same job as our **telnet** session.

```
import java.io.*;
import java.net.*;
        \
class TClient {
    public final static int PORT = 9999;
    int port;
    Socket talk;
    byte b[] = new byte[4096];
    int count;

    public static void main(String s[]) {
        port = PORT;
        try {
            talk = new Socket(InetAddress.getLocalHost(), PORT);
        }
        catch (Exception e) {
            System.out.println ("trouble");
        }
    ;   PrintStream lout = talk.getOutputStream();
        lout.println("This is only a test");
    }
}
```

We can see that it is an easy matter to open and manipulate sockets. The business of creating a second socket on a new port, to preserve the listener's function, has been automated. The business of connecting a stream to a socket is very natural. The **java.net** package supplies you with a very simple and yet fairly complete collection of what you need for stream-oriented communication between threads, processes, or even remote sites on the internet. You will see some other applications in which communications across the net will seem even simpler when we discuss Remote Method Invocation, but that is in the future and is not part of the first release of Visual J++.

EXERCISES

13-1   Write a pair of applications that each get input from **System.in**, and send that input to each other via **DatagramPackets**.

13-2   Expand exercise 1, so that some special command makes one
        application send a rapid numbered series of **Datagrams**. Write
        the receiver to test if any are received out of order.

13-3   Expand the **telnet** receiver application to forward its messages
        to a **DatagramPacket** receiver.

13-4   Build a client (applet) and a server (application) using sockets.
        Make the client draw colored polygons based on data received
        from the server (don't forget to call repaint).

CHAPTER 14

Connecting to Native Code

This chapter covers the following topics:

- **Native Methods**
- **Better Alternatives to Native Methods**
- **Java's javah Utility**

Native methods are external functions, written in C or C++, which are loaded outside the Java Interpreter by your Java application. They may be called as methods of a class which is otherwise running within the Java Interpreter. The keyword **native** is used to mark a stub within the class to make this kind of connection.

Java purists say that you should go to great lengths to avoid doing this because it destroys a lot of what makes Java good and useful. Still, depending on what you are using Java for, there may be times when using a native method will seem unavoidable. (Better alternatives are becoming available.)

When Java first became available, there were no alternatives to using Native Methods for issues related to using pre-existing libraries, talking to specific devices, or making system-specific calls to the operating system's features. Microsoft seems to have taken a middle of the road position on this. *Visual J++* supports the native keyword, but the Integrated Development Environment does not have any tool to generate the bits of C code required to make the connection. It does not even have more than one line of text on the subject in the on-line help. What

Visual J++ does do is provide facilities for connecting to ActiveX components.

> ### WARNING
>
> ### Don't Do It In An Applet
>
> Use of native code removes most of Java's best features. You can no longer be certain that there are no memory leaks, most of the portability issues are destroyed, and security is just a skeleton of its former self. As Java and Visual J++ develop, there will be much better ways to make these connections. Don't learn this very bad habit, unless there is some very timely and mission critical reason.

These warnings having been posted, let's look at how to do this evil thing.

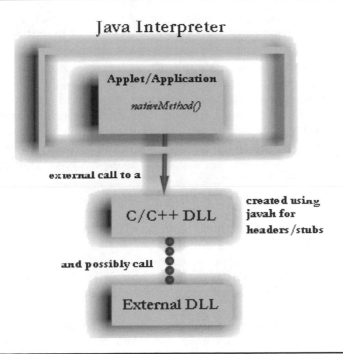

Figure 14.1   How a function in a DLL connects to Java code.

NATIVE METHODS

You may connect to a function written in C or C++ which is part of a dynamically linked library (DLL) by creating a stub for a method in a class of yours, and declaring it native. To invoke this method, you must be certain that the DLL containing the code for your native method is loaded using the loadLibrary method of the java.lang.System class.

There are of course a few other details that you must take care of, and there isn't any facility in *Visual J++* to help take care of these details. The CD-ROM on the back of this book contains a copy of *Sun's Java JDK, version 1.02*. This has a tool on it, which you should probably invoke from a DOS prompt, called **javah**, which is used to generate some helpful code fragments that must be present in the C or C++ code, whether you are calling a DLL or invoking Java from C or C++.

You may also invoke Java Methods from a C or C++ program. This also involves some detail work, which *Visual J++* also provides no facility for.

BETTER ALTERNATIVES TO NATIVE METHODS

No matter what you are doing, there is a way to do it without using the native method construct. Lets look at some of the alternatives:

- Make two separate applications (one C and one Java), which communicate using disk files.
- Make two separate applications (one C and one Java), which communicate through a socket. Let the C program handle everything that needs higher performance execution or direct to hardware interactions. (This may require some additional work, since many stand alone Windows95 systems do not have TCP available all of the time.)
- Use the VJ++ COM Wizard to let separate applications communicate.
- Use ActiveX components in your Java application. The means to do this are described in Part III of this book.
- Get Sun's package for connecting Java to CORBA (the IDL package). Put a CORBA wrapper around your C or C++ based application, and call it that way. (This is not described in this book in any detail.)
- Get Sun's Java Beans package, and connect to ActiveX, or other such interface objects in a way that Sun supports (probably will be the industry standard). (This is also not described in any detail in this book.)

There may also be some interesting third party tools which could get you around the need to make native methods. Consider your options, use of native methods is probably the worst choice you could make along these lines.

Just remember, if *Microsoft*, with its huge investment in C++ based software, didn't build in direct support for native methods, it must be a dead-end path in the evolution of software development.

JAVA'S JAVAH UTILITY

After all that, you are still interested in pursuing this approach? There are some details you will need to know, first of which is how to use the **javah** tool in *Sun's Java JDK*.

There are seven steps to follow to run a Java program with one or more native methods (but there is no twelve step program to stop doing it yet):

1. Write the Java part of the application.
2. Compile the Java part of the application to produce the **.class** file(s).
3. Run **javah** on the **.class** file to produce your **.h** file.
4. Run **javah** with the **-stubs** option to produce the stubs file for your C code.
5. Write the source code for your C or C++ function.
6. Compile and link to the C, stubs, and .h files to make a DLL.
7. Run the program.

Write the Java Part of the Application

This is a fairly simple matter. The only difference between this and what you have already done is that you must include a call to the loadLibrary method of the System class (**java.lang** package). This call must be invoked as a static part of any class that calls a native method. For example:

```
public class MyDevice {
    public native short readMyDevice( );

    static {
        System.loadLibrary("libmydevice");
    }
    // .. more methods
}
```

Note that in the above code fragment, we have declared a stub native method, which returns a **short**, and takes no parameters. The native method system permits the use of any valid return type, and any valid types as parameters.

The System.loadLibrary method loads a DLL into a space that the Java interpreter can access.

In some other part of your application (probably in a different class definition), you may invoke this native method. This might look like the following:

```
public void someOtherMethod ( ) {
    MyDevice md;
    Short newVal;
    md = new MyDevice( );
    // ... useful code
    newVal = md.readMyDevice( );
    // ... more useful code
}
```

As you can see, as far as any other part of your Java code is concerned, there is no difference between a native method and a Java method.

Compile the Java Part of the Application to Produce the .class File(s)

You can do this with *Visual J++* in the usual way.

Run javah on the .class File to Produce Your .h File

As we noted above, this will have to be done at the DOS prompt, using the javah utility that is on the CD-ROM in the Sun JDK. Consult the documentation on the CD-ROM in that directory to install the JDK on your system.

You actually create the appropriate file by using the command:

```
javah MyDevice
```

This command produces a small file which you should not edit. The file would in this case be called *MyDevice.h*. It should be included in the C file which contains the function which will be used as the *readMy Device* method.

Run javah with the -stubs Option to Produce the Stubs File for Your C Code

You must then run **javah** again to produce a stub file for your C application. Again this is a piece of code which you should not edit. You invoke this utility at the DOS prompt (again), this time using the following command:

```
javah -stubs MyDevice
```

This looks at your .class file, and produces a file called MyDevice.c. This code will have a reference to an external function which you must supply. In this case it would be named *MyDevice_readMyDevice*.

Write the Source Code for Your C or C++ Function

The C source code is fairly straightforward, after the above:

```
#include <StubPreamble.h>
#include "MyDevice.h"
#include <stdio.h>

void MyDevice_readMyDevice(struct HMyDevice *this) {
    // code to do that thing you do.
}
```

Compile and Link to the C, Stubs, and .h Files to Make a DLL

How you would do this depends on the **IDE** you are using, but should be well documented whatever you choose. With Visual C++ you could type the following command at the DOS prompt:

```
cl MyDevice.c readMyDevice.c -libmydevice.dll -MD -LD javai.lib
```

This will produce a file called libmydevice.dll, which is what your Java code want to load before executing the above described native method.

Run the Program

You run this program like any other Java program. The result should be what you would normally anticipate. There are two common exceptions that you may have to debug.

The first is the **NullPointerException** with a mention of an **UnsatisfiedLinkError**. This will often happen if you do not have the library path established at all.

The second is the **UnsatisfiedLinkError**. This happens when you do not have the Library path correctly established, or have otherwise put the DLL someplace the system isn't looking.

You may get other errors at run time, but it is beyond the scope of this book to help you troubleshoot those. We have, after all, recommended that you not use native methods at all.

EXERCISES

14-1   Name five good things that Java does that you lose if you use native methods.

PART II

Learning Visual J++

CHAPTER 15

The Visual J++ Developers Studio and the Build Process

In this chapter we cover the following topics:

- **A Comparison of the Windows and Java Programming Models**
- **Introducing the Visual J++ Developers Workbench**
- **Features of the Visual J++ Compiler**
  - **The Visual J++ Compiler**
  - **The Visual J++ Debugger**
  - **The Visual J++ Graphics Editor**
  - **The Visual J++ Source Browser/Editor**
  - **The Visual J++ Graphics Editor**
  - **The Visual J++ Resource Editor**
  - **Visual J++ and Source Code Control**
  - **The Visual J++ Help System**

A COMPARISON OF THE WINDOWS AND JAVA PROGRAMMING MODELS

The Windows Programming Model Revisited

Programming has changed incredibly over the last five to ten years. Gone are the days of batch—based and serial programming. Applications no longer have a single thread of execution, nor do they need to proceed serially from one task to the next. But rather, they can do many things at once and in any order based on external events. Old UNIX and MS-DOS programmers had to jump through many hoops if they wished to have a single application do more then one thing at a time or respond to an external event. As we shall see in the next few sections, Windows and Java applications can easily do several things at once, reacting to events as they happen. And, of course, we have glossed over the fact that Windows applications are normally built by being compiled to object code and then linked to produce a fully ready executable that is bound to the target machine's architecture. Java applications and applets have no such constraints and are designed from the beginning to be executable on any target that has a Java virtual machine developed for it.

The Event/Message Processing Model Historically, an application had a single entry point (under a C program normally called **main**) from which execution began. From there the application could make request for data via function calls and so on to do whatever it needed, normally in a serial fashion, moving from one task to the next in some predefined order. Windowing systems differ from this model in that they are **Message** or **Event Processing** based. That is, they react to events, generated externally or internally buy a user, the system, or other parts of the application.

A Windows program normally has a single entry point from which execution starts, *WinMain*, whose main task in life is to create the root or main window of the application. This window would then have code associated with it for processing messages. Today's Windows application differs from that done only years ago in that most applications are developed under a *Framework* that hides the underlying window's message—passing mechanism to some degree by associating messages and events with methods and using a routing mechanism to make sure the correct method is called when a event occurs.

> **NOTE**
>
> ### Frameworks and Windows Programs
>
> Discussion of Frameworks and Windows programming is beyond the scope of this book. However, many good texts exist on the subject. Readers interested in understanding more about native Windows programming are encouraged find a text and pursue this topic on their own.

When developing for native Windows, there is a set of predefined messages for creating and destroying windows, processing mouse events, and the like, as well as a mechanism for describing user-defined messages. Under today's *Framework-based* programming paradigm, those events that are interesting to the application are captured and some user-defined method is called to take action. As we shall see, the Java programming model is surprisingly similar.

Threads and Multiprocessing Windows has always been a multiprocessing environment (well, not always, but close enough). But multiprocessing and threads are not the same thing. Threads, sometimes called lightweight processes, have only recently come onto the Windows scene. An operating system that runs two tasks at the same time—such as a word processor and a spreadsheet—is multiprocessing. Whether you like it or not, the operating system schedules each of these tasks to get some CPU time. This, however, is not multithreading. Multiprocessing is something the operating system does for you. Multithreading requires effort on the part of the developer to split the application into parts that can be run at the same time as separate *threads of execution*. When 32-bit Windows arrived, the seeds were planted for multithreaded applications. Windows NT and Windows 95 now support a full-featured set of functions for creating, synchronizing, and otherwise managing threads. Java, on the other hand, was born and raised with multithreading in mind.

Resource-Based Programming Windows programming is heavily laden with resources. Under the Windows model, resources are a file or files that are combined and then bound by the linker into your application. Resources typically describe all your dialogs, menus, strings, and the like. All applications development environments provide text editors, and the Developers Studio is no different.

> **NOTE**
>
> ### Microsoft Developers Studio
>
> While not previously mentioned, Visual J++ and all its associated tools is collectively called Microsoft Developers Studio, or just Developers Studio.

But, in addition, Developers Studio also provides a *resource editor* that allows the developer to see what he or she is actually working with. Early versions of compilers for Windows required the developer to actually edit resources by hand, a tedious, time-consuming, error-prone process. Once you have built your dialogs, windows, buttons, and menus with the resource editor, you can bind them to your program, severing the link between the code and the resource, and allowing you to rearrange your dialogs, change strings, and do general reformatting, all without changing any code. Visual J++ embraces this model, providing similar features but implementing them in a slightly different fashion.

Memory Management Memory and its allocation have been, for the longest time, a difficult task for Windows developers including allocating selectors and handles, locking them in place, and freeing them. This is at best difficult, and at worst horrible. With the entrance of Visual C++, developers were freed from the hassles of memory management, as they could simply allocate what they needed and Windows did the rest. As will see shortly, the Java programming language takes this one step further.

Other Interesting Features Windows programming contains many other interesting features, one of the most important being DLLs. Other operating systems have had the concept of DLLs for a long time—Sun has had its runtime shared libraries for some time, and OpenVMS has had its version as well. DLLs, or dynamic load libraries, are special libraries that can be shared and are provided when your program runs, rather then being bound in at link time. Since DLLs are built separately, they can be tested and updated more easily, making your applications more manageable. Java, being an interpreted language, does not have a concept of DLLs per se, but compiles down to class files, which are remarkably similar, and are loaded as required and can be shared.

The Java Programming Model

The Java programming model is different from the Windows programming model from the very start. First and foremost, Java is interpreted on the remote machine under which the application runs. As you have previously seen, Java also has a Just-In-Time compiler. Byte code is delivered to the target machine and then executed in some fashion. And, of course, Java applets are normally embedded into a web page and executed from there. Java also supports complete standalone applications, which can be every bit as robust and function as any other application. Figure 15.1 below shows how a Java applet or application is built and run.

The Event/Message Processing Model Java supports events and message processing in a fashion similar to everyday Windows-based

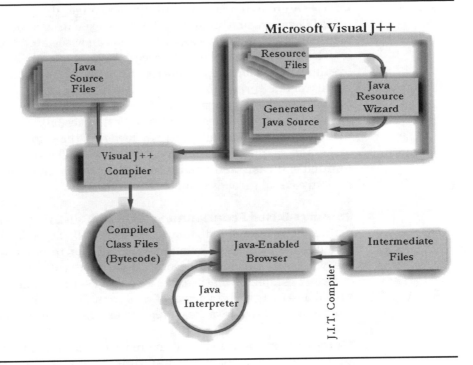

Figure 15.1   The Java Programming Model.

programming, right down to having a **static main** method where execution begins. Java also supports a rich set of events, such as **MOUSE_ENTER**, **MOUSE_EXIT**, **KEY_PRESS**, **KEY_RELEASE**, and many, many more, all via the **java.awt.Event** class. However, the Java model follows more closely the UNIX programming model in that most applications have a **main** that spawns one or more threads. Events and messages are encapsulated in the object concerned, with the threads of execution being the main application focus, rather then having a single message loop somewhere that processes messages and routes them to the correct window.

Threads and Multiprocessing Java was born to be multithreaded. We have just read about multiprocessing and how it differs from multithreading. To reiterate, multithreading is the process of having several sections of code executing at the same time, all within the same application. Threads themselves have been around for a long time, but Java is one of the first languages to have thread processing built right in. Synchronization is built into the language. By using the **synchronized** keyword, only one thread may be executing a method at a given moment. Each and every Java class has an associated **lock built** right in. These locks control thread access to objects and classes implicitly, freeing the developer from worries about synchronization and the possibility of one thread interfering with another. And support exists for synchronization right down to a block of code or a single statement! Java also has rich support for thread priorities, allowing the developer to manage threads intelligently by lowering the priority of background tasks and raising the priority of new tasks. Thread can also be **suspend**ed and **resume**d and can **wait** for, **notify**, and even go to **sleep**! And, of course, threads can be **destroy**ed.

Resource-Based Programming   Due to its distributed nature, Java is not normally considered resource-based at all. There is no concept of a resource file in normal Java development, nor resource DLLs. Rather, the windows, buttons and so on associated with a Java applet are described completely in the code. As we will see in the next few chapters, Visual J++ merges the concept of resources seamlessly into Java applets built by way of the Java Resource Wizard and Resource Templates.

Memory Management   Java memory management is simple and elegant. Rather than the **news** and **delete**s of C++, Java simply allows you to creates new storage as you need it. Gone is the destructor **delete** of C++—Java's Garbage Collection frees unused objects when there are no longer any references to them. As you have seen in Part I, Java has no pointers; rather, when you create an object you are actually creating a reference to it. You would need to do a corresponding **new** to actually create the object. Since there are no pointers to objects, there can be no dangling references to data, nor incorrect interpretations of pointers by casting. So we see that, again, Java makes our lives easier.

INTRODUCING THE VISUAL J++ WORKBENCH

The Visual J++ workbench will be a familiar site for those developers who have used Microsoft Visual C++, Microsoft FORTRAN, Microsoft Visual Test, and other Microsoft development tools. The workbench itself is quite full-featured, including an editor that is customizable and extensible with macros, configurable toolbars, dockable windows, and a host of other features. Figure 15.2 introduces the workbench and points out a few of its more important features.

Seasoned engineers and users of other Microsoft development products will be almost immediately comfortable with Visual J++ and may

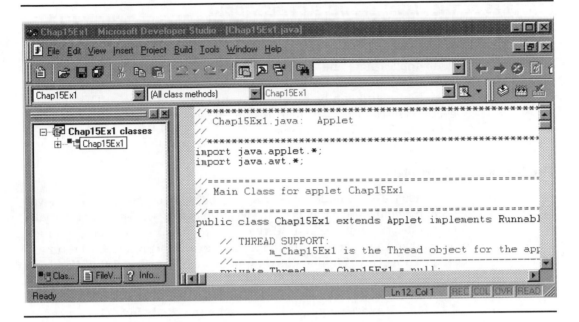

Figure 15.2   Visual J++ Developers Studio snapshot.

skip the next few sections or skim them for review. Others less familiar may wish to read these sections thoroughly to gain a better understanding of what a Visual J++ project is and how it is used to create a Java applet or application.

Projects are the central theme of many of the Visual line of products available from Microsoft. A project is a collection of files interrelated in some way and normally compiled to produce an end result, in our case the Java applet or application. In addition, a project contains a **make file** that describes how one file can be used to produce another. These are called dependency relations. Experienced engineers will be familiar with **make files**. A **make file** describes how a source file can be compiled or linked to produce an executable. In Visual J++ a **.Java** file would be compiled into its byte code equivalent—a **.class** file. Each and every application or applet you create will have an associated project file. Project files in Visual J++ have an **.mpd** or **.dsp** extension and make files have an **.mak** extension. Even though the **make file** is in fact just a text file and could be edited by hand, this is not recommended as it may render it unreadable.

FEATURES OF THE VISUAL J++ DEVELOPERS STUDIO

The Visual J++ Developers Studio contains new features as well as some tried and true. The tools allow you to develop, refine, debug, and enhance your applications and applets in a completely integrated fashion under Windows 95 or NT 4.0. Customizable tool bars make the environment easy to use and can be tailored to your own preferences. The following sections introduce these features and how each is used. First we introduce the Visual J++ Compiler.

The Visual J++ Compiler

The Visual J++ compiler (JVC.EXE) is the heart of the Visual J++ development environment. It is that special piece of software that actually translates or compiles your **.Java** files into their associated class files, which can then can be run under any Java interpreter. At the time of this writing the compiler was compliant with ***Version 1.0 of the Java Language specification***. Support for additional features may have been added after release. Check the online help supplied with Visual J++ for the exact language feature set supported. Java classes can be compiled one of two ways: either by compiling only a single source module or by building the entire project. The exact mechanics of building a project will be described in a later chapter.

The Visual J++ Debugger

Every good development environment, whether an integrated one or not, requires a debugger. A few select souls may be able to produce flawless, bug-free code from the beginning, but the rest of us will need a debugger from time to time. The Visual J++ Development Environment contains a full-featured debugger that allows the user to step through his or her code one line at a time, setting break points, stepping into methods, and examining variables (Figure 15.3). With the debugger you can manage multiple source code windows, debug multithreaded applications, and watch variables as they come and go out of scope. Add to that the ability to customize with your own preferences and you have the makings of an excellent tool.

The Visual J++ Graphics Editor

Java currently understands only Graphics Interchange Format (.GIF) or Joint Photographic Group format (.JPEG) files. The Visual J++ Development Environment provides a rich set of tools for creating, importing, and manipulating native .GIF and .JPEG format files. The

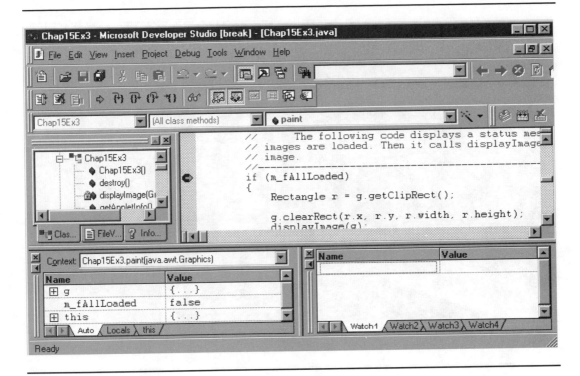

Figure 15.3   Visual J++ debugger snapshot.

graphics editor can convert .BMP files to .JPEG or .GIF format, customize colors and palettes, edit existing image files, or create new ones. In addition, the graphics editor is fully customizable, allowing you to set image properties and pane sizes, change the image magnification, and manipulate the pixel grid. Of course, you can also work with colors and select background and foreground colors for an image, as well make backgrounds transparent or opaque. These are but a few features of the graphics editor, which will be discussed in depth in Chapter 22. Figure 15.4 shows a snapshot of the Voyager 1 satellite and the various tools available for manipulating image files.

The Visual J++ Source Browser/Editor

In the past, an engineer needed to know what functions were contained in what source code modules and worry about where classes were defined and the like. If you worked on your own code, this was normally pretty easy. When another programmer was added, the task became more difficult. After all, people are unique and choose file and variable

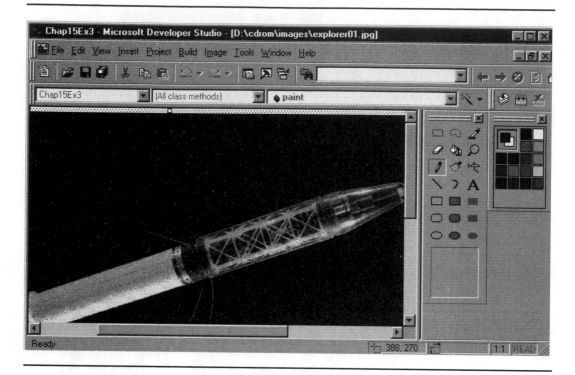

Figure 15.4   Visual J++ graphics editor snapshot.

names inconsistently. Add additional engineers and the task became quite daunting.

The Visual J++ Source Browser/Editor makes this difficult task more than a little bit easier. Since we are developing classes, we would much prefer a class view. Visual J++ shows hierarchically how your code lays out. The three main areas where Visual J++ improves over regular editors are **Base Class/Derived class display**, where you can easily tell which classes derive from which other classes; **Definitions and References**, where you can select any variable, class, or method and the browser can immediately take you to where it is defined or used; **Caller/Called Graphs**, where for any given method the browser can show you who calls it or, inversely, who it calls. And of course, if you know the name of the file where a method or class exists from the FileView you can easily open that file and editor as you have in the past.

Another exciting feature of the editor is emulations. If you are an Epsilon or Brief fan just change the editor emulation to use your editor of choice. Suddenly all the features you've grown to know and love are there for you.

The Visual J++ Resource Editor

The Visual J++ Development Environment, like it predecessor Visual C++, contains a full-featured resource editor (Figure 15.5). Actually there are several resource editors for manipulating various types of resources. Previously discussed was the graphics editor, which allows you to editor .JPEG and .GIF format files. But editors also exist for editing menus and dialogs and for creating resource templates. Each of these editors can be used to add new resources, manipulate existing resources, or copy/delete old unused resources. Anyone who has used Visual C++ has seen the dialog and menu editors before. The dialog editor can be used to add or arrange any sort of edit control, as well as set tab order, and is quite familiar. Likewise, the Menu Editor, which can be used to editor menu selection and assign accelerator keys, is also

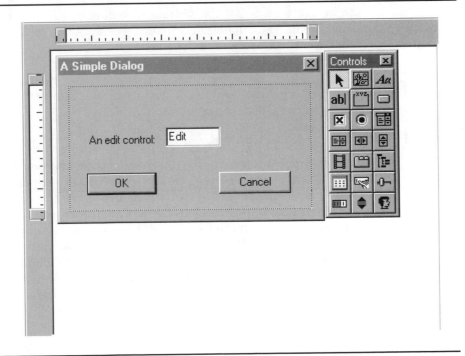

Figure 15.5   Visual J++ resource editor snapshot.

quite familiar. Property sheets are fully supported, so you can change the properties of an edit control as you wish.

One of the more basic yet useful features of Visual J++ is *Resource Templates*, which can be created and then reused to speed the creation of additional resources. These are especially helpful if every one of your dialogs needs to have a certain look and feel, such as containing the same company logo or icon. Just create a template for it, and then you know that all of your dialogs will look the same. The resource editors also share a common interface, making it easy to move from one resource editor to the next.

The Visual J++ and the Resource Wizard

At this point you know that you create and manipulate resources. But Java applets and applications don't use resources. Well, not directly. Enter the *Resource Wizard*. Normally, Java applications create their dialogs and menus on the fly using the Java Abstract Window Toolkit (AWT). What the resource wizard does for you is create Java code from an associated **.RES** (resource file) or **.RCT** (resource template). This is perhaps one of the most powerful features of Visual J++, allowing you to abstract away all the tedium of coding dialogs, menus, and such. Just create your dialog and Visual J++ does the rest, converting that dialog into its equivalent Java code.

However, there are problems: for example, not all Windows controls are supported. Chapter 18 describes in greater details the specifics of the resource editor and what limitations exist when creating Java code from its corresponding resource.

Visual J++ and Source Code Control

Every programmer at one time or another has had to work with a source code control system. Source code control systems are necessary, to allow for developers to manage source in such a way that revisions can be tracked, modules can be managed, so that multiple engineers are not working on the same module at that same time; and end builds can be managed. Visual J++ allows for integration of any source code control system that conforms to the Microsoft Common Source Code Control Interface. If you install a conforming product, such as Visual Source Safe, then you can directly access source code control functions from within Visual J++.

The Visual J++ Online Help

Visual C++ 4.0 introduced a new and exciting concept in online help— InfoView. InfoView integrates into the Visual J++ development environment all the currently available help. You can access help in many *different* ways. At the highest level of granularity is the book. When you choose **Contents** under the **Help** pulldown menu, the workbench changes to InfoView, or activates the InfoView tab, and presents you with a list of one or more books. You can then drill down into a book, looking chapter by chapter.

One of the more useful features of help is the **F1 Help** key. By just placing the cursor on any item and hitting the **F1** key, the user is presented with help for that item. You can select functions, classes, variables, macros, or other programming elements and get help on them. If several matches are found, the user is presented with a list box showing the various topics where the item was found, allowing you to choose the most appropriate one. This is arguably the most useful feature of the Visual J++ help subsystem.

Also supported is **Search** help, which allows you to enter a keyword or topic and get help on it. Everything under **Search** is listed alphabetically, so that it is easy to find a topic, even if you don't know the exact spelling.

A new feature of Help for Visual J++ is **Keyboard** help. By selecting **Keyboard** under the **Help** pulldown menu, you can see an entire list of the keyboard to function bindings supported by Visual J++.

EXERCISES

15-1   Using the help system, search for the keyword "public". Was it found? If so, how many times?

15-2   Open the resource editor and create an empty dialog. Add a few controls to it of any sort then quit the editor.

15-3   Open a .JPEG or .GIF file with the image editor. Make some noticeable change and save the image under a new name. Open the newly created image and verify your change.

Introducing The Visual J++ Developers Studio

In this chapter we cover the following topics:

- **Creating a Project with Java AppWizard**

CREATING A PROJECT WITH APPWIZARD

AppWizard (and wizards in general) is a special purpose tool that simplifies the process of building an application or applet. In Visual J++ AppWizard, you can build a skeleton applet and, optionally, an html page that is a starting point for further development. Let's jump right in and build our first application using JavaAppWizard and examine the result. It is strongly suggested that the reader work along with the example in this chapter, enter the text as shown, then build and finally run the result.

From the **File menu** choose New. The **New** property sheet will appear. Select **Project** tab and then **Java Applet Wizard**. The new **Project** tab is shown as Figure 16.1.

The New Project tab is used to create a new project workspace and the associated project files for that workspace. Initially, a project consists of a few project files, described a little later in detail, an .Html file, and the associated .java applet source file. Normally, these files are constructed in a subdirectory derived from the project name. However, you may specify whatever directory you wish with the **Location** box.

TIP

Visual J++ and other Developers Studio Products

If you have installed other packages that work in conjunction with Microsoft Developer Studio, such as Microsoft Visual C++ or Visual Test, click the **See Also** button (if it is active) to find related topics.

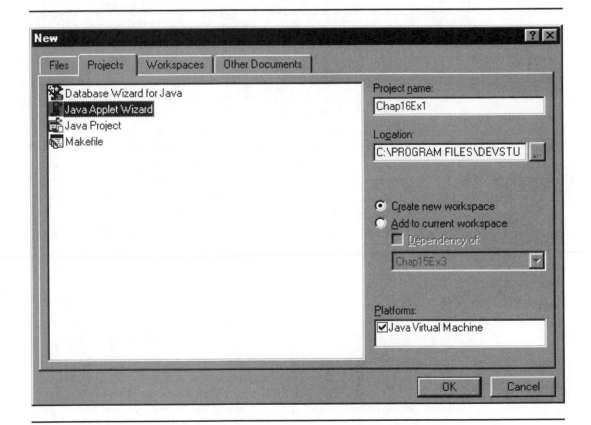

Figure 16.1   The New Project Tab.

Each of the fields in this dialog is described below. Simply select Java Applet Wizard and enter the name for the new project. In addition, select the location for this new project and hit the **Enter** Button.

Name

Enter the name of the project. Microsoft Developers Studio will automatically create the subdirectory and append the name to the path given in the **Location** box.

Type List

This specifies the type of the project you wish to create. Make sure you select Java Applet Wizard. Later on you may wish to build existing Java applets or applications using Visual J++. AppWizard can then be used to create an empty workspace under which an existing application can be build. If you have installed other Microsoft products, the **See Also** button will be added to this dialog. Selecting the **See Also** button will display other projects you can create (such as a Visual C++ project). "Using AppWizard for existing projects".

Platform

Select the platform. Currently only **Java Virtual Machine** is supported.

Location

A default project location will be provided for you, with the project name appended as a the files subdirectory. The default directory for project is the one under which Developers Studio was installed. If you enter a new directory, then this directory will become the default for future projects.

Browse Button

The browse button causes the **Choose Directory** common dialog to be displayed, from which you may browse for directories.

TIP

Java AppWizard and Subdirectories

Java AppWizard will happily create whatever directory hierarchy you enter into the directory box. This is fine if you wish to create the directory structure, but a minor annoyance if you make a typo. So make sure when entering a new or complex path that you type it correctly.

You are next presented with the Java Applet Wizard Step 1 of 5 dialog. This dialog tells the wizard how your programs will be run—as an embedded applet, an application, or both. In addition, you may specify that Developers Studio include comments in its generated code. You needn't make any changes to this dialog. Simply select the **Enter** button.

Step 1

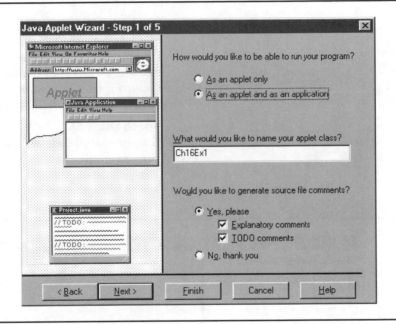

Figure 16.2   Java Applet Wizard step 1 of 5.

How would you like to be able to run your program?	**As an applet only** You are developing an applet that may only be embedded within a web page. **As an applet and as an application** The new application can either be embedded within a web page or run as a standalone.
What would you like to name your applet class?	The default name will be the same as your project name, without spaces. Change the class name to whatever you would like if you prefer something different from your project name.

Would you like to generate source file comments?

Yes, please
Java Applet Wizard will produce comments that are inserted into the applet source code.

Explanatory comments
The generated source code files will contain embedded comments that describe the use of the methods and variables generated by the wizard.

TODO comments
The generated source code files will contain TODO comments that make it easier for the developer to determine where to augment the generated code.

No, thank you
The generated code will not contain source comments.

Step 2

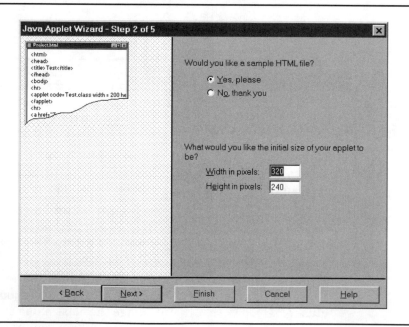

Figure 16.3   Java Applet Wizard step 2 of 5.

The next dialog presented describes how to build the .html file associated with the application. As with the first dialog, you needn't make any changes to the dialog—simply select the **Enter** button.

Would you like a sample HTML file?

Yes, please
This choice tells AppWizard to build an .html file for use with this applet.

No, thank you
AppWizard does not create an .html file. You must supply one yourself.

What would you like the initial size of your applet to be?

Width in pixels
If an .html file is generated, the width attribute is set from this field. The default for this option is 320 pixels.

Height in pixels
If an .html file is generated, the height attribute is set from this field. The default for this option is 240 pixels.

Step 3

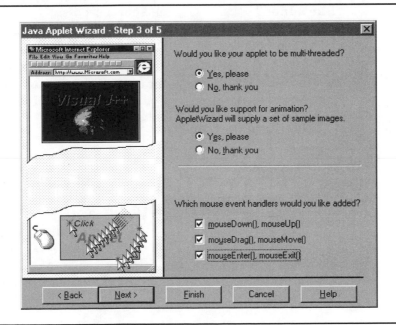

Figure 16.4   Java Applet Wizard step 3 of 5.

The next dialog presented describes how to build the .java class file which represents your application. As with the first dialog, you needn't make any changes to dialog simply select the **Enter** button.

Would you like your applet to be multi-threaded?	**Yes, please** Entry points will be added to the generated source file(s) to support multi-threading.
	No, thank you Multi-threading will not be supported in this applet.
Would you like support for animation? AppletWizard will supply a set of sample images.	**Yes, please** A set of images and code to support their display will be added to the application.
	No, thank you No entry points or default images will be displayed.
Which mouse event handlers would you like added?	**mouseDown(), mouseUp()** Code will be added to detect mouse up and down events.
	mouseDrag(), mouseMove() Code will be added to detect mouse add and mouse move events.
	mouseEnter(), mouseExit() Code will be added to detect mouse enter and exit calls.

TIP

Single-Threaded Applications

Single-threaded applications, while useful, will not be covered in this text. If the user selects *No, thank you* when setting the applications default parameter, the animation support is disabled, making for a much less interesting applet. All examples in this and subsequent chapters will have some animation associated with them.

Step 4

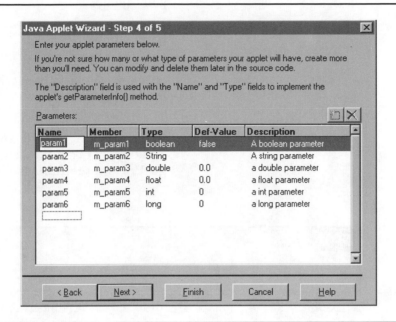

Figure 16.5   Java Applet Wizard step 4 of 5.

The step 4 of 5 dialog tells JavaAPP Wizard which parameters your applet will use. The **getParameter()** method will then be employed in the applet's initialization code to get and store parameter information. Add as many variables to your applet as you believe you may need later. The sample adds one of every available type.

Name	The external name of the parameter that will be passed via the Java **param name=** mechanism.
Member	The internal variable defined in your applet that will contain the value passed in via the external name.
Type	Select one of the five applicable Java parameter types: **String**—A string variable. **Boolean**—A true-false value.

Double—A double precision floating point number.

Float—A single precision floating point number.

Long—A 32-bit integer.

Integer—A platform-specific sized integer (normally a short).

Def-Value The default value for this variable.

Description Comments that describe this variable and that will be returned by the **getParameterInfo()** method.

NOTE

HTML and Parameter Passing

HTML only supports one parameter type as input to an applet—strings. What Java AppWizard does for you is marshal your parameters and convert them to their underlying native types using the numeric wrapper methods. If you specified a parameter of type **double**, then Java AppWizard would create for you a private variable in your applet of type **double** and then generate code to convert the **string** version to the **double** version.

This dialog supplies to AppWizard general information that will be returned by calls to **getAppletInfo()**. You may enter any text here you wish.

This is the final dialog displayed before your application is created. It shows all the selections you have previously made. Examine the result closely and make sure that it matches what you wished to do. If so, simply choose **OK** and the application will be created as defined. Otherwise, choose **Cancel** and then use the **Back** button to return to the dialog where you made an error.

Congratulations! You have successfully run the Java AppWizard to create your first application! In Chapter 17 we examine each of the files created by the Java AppWizard and then extend our basic applet to support simple mouse events.

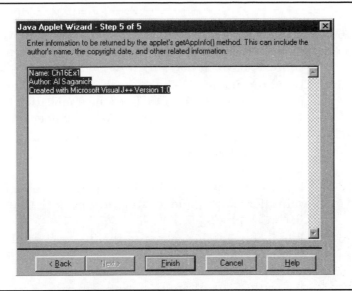

Figure 16.6 Java Applet Wizard step 5 of 5.

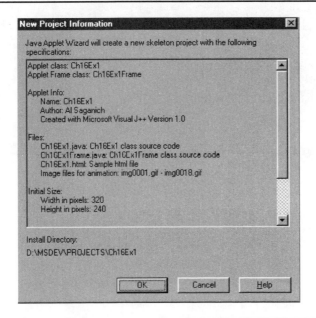

Figure 16.7 Java Applet Wizard finished.

EXERCISES

16-1   If you haven't already followed the steps above, create your first sample application. Did the files you got match the ones defined above? If not, why; what, if anything, was different?

16-2   Build the application by using the Build command in the Build menu item (or Shift + F7). Does the application build correctly? Artificially introduce an error. What happens now?

16-3   Run the application, using Execute in the Build menu (or Ctrl + F5). What happens when you run the application (pretty exciting, isn't it)?

16-4   Update the application to use a percentage instead of a fixed value for height and width. How does the new result look? Better? Worse?

16-5   What happens if you resize the browser window? Anything? Describe the result.

CHAPTER 17

The Java AppWizard Explained

In this chapter we cover the following topics:

- **What Java AppWizard Does for You**
- **Ch17Ex1.html**
- **Ch17Ex1.java**
- **Mouse Event Support**
- **A Few Final Notes**
- **Standalone Application Support**

In Chapter 16 we ran the Java AppWizard for the first time, creating a simple applet that supported animation. In this chapter we will examine in depth each of the files created by the wizard and extend the examples to add mouse support to manipulate the spinning globe causing it to stop turning for a moment.

WHAT APPWIZARD DOES FOR YOU

You have now successfully run the Java AppWizard, but what has the Java wizard actually done for you? This section details the files created by the Java AppWizard, what each is for and what the next steps are in building your own applet.

The following files are created by the Java AppWizard when steps in Chapter 16 are followed:

Ch17Ex1.html   A basic html file that contains sample code for embedding your java applet.

Ch17Ex1.java	The implementation of the java class Ch17Ex1.
Ch17Ex1.dsw	The Microsoft Developers Studio Project file.
Ch17Ex1.dsp	The make file used by **Ch17Ex1.dsp** to define the build process.
Ch17Ex1.ncb	Microsoft Developers Studio Program Database file.
Ch17Ex1Frame.java image directory and a set of image files	If you selected to run your application as a standalone, this file is also created.
	If you created an application that was multithreaded and contained animation, an images subdirectory was created for you containing a set of .GIF files.

CH17 EX1.HTML

How does the applet actually get started? Well, by now you should be quite familiar with basic HTML, or at least have seen a little HTML, perhaps enough to start your applet running. Let's look a the HTML file produced by the Java AppWizard and see how it starts the applet (Figure 17.1).

The HTML above creates a basic page. The page contains a header with a title as well as a body with a hotlink to the source code. In addition, it contains the one tag that we are really interested in—the **<applet>** tag. The first class we wish to actually instantiate is noted with the **code** attribute. The class denoted by the keyword is the name of the class that extends the default applet class; this should be loaded. The **width** attribute acts in a fashion similar to the width in the **<img>** tag. This attribute specifies how wide, in pixels, the window will be.

```
<html>
<head>
<title>Ch17Ex1</title>
</head>
<body>
<hr>
<applet
        =Ch17Ex1.class
    id=Ch17Ex1
    width=320
    height=240 >
    <param name=Param1 value="">
    <param name=Param2 value=false>
    <param name=Param3 value=0.0>
    <param name=Param4 value=0.0f >
    <param name=Param5 value=0>
    <param name=Param6 value=0>
</applet>
<hr>
<a href="Ch17Ex1.java">The source.</a>
</body>
</html>
```

Figure 17.1   The **.html** file.

Likewise, the **height** attribute specifies the window's height. Finally, we come to the parameter tag. The **param** tag is what makes it possible for your web page to pass parameters to the underlying applet. The param tag is actually three parts: the **param** keyword, **name = some name** and **value = somevalue. somename** may be filled in with any valid parameter name. Value must then be filled in with a value appropriate for the parameter. For example, true or false for a boolean, 3.14 for a float, and so on.

> **TIP**
>
> **Height and Width Can Also Be Defined as a Percentage**
>
> The height and width of window can also be defined as a percentage by following the number specified with a % sign.

CH17EX1.JAVA

The **.java** file is the starting point of our journey into actually developing interesting and exciting Java applications. In this section we will dig into our first applet, seeing what Java AppWizard has done for us and determining where to go from there to extend our applet.

The Class Generated By Java AppWizard

As we have seen in previous chapters, we must define our own class, which is runnable and derived from the class **Applet** in the **java.applet** package, in order to implement an applet of our own. The Java AppWizard does much of the grunt work for us by creating a skeleton subclass of the superclass **Applet**. Every subclass of **Applet** must contain at least two methods: the **init()** method and the **paint()** method. Of course, you are really overriding these two methods as **Applet** has itself has an **init()** and **paint()** methods. In addition, our applet was specified as **implements Runnable**, making a **start()** and a **stop()** method as well as a **run()** method necessary.

> **NOTE**
>
> #### Multithreading Example
>
> Had we not selected multithreaded when we were developing our sample, the **implements Runnable** keyword and, consequently the supporting methods,would have been missing our class. **implements Runnable** dictates that we must support those methods required by the **Runnable** interface. All that is absolutely required is the run method. In addition, without multithreading, our applet would contain little more then **start**, **stop**, and **init** methods. The **run** method would have been missing, and the only appropriate place for additional code would have been in the **init** and **paint** methods.

The **start** and **stop** methods are called when the applet appears and disappears, and in turn starts and stops the underlying animation thread. Once the thread is running, it executes the **run** method, which handles our animation. Let's look at each of these methods to better understand them.

> **NOTE**
>
> #### Animation Support
>
> The Java AppWizard has gone quite a bit beyond a simple applet in our first example. Our example is not only fully functional, but contains threads and support for display of a series of .GIF files that make for a nice animation.

Threads within the Skeleton Applet

As was previously mentioned, the class we are examining is implemented as threaded. In order to completely understand what's going on, we must have a better understanding of how multithreading is put to use. To that end, let's take an overview of our applet.

When the class is created, a main thread is started whose normal purpose is to handle events, or at a minimum do some other work. Since we would like to do some animation, it is advantageous to have another thread that will not get in the way of normal message processing. So our applet has a variable of type **Thread**, which is created when the **start** method is called. If this is not all clear, don't worry. Each of these methods will be discussed in more detail as the chapter progresses. The start method creates our underlying thread. If you look at the code, you will notice that the thread we create is just a standard thread object. It is not an object that is derived from the thread class and overrides thread class methods, but rather just an instance of a vanilla thread. What this means is that this thread will use the run method of the class it is created in (as a result of **implements Runnable**). This happens because we pass the constructor of the thread of the **this** object.

So what does this all mean? Well, when all is said and done, we will have two instances of our applet running: one doing the animation—the thread created by the start method—and one doing normal message processing—the thread created by the browser or frame when the applet is created.

As we look further into out sample, we will see how this all comes together to correctly load the images and do our simple animation.

With all of this now clear, let's continue.

The init **and** paint **Methods**

It was required that the **init** method be overridden when we implemented our applet. To do this, Java AppWizard implements this method and calls the **resize** method to resize the window (Figure 17.2).

The other required method is the **paint** method. The default Java AppWizard **paint** method simply waits until the thread has loaded all the animation images, displaying some simple text stating that the images are loading, and then displaying the given image. The entire method is shown in Figure 17.3. Once the applet is actually running, the **paint** method is called periodically to repaint the screen.

```
public void init()
{

    resize(320, 240);
    // TODO: Place additional initialization code here
}
```

Figure 17.2   The **init()** method.

> **NOTE**
>
> ### Your Mileage May Vary
>
> Several of the methods described here may differ from those you find, depending on the options you select when you create your skeleton Java applet. The **init** method is notorious for this with respect to the number of parameters actually passed to your applet. If you have several parameters, you may find a fair amount of additional code that manages those parameters.

```
1    public void paint(Graphics g)
2        {
3        if (m_fAllLoaded)
4            {
5            Rectangle r = g.getClipRect();
6            g.clearRect(r.x, r.y, r.width, r.height);
7            displayImage(g);
8        }
9        else
10            g.drawString("Loading images...", 10, 20);
11            // TODO: Place additional applet Paint code here
12        }
```

Figure 17.3   The **paint()** method.

Specifically, the method works as follows: line 9 checks to see if we have loaded all the images. If all the images are not loaded, then we just display a simple message (line 10). Otherwise, we determine the clipping region of the graphics context passed in via the call. We then clear the region (line 6) and finally display the image input (line 7). **displayImage** is actually a private method of our class that simply takes the current image and, using the input graphics context, draws it. It is left to the reader to examine the **displayImage** method.

> **NOTE**
>
> ### Place Your Simple Applet Code Here
>
> For applets that do not not support threads on animation, the most likely place to insert your code is into the **init** and **paint** methods. The **init** method will be called once at startup, and the paint method will be called once to paint the screen. Any additional code is up to the developer.

The start, stop, and run Methods

Next come the **start** and **stop** methods. The **start** method, shown in Figure 17.4, quite simply starts the thread that handles the display of the animation images. The **stop** method, shown in Figure 17.5, deletes the animation thread. The more interesting method is the **run** method, which implements the infinite while loop that displays the images making up the animation.

```
public void start()
{
    if (m_Ch20Ex1 == null)
    {
        m_Ch20Ex1 = new Thread(this);
        m_Ch20Ex1.start();
    }
    // TODO: Place additional applet start code here
}
```

Figure 17.4   The **start** method.

```
public void stop()
{
    if (m_Ch20Ex1 != null)
    {
        m_Ch20Ex1.stop();
        m_Ch20Ex1 = null;
    }
    // TODO: Place additional applet stop code here
}
```

Figure 17.5   The **stop** method.

> **NOTE**
>
> #### start, stop **and** init **Processing**
>
> It bears noting that the **start** and **stop** methods can be executed more than once for a given applet. Each time the applet's frame window is displayed, the **start** method is called. Each time the frame window is hidden or minimized, the **stop** method is called. This in contrast to the **init** method, which is called once when the applet is first initialized and before the first **start** call.

To support our animation, Java AppWizard created a class that contained a private variable of type **Thread**. This variable, **m_Ch17Ex1**, is the animation thread for our applet. Our applets **start** method will create this thread and start the animation for us. The **stop** method will stop the thread when our applet exits. Each of these methods is shown below.

Note that the thread object constructor takes as a parameter the **this** object. As a result the thread created runs another instance of the applet. Calling the **start** method ultimately causes the **run** method to be called to start our animation.

The run **Method**   The **run** method is the most interesting part of the applet we have created. It starts as a result of our applet's **start** method being called. It loads all the images and then loops forever displaying the images being animated. As previously stated, the **run** method is called when the applet's thread is started. Any ongoing processing is normally placed in this method. That is, processing that continues or does not require user input.

Let's look at the section that loads the images first. Then we will look at the code that follows that displays our images.

```
1    for (int i = 1; i <= NUM_IMAGES; i++)
2    {
3        // Build path to next image
4        strImage = "images/img00" + ((i < 10) ? "0" : "") + i + ".gif";
5        if (m_fStandAlone)
6        m_Images[i-1] = Toolkit.getDefaultToolkit().getImage(strImage);
7        else
8            m_Images[i-1] = getImage(getDocumentBase(), strImage);
9            // Get width and height of one image.
10           // Assuming all images are same width and height
11           //—————————————————————-
12           if (m_nImgWidth == 0)
13           {
14               try
15               {
16               // The getWidth() and getHeight() methods of the Image class
17               // return -1 if the dimensions are not yet known. The
18               // following code keeps calling getWidth() and getHeight()
19               // until they return actual values.
20               // NOTE: This is only executed once in this loop, since we
21               // are assuming all images are the same width and
22               // height. However, since we do not want to duplicate
23               // the above image load code, the code resides in the
24               // loop.
25               //—————————————————————
26               while ((m_nImgWidth = m_Images[i-1].getWidth(null)) < 0)
27               Thread.sleep(1);
28               while ((m_nImgHeight = m_Images[i-1].getHeight(null)) <0)
29               Thread.sleep(1);
30               }
31           catch (InterruptedException e)
32               {
33               // TODO: Place exception-handling code here in case an
34               // InterruptedException is thrown by Thread.sleep(),
35               // meaning that another thread has interrupted this one
36               }
37           }
38       // Force image to fully load
39       //—————————————————————
40       m_Graphics.drawImage(m_Images[i-1], -1000, -1000, this);
41   }
```

The code above loops for each image we expect to store. The basics of the code are simple: determine which image, load it into the appropriate array entry, and then go to the code that performs the animation.

> **NOTE**
>
> ### getImage **Works Asynchronously**
>
> It should be noted that **getImage** returns immediately after being called without waiting for the actual image load to complete. So how do we know when an image has actually loaded completely? The **imageUpdate** method will be called periodically as the image is loading, giving the developer a hook into the load process, and allowing processing to be done while the image is actually loading. An image might be displayed partially loaded. Or, as in our case, we can check if the image is completely loaded and then set, the **m_fAllLoaded** flag to true on the last image load.

Images are stored in a variable of type **Image**. Note that the first thing the run method does is create the storage for these images in the variable **m_Images**.

Lines 1 and 41 are simply the beginning and ending of the loop. Line 4 determines which image to load next. If this is not a standalone application, then simply call **getImage** to load the next image, specifying the directory and file name. Otherwise, the default toolkit is used to load the next image. Lines 12 through 37 simply get the height and width of an image and do appropriate error trapping along the way. Last, the previously loaded image is drawn.

> **NOTE**
>
> ### **Error Trapping is Important**
>
> A well-behaved application will not only do what is supposed to do when everything goes well, but also when things go astray. It is the developer's responsibility to make sure this happens by making good use of **try/catch** blocks. The best written code in the world is of no use if its fails even occasionally for no reason.

Lines 44 through 53 simply wait for image loading to complete. As previously mentioned, image loading is asynchronous and is signaled as complete through the **imageUpdate** method.

```
42      // Wait until all images are fully loaded
43      //————————————————————————————————
44      while (!m_fAllLoaded)
45      {
```

```
46        try
47        {
48        Thread.sleep(10);
49        }
50        catch (InterruptedException e)
51        {
52        }
53    }
54    repaint();
55
56    while (true)
57    {
58        try
59        {
60            // Draw next image in animation
61            // --------------------------------------------
62            displayImage(m_Graphics);
63            m_nCurrImage++;
64            if (m_nCurrImage == NUM_IMAGES)
65                m_nCurrImage = 0;
66            Thread.sleep(50);
67        }
68        catch (InterruptedException e)
69        {
70            stop();
71        }
72    }
```

The remaining lines handle the actually display of the animation images, and draw the current image, increment the image counter (line 63), check to see if we have run off the end and resetting back to the first image if we have, and sleep for a moment before displaying the next image.

NOTE

Threads and the Thread.sleep **Call**

All threads should be well behaved and our animation thread is no different. The purpose of the sleep call in a thread is twofold. First, we want our thread to consume only those resources it needs. Without the sleep call, the thread would spin wildly, consuming much more CPU time then it needs. The other reason is that without the wait, the animation would occur much too fast, causing the globe to spin much too quickly.

Mouse Event Support

When we created our first application, we specified that we wanted mouse support. Let's look at what we got as a result of that.

Five additional methods were defined as a result of selecting mouse support. They are:

```
public boolean mouseDown(Event evt, int x, int y)
public boolean mouseUp(Event evt, int x, int y)
public boolean mouseEnter(Event evt, int x, int y)
public boolean mouseExit(Event evt, int x, int y)
public boolean mouseDrag(Event evt, int x, int y)
```

These methods are called when the appropriate event occurs. In a nutshell, our application is derived from **Applet**, which is derived from **Panel**, which is derived from **Container**, which is derived from **Component**, which defines the five methods described above. Our defining these methods simply overrides them and causes control to be passed to our functions rather than the default functions.

Let's perform an exercise. Let's create an application that implements **mouseEnter** and **mouseExit** and supports threads and animation, then examine how we can update this application to cause the spinning globe to stop spinning when an mouse enter event occurs and start spinning again when a mouse exit occurs.

Create the application using Java AppWizard. On the examples CD, under Ch17Ex1, you will find the fully modified source code for this application. Use the **File/New** menu option and select **Project Workspace**. Choose **Java Applet Wizard** and name the application Ch17Ex1. From **Step 1 of 5** choose *applet and application*. Choose the defaults from **Step 2 of 5**. From **Step 3 of 5** choose **mouseEnter()** and **mouseExit()**. Choose next from **Step 4 of 5**, since we require no parameters for this application. In **Step 5 of 5** enter whatever text you would like and then choose **Finish**.

Now, taking the application you have just created, make the following changes:

Step 1	Add a variable as shown below, just below then **m_fAllLoaded** variable. **Private boolean m_fMouseInFrame = false;**
Step 2	In the run method find the section that actually manages the painting of images.

Replace statement **m_nCurrimage++;**
with

If (m_fMouseInFrame == false)

m_nCurrimage++

Step 3

Find the **mouseEnter** method and
add the following line before the
return:

m_fMouseInFrame = true;

Step 4

Find the **mouseExit** method and add
the following line before the return:

m_fMouseInFrame = true;

Now using the **Build/Build** menu entry, compile and run the
example. When the mouse pointer moves over the animation frame, the
frame should stop. When it moves off the frame, animation should continue. Congratulations! You have created your first application that
responds to Java events.

A FEW FINAL NOTES

Our applet class also contained a blank class constructor and destructor. From Part I, or from your familiarity with Java or C++, you can see
that every class is required to have a constructor and destructor. Our
classes are no different. The constructor can be used to do special setup
and the destructor to do special cleanup. You might create a network
connection in the constructor and delete it in the destructor, or something similar. In our simple example, we needed no special startup or
cleanup code, so these methods are empty.

STANDALONE APPLICATION SUPPORT

When we created our first test application, we selected "As an applet
and as an application". This resulted in an addition class being created,
as well as an additional member in the **Ch17Ex1** class. The additional
member is the **void main(String args[])** member, discussed in detail
below. In addition, a new class was created, **Ch17Ex1Frame**, which
simply extends the Java AWT class **Frame** and provides a container
for the applet.

> **NOTE**
>
> ### The Java AWT Frame Class
>
> The Java Frame class provides a top level window with a title and a border. It can also have a menu bar. The AWT sends all messages and events that happen within its boundaries to this frame. AWT Frame class

The main **Method**

The **main** method is only used when the application is run as a standalone. It is the starting point for the interpreter and creates a frame and then adds our applet to it. The **main** method is ignored when the applet is started from an HTML statement. An in-depth examination of the frame class is left as an exercise to the reader. The exact code for the **main** method is shown below, with a quick explanation following.

```
1 public static void main(String args[])
2 {
3      // Create Toplevel Window to contain applet Ch17Ex1
4      // --------------------------------------------------------
5      Ch17Ex1Frame frame = new Ch17Ex1Frame("Ch17Ex1");

6      // Must show Frame before we size it so insets() will return valid values
7      frame.show();
8      frame.hide();
9      frame.resize(frame.insets().left + frame.insets().right + 320,
10                   frame.insets().top + frame.insets().bottom + 240);
11     // The following code starts the applet running within the frame window.
12     // It also calls GetParameters() to retrieve parameter values from the
13     // command line, and sets m_fStandAlone to true to prevent init() from
14     // trying to get them from the HTML page.
15     //——————————————————————————————
16     Ch17Ex1 applet_Ch17Ex1 = new Ch17Ex1();

17     frame.add("Center", applet_Ch17Ex1);
18     applet_Ch17Ex1.m_fStandAlone = true;
17     applet_Ch17Ex1.init();
20     applet_Ch17Ex1.start();
21     frame.show();
22 }
```

Figure 17.6   The **main** method.

What does this method really do? Line 1 simply defines the method as **main**. As you have probably read from previous chapters, all stand-alone applications must have a **main**. Line 5 creates an instance of our frame, which was derived from the Java AWT **Frame** class. Examination of this class is left as an exercise for the reader. Lines 9 through 10 simply resize the frame to be 320 by 240, as specified when we created the application. Line 16 creates our actual applet line, and 17 uses the add method to add our applet, and into the frame. The applet is then initialized and started normally. Finally, the frame's show method is called to cause the applet code to be actually displayed in the frame.

EXERCISES

17-1   Experiment with Java AppWizard. What methods are missing if you do not specify that your application supports threads?

17-2   Examine the code created by Java AppWizard when an application is created as both "Applet and application". What exactly was done in the frame class that was created? What methods were overridden and why?

17-3   Play with AppWizard, creating applets with one, two, and more parameters. How does the **init** code change? What exactly resulted when you added parameters?

17-3   Update the modified Ch17Ex1 example (remember we modified it to stop spinning when the mouse entered the frame and start again when the mouse exited?) to change the direction of rotation of the globe when the mouse is clicked in the frame. Alternately, you could have the globe change direction when the mouse is held down in the frame. But beware, you now need to think about what to do when the mouse is moved out of the frame while held!

17-4   Create an application styled after the applet in exercise 17-3, but instead of using mouse events, use keypress events to change the direction when the user presses a key. Ignore all keys except for **f,F** for forward and **b,B** for backward. What method did you need to override? Where was it originally defined? (Hint: Look at the derivation of the class **applet**.)

17-5   Examine the **imageUpdate** call in the sample applet. When does it get used? What does it actually perform? Why would one wish to implement an applet's animation processing this way?

CHAPTER 18

Introducing the Visual J++ Resource Editors

In this chapter we cover the following topics:

- **The Resource Editors**
- **The Graphics Editor**
- **The Dialog Editor**
- **The Menu Editor**
- **String Tables**
- **Resource Property Sheets**
- **Resource Templates**
- **Creating Resources**

If the underlying code in an application is its heart, then resources are its soul. Resources, most simply put, are the dialogs, menus, and windows the user sees when he or she runs your applet. As we shall see, Visual J++ provides a rich sets of tools for manipulating resources in a wysiwyg format. An experienced developer, one who's familiar with dialogs and menus and such, might skip over this chapter and go straight to the next few chapters and the nitty gritty of editing resources.

THE RESOURCE EDITORS

The Visual J++ resource editors are powerful tools that allow you to define the dialogs, windows, and images associated with your application. In the most general sense, resources are used to interact with the user. They can be dialog boxes, windows of some sort, menus, or strings. Visual J++ provides four basic types of resources and associated editors.

- Image files (**.GIF** and **.JPEG** and the like)
- Dialog boxes
- Menus
- Resource templates

Resource templates are a new feature added to Microsoft Developers Studio with the release of Visual J++. Resource templates allow you to set up resources that can then be used as starting points for other new dialogs.

With the various editors, you can create new resources, edit existing ones, delete and manipulate the properties of a resource. The editors all share a consistent interface. While they are not quite the same, once you know one, the others will be familiar to you.

THE GRAPHICS EDITOR

Anyone who has done any web page development or Internet browsing has encountered **.JPEGs** and **.GIFs**, whether you have known it or not. As most of you know, **.JPEGs** and **.GIFs** are file formats for storing and displaying graphical images. Visual J++ provides a graphics editor for creating, manipulating, and otherwise viewing these types of resources. Figure 18.1 shows the graphics editor.

The graphics editor is a full-featured editor that anyone can easily use. The graphics toolbar contains all tools you can use for editing your image files. Let's concentrate on the graphics toolbar and each of its components first.

The graphics editor:

- Can edit and or create graphics resources.
- Can customize colors.
- Can convert between graphics formats.
- Has customizable toolbars.
- Has customizable workspace.

A graphics file, such as a **.JPEG** or **.GIF** file, can be opened in one of several ways. The most common is to choose **file/open** from the Visual J++ menu. From the **Open** common dialog, select a file to view by setting the file type to **Image Files** using the **Files of Type** drop-

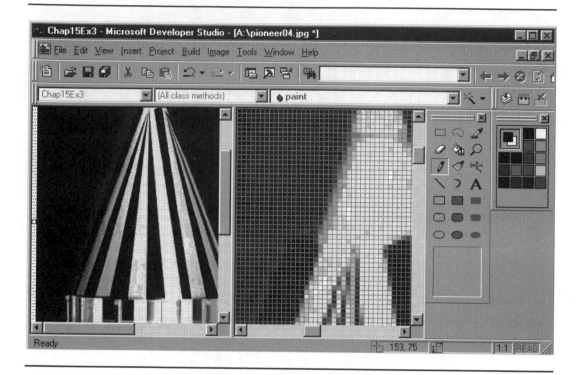

Figure 18.1 One of the Pioneer satellites.

down menu as shown in Figure 18.2, and then selecting a directory that contains a **.BMP**, **.JPEG**, or **.GIF** file. Remember that the CD contains image files in the *CDDRIVE:\VisualJ++\projects\images* directory. You can also select one of the previously created samples.

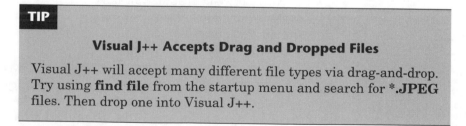

TIP

Visual J++ Accepts Drag and Dropped Files

Visual J++ will accept many different file types via drag-and-drop. Try using **find file** from the startup menu and search for *.**JPEG** files. Then drop one into Visual J++.

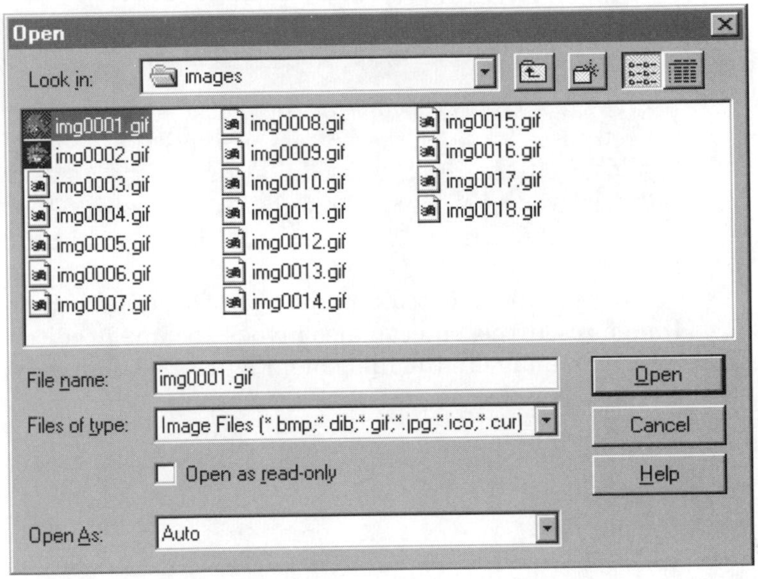

Figure 18.2   The Open dialog.

Once you have a set of image files showing, or have typed the path directly to one, double click it or choose it and click **Open**.

TIP

Sometimes Microsoft Developers Studio Is Too Smart

Sometimes Microsoft Developers Studio is too smart for its own good. For example, it will always try to open a file with a specific editor. If, for some reason, the editor associated with a file is not the one you would like to use (for example, you want to view a **.JPEG** file as a binary file), you can change the editor from auto to one of the other selections by simply using the **Open As** list box from the common file **Open** dialog. You will see a variety of file types including **Binary**. Simply choose the type you wish, and you are on your way.

For your efforts you are presented with the a screen similar to the one shown in Figure 18.1.

If you have created a project previously and that project contains Image resources, you can also invoke the image editor by double clicking on an image in the file pane. Figure 18.3 shows the file pane and a simple example.

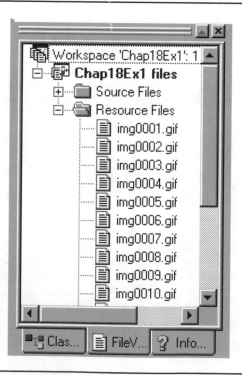

Figure 18.3   The file pane and its images.

Once you have loaded an image, editing is easy by using one of the many tools. The entire toolbar is shown in Figure 18.4.

You can add new detail, with the tools in the toolbar such as cut and paste, change colors and shades of gray, and so on. Chapter 19 covers the editor's features in detail.

TIP

Hiding a Toolbar

To hide or show the graphics toolbar, right click over the toolbar area on the right side of the screen. Check or uncheck the graphics setting to hide the graphics toolbar. If you inadvertently remove all the toolbar entries and cause the toolbar to completely disappear, simply right click on any toolbar above the image to display the toolbar popup again.

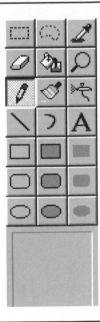

Figure 18.4   The graphics editor toolbar.

THE DIALOG EDITOR

The dialog editor helps you develop dialogs and windows for use in your applet or application. With the dialog editor you can create, edit, and test your dialogs and resource templates. You open a dialog template or resource file containing dialogs and resources in a fashion similar to image files, by using the **File/Open** menu entry. From the **Open** common dialog select a file to view by setting the file type to *resource files* using the **Files of Type** dropdown menu and then selecting a directory that contains a **.RES** or **.RCT** file.

If you are successful, you will be presented with a dialog that looks similar to the one shown in Figure 18.5.

From there you may open any of the individual resources by double clicking the folder containing the type or resource you are interested in. Figure 18.6 shows a sample dialog.

The dialog editor is much like the graphics editor. It contains a toolbar similar to the one for the graphics editor and in addition contains a second toolbar, the *dialog toolbar*, which contains tools specific to the manipulation of dialog controls, such as centering top to bottom or right to left entries and controls as well as aligning controls. The controls toolbar contains all the currently available controls for use in your dialog. Your dialog can contain picture controls; icon, bitmap, and the like controls; static text; and edit boxes. In Chapter 20 each of these components will be explained in detail.

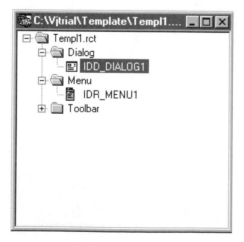

Figure 18.5   The dialog editor resource template pane.

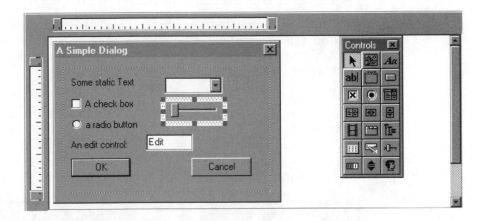

Figure 18.6   The dialog editor.

Almost every control contains properties that can be accessed by right clicking over the control. Figure 18.7 shows the result of right clicking a button control to show its properties.

THE MENU EDITOR

The menu editor is one of the simpler of the resource editors. Menus allow you to group together commands that make logical sense and present them to the user in a quick and easy-to-use format.

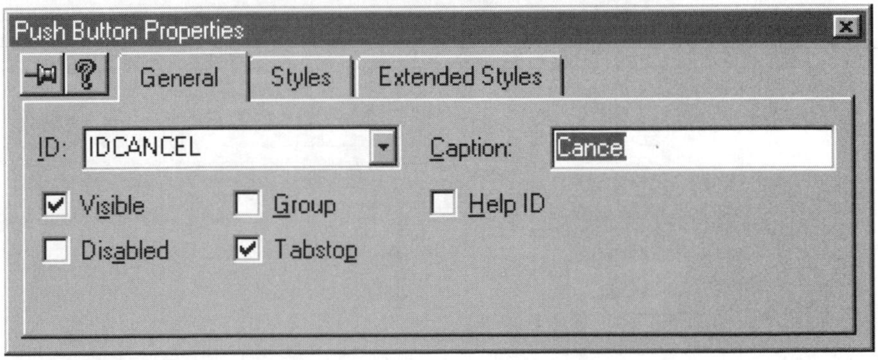

Figure 18.7   Properties of a button.

The menu editor features include such things as:

- Creating Menus (both single level and cascading).
- Converting a menu to a popup and back again.
- Assigning shortcut keys to menu selections.
- Moving and deleting existing menu entries.

You can open a menu resource in the same fashion that you open a dialog resource, with the exception of selecting menus instead of dialogs from the resource template pane and double clicking a menu resource. The menu editor is, again, a wysiwyg editor. That is, the menu you see when you edit is exactly the menu you see when you run your application. Figure 18.8 shows a sample menu.

> **NOTE**
>
> **Java Does Not Support Accelerators Keys**
>
> As of this writing, Visual J++ and Java did not support accelerators keys in menu selections. Perhaps a future release will.

> **TIP**
>
> **Adding and Deleting Resource Is Easy**
>
> If you find you have inadvertently added a resource you do not want, simply go to the resource template pane, select the resource you no longer need, and hit the delete key. To add a resource, simply choose **Insert** from the main menu and then choose **Resource**. You can also use the resource toolbar to add resources.

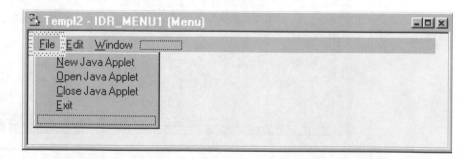

Figure 18.8   A sample menu.

STRING TABLES

One additional resource type is created when you develop either dialogs or menus—the string table. The string table is just that, a table of strings used by your resources. For example, when you add a new menu item and fill in the **prompt** property, a new string is added to the string table that contains this prompt. In normal Windows applications, the string table is invaluable as a single repository for all strings used in an application that can be viewed and translated into other languages easily. Java applications retain this value by continuing to place all of your strings in a single location that is easy to view and update.

RESOURCE PROPERTY SHEETS

To complete our introduction to resources it is important to understand resource properties. You can view the properties of a resource by either double clicking the resource or control or by right clicking and choosing properties from the edit functions popup. The *property sheet*, also often called a *property page*, for the resource or control is then shown. Figure 18.9 below shows the properties of a ComboBox.

Property sheets control several aspects of a resource, including behavior and appearance. In general, a property sheet will show the id of the control or resource as well as aspects particular to that control or resource type. For example, a ComboBox has a set of default entries that are entered in the list box to the far right of the ComboBox property sheet. In addition, it contains a styles tab that controls the type of

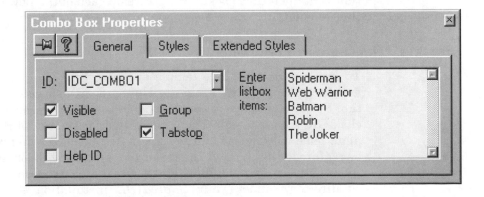

Figure 18.9   The ComboBox properties sheet.

ComboBox, and also an extended styles tab that controls other aspects of the ComboBox.

Other controls will have different properties associated with them. Slider controls may or may not display tick marks as determined by the styles tab of the slider property sheets.

> **NOTE**
>
> ### Property Changes Take Place Immediately
>
> Note that when you change the properties of a control those changes take place immediately. You are not queried with any sort of "are you sure" dialog.

The way a control functions, looks, and behaves are all controlled by these property pages.

As a last note on property pages, you can control how property pages are displayed by either pushing or releasing the pushpin in the corner of the property sheet. Once pushed, the property page dialog will remain displayed as you select different controls.

RESOURCE TEMPLATES

Resource templates are a new idea for Microsoft Developers Studios and were introduced in version 4.0 of Visual C++. Resource templates can speed the development of applications sharing common features by allowing the developer to create templates that can be copied and expanded. For example, if all dialogs were required to carry a company logo, then the developer might create a single dialog resource template that contained that logo and then create each of the new dialogs from that template.

Creating a New Resource Template

To create a new resource template, choose **File** from the main menu and then choose **New**. From the **New** property sheet select the **Files** tab. Select **Resource Template** from the list of resources and then click OK. A new template will be created for you and a resource template pane will appear on the screen. Add resources and modify them as required. Finally, save the resource template by choosing **File/Save As** from the main menu item. Make sure that you choose the *Template* subdirectory under your *SharedIDE* installation so that future requests to add resources will see these new templates.

TIP

Updating Resource Templates

You can update and add to a resource template just like you would any other resource by simply selecting the file using the **File Open** menu selection and then modifying your resource accordingly.

You can now copy and reuse your template resources as much as required, saving time and effort.

Creating a New Resource from a Template

Once you have create several resource template files and stored them, it is easy to insert these templates into your resource files.

If you have not already created a new resource script by using the **File/New** main menu selection, click on **Resource Script** from the **New** property pages. Make sure that you do a **File/Save As** on your script at some point placing it into a directory appropriate for the project you are working on.

Once you have a resource script to work on, you can add resources as described in the following sections.

CREATING RESOURCES

Most resources are created in a similar fashion. In this section we will quickly summarize the methods with which resources can be created. Later chapters will go into more depth about manipulating these resources once they have been added to a project.

Resources can be created in one of three ways:

- Via the resource toolbar, by clicking the resource type you wish to add.
- Via the **Insert/Resource** menu item, then selecting the resource type from the resource list.
- Via the resource template pane, by right clicking in the pane and then selecting the resource type from the displayed resource list.

Creating Resources from the Resource Toolbar

To create a resource from the resource toolbar, open a resource file using the **File** menu, click on **Open**, and then select an **.RCT** (resource

Figure 18.10   The resource toolbar.

template) file. Once the resource template file is open, select one of the
resource types from the resource toolbar shown Figure 18.10.

Creating Resources from the Insert/Resource Menu Selection

To create a resource from the resource toolbar, open a resource file using
the **File** menu, and click it open, and then select an **.RCT** (resource template) file. Once the resource template file is open, select **Insert** from
the main menu and then the resource. Select one of the resource types
from the **Insert Resource** dialog, shown in Figure 18.11.

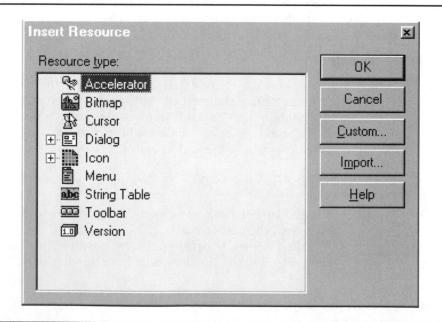

Figure 18.11   The **Insert Resource** dialog.

You will note that the **Dialog** resource type has a plus (+) sign next to it. The plus sign is an indicator of the existence of resource templates for that resource type. By clicking on the plus sign, a hierarchy of underlying template types will be displayed. You may choose to insert a generic resource type by clicking the high level entry or select one of the previously entered templates and then work from there. Microsoft Developers Studio will do all the required work to insert the appropriate copies of the template into your resource script, and you can begin editing from there.

As we have seen resources are really an exciting part of an application. Resources help the developer immeasurably by decoupling the screens and windows the user sees from the code that implements them, making dialog and window development quick and easy. With resource templates we can remove some of the drudgery of creating resources by doing those tasks once that should be done only once.

EXERCISES

18-1 Create or open an existing Graphics resource. One of the images created by the Java AppWizard would be a good example. Update the resource to replace one of the images with nothing but a white space and rerun the applet. Note the result.

18-2 Create several resources in a resource template file. Create at least a dialog, a menu, and an icon file. Save your resource template for later use.

18-3 Create a resource script and add several resources to it. Make sure one is from a previously defined resource template. What would you expect to happen if the template was changed after you created a new resource from it? Change a template and review your previously added copy. Did it change at all? Was this as you expected?

18-4 Experiment with the property sheets of some of the dialogs and resources you have created. What are the properties most common to all controls? What are the some of the differences. How do the properties of a dialog, in general, differ from those of an icon or other dissimilar resource?

CHAPTER 19

The Visual J++ Workspace

In this chapter we cover the following topics:

- **The ClassView Pane**
- **The FileView Pane**
- **Projects and Subprojects**
- **Project Configurations**

As we have seen, the Visual J++ is not a new product per se, but rather a new and exciting addition to an existing family of products. In order to better understand how we can use Visual J++, it is better to understand how Developers Studio works together with those things that are specific to Java and how a project is really put together. The project workspace consists of a directory and files in that directory representing individual projects that you add to the workspace.

Project Workspaces come in three sizes. The first is a single top-level project; the second is a top-level project with one or more subprojects; and the final size is an empty top-level project with many subprojects. We shall concentrate on the most common of these three possibilities, the top-level project with no subprojects.

When you create a project or open an existing project, you are presented with screen similar to the one in Figure 19.1.

A workspace is made up of three main panes. Then **ClassView** pane, the **FileView** pane, and the **InfoView** pane. Each of these *views*, or *panes*, as they are more commonly called, describes a project from a

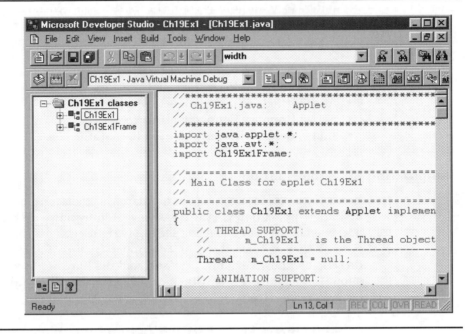

Figure 19.1   A sample project workspace.

different point of view. From past chapters we have seen some of this already. Let's look more closely at each of the panes to understand what each one is for and provides to the user. We shall omit the InfoView pane from our discussion at this point, because its primary purpose in life is to provide help and information, not about the workspace or applet, but rather in general.

THE ClassView PANE

The **ClassView** is an exciting addition to integrated development environments. While it's not new to Microsoft Developers Studio, its allure hasn't changed. The **ClassView** is a hierarchical view of all the classes defined in your project. Each of the projects within the open workspace will have a folder associated with it. Upon opening a workspace, the default configuration for that workspace will be selected and is indicated by the folder name being bolded. If you click on the **+** sign next to a given class, it expands to show the underlying members and variables of the selected class. One of the most interesting features of the **ClassView** is its ability to manipulate your class's direction without regard to the files the classes are stored in.

Within the **ClassView** pane you can:

- Add new classes to your project.
- Expand and contract the class hierarchy.
- Add methods and variables to your class.
- Set and remove debugging breakpoints.
- Add folders which may be used to contain class groupings.

Manipulating Class Information

You can easily change and manipulate the classes that make up your applet or application via the class view. Adding new variables, methods, and even new classes is a snap! Simply right click over the **ClassView** pane, either a class itself or the upper Classes folder, and you can directly add new variables, classes, and the like. Figures 19.2 and 19.3 show the **Create New Class** dialog and the **Class Manipulation** dialogs, respectively.

Adding Classes to an Existing Application   Adding a class to your application is easy. Let's add a new thread class to our application that can handle all the actual animation associated with our applet.

Start by right clicking over the classes folder icon and then choose **Create New Class**. In the **Create New Class** dialog, displayed in Figure 19.4, enter **CMyThread** as the class name, and in the **Extends** box type **Thread**. Then hit the OK button.

Enter appropriate data.

Figure 19.2   Create New Class popup.

Figure 19.3   **Class Manipulation** dialog.

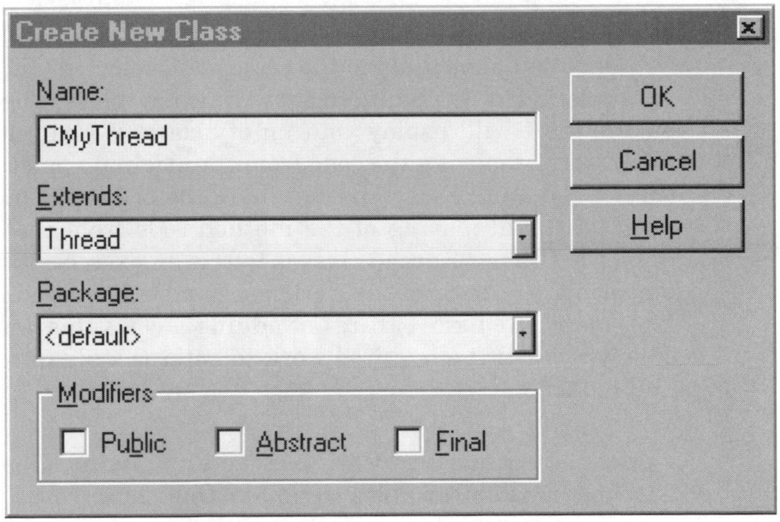

Figure 19.4   **Create New Class** dialog.

Name	Enter the name of the new class, typically prefixed with a "C" to indicate that it is a class file.
Extends	Enter the name of the class you wish to have as the parent, or superclass, of this new class.
Package	Enter the name of the package you wish to include this class as part of. Or, alternately, select one of the packages in the list.
Modifiers	Select an appropriate set of modifiers from the given set.

TIP

Enter an "*" in the Extends **Box**

After you have entered your class name, you can see all the classes that are available for extending by entering an "*" in the **Extends** box and hitting the OK button. The **resolve class** dialog will appear with a listing of all the known classes you can extend from.

Once you have filled in the dialog and selected OK, the **ClassView** will automatically update to show your new class. The file editor pane on the right will display your empty class. We can now go about the mechanics of moving the code from the original applet class to the new thread class and encapsulating there the process of building a thread.

The actual moving of the method code from the original generic applet to the new thread class is left as an exercise to the reader since our primary concern is the workspace and its panes and how they work.

One of the best features of adding a class this way is that Visual J++ will do all the required work to enter the file into the project files and makefiles.

Adding Methods and Variables to an Existing Class   To create add new methods or variables to an existing class, you simply right click over the class of interest instead of the class folder. Figure 19.5 shows the **AddVariable** dialog box.

Enter the data into the new variable dialog.

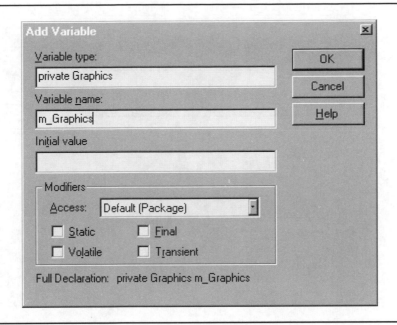

Figure 19.5   The **AddVariable** dialog.

Variable type	Enter a user-defined type or a Java native type variable.
Variable name	Enter any name you wish.
Initial value	If you would like an initial value, define it here.
Modifiers	Select the appropriate modifiers.
Access	Select the appropriate access rights.
Full Declaration	This read only editor box shows the result of you have entered. Select OK to continue.

You can add methods to your classes as easily as you add variables by simply right clicking over the class and then selecting **Add Method**. The **Add Method** dialog, shown below in Figure 19.6 will be displayed. Enter data into the **Add Method** dialog.

Return Type	Enter the return type for the new method.

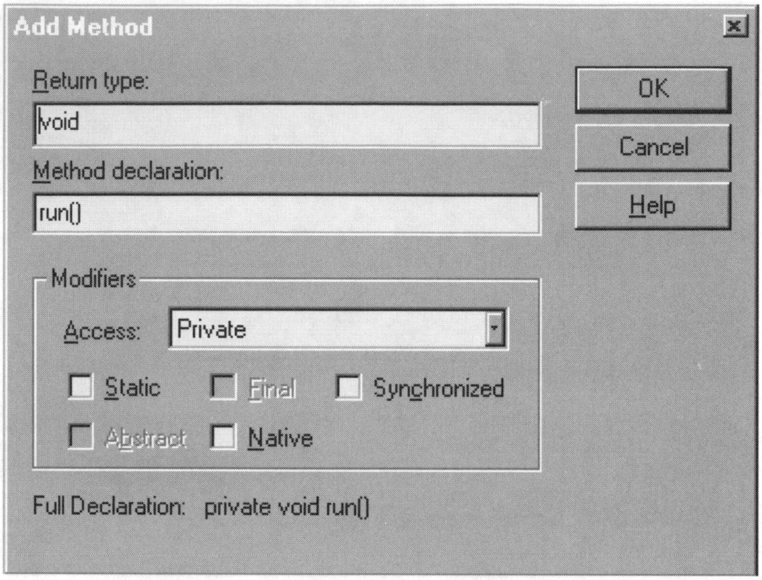

Figure 19.6 The **Add Method** dialog.

Method Declaration	Enter an appropriate declaration.
Modifiers	Select the appropriate set of modifiers
Access	Set the access for this method.
Full Declaration	This read only editor box shows the result of your choices. Select OK to continue when you are happy with the result.

TIP

Visual J++ Knows What Goes with What

Visual J++ knows what goes with what, with respect to access modifiers. If you select a certain modifier, then others become gray, ensuring that you do not enter something that makes no sense syntactically.

Setting Breakpoints from within the ClassView One additional thing supported by **ClassView** is setting breakpoints for the debugger. You can set a breakpoint on a method within a class almost as if you were adding a new method to that class. Simply expand the class in question and then select the method you wish to break in. Right click the method name and select **Set Breakpoint** from the menu. Your breakpoint it now set.

THE FILEVIEW PANE

The **FileView** pane shows files making up the currently open project—the folder at the top of the file hierarchy—and shows the relationships between files. Like the **ClassView** pane, the **FileView** pane will show a top-level folder for each of the projects in a workspace. If a project contains subprojects, then those will be shown as folders within the parent project. It bears noting that the shown relationship is a logical and not a physical one. A file related to another need not be in the same directory, nor even on the same physical device. The only requirement is that Visual J++ be able to access both files. Like the **ClassView** pane, the default project in the **FileView** pane is shown bolded.

Figure 19.7 shows a typical **FileView** pane for a simple project with no subprojects.

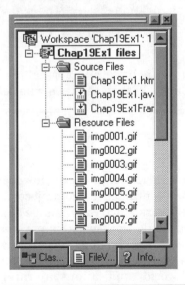

Figure 19.7   The **FileView** pane.

If your project contains dependencies, the norm for most projects, then these dependencies will show up as subfolders within the given project. Clicking the dependency folder will cause it to open and show the files contained there.

NOTE

Source Code Control and the FileView Pane

If you have installed source control on your computer, then some of the **FileView** icons may look or act differently than you expect. If you display the file list and one or more of the files is locked by another user, then its icon may be grayed to indicate this state. Likewise a checkmark next to a file indicates that you have that file checked out.

TIP

Adding Existing Files to Projects

If you have opened an existing file with one of the editing tools and wish to add it to the project that is currently open, simply right click in the editor pane and select **Insert File Into Project**. From the cascading list of configurations, select the configuration you wish to add to.

Now that we understand a little bit more about how files and classes are viewed within a workspace, let's see what else workspaces provide us.

PROJECTS AND SUBPROJECTS

At this point we have built a variety of projects. However, each of these projects was quite simple and contained no subprojects or other levels of dependency. The Visual J++ workbench can manage a much more complex set of projects within a single workspace than we have yet seen.

The most common project has no subprojects but rather only files that are interdependent in some way and come together to build a single application. In the real world, applications are rarely this straightforward but rather have lots of subcomponents and assemblies that come together to make up a cohesive whole. The following sections give a brief introduction to how you can take advantage of the Visual J++ environment to set up interdependent projects and subprojects.

The Simplest Configuration

A single project workspace is all we have built so far using Visual J++. In actuality these projects have contained two configurations: one for doing release builds (without debugging information) and one for debug builds (containing debug information). You can switch between configurations easily by simply clicking the arrow in the **Project** workspace toolbar configuration list box, shown below in Figure 19.8.

The meanings of entries in the toolbar are, from left to right: compile the currently selected file; build the currently selected configuration; stop the current build; select a configuration; go until next breakpoint; insert or remove a breakpoint; and lastly, remove all breakpoints.

In general, **Project** workspaces have two parts.

- A *project* is a set of some number of source files and at least one configuration. The project itself specifies what will be built, a **.class file**, an **.exe**, or something else.
- Within projects you normally have one or more *configurations* that contain settings and control the way the end result is built. Projects start with both a debug and a release configuration, and you can add additional configurations and change the settings associated with a configuration as required.

Projects normally have a *top-level project*; within that project there can be *subprojects* that the top-level project depends on. If a project has subprojects, then they are built first if the top-level project is determined to be out-of-date for some reason.

Creating a Simple Project Workspace Without knowing it, you have been creating simple top-level project workspaces all along. The Java AppWizard, when run to create an applet, creates a top-level project and all its associated files.

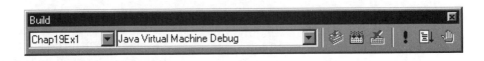

Figure 19.8   The **Project** workspace toolbar.

To create a standalone project without using Java Applet Wizard, select **File** and then **New** from the main menu. From the **Type** list in the **Projects** tab, choose **Java Project** and enter a new project name. Make sure that Java Virtual Machine is selected in the **Platforms** list. Make sure you check *Create a new workspace*. And lastly click OK to create the new workspace.

You now have an empty project where you can insert existing files or add new files and classes from scratch.

Creating a Project Workspace with Subprojects Applications with no dependencies are rare. To build most anything, you normally start with a set of parts—a satellite is made up of many interconnected assemblies. Projects are no different. For example, you may wish to create a new applet that uses a new networking package you have been working on. The new applet would have as its subproject the networking package.

To create a project that contains subprojects, you need first create a regular top-level project, after which you may add subprojects to it. Follow the instructions for creating a top-level project and then From the **FileView** pane select the project workspace and right click it. Select *Add a new project* from the popup. You will be presented with the **Project** tab of the **New** properties sheet, shown as Figure 19.9.

The **Project** tab is used to add new projects to an existing workspace. After the project is added, two configurations are set up: release and debug. In addition, a subdirectory of the current project is created where all the subproject files and settings will be placed.

The fields in the **Project** tab are described below.

Name

Enter the name you would like associated with the subproject. This name will be used as the subdirectory name for the subproject within the current project workspace.

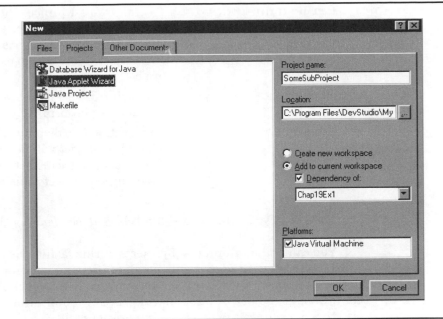

Figure 19.9   The **Insert Project** dialog.

Type **List**	Select the type of the project to create or update. Displayed project types come from the list of installed products.

The two possible options are: **Top-level project** (select this option to insert into the current workspace an additional top-level project). or **Subproject of** (this setting will gray if the **Top-level project** option is selected).

Select **Subproject of** to create a subproject of one of the existing projects in this workspace. From the subprojects that drop down, select one of the currently existing projects. Note that the subproject need not be a subproject of a top-level project but can be a subproject of an existing subproject.

Create a new/Add to current	To create a new project check and create a new project box. To add to the existing project workspace or create a sub project select add to existing project.
Platform	Make sure Java Virtual Machine is selected as platform.
Location	The location box displays the directory where the project will be created. You cannot change the directory when inserting subprojects this way.

Make sure you enter a name and check *dependency of* then click OK to create sub project.

You can add additional subprojects in this fashion as required.

These are just two possible configurations of subprojects. There's nothing to say that you wouldn't have multiple top-level projects, each containing some set of subprojects. The only limitations to how you create a project are the ones you impose yourself!

Building Your Projects and Subprojects When a top-level project is built by default, all its subprojects are also built. However, you can build any subset of the projects within a workspace.

Building a Subproject To build a subproject, simply select it from the **Select default project** dropdown menu of the **Build** tool bar, or use the **Set Default Configuration** choice from the **Build** menu selection. Then either choose **Build** from the **Build** main menu or hit the **Build** key on the **Project** toolbar.

TIP

Shortcut Keys Are Your Friends!

Many shortcut keys exist to speed the development of your application. To build the project currently selected you need only hit **[Shift + F7]**. To compile the current file you can hit **[Ctrl + F7]**. Many additional keyboard equivalent commands exist for menu and toolbar commands.

Building a Top-Level Project To build a top-level project you simply follow the steps outlined above, selecting the top-level project as the default project. If any subproject associated with the top-level project is out of date, it will be built first.

If, for some reason, you are not getting the result you want, you can always force the entire project to be rebuilt by choosing **Rebuild All** from the **Build** menu. This will force all underlying projects to be rebuilt regardless of whether Developers Studio thinks they are out of date.

NOTE

.class .class, **where is my** .class?

Developers Studio needs to know where to find classes that are used by other classes. The easiest way to make sure that this happens is to place the subproject output into the same directory as the top-level project output. However, there are other ways. For example, you could add the output file directory to your class path (messy at best), or perhaps copy the result to a known directory after having built the **.class file**.

Project and Subproject Settings We have spent some time understanding projects. Visual J++ will create nice neat projects and subprojects for us. However, the only thing Visual J++ knows about is simple default configurations. It cannot take advantage of special situations that you, the developer, know about. Enter project settings.

Project settings allow you to change the default behavior of the workspace to better suit your needs. You can add special build commands to a project, specify directories to search, and set output file directories, as well as change compiler options and more.

Let's examine project settings and how we might use them for in order to tailor our projects to better fit our needs.

Before we get into how to change settings, it's important to understand how settings take effect. Settings are applied to a specific configuration and can be applied at either the *project level* or the *file level*. Settings applied at the project level apply to all files in the project configuration unless overridden by file level settings. File level settings only apply to the file specified and control actions such as excluding a file from a build or generation of dependencies, setting up custom built tools, and so on.

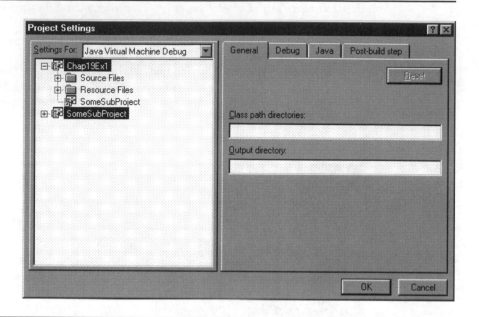

Figure 19.10   The Settings dialog.

To change the settings associated with a specific configuration choose **Project** and then **Settings** from the main menu. You will be presented with a dialog that looks like Figure 19.10.

The **Settings For** pane of the **Project Settings** dialog contains a list of the current configurations in the open workspace. You can expand or contract any configuration that is preceded in the list by a the **"+"** sign. Simply click on the plus sign. Only those projects containing sets of files will have the **"+"** sign associated with them. You can change the settings associated with a single file by selecting the file in question.

The **Settings** dialog contains three tabs: the **General** tab, which controls general settings; the **Debug** tab, which manages debug settings such as optimization; and the **Java tab**, which contains Java specific settings.

The Settings Tabs   Settings are managed for three different areas of your project. **General** settings, **Debug** settings, and **Java** settings. Within the **General** settings tab you can add to your class path by inserting semicolon-separated path entries into the **Class path direc-**

tions edit. These directories will be searched in addition to any listed in the **Directories** tab of the **Options** dialog box. If you had selected a single file, then you may also check the **exclude from build** checkbox and future builds of this configuration will not include this file. You can also control the output directory for the generated class by entering a existing directory into the **Output Directory** edit.

The **Debug** tab has several categories of settings that are user settable. Under the **General** category you can select the **Class for debugging session** and whether you would like to debug under a standalone interpreter or under the selected browser. The **Browser** category allows you to select the browser you wish to debug with, the name of the HTML page you wish to launch your applet from, and the set of parameters to pass to it. The **standalone interpreter** category lets you choose the standalone interpreter you wish to use (**Jview.exe** is the default), what parameters you would like to pass to the applet or application, and any additional parameters you wish to pass to the interpreter itself.

> **TIP**
>
> ### Standalone Debugging
>
> If you wish to use a stand alone interpreter for debugging your base class must have a **main** method to start debugging from. Its easiest if you always set the 'as an applet and application' flag when creating your applications and then you will always be able to use the stand along debugger.

In addition to the configuration-specific settings, you can also set workspace-specific options and options common to Visual J++ by selecting **Tools** from the main menu and then **Options**.

PROJECTS AND CONFIGURATIONS

During our discussion of projects we have ignored that fact that each project is actually two projects—or as they are more commonly called, *configurations*—a debug configuration and a release configuration.

A debug configuration, by default, contains settings that make sense for debugging. Normally, all optimizations are turned off and settings are set for generating symbolic debug information that the debugger can use when testing your code.

A release configuration, by default, has optimizations turned on and no symbolic debugging information is generated. You can optimize for speed, size, or both, as well as many other options.

You can add, change, and delete configurations by selecting **Build** and then **Configurations** from the main menu. The **Projects and configurations** list box shows all the current projects and subprojects. You can add a new configuration by first selecting an existing configuration to base your addition on and then hitting the **add** button. Your will be presented with the **Add Configuration** dialog, which allows you to name the new configuration, select an existing configuration to base it on, and choose a target platform type (all that's currently supported is Java Virtual Machine). To remove a configuration, simply select the configuration to remove and hit the **remove** button. Once you are done manipulating adding, and removing your configurations, make sure you check the settings to be sure that any new configurations have appropriate settings and options for what you wish to perform.

Well, we now know all there is to know about projects, subprojects, configurations, and settings. In the next few chapters we shall look at Visual J++ from a debugging point of view, understanding how applets can be debugged and learning simple, and then advanced, debugging techniques.

EXERCISES

19-1   Update the thread class that was created early in the chapter by using the **Add Method** entry in the **Class Manipulation** dialog to add the required methods.

19-2   Using cut and paste, cut each of the required methods and code from the original applet class and insert them into the new thread class.

19-3   Build your new applet and test it. Does it work as expected? What, if anything, didn't work? Is this result better then the original generic application with an embedded thread?

19-4   Discuss the pros and cons of the two methods of using threads. Which would you ultimately choose and why?

19-5   Create some additional configurations of a sample applet or application. Look at the settings and change a few. What result, if any, does it have on your build? Why might you want to have several additional configurations of an existing project?

CHAPTER 20

Introducing the Visual J++ Debugger

In this chapter we cover the following topics:

- **Debugger Basics**
- **The Debugger Interface**
- **Debugger Windows**
- **Breakpoints and Watches**
- **Controlling Execution in Other Ways**
- **Using QuickWatch, Watch, and the Variables Window**

Unless you write perfect code from the beginning—and I know I don't—then at some point you will need a debugger. With object-oriented programming and Windows-based applications, old styles of output-based debugging simply don't work. A great development environment without a great debugger is doomed to failure. Visual J++ contains an exceptionally feature-rich debugger. With it you can look deep into your code, even to the point of examining disassembled byte codes! In this chapter we introduce the basics of debugging and in Chapter 21 we will see how we can expand those skills to debugging even the most complex applets and applications.

DEBUGGER BASICS

In order to use the debugger, it is helpful to have a better understanding of its components. Interaction with the debugging environment happens in many ways. The debugger main menu and toolbar control the action, while tools like the **Watch** windows and **QuickWatch** allow to see what your code is doing. Dialog boxes help you manage threads, breakpoints and exceptions. Let's take a closer look a these debugger components.

> **NOTE**
>
> ### Applets, Applications and Debugging
>
> When debugging Java applications you have no choice but to use a standalone interpreter such as **JView.exe**. In fact, its often easier to use a standalone debugger to debug most applets as well, because you don't have the overhead of a browser. For the remainder of this chapter and the next, all the examples are given with the expectation that you are using the standalone interpreter for your debugging. If you cannot run your application standalone, then refer to Chapter 17 for a description of application specific code, or simply generate a new Java Applet Wizard application and steal the frame class and main method for use in your existing applet. However, if you are more familiar or comfortable with using a browser, then by all means do so, Visual J++ supports both!

Setting up Your Applet or Application for Debugging

Before we jump right in to debugging, you need to prepare your application. In the previous chapters we always built our applets **as an applet and an application**. There was a method to this madness. Applications can be started by the **JView.exe**, the standalone debugger, while applets can only be started by a browser. While you should do your final testing in a browser, it's often easier to do the first compile, test, and debug loops using the standalone interpreter.

To enable your application for debugging using the standalone interpreter, first choose a configuration to debug using the **Project** workspace toolbar, then select **Build** from the main menu and click on **Settings**. From the **Project settings** dialog choose the **Debug** tab. Making sure that you check **standalone interpreter**.

Now all you need is a bug and you're ready to go!

THE DEBUGGER INTERFACE

The Visual J++ debugger is made up of many different components, such as windows, information panes, dialog boxes, popups, menus, and dockable toolbars. We have seen the **ClassView** and **FileView** panes already and know how they function and what can be done with them. Let's examine, quickly, those interface elements unique to the debugger so we can get an overall understanding of how debugging actually happens.

The Elements

The debugger is primary composed of two menus, some settings values, a set of windows, several popups, and four special-purpose dialog boxes. The menus you have mostly likely already encountered. The first is the **Build** menu, not really part of the debugger per se, but it starts execution of an application. The **Debug** menu controls execution of the application while it is running under the debugger. And the **Debug** menu toolbar contains debug menu commands as pushbuttons.

Debugger Dialogs The four new dialog boxes, some of which have sub-dialogs, are:

- **Breakpoints** dialog
- **QuickWatch** dialog
- **Thread** dialog
- **Exceptions** dialog

The **Breakpoints** dialog controls the setting and manipulating of breakpoints. With it you can set, clear, modify, and disable breakpoints. The **QuickWatch** dialog shows the value of a displayed expression or variable. With it you can enter new values for data or save a variable into the watch window. The **Thread** dialog allows you to view what threads are running in your application and also control threads by suspending, resuming, and setting focus to a specific thread. The **Exceptions** dialog controls how the debugger handles exceptions, determining how the debugger will handle exception processing in general.

Debugger Windows In addition to the debugger dialogs, Visual J++ also contains several windows that display information about application state. These seven informational windows are:

- **Output** window
- **Watch** window
- **Call Stack** Window
- **Register** Window
- **Variables** window
- **Disassembly** Window
- **Memory** window

The **Output** window contains four tabs describing different output information, providing information on the build process, showing compiler statements; on the debug process, showing debug information such as errors, exceptions, and termination codes. It also displays the results of doing **find in files** so that you can step from result to result and supplies information about Java Type Libraries. The **Watch** window allows you to view variable names and values, and set and evaluate expressions. The **Call Stack** window shows a hierarchy of function calls that can be used to jump from method context to context. The **Register** window shows the current state of the machine registers. The **Variables** window contains three tabs for displaying information about automatic variables, local or stack variables, and the implicit **this** object. The **Disassembly** window contains byte codes created by disassembling the currently running compiled program. The **Memory** window shows information about memory used in your application.

TIP

Debugger Windows Are Drag-and-Drop Aware

It is easy to use the debugger windows, because they are fully drag-and-drop and cut-and-paste aware. For example, you can select a variable in the **Variables** window and drag it to one of the **Watch** windows. When you select a variable or other window item that can be dragged, the cursor will turn to an arrow with a rectangle at the bottom. As you move the cursor over a location that does not accept drops, it will become a circle with a slash through it, indicating this target cannot accept the drop.

NOTE

Memory and Register Windows Are Disabled

Registers and memory are concepts specific to a specific type of computer. Java does not support them and as a result Visual J++ disables these features.

Debugger Popups Almost all the windows used by the debugger support right clicking in some fashion. When you right click over a window or pane in the debugger an appropriate popup will be displayed showing the most commonly used commands for that window. For example, right clicking over the **Edit** window allows you to cut, copy, and paste; whereas right clicking over the **Help** window allows you to set bookmarks, print the topic, do search, and perform other help-related commands.

The Menu

Let's return to the applet we created in Chapter 17 that would stop and start the animation when the mouse entered and exited the window. In the following sections we will learn how to start the debugger and stop execution of the applet, as well as examine and perhaps change a variable and resume the applet.

If you can remember back that far, in Chapter 17 we created an applet and then extended it so that when the mouse entered the applet's frame the globe stopped spinning and when it exited it resumed spinning. This will be the starting point for our excursion into debugger. For starters, either open that exercise or create a new applet that contains animation support and mouse events.

Once you have selected the debug configuration and built your applet you can start the debugger by either hitting the **[F5]** key or by choosing **Build** from the main menu, then **Debug**, and selecting **Go** from the popup menu.

Be patient for a moment, the image loads take a while, and you will be presented with the applet frame window with the spinning globe. If everything went as planned it should look something like Figure 20.1.

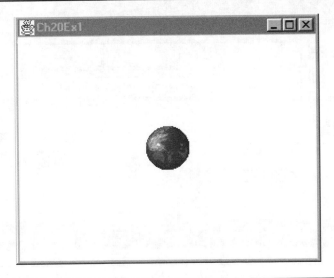

Figure 20.1   The Java Applet Wizard skeleton applet running under **JView.exe**.

The debugger itself will look something like Figure 20.2 below. The **ClassView** pane and the editor pane to its right should be quite familiar to you by now. Some new additions, however, are the debugger toolbar, the **Watch** window (lower right) and the **QuickWatch** variables window (lower left) In addition, nestled neatly in the middle of the code window is the debugger toolbar. The entries are the same as those shown on the debugger menu, but represented as toolbar icons. From left to right they are shown in the following table.

NOTE

The Debug and Build Menus

Those of you with sharp eyes may have noted that the build menu was replaced with the debug menu when the debugger was running. While the debug toolbar contains all the same commands as the debug menu, it's often nice to see the menu and learn the keyboard equivalent commands.

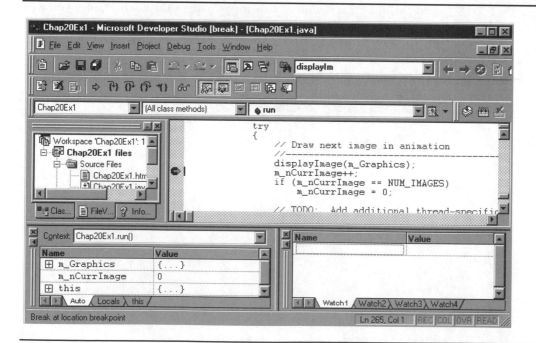

Figure 20.2   The Visual J++ debugger.

Icon	Tool	Menu Selection	Description
	Restart	Ctrl Shift + F5	Restart the application from the start.
	Stop Debugging	Shift + F5	Stop the debugger.
	Step Into	F11	Step into a function.
	Step Over	F10	Step over a function rather than into it. For normal statements just single step.
	Step Out	Shift + F11	Step out of a function. Execution stops at the first line following the function call.
	Run to Cursor	Ctrl + F10	Run the application until execution reaches the line the cursor is on.
	Quick Watch	Shift + F9	Show the value of the variable the cursor is sitting on in a popup window.
	Show/Hide Watch	None	Show/hide the **Watch** window from visible to hidden and back.
	Show/Hide Variable	None	Show/hide the **Variable** window from visible to hidden and back.
	Show/Hide Register	None	Show/hide the **Register** window.
	Show/Hide Memory	None	Show/hide the **Memory** window.
	Show/Hide Stack	None	Show/hide the **CallStack** window.
	Show/Hide Disassembly window	None	Show/hide the **Disassembly** window

Breakpoints and Watches

Now let's look at what's going on. The two most useful things a debugger can do is stop execution at a particular line of code and allow you to examine variable states. Telling the debugger to stop at a particular location is called setting a *breakpoint*. Visual J++ can set breakpoints in any of several ways.

Breakpoints can be set at the entrance to a method, stopping at the first line as the method is entered, or setting at a code label or a specific line of code. Perhaps one of the more powerful features of the Visual J++ is setting *conditional breakpoints*, where you can set a break based on an *expression*. An expression can be based on any variables within the scope of the breakpoint and uses normal Java syntax.

Let's look at breakpoints closely now and how we can set and remove them, view existing breakpoints, and add conditions and expressions further refining our debugging session.

Setting Simple Breakpoints Breakpoints can be most easily set by finding the line of code where you wish to set the breakpoint and then hitting the **[F9]** key. Let's set a few breakpoints in our example applet and then examine the program state at that point.

TIP

Toggle Breakpoint with the [F9] **Key**

You can toggle breakpoints on and off with a touch of the **[F9]** key. Simply place the cursor on the line that contains a break and hit the **[F9]** key to remove it. If no break is already set, then hit **[F9]** to set one.

Figure 20.3 shows two code samples, side by side, with a breakpoint set in each, one in the **main** method and another in the **run** method. Find the sections of code in the sample and set the two breakpoints using the **[F9]** key. Simply place the cursor on the line where you want the breakpoint set and hit **[F9]**. Then start the program executing by hitting the **[F5]** key. Set the breakpoints on line 2 of the **run** code and line 1 of the **main** code.

TIP

Identification of Breaks in Code

There are many ways to identify breakpoints in your code. The most visible is the red dot. The red dot will appear to the left of any line of code that has a breakpoint set there. When your application is running and reaches that point, you will see the yellow arrow. This is the debugger current line.

Run	*Main*
| ```
1    displayImage(m_Graphics);
applet_Ch23Ex1);
2    m_nCurrImage++;
true;
3    if (m_nCurrImage == NUM_IMAGES)
4        m_nCurrImage = 0;
``` | ```
frame.add("Center",

applet_Ch23Ex1.m_fStandAlone =

applet_Ch23Ex1.init();
applet_Ch23Ex1.start();
frame.show();
``` |

Figure 20.3   Simple breakpoints.

Occasionally you will set a breakpoint somewhere that Visual J++ does not support. For example, on a comment. This is normally done by accident. The Visual J++ debugger is smart enough to recognize this and will move your breakpoint to the next valid line of code!

After setting the breakpoints, start the application running with the **[F5]** key or from the **Build** main menu item and then click **Execute**. The application should run for a moment, starting up **JView.exe** and then jump back to Visual J++, showing a yellow arrow next to line 1 above.

TIP

Lets Get Going! Wait! Stop!

You can resume execution of a program quickly after stopping at a breakpoint by hitting the **[F5]** key or using selecting menu **Debug** entry and then **Go ([F5])**. You can suspend execution of an application at any time by selecting the **Debug** command and then **Break**. But be careful! If you are in the middle of a windows function, the result could be unpredictable.

Managing Breakpoints with the Breakpoints **Dialog** The most feature-laden way to manage breakpoints is via the **Breakpoints** dialog. To bring up the **Breakpoints** dialog either hit **[Alt + F9]** or use the **Edit** command from the main menu and hit **Breakpoints**. The **Break points** dialog, displayed in Figure 20.4 will be then be displayed.

Breakpoints can be used to manage breakpoints by allowing the user to set, remove, enable, and disable existing breakpoints.

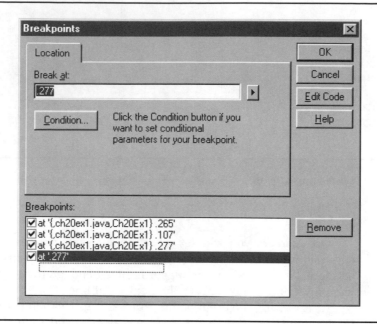

Figure 20.4   The breakpoints dialog.

The **Breakpoint** dialog contains the following fields:

Breakpoints

Shows all the currently set breakpoints. Enabled breakpoints will have a check in the box to the left of the breakpoint. You can disable a break point by unchecking this box.

Break at

Enter the memory address, line number, label, or method to break at. When specifying a break by method, you must fully qualify the method. See the tip box below. Just to the right of the **Break at** box is the line number dropdown. Clicking this box shows the current line number, and if the application is running the current method. Click either of these to set a break at that location.

	When entering line numbers don't forget to precede the line number with a period.
Remove	Remove the selected breakpoint.
Edit	Jump to the location in the code where this breakpoint is set and set the cursor there.
Condition	You may enter expressions that represent conditions when this break will be enabled. Clicking this button causes the **Breakpoint Condition** Dialog to be displayed.
OK	OK accepts any changes you have made.
Cancel	Cancel cancels any changes you may have made.

TIP

Entering Method Names into the Break at Box

You can enter method names into the **Break at** box of the **Break points** dialog if the function is specified as a fully qualified method name. That is, you must specify the complete name of an instantiated class and the name of the method. **Ch20Ex1.main()** for example.

NOTE

Setting Breakpoints in Source Files Other Than the Current One

The easiest way to set a breakpoint is to place the cursor on the line and hit the **[F9]** key to toggle the breakpoint on or off. However, you can use the **Advanced Breakpoint** dialog to set these breakpoints as well. The Visual J++ Beta did not support the advanced dialog, but the documentation associated with debugging states that you may select **Advanced** in the list box next to the **Break at** box and enter the file name, location, class, and method associated with the break you wish to set.

Setting Conditional Breakpoints The one feature of breakpoints that was not covered in the previous sections was that of *conditional breakpoints*. A conditional breakpoint is one with an associated condition. The break only occurs when the expression or condition associated with the break is satisfied. To set a conditional breakpoint use the **Breakpoints** dialog to set a normal break and the hit the **Condition** button. Figure 20.5 shows the **Breakpoint Conditions** dialog.

This subdialog allowed you to specify a condition or expression to apply to the selected breakpoint as follows:

Enter the expression to be evaluated:	You may enter either an expression or an actual variable into this field . For variables, execution will break when the value of the variable changes. This is also true for an expression without a true/false value such as **a+b**. For actual expression, execution will break when the value of the expression is true. For example if you entered **a>b** then when the expression evaluates to true execution will halt.

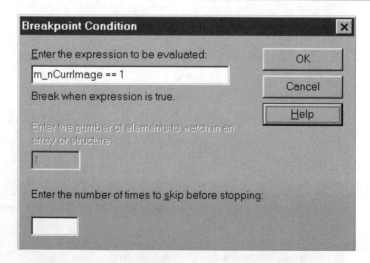

Figure 20.5   The **Breakpoint Conditions** dialog.

Enter the number of times to skip before stopping:	If you wished to stop every tenth iteration of a loop, then enter the number of times to skip here. You can combine this field with expressions that evaluate to **true or false** but not to those that are only associated with variables.

TIP

Setting Breaks on Method Start via the ClassView **Pane**

In the **ClassView** pane of an application you may set breaks on the entrance to methods by clicking on the class name to display all the methods in that class and then right clicking on a method. Then select **Set Breakpoint** from the popup menu displayed. Note that until the debugger stops for the first time you will only see your breakpoint by selecting **edit** and then **breakpoint([CRTL + B])** and not as the customary red dot next to the line of code where the break is set.

Controlling Execution in Other Ways In addition to breakpoints, you can control execution of a program to a finer level by use of the step functions. These functions are all available from the Start **Debug** menu, shown as Figure 20.6.

The commands work as follows.

Go(F5)	Executes the application until a breakpoint is reached or until the application exits.
Restart(Ctrl+ Shift+F5)	Restarts the application and automatically halt at the **main()** method. All breakpoints are retained but all variables are reset to their original values.
Stop Debugging (Shift+F5)	Stops execution of the application and returns control to the editor.
Break	Halts execution of the application immediately.
Step Into(F11)	Steps instruction by instruction through the application, and steps into any method encountered.

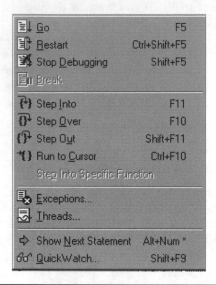

▤⬇	<u>G</u>o	F5
▤➡	<u>R</u>estart	Ctrl+Shift+F5
▤✖	Stop <u>D</u>ebugging	Shift+F5
▤‖	<u>B</u>reak	
{→}	Step <u>I</u>nto	F11
{→}	Step <u>O</u>ver	F10
{→}	Step O<u>u</u>t	Shift+F11
*{}	<u>R</u>un to <u>C</u>ursor	Ctrl+F10
	Step Into Specific Function	
▤✖	<u>E</u>xceptions...	
▤	<u>T</u>hreads...	
⇨	Show <u>N</u>ext Statement	Alt+Num *
66ʳ	<u>Q</u>uickWatch...	Shift+F9

Figure 20.6   The **Debug** menu.

Step <u>O</u>ver(**F10**)	Steps instruction by instruction through the application, and steps over any method encountered as if it were a single instruction.
Step o<u>u</u>t(**Shift+F11**)	Runs until the end of the current method, stopping at the first line following the original method call.
Run to <u>c</u>ursor (Ctrl+F10)	Executes until the debugger reaches the line on which the cursor sits.
Step Into Specific Function	When the debugger is running, select a method in the edit pane and either single step to it or set a break before it. Then select **Step Into Specific Function** and step into the function.

The remaining commands will be detailed in the Chapter 21.

Using QuickWatch, Watch, **and the** Variables **Windows** We have spent a great deal of time examining how to control an application under the debugger. But that's only half the story. In addition to starting, stopping, and otherwise controlling the way an application runs, we need to be able examine variable and class values. The **Watch** window and the **QuickWatch** command provide us with the tools we need to be examine and change program state.

Let's look back to our sample for a moment and examine some variables. Start the applet and wait for it to break in the **main** method. Then hit the **[F5]** key and wait for it to stop in the **run** method. Once the applet has stopped, we can look at a variable.

> ### NOTE
>
> ### Changes for the Purpose of Debugging
>
> For the purposes of debugging, a very simple change was made to the default skeleton applet created by the Java Applet Wizard. A new variable defined as **private int m_nSleepInterval** was added to Ch20Ex1 example. This variable controls the thread sleep interval in the run method so that we can make a debugger change and see its effect immediately.

Using QuickWatch   Select the variable **m_nSleepInterval** and hit bring up the **QuickWatch** dialog by either hitting **[Shift + F9]** or by choosing **Debug** from the main menu and then **QuickWatch**. You will be presented with a dialog that resembles Figure 20.7 below.

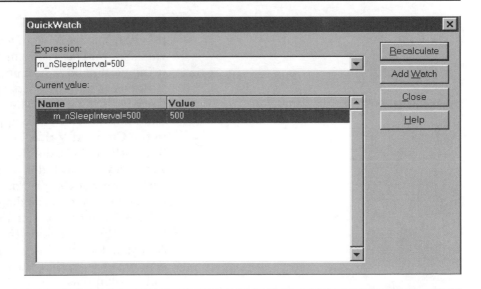

Figure 20.7   The **QuickWatch** dialog.

From within the **QuickWatch** dialog you can view and modify variables by entering valid Java expressions into the **Expression** box and choosing enter. Notice that the **Expression text** box is initially displayed containing the variable selected. Enter the expression **m_nSleepInterval = 10** and then hit enter.

The **QuickWatch** dialog can do several other things, which we will address in a moment. But right now let's see what happens when we change the sleep interval associated with our animation.

Once you have entered the expression and hit the enter key, the value of **m_nSleepInterval** will be changed. Clear any breakpoints in the run method, remember the **[F9]** key to toggle breakpoints, and hit **[F5]** to start the application executing again.

Whoa! That's way too fast! I can't even tell any more what the spinning thing is (50 was actually a pretty good value). Let's slow things down a little. Place the cursor on the **Thread.sleep(m_nSleep Interval)** sleep statement and hit the **[F9]** key to reset a break there. After a moment, execution should stop and you can enter a new value. Try 500 this time, then remove the break and restart execution. What happens now?

Tooooo slooooow. OK, so 50 wasn't bad. Stop the application completely by selecting **Debug** from the main menu and then select **Stop Debugging** or use **[Shift+ F5]**.

Now what else can with do with **QuickWatch**? Well, in its entirety the **QuickWatch** dialog works as follows:

Expression: Enter an expression to evaluate into this box. You can assign values to variables and structure members by using normal Java language statements and then hitting the **Recalculate** button. The expression and its (new) value will appear below in the **Current Value** spreadsheet-like portion of the dialog. If the variable you selected is an object, array, or other complex data item, it will be preceded in the display with a "+" sign. You can expand and contract the variable by clicking this plus sign. An expanded variable will have a "–" sign next to it rather then a "+" and can be compressed by clicking the "–" sign.

Current Value:	This field displays the contents of the variable in question. You may enter a new value for a variable, a structure, or an array member by clicking in the right column. The old value will highlight and you can enter a new value and then hit the return key. Once you hit the return key, the variable will take on the value you enter. To return a variable to its original state you must reenter the value. Values entered cannot be undone.
Add Watch:	To add a variable or an expression to the **Watch** window simply enter it in the **Expression** box and hit the **Add Watch** button.

TIP

Selecting Previous Expressions and Cut-and-Paste within the QuickWatch **dialog**

When you add an expression to the **Watch** window or enter an expression into the **Expression** box, the **QuickWatch** dialog remembers it and displays it for you in the **Expression** dropdown box when you hit the down arrow button. You may select any previous expression and execute it by selecting one of these entries and hitting **Recalculate**.

The **QuickWatch** dialog is also cut-and-paste aware. You can cut an expression and then paste it into the expression box, saving valuable keystrokes (not to mention a little sanity) for those long expressions.

Using the Watch Window With the **Watch** window you can set up to four sets of variables (via the four watch tabs) you wish to watch as your application executes. Each window could represent a different aspect of your debugging session and each is saved when you close your workspace. The **Watch** window is completely drag-and-drop aware and can take advantage of your selecting a variable from the **Variables** window and then dropping it into a watch tab. You can enter variables into the watch window by either drag-and-drop from the **Variables**

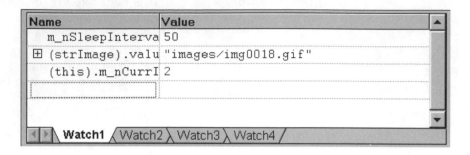

Name	Value
m_nSleepInterva	50
⊞ (strImage).valu	"images/img0018.gif"
(this).m_nCurrI	2

◄► Watch1 Watch2 Watch3 Watch4

Figure 20.8   The **Watch** window.

window or by entering expressions directly. Figure 20.8 shows a sample **Watch** window.

For complex variables such as structures and arrays, the variable will be preceded with plus sign (+) if not expanded, and a minus sign (–) if expanded. If you wish to expand or contract a variable, simply click on the plus or minus sign. Values added to the **Watch** window are evaluated immediately and then every time application executions halts, for example, when a breakpoint is reached. By default **Watch** window variables are displayed in their native format—strings as strings, floats as floats, and so on. However, through the use of formatting characters, you can specify the format in which a variable can be displayed. To change the format a variable is displayed in, simply select the variable in the right column of the watch window and then enter a comma (,) followed by the appropriate formatting character. Figure 20.9 shows the list of allowed formatting characters. Note that all formats are not interchangeable . The debugger will not let you display variables in formats that it thinks make no sense, such as trying to display a short integer as a float. Often its useful to view a variable in some format other then its native one. Visual J++, through the use of formatting characters, allows you to do this thoroughly and completely!

You can change the value of a variable or expression in the **Watch** window in much the same way as you would change the value in the **QuickWatch** dialog. Simply click on the right column of the variable and the current value will be displayed in an edit box. Enter a new value and hit the return key. Hit the escape key **[ESC]** if you want to quit. You cannot retrieve an old variable state once you have changed it, so make sure you know what you are changing before you change it.

Formatting Character	Meaning	Displayed as
d,i	signed decimal integer	signed
u	unsigned decimal integer	unsigned
o	unsigned octal integer	octal format 3 characters to the byte
x,X	Hex integer	0X preceded base 16 number
f	signed float	integer with decimal
e	signed scientific notation	integer with decimal and exponent
g	f or e, whichever is shorter	see f or e
c	character	display as it variable was a single character
s	string	display as a string
su	unicode string	display as a Unicode string

Figure 20.9 **Watch** window formatting characters.

NOTE

Integer Modifiers

For integer values such as d, I, u, o, x, and X, you may enter either h (for short) or l (for long), further refining the specification.

TIP

Properties of a Watched Variable

If you wish to see the type and associated properties of a watched variable, simply select the variable in the **Watch** window and then right click and choose properties. The properties of the variable will be displayed, including its type, access rights, and current value.

Using the Variables Window   The **Variables** window is sort of like a predefined **Watch** window. It contains variable combinations that are almost always of interest. The three tabs in the **Variables** window are:

- **auto tab**   Displays variables from the previous and current statement as well as the return value of methods just exited.
- **locals tab**   Displays variables that are local to the current method or context.
- **this tab**   Displays variables for objects referenced by the **this** object.

While you cannot add or remove variables from the **Variables** window, you can change the value of variables and expand and contract complex expressions and variables through the plus and minus signs. In addition to the variables themselves, the **Variables** window also contains a **context** box, which is like a mini-call stack and displays the current context. You can change the context of the **Variables** window by clicking the **context** dropdown and then selecting a class higher up in the call tree.

So now we are all debugger experts, right? We know how to start, stop, and otherwise control the execution of our applications. We can set breakpoints and know how to make them conditional. We can examine and change program variables. In the next chapter we will develop another simple example, one in which we use mouse events to change the direction of the spinning globe, inadvertently introduce a bug, find it with the debugger, and then correct it.

EXERCISES

20-1   Discuss at least three methods of setting breakpoints. What are the pros and cons of each?

20-2   Discuss at least three methods of controlling program execution, one of which must be **Step to Cursor**. What are the uses of each?

20-3   Drag and drop a variable from the **Variables** window to the **Watch** window and the **Code** window. What happens when you drop the variable into the **Code** window? Is it what you expected?

20-4   Add an expression to the **Watch** window then set a break. Examine the result of your expression as each break occurs. In general, exercise your knowledge of the **Watch** window and **QuickWatch**.

More Debugging Techniques

In this chapter we cover the following topics:

- **Debugging Compiler Errors**
- **Debugging A Sample Application**
- **Advanced Debugger Features**
- **The Disassembly Window**

In the previous chapter we learned some basic techniques for debugging. In this chapter we will put those techniques to use by developing an application, finding and correcting the bugs in the application, and then expanding our debugging techniques to understand how to use the call stack as well as learning how to debug *Threads* and *Exceptions*. Finally, we shall look at some additional features of the debugger and what each provides.

DEBUGGING COMPILER ERRORS

In the prior chapter we did not cover compiler errors. Compiler errors are a form of bug just like any other bug. They are just a much more rudimentary form.

After building your applet, typos and syntax errors will be displayed line by line in the output window. These errors, of course, stop your code from being executed properly. You can easily navigate between errors in the output window by double clicking the error with the mouse, selecting the error, and then hitting the enter key or hitting the **[F4]** key (my personal favorite). The cursor will then be moved to the beginning of the line containing the error. In addition to hitting **[F4]** to move forward by errors you can move backward by error by hitting **[Shift + F4]**. Lastly, if you have selected an error message, you can also right click in the output window and then choose **goto error/tag** from the popup to jump to the error.

TIP

Huh? What Error Is That?

If you do not understand an error message, simply place the cursor on the error number and hit the **[F1]** key. Any online help available for that error will be displayed for you.

DEBUGGING A SAMPLE APPLICATION

We have done some experimenting with the debugger, but here is where we will really take a stab at it. Using Java AppWizard, create an application that supports animation and mouse down and mouse up events. Our purpose with this application will be to make the globe spin backward when the mouse button is pressed and then resume its normal rotation when the mouse is released.

A Buggy Applet

If you have not already created your application, example application **Ch21Ex1** already implements a starting point for this applet, doing most of the work for us but containing—gasp!—a bug! Open your application or the **Ch21Ex1** sample. You will notice some changes.

1. Add a new variable to the class that controls the spin direction. Since we are interested in spinning only forward and backward, a simple boolean will do fine. **m_fSpinForward** is declared as a boolean and initialized to true.
2. In the **mouseDown** method set **m_fSpinForward** to false. Our definition says that when the mouse is pressed the globe should reverse direction and spin backward.
3. In the **mouseUp** method reset **m_fSpinForward** to true. Our definition says that when the mouse is released the globe should spin forward again.

4. In the run method replace the code shown with the following fragment.

Replace

```
m_nCurrImage++;
```

with

```
// Chapter 21 debugging example 1
// Change 3
// If spinning forward then increment the image count
// Otherwise decrement.
if (m_fSpinForward == true)
    m_nCurrImage++;
else
    m_nCurrImage—;
```

Now build and run the applet. On first appearances everything seems to work fine. The globe is happily spinning. We place the mouse into the frame and click it. It reverses direction! But wait! After a moment it stops! That's not right! Let's set a breakpoint and see if we can tell what went wrong.

Set a break on entrance to the **mouseDown** and **mouseUp** events and restart the application. Let's see what happens.

The **m_fSpinForward** seems to be getting set properly, and that is borne out by the fact that the globe starts to spin backwards and just stops. Perhaps its getting changed in some other way? Set a watch on in and let's break every five or ten iterations of the display loop in the run command and look to see what happens. Seems to change and stay changed. It must be something else. Set a break in the **displayImage** routine. Let's see what image is being drawn when the animation stops. Set the break, and on the first instance add the variable **m_nCurrImage** to the **Watch** window using **Quickwatch**.

Rerun the application. What do you find? The image numbers cycle from 0 to 17 and then start going down from 17 or less, depending on when we hit the mouse button. Aha! Suddenly we are asking **displayImage** to display image –1!

Something was left out of our applet. Java handled the error well enough—the applet never completely failed, but it still didn't work correctly. The real problem was in the code fragment shown below.

Buggy Code

```
// Chapter 21 debugging example 1
// Change 3
// If spinning forward then increment the image count
```

```
// Otherwise decrement.
if (m_fSpinForward == true)
    m_nCurrImage++;
else
    m_nCurrImage—;
```

Or, more precisely in the fragment that follows.

```
if (m_nCurrImage == NUM_IMAGES)
    m_nCurrImage = 0;
```

The original skeleton code handled the upper boundary condition fine. Specifically, when we got to the last image in the loop it would start over at the first. However, we have introduced a logic change. We now have a lower boundary condition as well. What we really need to have done is something else—change number 5, shown below completed in the example **Ch21Ex2**.

Corrected Code

```
// Chapter 21 debugging example 1
// Change 3
// If spinning forward then increment the image count
// Otherwise decrement.
if (m_fSpinForward == true)
{
    m_nCurrImage++;
    if (m_nCurrImage == NUM_IMAGES)
        m_nCurrImage = 0;
}
else
{
    m_nCurrImage—;
    if (m_nCurrImage < 0)
        m_nCurrImage = NUM_IMAGES-1;
}
```

ADVANCED DEBUGGER FEATURES

So now we've seen the debugger at work and used its features to correct a bug, albeit a simple and convenient bug. And had a taste of its power. But real applications are much more difficult to debug. They are multi-threaded; they have exception handling code. Real applications are complex. We will now take some time and look at some additional features of the Visual J++ editor and how they are used to help debug even the most complex applications.

The Call Stack Window

The call stack is an area where we have not spent much time. Most of us take for granted that one function calls another and so on. With the call stack we can tell exactly where in an application we were called from, move up and down the call tree examining variable states at the various levels, and other operations. Figure 21.1 shows the **Call Stack** window.

While the debugger is running, the call stack shows all the currently active methods for the current thread (more on debugging threads later). Call stack order is top down with the top-most method the most recently called. More specifically, the more recent calls are shown first. The default **Call Stack** window displays not only the methods but their arguments and associated values.

The call stack can be used in many ways. The simplest way is to stop in a function and the select **View** from the main menu and then **Call Stack**, from **Debug Windows** or by hitting **[Alt+7]**. This will display the call stack whether the debugger is stopped in a method or not.

The call stack is automatically updated whenever a breakpoint is reached.

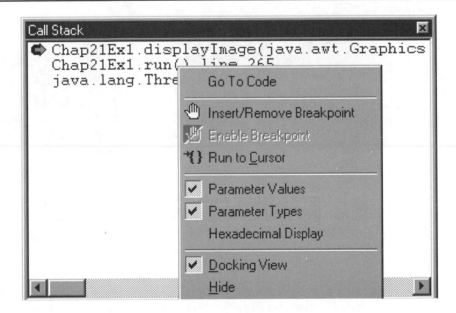

Figure 21.1   The **Call Stack** window with popup showing.

TIP

Changing the Call Stack Display

You can change the way the call stack is displayed by using the **Debug** tab of the **Tools/Options** menu or by right clicking over the **Call Stack** window. You can choose to display method parameters, values or both.

You navigate up and down the call stack by simply doubleclicking a method in the currently displayed **Call Stack** window. You will be brought to the line of code immediately following the previous stack frame entry. For example, If **A** called **B**, **B** called **C**, and you doubledclicked on method **B**, the cursor would be placed on the next line after the call to **C**. If the source is not available for the method, then the disassembled byte codes will be displayed instead.

Changing to a different stack frame causes the debugger context to change also to that context. For example, the **auto tab** and the **locals tab** from the **Variables** window are automatically updated to reflect the new stack frame, now displaying variable state for the newly selected methods.

TIP

Setting Breakpoints in the Call Stack **Window or Running to the End**

You can set breakpoints in the **Call Stack** window by selecting a stack frame and then right clicking and choosing **insert/remove breakpoint**. If no breakpoint is set for the *return* of the method, then one will be added there. Otherwise, an existing breakpoint on the *return* of the method will be removed.

You can also run to the end of method by selecting the method in the **Call Stack** window and then choosing **Run To Cursor** from the **Debug** menu or hitting **[F7]**. The debugger will then run, stopping on the first line following the selected call.

The call stack can be an invaluable tool in determining where errors are occurring your code. For example, if you are dealing with an application that appears to fall into an infinite loop, then it may be possible to isolate the spot where the code is in error by selecting **Break** from the **Debug** menu when the application is in the loop and then displaying the call stack. By navigating up and down the call stack and examining the program state in the calling methods, it may be possible to find the cause of the problem.

Debugging Threads

Java is by nature multithreaded. Threads and the thread class are well integrated into Java and not just an afterthought as with most languages. Let's review for a moment. *Threads*, sometimes called *lightweight processes*, are simply paths of execution with in a single process. Under most operating systems, creating a new process is a time- and resource-consuming task. Processes must have their own memory space as well as an entire set of housekeeping data to be managed by the OS. Threads, on the other hand, are *lightweight*—that is, they share many, sometimes all, the attributes of the parent process. A thread may only differ from its parent in that it has its own call stack and thread identifier. A great debugger must have an intimate understanding of threads and how they are managed and interact. The Visual J++ debugger is such a tool. When the operating system starts an application, the applications main thread starts running. In a multithreaded application, the main thread then starts one or more worker threads, perhaps to handle GUI input or some background processing.

In this section we will examine how Visual J++ manages threads and see how we can debug a process that contains threads, swapping context from one thread to another and examining thread interaction.

You can display the **Threads** dialog (Figure 21.2) by selecting **Threads** from the **Debug** main menu. There is no hot key for display-

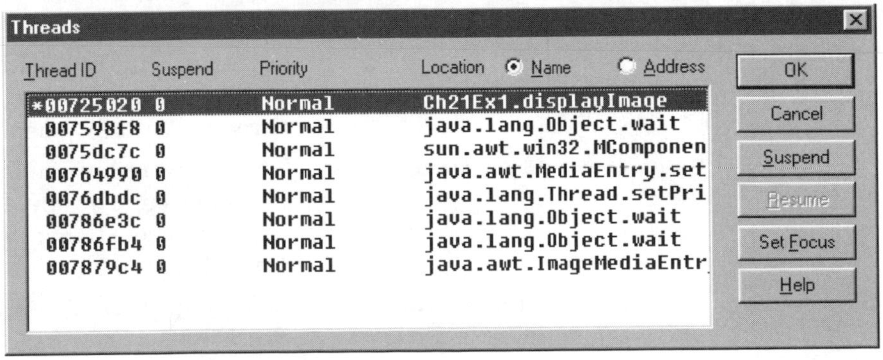

Figure 21.2   The Threads dialog.

ing the **Threads** dialog. Note that your application must be stopped at a break in order to display the threads dialog.

The **Thread** dialog is a multiline dialog, where each line represents a single thread of execution. Note that even if you don't create any additional threads, Java creates some for you.

Thread ID	An unsigned long that uniquely describes a thread. An asterisk appears next to the thread that currently has focus.
Suspend	Some value between 0 and 127. Each time a thread is suspended its suspend count is increased; reach time it is resumed, its suspend count is decreased. A thread with a suspend count of 0 is executing.
Priority	One of seven priorities representing the priority of this thread with respect to other threads and the system. Priorities, listed from lowest priority to highest, are: Idle, Lowest, Below Normal, Normal, Above Normal, Highest, and Time Critital.
Location	The current location of the thread. This is normally displayed as a method name but can displayed as an address depending on whether the Location radio button is set to **Name** or **Address**.
Suspend Button	The **Suspend** button increases the suspend count by one. If the suspend count was previously 0, then the thread is actually suspended.
Resume Button	The **Resume** button decrements the suspend count by one. If the suspend count reaches 0, then the process is actually resumed.
Set Focus Button	Selecting a thread and then choosing **Set Focus** causes focus to be set to the selected thread. All values for that thread become current, such as the **Variables** window **local** and **auto** tabs.

Cancel Button	Remove the dialog box, ignoring any changes.
OK	Remove the dialog box, accepting any changes made.

TIP

Jumping to Source Code from the Threads Dialog

You can jump directly to the source code line associated with the displayed thread by double-clicking the thread you are interested in. You will immediately be brought to the source code module currently executing the thread method. If no source code is available, then the disassembled byte codes are displayed.

Once you have selected a new thread to monitor all variable and program state context changes to the context associated with the thread. The call stack, when shown, will display calls pertaining to that thread as well as the **Variables** window **local**, **auto**, and **this** tabs displaying variable information specific to the selected thread. In short, when you select a new thread to monitor, all aspects of the debugger switch to that thread.

Debugging Exceptions

Life is full of exceptions, C++ is full of exceptions, why should Java be any different? Just as a matter of background, exceptions are a way to handle unexpected conditions in an application in a "normal" fashion.

Applications normally signal some sort of unexpected condition via a mechanism called *throw*. In C & C++, we were always **new**ing memory. It was not uncommon to see an application *throw* a memory error when a call to allocate memory failed. Once an exception has been thrown, the underlying exception handler looks to see who has registered as interested in the exception by using *catch*. The exception handler then directs the exception to that method or code fragment for processing. If no catch handler has been registered by the application, then the interpreter will normally print a message about *unhandled exception xyz* and then typically exit.

This, of course, is the case when an application is not running under the debugger. The debugger has two other options for handling exceptions. By use of the *Exceptions* dialog, show below as Figure 21.3, you can specify how you would like Visual J++ to handle exceptions.

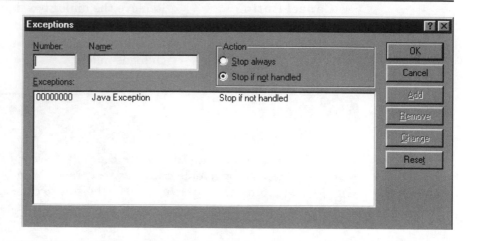

Figure 21.3   The Exception dialog box.

Your two choices are:

- Stop Always
- Stop If Not Handled

These are the elements of the **Exception** dialog box.

Number	A unique number representing the exception. Exception 0000000 representing all Java exceptions is the default here.
Name	The name associated with the exception.
Action	Either **Stop Always** or **Stop If Not Handled**.
Add Button	If a new exception is entered in the **Number** and **Name** boxes, the **Add** button becomes available. You may add this exception to the list and set the default action associated with it.
Remove Button	Remove the selection exception from the list.

Change Button	Accepts the name or action change associated with the selected exception.
Reset Button	Resets all system exceptions back to their default states. User-entered exceptions are not changed in any way.

Associating Actions with Exceptions If you choose **Stop If Not Handled** as the action for an exception, the debugger does nothing more the write an error message into the output window and continue. You have no choice about looking at the code that generated the exception, variable states, or any other options. The debugger simply continues on.

If you choose **Stop Always** as the action associated with an exception, the debugger stops immediately when an exception is raised. You may at this point look at the call stack, examine and change variable states, or take other actions. This is the preferred action, because it gives the user the most control as to how to handle an exception. **Stop Always** alerts the debugger immediately and before any handler code is called.

If you have selected **Stop Always** as the action for an exception, then you may be able to correct the problem and resume execution of your application. For example, if you were encountering a divide by zero error in you applet because some variable was going out of range, you can change that variable (and normally the code in error) and continue. If you fix an error and then continue the application by hitting **[F5]** or in some other fashion, then you will be prompted to pass this exception on to the applications exception handler. If you have fixed the problem respond **no** to the dialog. If you have not, respond **yes**. If some other handler is defined for this exception, then that handler will get a chance to resolve the error and processing will continue. If no handler is defined for the exception, the debugger will print a message about an unhandled exception and then exit.

NOTE

Visual J++ Only Supports the Global Java Exception

Java has a robust exception mechanism with most packages having well defined exception behavior and allowing the developer to define his/her own exceptions. Visual J++ supports Java exceptions by trapping the global *Java Exception* only. You may choose to ignore this exception or change it behavior using the Exceptions dialog.

THE DISASSEMBLY WINDOW

The last feature of the debugger we are going to examine in any detail is the disassembly window. The disassembly window shows the disassembled byte codes associated with an application method. The disassembly window has a decided advantage over a source code window in certain situations. Often developers will place several source code statements on a single line. Since the debugger normally can only step line by line if one of the statements causes an error, it's hard to see that error individually.

With the disassembly window the unit of work is the byte code. When the disassembly window is being displayed you can set breakpoints at a much finer level of granularity, looking at variables as each byte code is executed, rather than as each source line is executed. This is especially true when you are debugging optimized code and the optimizer has done something to your code that was unexpected.

You display the Disassembly window, shown in Figure 21.4, by selecting **Disassembly** from the **Debug Windows** selection of the **View** menu or by hitting **[Alt + 8]**.

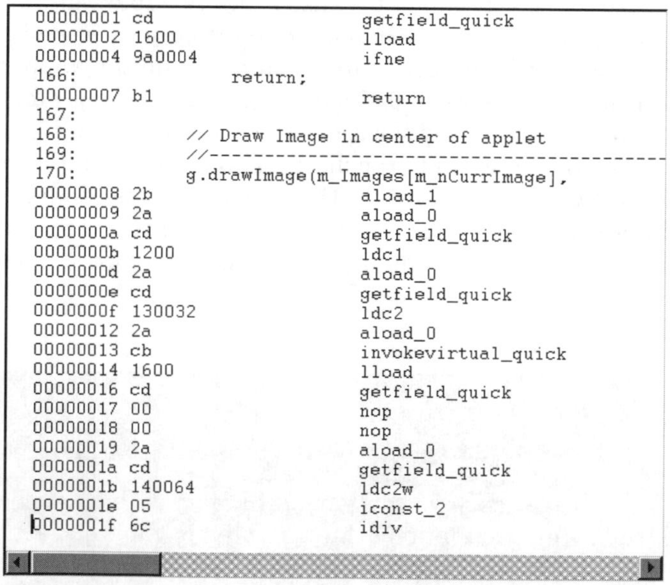

```
00000001 cd                        getfield_quick
00000002 1600                      lload
00000004 9a0004                    ifne
166:              return;
00000007 b1                        return
167:
168:              // Draw Image in center of applet
169:              //-------------------------------------
170:              g.drawImage(m_Images[m_nCurrImage],
00000008 2b                        aload_1
00000009 2a                        aload_0
0000000a cd                        getfield_quick
0000000b 1200                      ldc1
0000000d 2a                        aload_0
0000000e cd                        getfield_quick
0000000f 130032                    ldc2
00000012 2a                        aload_0
00000013 cb                        invokevirtual_quick
00000014 1600                      lload
00000016 cd                        getfield_quick
00000017 00                        nop
00000018 00                        nop
00000019 2a                        aload_0
0000001a cd                        getfield_quick
0000001b 140064                    ldc2w
0000001e 05                        iconst_2
0000001f 6c                        idiv
```

Figure 21.4   The Disassembly window with source code annotations.

> **TIP**
>
> ### Jumping between the Source and Disassembly
>
> You can right click in the source code pane and select **Go to Disassembly** to jump directly to the disassembly pane as well as right clicking in the disassembly pane and selecting **Go To Source** to return to the source code windows.

One of the better features of the disassembly window is its ability to display source code annotations. When source code annotations are enabled, you will see your source intermixed with the byte code instructions it generated. You can then set breakpoints in the disassembly within an instruction as well as on single source lines.

Well, now we know all there is to know about debugging, so it's time to move on to bigger and better things. In the next few chapters your newly acquired debugger knowledge will be tested as we add resources to our applications, use Resource Wizard to generate code from those resources, and then integrate that code into our application.

EXERCISES

21-1   Examine the example in this chapter. Can you extend it to handle mouse drag events? Set a break in you mouse drag event and using the call stack see how you got there.

21-2   How many threads are normally associated with an applet? Determine which thread handles your animation and suspend it. What happens?

21-3   When you disable the animation thread, is the applet otherwise responsive? Does it still minimize and maximize normally? What about when you close it down completely?

21-4   Use the disassembly window to examine a simple statement such as incrementing a variable by one. How many instructions are required to do this? What about making a method call?

21-5   What can we say about the overhead of making method calls versus simple statements?

CHAPTER 22

The Visual J++ Graphics Editor

In this chapter we cover the following topics:

- **The Graphics Editor**
- **The Graphics Toolbar**
- **The Color Palette**
- **The Image Menu**
- **The Status Bar**
- **Tips and Tricks**

THE GRAPHICS EDITOR

In Chapter 18 we first encountered the Visual J++ resource editors. A good graphics editor should be well integrated into the development tool, providing the tools necessary to create, edit, and otherwise manipulate graphics images. In this chapter we shall examine the Visual J++ graphics editor in depth, seeing how it can create and manipulate **.JPG** and **.GIF** files, and otherwise fully explore graphics resource editing. And as we shall see, Visual J++ implements not only a good graphics editor, but a great one.

The Graphics Editor Interface

The graphics editor is made up of a single window, split down the middle with two versions of an image shown. An extensive set of tools for adding text, selecting images, changing colors, and performing other tasks is available through the graphics toolbar. The color palette provides support for changing foreground and background colors and selecting the current drawing color. A set of menu entries with the status bar ties all of this together into a single integrated graphics editor. We will now look at these components in detail and understand how they make up the Graphics Editor as a whole.

Viewing an Image When you first open an image you will see a display similar to Figure 22.1. The image window is split into two frames, the active frame surrounded with a dotted border. A split bar separates the two and can be grabbed and moved back as forth to change how much of one image or the other is displayed.

The two frames are normally used as closeup and normal views (magnifiable view but initially displayed as 1:1), making it simple to see both a large and a normal size view of an image. By default the editor shows the right pane magnified 6x and the right pane as normal size. Of course, you can use the panes in whatever way you see fit, such as viewing two sections of the same file at the same magnification fac-

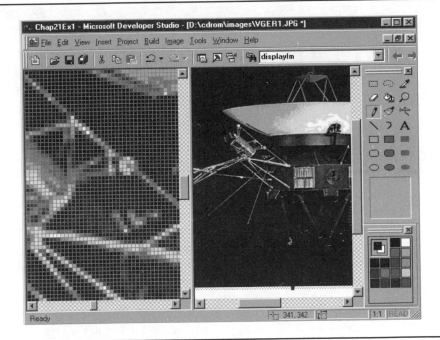

Figure 22.1   The graphics editor interface.

tor. You can change the magnification of the image by selecting the magnifying glass tool and then selecting a section to zoom in or out on.

> **TIP**
>
> ### Creating a New Image File
>
> To create a new image file, choose **New** from the **File** menu. In the Files tab of the New property sheet choose **Bitmap** and then hit OK. The graphics editor will open with an empty file. Make sure when you are done you choose **Save As** under the **File** menu and add an extension of **.jpg** or **.gif**.

Specifically, you select the pane where you wish to change the magnification factor and then select the magnifying glass from the toolbar. The pointer will become the magnify tool and the magnification factors will appear in the options portion of the toolbar. Finally, select the correct magnification and the area to zoom in or out.

> **TIP**
>
> ### Quick Zoom
>
> You can quick zoom an image by selecting the pane to view and then hitting the shift key followed by either less than [<] to zoom in or greater than [>]to zoom out.

THE GRAPHICS TOOLBAR

All drawing tools work in the same fundamental way. You select the tool of choice and apply it to the current image. The Toolbar is actually made up of two parts. The top section shows the tools for image manipulation and the bottom part represents an options section. Figure 22.2 shows several toolbars with various options for the tool selected. The options selector portion of the toolbar allows you to select brush width, pen size, and various other options.

The toolbar is actually broken down into four basic tool types: those tools designed to work with simple freehand drawing and erasing, those tools allowing you to draw closed images, and selection tools and the remaining tools.

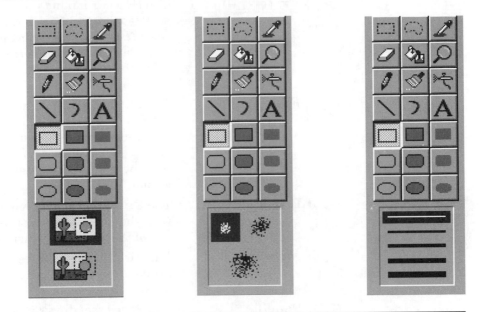

Figure 22.2   Sample toolbars with options.

You select a tool by clicking over the tool you wish to use. The currently selected tool is shown depressed with its appropriate options displayed in the options section.

The Freehand Drawing and Erasing Tools

The freehand drawing tools are Select Color, Eraser Fill, Brush, Air Brush and the Pencil tool. All the tools work in the same basic fashion. You select a tool, set any optional attributes of that tool, and then begin drawing by moving the cursor into the image and then pressing the left mouse button to draw in the foreground color or pressing the right mouse button for background color.

The freehand drawing and erasing tools are shown below.

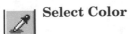 **Select Color**   Select Color allows you to "adopt" a color for drawing. Choose it and then select a tool and the color selected will be used with that tool.

Eraser

The Eraser "paints over", using the selected foreground color. Simply place the cursor into the image, press the left mouse button and erase. You can swap the foreground and back ground colors by right clicking.

 Fill

The Fill tool fills a bounded area with the foreground color selected. You can select foreground color in the color palette by left clicking or background color by right clicking and then select a color.

 Brush

The Brush tool allows you to draw with the foreground color using any one of the displayed brushes.

 Airbrush

The Airbrush distributes colors pixels randomly about the center of the brush.

 Pencil

The Pencil tool draws in a width of one pixel in the selected foreground color as you move the mouse.

TIP

Changing Tool Sizes

You can change the Eraser, Brush, or Airbrush size by using the minus [-] and plus [+] keys. The minus key reduces the size of the tool, and the plus key increases the size. You can always choose the period [.] to select the smallest size.

TIP

Changing Foreground and Background Colors

You can change the foreground color by left clicking the new color in the color palette. Choose a background color by right clicking a color. Bring up the custom color palette by double clicking a color. You may then choose a custom color to replace the selected color.

The Closed Figure Drawing Tools

The closed figure drawing tools allow you to draw lines and figures such as ellipses, squares, and rectangles. These figures can have borders or not, but filled or not, all based on the tool selected.

All drawing tools work in the same basic way. Select a figure tool and click the left mouse in the bottom pane. Holding the mouse button, stretch the image to the desired size. For lines, the first click represents the first end point of the line and the release the second. For circles, ellipses, squares, and rectangles, the mouse press represents the corner of the bounding rectangle and the mouse release the opposite corner.

> **TIP**
>
> ### Drawing in Background and Foreground Colors
>
> The closed figure filled drawing tools and the line tool will normally draw in the foreground color when you use the left mouse button. However, you can draw the figure in the background color by using the right mouse button instead!

The closed figure drawing tools are shown below.

Line

The Line tool draws a line by placing the mouse on the first end point and holding the mouse down and dragging the line. When the mouse is released, the cursor position represents the second end point of the line.

Rectangle

The Rectangle tool draws an opaque rectangle using the left mouse button for foreground color, right mouse button for background.

Filled Rectangle

The Filled Rectangle draws a rectangle, filled with the foreground color when drawn with the left mouse button, and filled with the background color when drawn with the right mouse button.

Outlined Rectangle   The Outlined Rectangle draws a filled outlined rectangle, filled with the foreground color and outlined with the background color if using the left mouse button, and reversed if using the right mouse button.

Round Corner Rectangle   The Round Corner Rectangle is exactly like Rectangle only with round corners.

Filled Round Corner Rectangle   The Filled Round Corner Rectangle is exactly like Filled Rectangle only with round corners.

Outlined Round Corner Rectangle   The Outlined Round Corner Rectangle is exactly like Outlined Rectangle only with round corners.

Ellipse   The Ellipse tool operates exactly like Rectangle tool only it draws an ellipse.

Outlined Ellipse   The Outlined Ellipse tool operates exactly like Outlined Rectangle tool only it draws a outlined ellipse.

Filled Ellipse   The Filled Ellipse tool operates exactly like Filled Rectangle tool only it draws a filled ellipse.

Remaining Toolbar Tools

In addition to the drawn and closed figure tools there are several other tools of interest. Two selection tools, select a rectangle and select a region, allow you to select portions of images that can then be the focus of cut, paste, copy, clear, resize, move, or invert operations. The text tool allows you to enter text, choosing font, size, and other text attributes. The curve tool allows you to draw complex curves, and the magnify tool allows you to zoom in and out on images.

Let's look at each of these tools a little more closely.

Selecting a Rectangle Region

The Select tools allow you to select a rectangular region of the screen and then perform operations on it such as cut, paste, copy, clear, invert, or move. Select the upper left corner of the desired area and then, holding the left mouse button down, drag the bounding rectangle to select an area. The area will be selected when you release the mouse button.

 Select a Region

The Select a Region tool works very much like the Pencil tool. Draw a line around the area you wish to select by placing the cursor into the pane and then holding the left mouse button down to enclose an area. When the mouse button is released, a bounding rectangle will be generated that borders the area you have selected. You may now cut, paste, copy, or perform other operations on the selected area.

 Insert Text

The Insert Text tool allows you to insert text into an image. When you select the text tool, the text box (shown in Figure 22.3) will be displayed. Enter the text you wish to insert into the box. You can set the font, font style, and size via the Font button, which brings up the Text Tool Font dialog, shown in Figure 22.4. All installed fonts will be displayed in the Text Tool Font dialog and you need only choose the one you wish to use.

 **Magnify**

As was stated in the Viewing an Image section, the Magnify tool controls the current zoom of an image. To zoom an image, simply select the Magnify tool and place it over the section of the image you wish to zoom. Select the magnification factor from the choices shown in the toolbar options section, or use the less then [<] or greater then [>] symbols to decrease or increase the magnification.

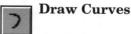 **Draw Curves**

The Draw Curves tool is one of the most interesting of the tools available to you. With the curve tool you can draw complex curves around two distinct points. To draw a curve, select the Curve tool and then select the first and second curve end points. Move the mouse to drag the curve around the selected end points. Click the mouse a second time to select a second anchor point and the drag the curve again.

Figure 22.3   The Text box.

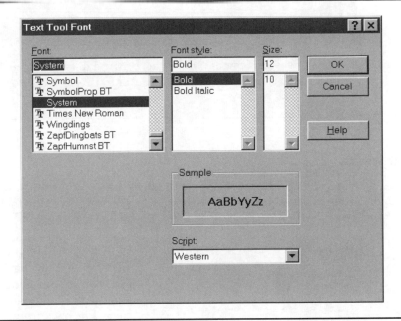

Figure 22.4   The Text Tool Font dialog.

TIP

The Curve Tool

The curve tool is one of the most interesting tools in the graphics editor. It allows you to draw complex curves around several points. However, its function is fairly hard to describe. Try adding a few curves into your image. Play with the tool and see how it works!

TIP

Line Breaks in the Text Box

You can insert line breaks into your text by hitting **[Shift + Enter]** where you want a line break.

Select and Custom Brushes

You can select a portion of the screen and use it for a custom brush! See the Custom Brushes section later in this chapter for more information.

Toolbar Options

Since we now understand the basics of the toolbar tools, we can delve a little further into their functions by examining the toolbar options. There are seven toolbar options, each shown below.

Selection & Text

With this option, you can select either opaque or background/foreground. For opaque, the text has the existing background color. For background/foreground, the text is in the foreground color and the background uses the background color.

Erase

Using Erase, you can select one of the four erase sizes.

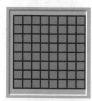

All Filled Images & Fill

This option shows the current fill color. If the pixel tile grid is enabled, it shows the grid as well.

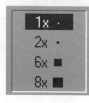

Magnify

The magnify tool selects new magnification rate.

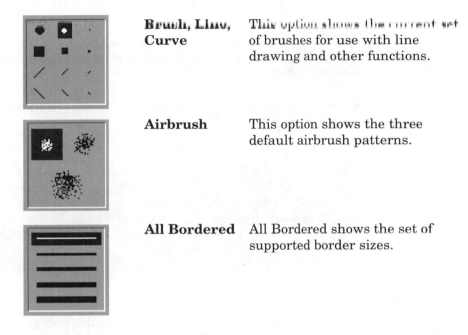

Brush, Line, Curve   This option shows the current set of brushes for use with line drawing and other functions.

Airbrush   This option shows the three default airbrush patterns.

All Bordered   All Bordered shows the set of supported border sizes.

All simple enough. Let's take a closer look now at the color palette and what we can do with colors.

THE COLOR PALETTE

When you first open an image, you are presented with a color palette, similar to the one shown in Figure 22.5 containing sixteen "standard" colors and another eight dithered colors. You can create and save your

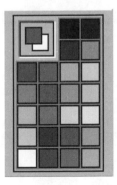

Figure 22.5   A sample color palette.

own color palettes. The last used palette is saved into the registry and restored as the default when you open an image. It's simple and easy to manipulate the colors in an image, either through the color palette or via the properties page for the image.

> **NOTE**
>
> ### Color Changes are Global and Immediate
>
> You can manipulate the colors associated with an image via the image property page (**[Alt + Enter]** or select **Properties** under the **Edit** menu). Try double clicking on one of the 256 colors stored for an image. You can change a color subtly or drastically. But remember your change is permanent (assuming you save your changes) and immediate.

Custom Colors

You can change a color in either the color palette or on an images property page by selecting **Adjust colors** from the **Image** menu. The Custom Color dialog box, shown in Figure 22.6, will be displayed and works as follows.

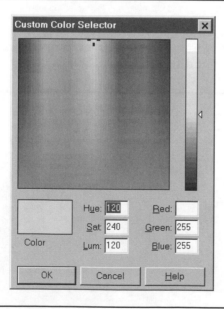

Figure 22.6   The Custom Color dialog.

With the **Custom Color** Dialog you can you can select a new color via RGB triplets or Hue, Saturation, and Luminance triplets; or via the cross hairs and sliding luminance scale.

The dialog fields are

Cross Hairs	Selects the color you wish to change using the cross hairs.
Luminance Slider	Moves the luminance slider up and down to change the luminance values for the selected color.
Red	The red value for the color you have selected, in the range 0 to 255.
Green	The green value for the color you have selected, in the range 0 to 255.
Blue	The blue value for the color you have selected, in the range 0 to 255.
Hue	The hue of the color you have selected, in the range 0 to 240.
Sat	The saturation of the color you have selected, in the range 0 to 240.
Lum	The luminance of the color you have selected, in the range 0 to 240.
Color	Displays the solid color closest to the dithered color displayed.

Once you have either entered the values you want or selected them via cross hairs and slider, you may select the solid color by clicking the color window, or simply click OK to replace the original color entry with the dithered value.

Selecting Foreground and Background Colors

Whether you have created your own custom colors or simply used the existing ones, you select foreground or background colors the same way, by either left clicking a color in the color palette for foreground or right clicking for background.

Saving and Restoring Color Palettes

It is often useful to have a set of color palettes available for different uses. Shades of gray are often useful as well as your own special combinations. To save a custom color palette after you have created one choose **S̲ave** from the **I̲mage** menu and then enter a file name. To load a custom color palette chose **L̲oad** from the **I̲mage** menu and then enter the directory and file name of **.pal** file to load.

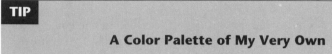

A Color Palette of My Very Own

Creating color palettes is easy and very convenient at times. But finding that color palette isn't always as easy. Do yourself a favor and create a directory (**c:\palettes** comes to mind!), then store ALL your color palettes there, and give each a distinctive name like **ShadesOGray.pal**. Then the next time you want that nifty palette you created, you will be able to find it quickly and easily.

THE IMAGE MENU

We've talked about colors, tools, and the graphics editor interface. Now we will cover the Image menu, which provides a few additional commands to manipulate your images (see Figure 22.7).

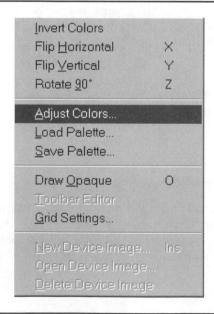

Figure 22.7   The Image menu.

The image menu contains thirteen commands in three broad categories.

Image Manipulation Commands

You can manipulate either an entire image or a section of the image using the first four image menu commands.

Invert Colors	Inverts the currently selected colors: black becomes white, and a "negative" of each selection is created.
Flip Horizontal	Flips an image from left to right: the right side becomes left and vice versa. This is useful for creating mirror images.
Flip Vertical	Flips an image top to bottom: the top becomes the bottom and vice versa. Again, useful for creating mirror images.
Rotate 90	Rotates a selection 90 degrees.

Color Manipulation Commands

Adjust Color	Bring up the Custom Color Selector dialog to manipulate the currently selected foreground color.
Load Palette	Loads an existing color palette.
Save Palette	Saves a color palette to disk.

Drawing/Toolbar Commands

Draw Opaque	Selects either draw opaque or transparent. Opaque drawing complete obscures the background. Transparent lets the background color show through.
Toolbar Editor	Bring up the toolbar editor to edit a toolbar.
Grid Settings	Bring up the Pixel Grid Settings dialog. See the pixel grid section later in this chapter for more information about the grids.

And that's it for the Image menu! Let's take a quick look at the status bar.

THE STATUS BAR

The status bar is perhaps the simplest part of the graphics Editor. It displays useful information about the cursor's current position. The status bar itself is broken down into four panes and the ever-present tool tips. The first pane shows the position of the cursor in the window. The second pane shows the size of any area selected during a cut, paste, or drag type in pixels, relative to the upper left corner. The third pane shows the current magnification of the selected window pane, and the last pane shows **read** grayed or not depending in whether the file you are view has the read only attribute set.

TIPS AND TRICKS

OK, we've tried to cover all the topics related to the graphics editor in some sort of coherent fashion, but there are a few more things you need to know. Take a few more moments and finish up the remaining sections. They will help you get the most out of the Image editor.

The Pixel Grid

When displaying an image with a magnification factor of 4x or greater, you can display the pixel grid. The pixel grid separates individual pixels and can easily be changed by selecting **Grid Settings** from the **Image** menu. The **Grid Settings** dialog appears, in Figure 22.8.

Pixel Grid	Toggles the pixel grid on and off.
Tile Grid	If you have turned on the pixel grid, you may also toggle on the tile grid. The tile grid is much larger grid then the pixel grid.
Width	If you have toggled on the Tile Grid, then you may select the width, in pixels, of the tiles to display.
Height	As with Width, if you have toggled on the Tile Grid, then you may select the height, in pixels, of the tiles to display.
OK Button	Accepts any changes to grid settings.
Cancel Button	Cancels any changes to grid settings.

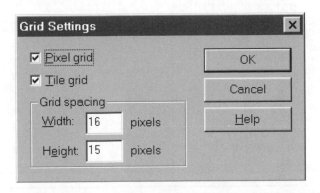

Figure 22.8   The Grid Settings dialog.

Using Custom Brushes

A custom brush is basically an area of an image that you have "picked up" and then can draw with. Create a custom brush by selecting an area of an image and then pressing **[CTRL + B]**. You can now "draw" with this brush, either transparently or opaquely, and produce a number of interesting effects.

> **TIP**
>
> **Custom Brushes and Selections Are a Lot Alike**
>
> Almost all of the actions you can perform on a selection you can perform on a custom brush. Try stretching it, compressing it, or manipulating the brush in some other way to see what happens.

Image Properties

The properties of an image include its size (height and width in pixels), the number of colors used, and the color palette associated with the image. For **.JPG** images, the image may also be stored compressed.

You can view the image's properties, changing them if you wish, by selecting **Properties** from the **Edit** menu. The image property sheet is shown in Figure 22.9.

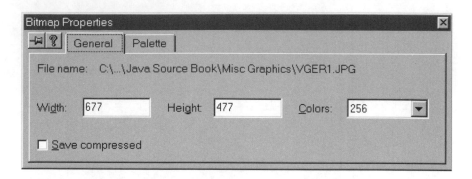

Figure 22.9   Properties.

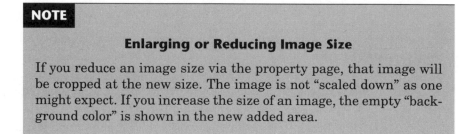

Enlarging or Reducing Image Size

If you reduce an image size via the property page, that image will be cropped at the new size. The image is not "scaled down" as one might expect. If you increase the size of an image, the empty "background color" is shown in the new added area.

Resizing Images

Often it's nice to be able to show a thumbnail sketch of an image. A thumbnail is really just a very small version of an existing image, often displayed as a preview for another, normally full-scale, image. You can resize an entire image or just part of one. What exactly happens depends on what you have selected. There are two ways to resize an image. The first has already been explored—simply manipulating the properties of the image—and only applies to the image as a whole. The second is using the resizing handles on a selection. Resizing handles are those little squares on the edges of a selection. By grabbing a resizing handle you can stretch or shrink an image. You can only resize by grabbing solid resizing handles, you cannot grab opaque handles.

Shrinking or Expanding an Entire Image You can resize an entire image by hitting the **[esc]** key outside an already selected image area. Then grab a resizing handle, and while holding down the **[shift]** key, shrink or extend the image. The entire image will shrink or expand according to what you have done.

Extending or Cropping an Entire Image You can crop or extend an entire image by following the prior procedure; that is, grab a resizing handle and pull. However, do not hold down the **[shift]** key. If you expand the image, the new area will be filled with the selected background color. If you contract the area, the image will be cropped as specified.

Shrinking or Expanding a Selection Simply select the area you wish to expand or contract and drag a resizing handle in or out as required. Note that you cannot crop a section per se, as you can with an entire image, but rather you need to cut and paste the area to be cropped.

TIP

Resizing to the Grid

If you wish to resize to a specific size, try turning on the pixel grid. Images resized while the pixel grid is displayed are automatically snapped to the grid.

Applying Actions to Selected Images

Selected text can have standard operations—such as cut, paste, clear, or move—applied to it. Since the graphics editor is an integrated Microsoft product, the selections you cut, copy, or paste are stored on the clipboard and can be inserted into other clipboard-aware products.
Operations on selections include the following:

Cut	You can choose **cut** from the **edit** menu or **[CTRL+X]**. The original area of the selection is filled with the current background color.
Paste	When you choose **paste** from the **edit** menu or **[CRTL+V]**, the current clipboard image, cropped by the selection size, is displayed in the upper left corner of the screen and can be moved and deposited wherever required.
Clear	You can choose **clear** from the **edit** menu or **[delete]**.

Move	To move, you can select anywhere within the desired area and drag the selection to its new location. The original area of the selection is filled with the current background color.
Copy	When you choose **copy** from the **edit** menu or **[CTRL+C]**, a copy of the currently select region is placed on the clipboard.
Draw With	You can place the cursor anywhere within the selected area and hold down the shift key. The currently selected area will be used like a drawing tool and will insert repeatedly copies of itself into the document. When the mouse is moved faster, fewer images are entered and vice versa.
Rotate/Flip	You can rotate flip an image by choosing **Flip Horizontal**, **Flip Vertical**, or **Rotate 90** from the **I̲mage** menu.

Converting a Bitmap to an Image File

The image editor can easily covert a **.bmp** (bitmap) to a **.jpg** or **.gif** file easily. Simply chose **O̲pen** from the **F̲ile** menu and select a bitmap. Make any changes you wish to the file and then choose **Save A̲s** from the **F̲ile** menu. Set the directory as you wish and then update the file extension from **.bmp** to **.gif** or **.jpg**, and then save the file.

EXERCISES

22-1   Open an existing image and invert the colors. Compare it with the original. What use might there be for this "negative" image?

22-2   Exercise each of the drawing tools, especially the curve tool.

22-3   Experiment with shrinking and expanding images. Did what you expect happen when you selected an entire image and squeezed it down? How about expanding selections?

22-4   Create a custom brush. Draw with it in both transparent and opaque modes. How does the result differ?

CHAPTER 23

The Visual J++ Dialog and Menu Editors

In this chapter we cover the following topics:

- **The Dialog Editor Interface**
- **The Menu Editor Interface**
- **Resource Templates Reviewed**

Dialogs and menus are an integral part of any windowing application. Visual J++ allows you to create and manage dialog and menu resources quickly and easily with a wysiwyg interface. You can easily insert, manage, and modify controls as well as view their properties and test your dialogs, all from within the Dialog editor. In addition, the Dialog editor fully supports templates so you can save your basic dialogs and then have a base to start from when you do new development.

As you read this chapter, it's important to understand that we will not cover some things. We are specifically leaving out a description of how to run the Java Resource Wizard. For those of you familiar with dialog editing, you can skip this chapter and move directly to the next, but be forewarned if you do. In this chapter we will begin to touch on the relationship between controls and the underlying Java code created by Java Resource Wizard and how the generated code represents the original dialog, as well as examine which controls are supported by Java.

THE DIALOG EDITOR INTERFACE

When you open a dialog resource file, you will be presented with a screen that looks something like the one in Figure 23.1.

TIP

Creating an Empty Dialog

If you have never before created a dialog box, it's easy. Simply choose **Resource** from the **Insert** menu (or hit **[Ctrl+R]**), and then choose a dialog resource from the **Insert Resource** dialog. If dialog templates exist, any of the standard dialog types then a plus sign **(+)** will be displayed to the left of the resource. Click the plus sign to expand the resource type to show all the resource templates of that type.

The Dialog editor basically is made up of the dialog display pane, a single menu (the layout menu), the layout toolbar, the controls toolbar, and a status bar.

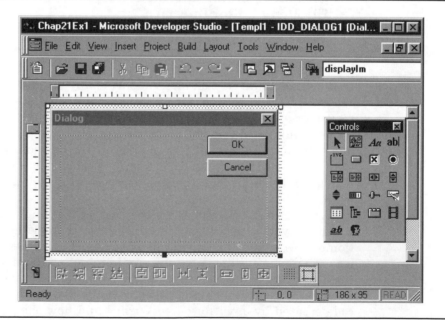

Figure 23.1   The Dialog editor.

- The layout menu and the layout toolbar basically allow you to do the same things. Control the layout of controls within a dialog by providing you with tools to align, size, and otherwise manipulate controls.
- The dialog display pane shows a wysiwyg display of the dialog you are working on. Grid lines and rules may or may not be displayed.
- The controls toolbar contains all the controls you will ever need to create a fully functional dialog.
- The status bar tells you the size of your dialog, the current location of the mouse, and other important information.

A default new dialog contains nothing more then an OK and a CANCEL button. Not too exciting! Let's look at adding controls to our dialog.

TIP

Right Click Often

As we have seen in the past you can right click almost anything. Try right clicking over your dialog, a button or a control. Almost all parts of the Dialog Editor support some display of most frequently used commands.

Adding and Positioning Controls

To add a control to a dialog, simply choose the control you want from the controls dialog and then drag it to the place you want to see it in the dialog. The cursor will change to look like the control you have selected and are inserting. In addition, a control outline will appear, showing the approximate size of the control selected. When the cursor is where you want the control, release the mouse button and the new control will appear.

Supported Controls As it stands today, only a subset of the total set of controls shown in the controls toolbar will produce Java code when placed into a dialog box. You may insert any type of control you wish, but unsupported controls will not have code generated for them.

They are:

Tool	Name	Description	Implemented Via Java Class
	Select	Selects a control	N/A
	Picture	Inserts a picture, icon or bitmap	None, **.jpg** or others inserted directly
	Static Text	Inserts a static text item	Label Class
	Edit Box	Inserts an editor box	TextField Class or TextArea Class for multi-line edits
	Group Box	Causes Java Resource Wizard to group controls	N/A
	Push Button	Inserts a push button.	Button Class
	Check Box	Inserts a check box	CheckBox Class
	Radio Button	Inserts a radio button	CheckBox with accompanying CheckboxGroup as required
	Combo Box	Inserts a combo box	Choice Class
	List Box	Inserts a list box	List Class
	Vertical Scroll Bar	Inserts a vertical scroll bar	Scrollbar Class with VERTICAL property set
	Horizontal Scroll Bar	Inserts a horizontal scroll bar	Scrollbar Class with HORIZONTAL property set

As it stands today, Visual J++ and the Java programming language only support a subset of the controls and styles supported by Windows. In the future you can expect a much richer set of controls and much greater control over the style of those controls.

TIP

Other Methods of Adding Controls

There are other methods of adding controls to a dialog box. For example, you can select a control and then, without dragging, simply click in the dialog box. Where you click will be the upper lefthand corner of the newly added control. You can also extend this idea by "drawing" your control; that is, click where you would like the upper lefthand corner to be, and then hold the mouse button down and draw out a bounding rectangle for the control you are inserting. The rectangle will be the original control size when you release the mouse button.

Once you have inserted your control, you are certainly not done. Normally, you need some method to either get or set the state or contents of the control, so you really would like to know the id of the control and perhaps change its caption.

Right clicking over a control will cause its properties box to appear. All controls share some basic properties, such as an id, whether they are visible or not, and almost all have a caption. In addition, all controls have a size and a position. The size and position are controlled by the resource editor. The name and other properties are controlled by you and can be manually set through the controls properties.

Open or create a dialog if you have not already done so, and then drag onto it a radio button. Right clicking the new button will display a dialog similar to the one shown in Figure 23.2. You may set the dialog id to any name which has not been already used.

The properties common to all controls are:

ID	The resource id of the control. Enter any valid quoted string or name or an integer.
Caption	Some caption associated with a control, for example "Radio Button 1".

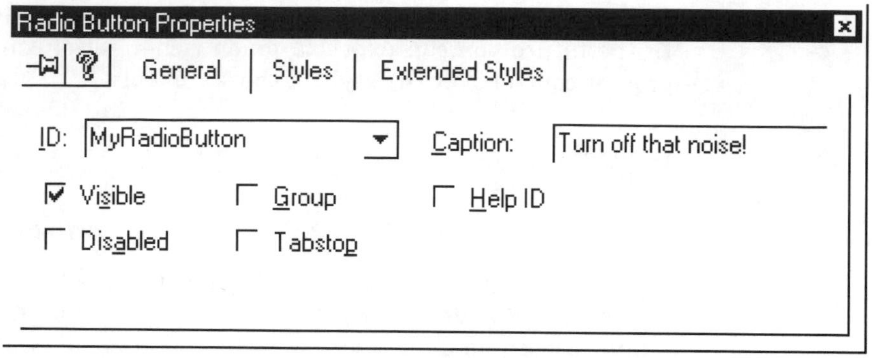

Figure 23.2 Properties of a radio button.

Visible	Is this control visible or not? Boolean, default = true.
Disabled	Will this control be disabled when displayed? Boolean, default = false.
Group	Specifies that this control is first of a group. Controls grouped together are treated as one control when tabbing between controls. If you placed several radio buttons together, then you might want them grouped together; for example, one as on and the other as off. The next control in the tab order specified as a group indicates the start of a new group.
Tabstop	Notes that the user can move to this control or group of controls with the tab key.
Help ID	Specifies that a help id should be associated with this control.

Selecting Controls Once you have added some controls, it's important to understand how to position controls such that they align together, to a grid, or in some other configuration. But first you need select one or more controls. To select a control, first choose the selection tool and simply click on a control. The selected control will appear, surrounded by a border, much like Figure 23.3 below. The small squares in the corners and edges of the border are called sizing handles and allow you to pull, stretch, and resize the control as you require.

> **TIP**
>
> ### Controlling Tab Order
>
> The tab order of a dialog is the order in which controls are selected when the user hits the tab key. You can toggle between displaying tab order or not by hitting the **[Crtl+D]** keys. The dialog tab order will be displayed. Click the mouse on the control you wish to be first in tab order, then second, and so forth to cover all controls. Normally, the **OK** button is first in the tab order, but almost as often the **CANCEL** button is first.

Sizing and Positioning Controls Once you have selected a control, you can perform operations on it. Grab any sizing handle and you can either expand or contract the control in the direction supported by that handle. Corner sizing handles allow you to resize a control's height and width at the same time. Top, bottom, and side sizing handles allow you to make a control taller/shorter or wider/narrower.

You can also position and align controls easily using either the **Layout** menu or the layout toolbar, shown in Figure 23.4.

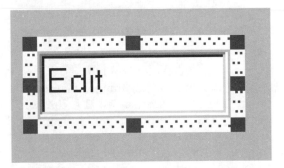

Figure 23.3   A selected control.

Figure 23.4   The Layout toolbar.

> **TIP**
>
> ### Selecting Multiple Controls
>
> In order to align controls together, you need to select the controls you wish to align. You can select additional controls by "shift clicking", that is, holding down the shift key and clicking another control. The additional controls will also be selected, showing their sizing handles just like the first control. You may now apply positioning, alignment, or resizing operations to the selected controls.
>
> You can also select multiple controls by pointing to a position near one of the controls and then holding the mouse down and dragging a rectangle around the controls to be selected. When the mouse is released the controls in the bounding rectangle will be selected.

> **NOTE**
>
> ### Dominant versus Inactive Controls
>
> When you select more than one control, the first control is said to be *dominant*, while the others are said to be *inactive*. All operations will be performed in terms of the dominant control. For example, if you choose to resize the height of all the controls, the size that would be used would be that of the dominant control. The dominant control in a multiple selection is always shown with solid sizing handles, and the inactive controls are shown with hollow handles. If you wish to choose another control as the dominant control, simply click it while holding down the **[Crtl]** key, and the selected control will become the dominant control.

The tools work as follows:

Tool	Layout *Command*	*Description*
	Test	Tests the dialog box.
	Align Controls	Aligns controls left, right, top, or bottom with respect to active or dominant control; that is, all controls will line up with the dominant control on the side selected.
	Center in Dialog	Centers the controls left to right or top to bottom in the dialog; that is, all controls are aligned to the center, right to left, or top to bottom of the dominant control.
	Space Evenly	Spaces the controls evenly either from top to bottom or side to side between the leftmost and rightmost control or the topmost and bottom most control.
	Makes Same Size	Make the controls the same height, width, or both.
	Guide Settings	Toggles the grid settings on and off.

In addition, the **L**ayout menu also contains several other commands that can be applied to controls but that have no toolbar equivalents. They are:

Arrange Buttons	Arranges buttons either on the bottom of the dialog or into the upper right corner.
Size to Content	Sizes text fields to content; that is, expand or contract the control to fit the text entered.
Flip Horizontal	Takes all the controls on the right and places them on the left, and all the controls on the left and places them on the right.

Tab <u>O</u>rder   Shows the tab order of the dialog
box.

> **TIP**
>
> ### Sizing in Dialog Units (DLUs)
>
> Controls can be resized in intervals of dialog units by holding the
> shift key down and hitting an arrow key. Each time you hit the arrow
> key the control's size will change by one DLU. A dialog unit is based
> on the size of the display font for the dialog and defaults to 8-point
> MS San Serif. A vertical dialog unit is the average height of the font
> divided by 8 and the horizontal size is the font size divided by 4.

Sizing Dropdown Combo Boxes Dropdown combo boxes are a little
different from other controls in that in addition to the size of the control, you can also resize the dropped view of the combo box. To resize
the dropdown portion of the combo box, select the control and then click
the down button. The combo box will then be displayed looking something like Figure 23.5. Simply grab one of the sizing handles and
extend or contract the dropped version of the combo box.

Aligning Controls Using Guides and Margins Aligning controls
together and within a dialog is often a tedious and time-consuming
process. Guides, margins, and rulers can speed the process of making
controls align within a dialog.

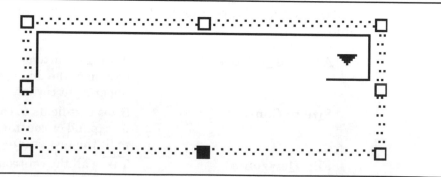

Figure 23.5   A dropdown combo box, shown dropped with sizing handles.

By default, when you first create a dialog box, four guides are provided—top, bottom, right, and left—and are shown as dotted blue lines. Figure 23.6 shows the dialog editor and with default guides.

Using guides, you can

- Align controls
- Move and change guides
- Create your own guides
- Size controls
- Move controls as guides move or independently

Snapping Controls to Guides　　Controls are "snapped" to a guide by selecting a control or group of controls and then bringing them right up next to a guide line. When the control is close to the guide, it will automatically "snap" to that guide. Until removed from the guide, the control and guide will move as one.

Moving a Guide and Its Controls　　Once you have snapped a control or two to a guide line, you can move them as a group by grabbing the margins on one of the rulers and then dragging it left/right or top/bottom. The guide line and all the controls associated with it will move. Alternately, you can move the guide by grabbing the guide itself, rather than the ruler, and moving it one way or the other.

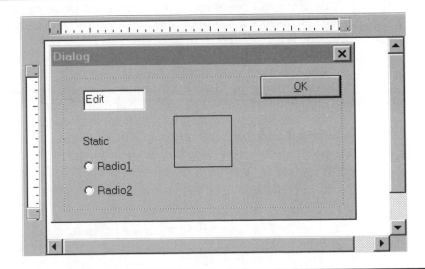

Figure 23.6　　Dialog editor and guides.

When you select a guide or ruler, the actual position of the guide will be displayed in both the ruler and the status bar. Horizontal guides will show distance from the top in the left pane and the bottom in the right, all referenced from the upper lefthand corner of the dialog box. Vertical guides will show distance from left on the left and right on the right.

Creating Your Own Guides   You can easily create your own guides by clicking in the ruler. Wherever you click, a new guide will be entered that can be moved left and right or up and down. Additional guides are very useful for sizing controls.

Sizing Controls with Guides   You can size controls with guides by creating, or using existing, guides. Simply snap one side of each of the controls to one of the guides. Then bring the second guide up next to the controls. Now, by grabbing and moving the guides, the controls will resize. For example, dragging the rightmost guide right would cause the controls to grow to the right.

We've now seen how to add guides, manipulate guides and controls, and even size controls to guides. But what about moving guides and controls independently? What if I add a guide and no longer want to use it?

Moving Guides and Controls Independently   If, for some reason, you wish to move a guide, but want to leave the controls behind simply press the **[shift]** key as you select the guide. When you move the guide, the control positions will stay fixed.

Sometimes the snapping of controls to a guide can also be inconvenient! To disable the snapping effect while you move a guide, simply hit the **[alt]** key first and then drag the guide. Controls will not automatically snap to a guide when it is moved with the **[alt]** key.

You can turn guides off completely by right clicking in one of the rulers and choosing **Guide Settings**. From the **Guide Settings** dialog, choose **none**. After you click OK, all the guides will be removed.

And you can always simply *pull away* a control from a guide by selecting it and dragging it separately.

TIP

Removing Guides

You can remove an individual guide by dragging it to the 0 position of a ruler. Remember to **[alt]** drag the guide if you don't want to move the controls that are snapped to it. In addition, you can clear all guides by right clicking in a ruler and then selecting **Clear All** from the popup menu.

You can move a control independently of a guide by selecting it and dragging it.

> **NOTE**
>
> ### Guides, Sizes, and Dialog Units (DLUs)
>
> Guides, sizes, and other information are displayed in a dialog box in dialog units or *DLUs*.

> **TIP**
>
> ### Changing the Ruler Interval
>
> You can change the tick interval displayed on the guide rulers by right clicking in the ruler area and then choosing **Guide Settings**. From the **Guide Settings** dialog you may change the horizontal or vertical ticks. The default is 5 DLUs for each, but it can be changed as required.

Of course, using guides and margins is not the only way to align controls. You can also use the layout grid.

The Layout Grid The layout grid is just that—a series of grid lines that controls are drawn to automatically as if magnetized. When the layout grid is active, controls will be *snapped* to the grid as they are moved.

You enable the layout grid by selecting <u>G</u>uide Settings from the **<u>L</u>ayout** menu. From the **Guide Settings** menu choose **Grid** and hit the OK button. Your dialog will be overlaid with a grid, and controls will snap to the grid as they are moved.

You can always change the settings on the grid by returning to the **Guide Settings** dialog and changing the grid spacing as desired.

Defining Mnemonic Keys

Most often users will move about in a dialog by either using the mouse, the tab keys, or the arrow keys. Windows supports another method known as *mnemonic keys*. Mnemonic keys allow the user to select settings, buttons, and so on with the keyboard, normally by hitting the [alt] key, followed by another key known as the mnemonic key. While mnemonic keys are not truly supported in the Java Resource Wizard, they can still be implemented from within an application. In the

Chapter 24, we will return to how to implement mnemonic keys. But for now, let's see how we can display mnemonics in our dialog using standard dialog editing principles.

> **NOTE**
>
> ### Mnemonic Keys Not Supported in Visual J++ 1.1
>
> Mnemonic keys are not truly supported in Visual J++ 1.0. That is, the Java Resource Wizard does not generate native code to capture and process a mnemonic key as it is pressed. However, we can certainly learn to implement this functionality ourselves.

Controls are typically of two types—those with an associated caption and those without. Radio buttons, check boxes, and buttons are examples of controls with associated captions. Combo boxes, list boxes, and edit boxes are examples of controls without associated captions.

To create a mnemonic key for a control with an associated caption, simply display the properties for the control in question (If you have forgotten, simply right click and choose properties from the popup or hit **[Alt + Enter]**). In the **General** tab of the control properties you will see the caption displayed. Simply type an ampersand **[&]** before the character you wish to use as the mnemonic. When the dialog is displayed, the mnemonic key will be displayed underlined. For example, the caption "Click & Me" would result in "Click <u>M</u>e".

Creating mnemonics for controls without associated captions takes a little more work but is still quite simple. In addition to the control in question add a static text field that represents the control. Enter whatever caption you would like and precede the mnemonic key with an ampersand as before. Last, make sure that the static text control immediately precedes the control in the tab order.

Even though Visual J++ 1.0 does not support mnemonic keys, by following these simple procedures, when it does your dialogs will automatically support them.

> **TIP**
>
> ### Check Mnemonics
>
> You can check the mnemonics you have added to a dialog box to see if there are any conflicts quickly and easily. Simply right click inside the dialog box and then choose **Check Mnemonics** from the popup. Any conflicts will be pointed out immediately.

Control Properties

We have seen some of the common properties of dialogs, but it's important to know how these properties affect the way our controls work and how the Java Resource Wizard uses these properties to build its Java code. For the most part, Windows properties and Java don't mix. That is to say Windows has a much broader supported set of control properties than the Java Resource Wizard supports. That's not to say that you cannot implement a property in some way—often you can—but the Java Resource Wizard will not do it for you. For the remainder of the section will look at the general properties of a control. So when you set a property, make sure you test it to be sure it does what you expect.

The first of the control properties is the **Control ID**. The control ID will become the name of the object associated with your control. When you select a Control ID for a control, make it something that reflects what the control does. For example, why not *OkButton* for the OK button?

We have already covered the caption and how it effects mnemonic keys, so no more need be said about it.

The **Visible** and **Disabled** properties don't do anything to change the code generated by Java Resource Wizard, nor does the **Help ID** property.

The **Tabstop** and **Group** properties do in fact cause changes to the code. Java fully supports groups and the concept of tab stops.

So what did we really get from the resource editor? A graphical method of creating and manipulating dialogs, which can be expanded and most likely will be in future releases of Visual J++.

Testing a Dialog Box

The last interesting piece of the Dialog editor is the test button on the Dialog editor toolbar. The test button allows you to exercise your dialog, seeing how controls work, and how text entered into edits is displaced. The test button exercises the tab order and points out mistakes in it as well as allowing you to see control groupings and make sure that radio buttons, check boxes, and the like are grouped correctly.

To test a dialog simply hit the test button in the dialog toolbar, choose **Test** from the **Layout** menu or hit **[Ctrl +T]**. Your dialog will be displayed in all its glory. Click, enter text, tab, and otherwise exercise your dialog all you want then either hit the **[Esc]** key, the upper right close button, or the dialog's IDOK or IDCANCEL buttons to end the test. Make whatever changes are required and then retest.

THE MENU EDITOR INTERFACE

Menus allow you to present commands in a simple, concise fashion. The Visual J++ menu editor allows you to lay out menus that will match almost exactly those in the resulting application. Note that due to differences in how browsers display menu's, what Visual J++ display's may not match the end result exactly. The menu editor interface is much simpler than dialog editor, containing new special commands other than cut and paste.

We have already seen how to create resource templates. Open or create one now if you have not already done so. Then, from the **Insert** menu, choose **Resource [Ctrl + R]**, and from the **Insert Resource** dialog, choose **menu**. You will be presented a menu that looks something like the one in Figure 23.7.

To add an entry to the menu, select the empty menu item box and hit enter. Fill in the name of the menu entry in the caption box and hit the return key. If you want to add a mnemonic key, now would be a good time. Figure 23.8 shows a menu with several top-level choices, some intermediate choices, and a cascading submenu.

> **TIP**
>
> ### Don't Forget Right Click
>
> As with almost everything else, most items in the menu editor can be right clicked to show the list of most frequently used commands. When you right click a menu selection, a popup containing cut, paste, and copy, as well as other selections, will be displayed.

Creating and Manipulating Menus Entries

To actually create a menu entry you need only double click one of the new item boxes, which are show in Figure 23.9 as empty entries. You will be presented with an properties sheet something like the one shown in Figure 23.9. Note that for top-level menu items (**File**, **Edit**, and **Third Menu Choice** in Figure 23.8), you will not be able to choose an ID for the menu item.

So, to add a new menu item, either select one of the new item boxes or, using the mouse or arrow keys, select the top-level menu and hit the **[ins]** key. The menu item properties page will immediately be displayed.

The properties of a menu entry control how that menu entry will be displayed and function. Each of the properties is detailed below.

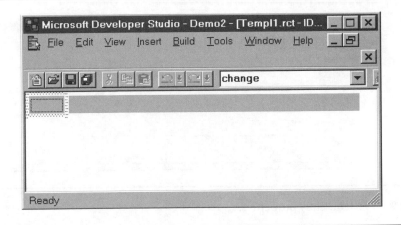

Figure 23.7   An empty menu.

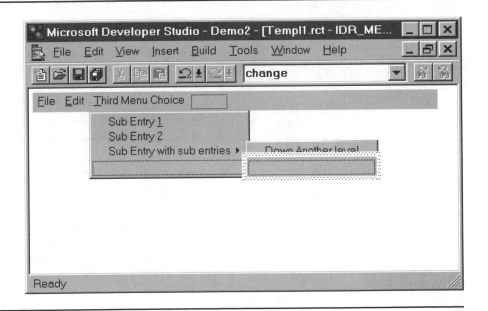

Figure 23.8   A more useful menu showing new item boxes.

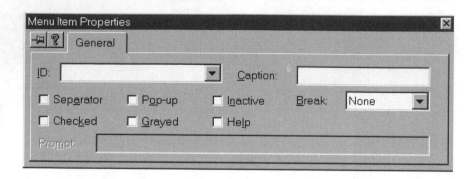

Figure 23.9   Menu entry properties.

Property	Description
ID	The id that will be assigned to the menu entry. If not filled in, then the menu editor will choose a name based on the caption. An ID can normally be a symbol, a quoted string, or an integer.
Caption	The text displayed in the menu for this entry. Place an "&" into the caption before the mnemonic you would like to associated with this entry. Enter "\t" followed by a quick key sequence if so desired.
Separator	If set, this entry is not really a menu choice but rather separates sets of menu choices.
Checked	If set, this menu choice is displayed with a left check mark.
Pop-up	If set, this menu is a cascading hierarchical menu with a popup submenu. Checking this box causes the ID box to gray and a submenu to be displayed to the right.
Grayed	If true, then this menu item is initially inactive.
Inactive	If true, then this menu is always inactive.

Help	Right justifies the menu at runtime.
Break	One of three different values: none; column: for static menu-bar items this item will be placed on a new line; bar: the same as column except that for popup menus separate the menu from its sub menu with a bar or vertical line.
Prompt	Not used by Visual J++.

Cascading Menus

Cascading menus are those that are hierarchical in nature. For example, menu entries may have submenus, and those submenus may have submenus. Figure 23.8 shows an example of a hierarchical menu. An entire menu may be cascading or may have one or more cascading submenu items.

To make the entire menu cascading, select the entire menu (click to the right away from any menu entries), and then set the **View as Popup** property. Figure 23.10 shows a fully cascaded menu.

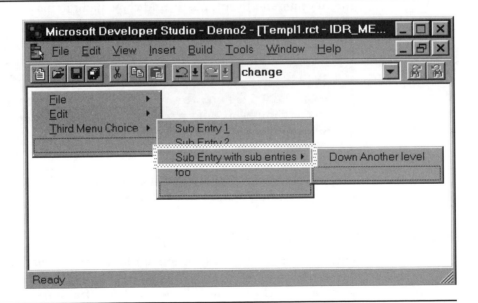

Figure 23.10   Cascaded menu.

To return the menu to a noncascading format, simply repeat the procedure and unset the **View as Popup** property. To make an individual menu entry cascading, simply set the popup property.

Moving and Manipulating Menu Items

You can move individual or groups of menu items around simply using drag-and-drop techniques. Select a menu item or several menu items by shift clicking, and then while holding the mouse down, move them from one place to another. You can move items to a different place in the same menu choice or to a wholly different menu entry.

> **NOTE**
>
> ### Moving Main Menu Entries to Submenus
>
> If you cut and paste or otherwise move main menu items (and their submenu choices) to a position within a submenu, the entire menu choice will become a cascading submenu of the selected submenu. Try it! It's cool!

In addition to selecting and dragging, you can also used the **Edit** menu command to cut, paste, and copy menu items.

> **TIP**
>
> ### You Can Cut and Paste between Different Menus
>
> It's easy to move an entire set of menu choices from one menu to another. Simply open both menus and either select and drag or cut and paste the menu entries from one menu to another.

And that's it for menus! In Chapter 24 we will see how we can integrate menus and dialogs into our Java applications.

RESOURCE TEMPLATES REVIEWED

Once you have created a resource file it can be saved it several ways. The first and most common way is to save your file as a **.rct** or resource template file. From the **File** menu choose **Save As**. At this point you need to choose whether you want to use this resource file as an actual template; that is, one that you will derive future resources from, or one that will be project specific. If this resource file is project specific, then change the directory to whatever is appropriate for the project. If the resource file is going to be used as an actual resource template, then you need to change the directory to **c:\msdev\template** and save it there. In either case, save the resource file with a name applicable to the project or class of templates that the resource file provides.

> **NOTE**
>
> ### Saving Resources as Binaries
>
> You can always save a resource file as a binary or **.res** file. However, some of the flexibility of the resource editor is lost when you do. For example, you can no longer use symbolic names for resources, but rather you will need to use resource numbers. For this reason alone it is strongly suggested that you always save your resource files as **.rct** files.

In the next chapter we will continue looking at dialog and menu resources and see how they can be integrated into our applications using Java Resource Wizard. We shall see what Resource Wizard has done for us, and what it has not, and take another step further in our understanding of Visual J++.

EXERCISES

23-1 Create your own resource template containing a dialog template. Save it in the common location and then create a new dialog from the template.

23-2 Change the size of the font associated with a dialog box (Hint: use the dialog box properties). What happens to the dialog? What about the size of the dialog's DLUs?

23-3 Add two additional guides to a dialog box. What could you use these additional guides for? How many additional guides would be optional for aligning and sizing controls?

23-4 Create a main menu. Add several menu entries to it. Make sure one has cascading submenus.

23-5 Create a second menu. Grab one of the entries in another menu and drag them to this menu. Then change the menu so that it is viewed as a cascading menu.

23-6 Experiment with dialog boxes and properties. What kinds of properties effect the generated code? Which do not? What properties might be candidates for providing support for your application?

The Visual J++ Java Resource Wizard

In this chapter we cover the following topics:

- **The Java Resource Wizard**
- **Integrating a Generated Dialog**
- **Integrating a Generated Menu**
- **Simulating Mnemonic keys**
- **DialogLayout.Java Class**

In the last chapter we took a long and extensive look at dialogs, menus, and popups. In this chapter we shall see how to run Java Resource Wizard to integrate these items into our applets. However, before we go any further, it's important to understand controls and menus and how the Java AWT uses these components. Within the Java AWT there is nothing that says controls must be placed solely into dialogs. Rather, controls can be found within any class derived from the Java AWT's **container** class. Predefined containers are applets, panels, windows, and—of course—dialogs.

Since there are many kinds of containers, Java Resource Wizard does not generate a class derived from a single container class. This would be just too limiting. In order to allow you to add controls to any container, Java Resource Wizard generates a class that takes the **container** for the controls into its constructor. Once you have created your dialog object, you then need to execute the **CreateControls** method, which actually creates and positions the controls into the container specified in the constructor.

Java Resource Wizard also generates an additional class, used by dialogs, that implements the Java AWT **LayoutManager** interface. This class is used by every dialog and mimics the windows positioning of controls in a container. Every control creator type class generated by Java Resource Wizard will use this class to lay out its controls.

Menus are not handled exactly like dialogs for one obvious reason— Java AWT requires that menus appear within a frame. Thus, Java Resource Wizard creates classes which can be contained within **Frame** classes and implements a constructor and CreateMenu method, both similar to the constructor and **CreateControls** methods of a generated dialog class.

With these thoughts in mind lets move on and actually create and test a dialog!

THE JAVA RESOURCE WIZARD

Before you can run the Java Resource Wizard, you must first have a resource file to use as input. If you have not previously created a resource file, then you need to read Chapter 23, and create a resource file with a dialog in it for testing.

Now you are ready to run the Java Resource Wizard by choosing **Java Resource Wizard** from the **Tools** menu. The Java Resource Wizard Step 1 dialog, shown in Figure 24.1 will be displayed.

Enter the resource script file name or use the browse button to select a resource template (**.rct**) or a binary resource file (**.res**) and then hit the **finish** button. Java Resource Wizard will then present you with a dialog that tells you what **.java** files were created from your resource file. An example is shown in Figure 24.2.

NOTE

Generated Files

When you use Java Resource Wizard to generate files from a resource script, you will get a single file for each dialog, menu, defined. In addition, you will also get a copy of the **DialogLayout. java** class used by all control-based classes.

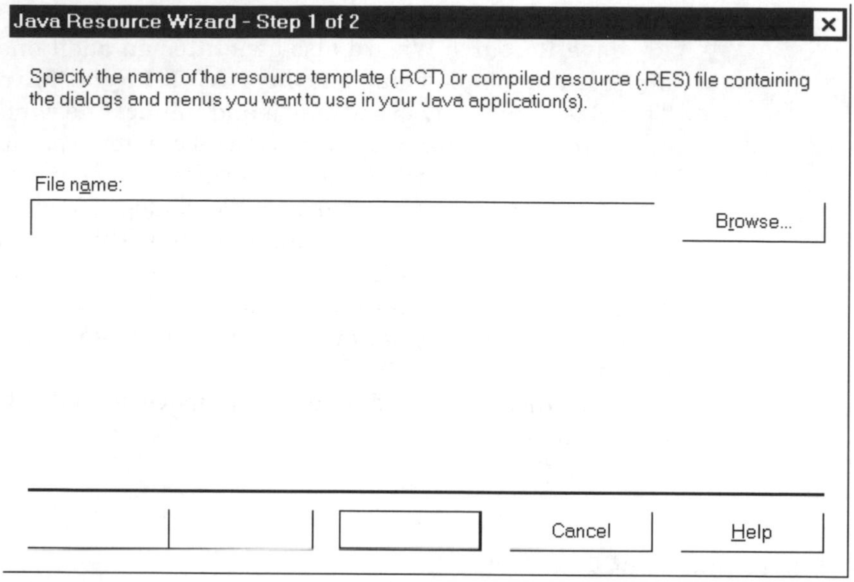

Figure 24.1   The Java Resource Wizard Step 1 dialog.

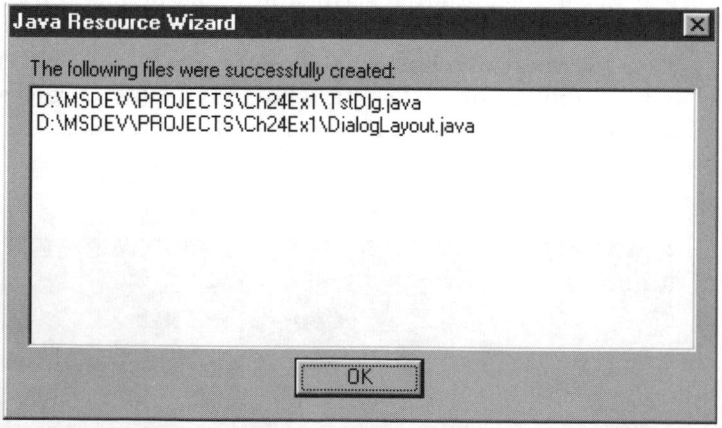

Figure 24.2   Sample generated .java file listing.

INTEGRATING A GENERATED DIALOG

Once we have generated our classes or dialogs, we need to use that generated code. Let's create an empty application that we will use for testing our menus and dialogs. From the File menu, choose **new** and then create a Java applet using Java Applet Wizard. Select **Applet and application** and animation support (not that we really need animation, but I happen to like the way it looks spinning away).

> **NOTE**
>
> ### Chapter 24 Samples
>
> Chapter 24 samples can be found on the accompanying CD ROM as **Ch24Ex1** and so on. The dialogs and underlying **.java** files and class names are based on **NewDialog** (a dialog) and **AMenu** (a menu). You may use any names you wish. And don't forget that the Resource ID controls the name of the dialog, menu, or control in the generated **.java** file.

Import Your New Class

Once you have created an empty applet, open it and find the import section. Add the name of your dialog class as an import (in our example **NewDialog**):

```
import NewDialog;
```

Define an instance of your new dialog: Near the definition of the animation thread define an instance of the dialog.

```
NewDialog dlg;
```

Find the application's **init** method and remove the **Resize** call. We remove the resize call because the dialog size will control the container size. Add the following lines of code:

```
dlg = new NewDialog( this );
dlg.CreateControls();
```

If you wish, remove the call to **drawstring** in **paint** method. It will just confuse the look of the dialog (You can actually leave it in. It won't hurt, but will just look a little strange.)

Add the New Class to the Project

Last, add the new class to your project by opening the file using **Open** from the **File** menu and then selecting the new class file. Once the file has been opened, place the mouse into the code pane and right click. Choose **Add to Project**, select the current project, and the file will be added to your project.

Build and test the applet by choosing **Build** from the **Build** menu.

Now execute your applet. If you used the source code for the **Ch24Ex1** you should see something like Figure 24.3.

We have done nothing to handle the buttons or radio buttons on our menu. And remember the classes associated with the various controls and how you might use them to access your dialog data.

Controls and Their Underlying Classes

Control	Underlying Java AWT Class
Static Text	Label Class
Edit Box	TextField Class or TextArea Class for multi-line edits
Push Button	Button Class
Check Box	CheckBox Class

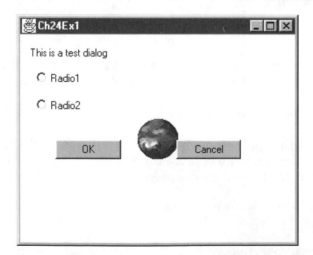

Figure 24.3   Sample dialog.

Radio Button	CheckBox with accompanying CheckboxGroup as required
Combo Box	Choice Class
List Box	List Class
Vertical Scroll Bar	Scrollbar Class with VERTICAL property set.
Horizontal Scroll Bar	Scrollbar Class with HORIZONTAL property set.

Accessing Dialog Controls Data

We have now seen how to position controls into a dialog and then how to integrate that dialog into our applets and applications. But how do you actually access the data in the dialog? Or set and get the various values? Well, the key is in the Resource ID of the dialogs. Remember way back in Chapter 23 when we discussed how to set the Resource ID of a control? Well, when Java Resource Wizard ran that ID, it became the variable name of our control, so the radio button that we named **radio1** has resulted in a **CheckBox** being generated as a member of our dialog box and its name, strangely enough, is **radio1**!

Each variable in our dialog can be referenced through the dialog itself by its ID name. If we had defined a dialog as **somedlg**, then we could reference our controls as **somedlg.control**.

For example, if we had a edit control named **AnEdit**, which has as underlying type **TextField**, we could get its content as follows:

```
String value = somedlg.AnEdit.getText();
```

where **value** would end up containing whatever use had entered the dialog when the data was returned.

All the controls in a dialog are referenced in a similar fashion. Let's look now to menus and see how they are processed.

INTEGRATING A GENERATED MENU

The other major thing that Java Resource Wizard does is produce menus. Let's build on our previous example by adding a menu. If you have not already done so, add a simple menu to your resource template by selecting **Resource** from the **Insert** menu (or **[Ctrl + R]**). Add a few top-level entries and a few dropdown entries.

There are several ways to add menus to an applet. Since menus are inserted into a frame, you must first have a frame. If you have been following along with the examples, then you already have an application that contains a frame. For those of you who have not, we will examine how to create a frame for use in our applets.

Creating a Simple Frame

If your applet does not have a main method or an associated frame, then you need to create one. Simply derive a frame as follows:

In the file containing your applet class, at either the start or the end add the following **handleEvents** method.

```
Class AFrame extents Frame
{
    Aframe(String title)
    {
        super(title);
    }

    //
    // To capture action events add an action method
    //

    public boolean action (Event evt, Object obj)
    {
        Object target = evt.target;
        if (target instance of MenuItem)
        {
            //
            // Add your action specific code here
            //
            return true; // Since we handled this action
        }
    }

    //
    // Alternately you can catch all frame events such as WINDOW_DESTROY
    // and ACTION_EVENT, MOUSE_DOWN etc. with a handleEvents method.
    //
    public boolean handleEvents (Event evt)
    {
        switch(evt.id)
        {
            case Event.WINDOW_DESTROY:
                dispose();
                System.exit();
                return true;
```

```
    case Event.ACTION_EVENT:
        if (evt.target instanceof MenuItem)
        {
            // Handle menu picks
            String menupick = (String)evt.arg;
            if ( menupick.equals("exit"))
            {
                dispose();
                System.exit();
                return true;
            }
        }
        else if (evt.target instanceof Button)
        {
            // Handle buttons picks
            return true;
        }
    case default:
        return super.handleEvent(evt);
} // end switch on event id.
}
}
```

If, when you were creating your application originally, you choose **As applet and application**, then Java AppWizard already created a frame for you. You can add the **handleEvents** method displayed above to this class and update it as required to catch your menu entries and such.

Adding the Menu to a Frame

Now that we have a frame we can add our menu to it. Add a new menu variable to either the **main** method, for applications, or into the applet as shown below.

For Applets Declare two new variables in your applet, somewhere near the top, perhaps near the **Thread** declaration.

```
AFrame aframe;
AMenu amenu;
```

In the applets' **init** method add,

```
// Create our frame
aframe = new AFrame ("This is a test of the emergency menu system");
aframe.resize(100,100);
```

```
// Insert the menu into it.
amenu = new AMenu(aframe);

// Now create the menu items
amenu.CreateMenu();

// And finally show the frame and its associated menu.
aframe.show();
```

Important! Before you compile and run your applet, make sure that you have added the **import AMenu**; statement to your imports section so the Java compiler knows about your menu.

NOTE

Layoutcontrol.java

As was stated in the introduction, when you generate a dialog, you also automatically get a **Layoutcontrol.java file**. If this is your first application then you need to add **Layoutcontrol.java** to your project so that it will be built correctly.

If all went well when you ran your applet, a new frame will appear with your menu entries in it. Experiment for a while and see what happens.

One of the disadvantages of this method is that the frame and the dialog are separate. Let's look for a moment at an application instead and see how we might insert our menu into the applet's dialog.

For Applications As previously mentioned, when you create an application using Java AppWizard, a frame class will be created to house your applet. There is nothing stopping you from actually creating your own frame in your applet and then adding both your dialog and your menu to it. But for now, let's look at the code created by Java AppWizard.

Find the main method and add the menu variable directly below where you the frame variable.

```
Ch24Ex2Frame frame = new Ch24Ex2Frame("Ch24Ex2"); // Existing code
AMenu amenu = new AMenu(frame);                    // add this line
amenu.CreateMenu();
```

Again, don't forget the import statement, **import AMenu**;.

> **NOTE**
>
> ### Rebuild All
>
> If you are having problems running an application or applet, try doing a **rebuild all**. It's easy to get things out of sync and not always easy to tell that you have.

Did we forget anything? Yes, don't forget to add the menu class to the project.

Add the New Class to the Project Ad the menu class to you project by opening the file using **Open** from the **File** menu and then selecting the new class file. Once the file has been opened, place the mouse into the code pane and right click. From the popup choose **Add to Project** and then select the current project.

> **TIP**
>
> ### Resource Templates Are Not Part of Your Project's Dependencies
>
> Under normal circumstances resource templates are not part of your project's dependencies. So, when you update a resource template, the code generated from it is NOT automatically updated. Each time you update your resource file, rerun the Java Resource Wizard to make sure that generated class files are in sync with your application.

And so you see, menus are not hard to implement and use, but they are not free, either. Java Resource Wizard happily provides the graphical part of the menu. But it's up to the developer to add command handlers for the menu choices.

> **NOTE**
>
> ### The Future?
>
> Even though it's not handled today, I wouldn't be a bit surprised if the next release of Visual J++ added a class wizard like interface to support building frames and whatnot for your dialogs and menus. It would be a relatively simple extension and something already supported in the other Visual products.

SIMULATING MNEMONIC KEYS

We have seen how to create dialogs, menus, and some simple dialog handlers. One of the more common windows interface tools is the *mnemonic key* or *keyboard equivalent*. As we've seen before, a mnemonic key is just a keyboard way of using a dialog or menu selection. But Visual J++ doesn't handle mnemonic keys in a built in way. So what can we do? Well, simulate them, of course! This section will give a quick introduction to mnemonic keys so that you, the developer, can get up and going quickly.

First, a little background.

A mnemonic key is one where you hit the key and something happens immediately or you hit the **alt** key followed by a key (or the **[Ctrl]** key followed by a key). We will concentrate on using the **[Ctrl]** key to kick off commands. We could use simple single keys, but when you have one or more edit boxes, then the keystrokes are directed to those boxes and would confuse the user. So, for the purposes of this section we shall limit our discussions to the **[ctrl]** key.

One more thing—Java is still an emerging standard. Nothing has been defined concerning how a user interface *should* look or feel or act, so for our menus and controls we will require that the user enter and hold down a special purpose key before using a keyboard equivalent.

NOTE

Avoid Function Keys

While Windows, Java, and Visual J++ all support the use of function keys, there general use is strongly discouraged. Not all operating systems support the concept of function keys, and we want our Java applets to work across all platforms. So it's in everyone's best interest if we avoid the use of function keys.

Supporting Mnemonic Keys

For our support of mnemonic keys we shall primarily rely on the **handleEvents** method of the frame class. By always embedding our dialogs and menus in frames, we can always have the full frame functionality available to us. With this in mind let's look for a moment at events.

When then user presses a key, any key, a **KEY_PRESS** event is generated. Likewise, when the key is released, we get a **KEY_RELEASE** event. The first event will be the basis for our support of mnemonic keys. When the user presses the **[ctrl]** key, we will note it and the key pressed along with it. The following snippet of code, from a class that extends a frame, shows the processing of these keys to simulate mnemonic keys.

```
//
// Handle the mnemonic keys
//
private handleMneKeys(int key)
{
    switch (key)
    {
        case 'x':
        case 'X':
        {
            dispose();
            System.exit(0);
            return true;
        }
        default: return false; // Unknown control key sequence
    }
}
```

And in the event switch in the **handleEvents** method of the frame class, add the following **KEY_PRESS** events:

```
...
case Event.KEY_PRESS:
{
    if (evt.id == Event.KEY_PRESS &&            // Not a function key
        (evt.modifiers & evt.CTRL_MASK) != 0) // and user hit ctrl key
    {
        return handleMneKeys(evt.key);          // Pass off to handler
    }
}
```

Simple and straightforward enough, and easily extensible to handle all the special keys that you might want to process.

THE DialogLayout.java CLASS AND USER CLASSES

The **DialogLayout.java** class is generated each and every time you create a dialog class from a resource file. However, you need not keep adding it to your projects and then rebuilding it. Rather, you can build it once and use it forever. You can do this by creating your own class directory, adding class files to it, and then making Visual J++ and the Java Virtual Machine aware of your new class directory.

The Java Virtual machine uses a registry entry to find the Classpath, specifically **HKLM\Software\Microsoft\Java VM\Classpath**. This registry entry normally points to **c:\windows\Java\classes\ Classes.zip**.

You can specify additional classpath variables through the CLASS-PATH environment variable and the **Options** dialog of the **Tools** menu. More on that in a moment.

Its important to understand where the Java Virtual Machine and Visual J++ look for class files. If you understand this mechanism, then it will be easier to debug problems that arise from not knowing which **.class** file is being user by your applet or application. Visual J++ uses the aforementioned registry variable to find classes. In addition, any paths set in the options dialog are searched. The Java Virtual Machine, when run from the command line, will first look in the directory pointed to by the classpath registry variable and the CLASSPATH environment variable.

NOTE

Classpath, Classpath, Which Classpath?

If you want to save yourself time and headaches, then create a single classpath directory and use it both for completed classes and as your CLASSPATH environment variable. If you use only a single directory and point all things to it, then there will never be any question as to what your application is finding when you search for a class.

To create your own supplementary class directory you need only create the directory and add it to your classpath. I suggest **c:\windows\ java\extclass**, but you can use anything you like. Add it to your classpath variable as follows: For Windows 95, in your **autoexec.bat** add the following line.

```
SET CLASSPATH=somedevice:\somepath
```

For Windows NT, use the control panel system applet and using the environment tab set

```
CLASSPATH=somedevice:\somepath
```

In addition, using the Visual J++ options dialog, you can add additional directories by selecting **Options** under the **Tools** menu and then clicking the **directories** tab. Make sure Java Virtual Machine is selected for **Platform** and **Class Files** is shown in the **Show For directories** . Select a blank entry, denoted by the dotted line box, and double click it. Then enter your path.

TIP

Classpath Search Order

You can change the search order of class paths added in the **Tools/Options** dialog by selecting an entry and hitting the up arrow to move it forward in the hierarchy or the down arrow to move it backward. You can delete entries with the X button. The dotted line box adds a new entry.

EXERCISES

24-1   Update the **Ch24Ex1** example to rename the buttons to *forward* and *backward*. Also add a static text field that tells the direction the globe is spinning. Capture the button presses and have the backward button change the direction to backward and the forward button to forward. Clicking a button twice should do nothing. (Hint: You will need to add an action method to your class.)

24-2   How might you automatically detect changes to a dialog. (Hint: Think threads.) What are the pros and cons of this method? What about specifying the threads as **synchronized**?

24-3   Add a handler for your menu items. What would happen if had two main menu choices with similar submenu choices? Could you handle this? If so, how?

24-4   Extend the sample mnemonic key hander to handle **[meta]** keys as well. What happens if you override the **action** or **keyPress** method in your main applet? Do they get called? Or does just the frame **handleEvents** method get called? What are the pros and cons of using the **keyPress** versus the **handleEvents** methods?

24-5   If you use the same keys for two menu items, what happens? Can you tell which was in use? Can you simulate the windows behavior of the **[alt]** key opening the menu and then dropping down the selection that with the next key pressed?

The Visual J++ Source Editor

In this chapter we cover the following topics:

- **Basic File Operations**
- **Basic Editing Operations**
- **Using Multiple Source Windows**
- **Tips and Tricks**

By now you have used the text editor quite a bit—adding and deleting text, perhaps creating new source files, and certainly editing and saving files. In this chapter we will see just how full featured the Microsoft Developers Studio editor really is and learn about editing files, doing searches, and, in general, using the editor features.

BASIC FILE OPERATIONS

Basic file operations are those that you need every day, such as opening one or more files, creating new files, saving open files, and often printing files. You have been using some of these operations for a while, but now let's look at the specifics of each.

Creating New Files

To create a new file, just follow these steps: (1) Choose **New** from the **File** menu or **[Ctrl+N]**. (2) Choose **Text File** from the **Files tab** of the

New property sheet and then hit the OK button. You will presented with a new completely empty file to work on.

Opening Existing Files

You open a file, in a fashion similar to creating a new file. Choose **Open** from the **File** menu or **[Ctrl+O]**. The common **File Open** dialog will appear, shown in Figure 25.1.

With the **File Open** dialog you can do many things, such as:

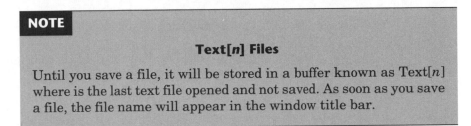

Figure 25.1   The common File Open dialog.

- Specify the file types to display
- Control whether file details are shown
- Choose how the file will be opened
- Select other directories for browsing
- Perform file operations such as delete and others

Let's look quickly at what each of the fields does. Figure 25.2 shows the expanded version of the Look in field (with the dropdown pressed).

Icon	Name	Description
N/A	**Look in**	The Look in drop down combo shows the current folder being displayed in the window directly below it. Click the down arrow to see the exact path or to navigate up and down.
	Up One	Moves up one level from the current directory.
	New Folder	Creates a new directory at the current directory level.
	List/Details	Toggles between showing a list of files (the default) and showing file details (size, etc.).

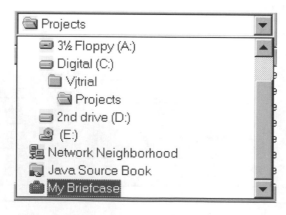

Figure 25.2   The Look in field.

Icon	*Name*	*Description*
N/A	**File/Dir List**	The large window in the middle of the common dialog shows the contents of the current directory including subfolders. See the tip box below for additional information about this box.
		You may double click a file in the box to open it.
N/A	**File name**	Enters a fully qualified file name, a wildcard specification, or a network path to a file that you would like to open.
		If you enter a wildcard specification and hit the return key, then the files that match will be displayed in the file/directory window. You may enter any number of wildcard masks by separating them with semicolons.
N/A	**File of types**	Selects one of a set of predefined file masks. Supplied masks are for HTML files, Java files, and a score of others.
N/A	**Open as read only**	Sets the open as read-only check box to set the read-only attribute on the file being opened. You may still edit a file marked as read-only, however, you will be prompted to "Save As" if you choose to save the file.
N/A	**Open As**	You may allow Microsoft Developers Studio to try to open the file with the correct editor (Default or Auto) or you may choose one of the supplied editors to open the file.

TIP

You Can Do Things with the File/Dir List **Window**

When you open a file with **Open** from the **File** menu, try right clicking in the **File/Dir List** window. Or select a file and hit the delete key (make sure it's one you don't want!). What happens? The **Open File** dialog supports quite a bit more then just opening files.

CHAPTER 25

NOTE

Most Recently Used File List

Beneath the list of standard files operations are two *Recent File* lists. You can select either **Recent Files** or **Recent Workspaces** and quickly return to a recently edited file or project. In addition you and quickly open a file or workspace by typing the assigned hotkey sequence.

Opening Multiple Files

You can select and open more then one file at a time easily by selecting **Open** from the **File** menu. When the **Open File** dialog is displayed, either (1) **[shift]** click: To select contiguous files (those listed next to each other) select the first one and then **[shift]** click to highlight additional files—that is, hold the **[shift]** key down as you select one or more files. Once you have highlighted the files you wish to open, hit the return key or the OK button. Or, (2) **[ctrl]** click: To select noncontiguous files (those separated by files you DO NOT want to open) you can **[ctrl]** click—that is, select the first file by clicking it and then hold the **[ctrl]** key down as you click on the other files you wish to open. Once you have selected the files you wish to open, hit the return key or the OK button and the files will be opened.

TIP

Shift Clicking and Files Displayed

Note that you can only open multiple files if they are displayed in the file/directory window. You may wish to select files to display by entering your own file open mask in the File name window and then selecting from the files matching your mask.

Saving Files

Once you have opened a file and changed it, you most likely will want to save it. You can save files in many ways: all changed files, selected changed files, individual files, or files with new names. Let's take a look at how to do each of these things.

Note that changed files have a asterisk (*) displayed next to the file name in the title bar or in the Windows display dialog.

Save All Files	Selects **Save All** from the **File** menu to save all changed files.
Save Selected Files	Brings up the **Windows** file dialog by selecting Windows from the **Window** menu. From the **Windows** file dialog choose the files to save by either clicking, shift-clicking, or control-clicking.
Save as a New File	Selects **Save As** from the **File** menu. When prompted, select an appropriate name.

TIP

Save Related Options

A group of options is related to saving files. To see or change files options, choose **Options** from the **Tools** menu. From the **Editor** tab you can view and change file-save related options.

Printing Files

We've talked about creating new files, opening existing files, and saving changed files. Sometimes it's just easier to have printed copy of a file. With Developers Studio you can print a selected portion of a file, print an entire file, or print on-line documentation.

Printing a Complete Source File Make sure the file you want to print is active and then choose **Print** from the **File** menu. The **Print** dialog will be displayed. Click OK to print or cancel to cancel.

Printing Selected Text If you had selected some amount of text and chosen **Print** from the **File** menu, the **Print** dialog will be displayed, but instead of the **Print Range** field defaulting to **All** and graying out the **Selection** check box, **Selection** will be the default. Choose OK to print the selection. Choose Cancel to cancel.

> ### TIP
>
> ### Printing On-Line Documentation
>
> If you had opened a book on-line or other help source, by for example placing the cursor on a keyword and hitting the **[f1]** key, you can print the entry by choosing **Print** from the **File** menu or right clicking the mouse in the InfoPane and then selecting **Print Topic** from the popup menu.

BASIC EDITING OPERATIONS

Opening and closing files is good, but we really need to be able to edit, replacing strings as required, cutting code, pasting to other places, and things like that.

Cut, Paste, Copy, and Delete

All cut, paste, copy, and clear operations all start with the same thing—selected text. Select text by placing the mouse cursor at the point of the selection and then pressing the left mouse button and dragging the mouse. Text will be selected and then shown as white letters on a black background.

Once you have selected text then you can perform operations on it. Each of these operations is described below.

Action	Keyboard Shortcut	Description
Cut	Ctrl + X	Select **Cut** from the **Edit** menu. This option cuts the selected text and places it into the clipboard.
Paste	Ctrl + V	Select **Paste** from the **Edit** Menu. This option pastes the contents of the clipboard into the document.
Copy	Ctrl + C	Select **Copy** from the **Paste** Menu. This option copy the current selection to the clipboard.
Delete	Del key	Hit the Delete key. This option deletes the current selection from the file.

Editing with Drag-and-Drop

You can edit by using drag-and-drop within a single Visual J++ window, or if multiple windows are displayed across windows.

To use drag-and-drop editing, select the text you wish to move, then, holding the right mouse button down, drag it to its new location. You can also drag a copy of text to another location by holding down the [ctrl] key as you drag the text to its destination.

TIP

Undo and Redo

You can always undo the last editor operation by selecting **Undo** from the **Edit** menu or by hitting [**Ctrl+Z**]. You can redo the last editor operation by selecting **Redo** from the **Edit** menu or by hitting [**Ctrl +Y**]. Certain operations, such as simple text editing, can be undone several commands back. Other operations, such as replace all, can only be undone backward a single command.

Search and Replace

Often when writing code it's important to be able to search for and replace strings. Developers Studio supports search and replace within the currently active window as well as a Find in Files functionality that we will discuss a little later.

Regular Expressions For those of you with a Unix background, regular expressions will be an old familiar sight. For those who have never seen once before, a *regular expression* is a text pattern that matches text programmatically rather then as an exact match. Developers Studio supports regular expressions in both **Search** and **Replace**. Before we look at **Search** and **Replace** we need to understand a little about regular expressions and how they work. A few simple examples follow.

Expression	*Matches*	*Description*
`foo[a-z]`	fooa, foob, fooc, through fooz.	Matches any string starting with foo and ending in any character in the range a to z.

Expression	*Matches*	*Description*
`.oo[a-zA-Z]`	aooa, aoob, aooc, as well as booa, boob, booc, and so on.	Matches any string that starts with any character containing two o's in a row and ends in any character.
`[^0-9][a-zA-Z]bar`	fbar, Fbar etc, but not 1bar.	Matches strings that do not start with a number, are followed by a character, and end in bar.

Each of the editor emulations in Microsoft Developers Studio supports regular expression **Search** and **Replace**. The following list of expressions is supported by Microsoft Developers Studio.

.	Matches any SINGLE character.
[ ]	Matches any of the set of characters contained in the brackets. Use the caret symbol (**^**) to indicate NOT. For example **[^abc]*** would match any string not starting in a,b, or c.
^	Matches the beginning of a line. **^[a-z]** would match any string starting on a new line starting with a lower case letter in the range a through z.
$	Matches the end of a line.
\(somestring\)	**somestr** is a tagged expression to be retained for replacement. When used with a replace string, the **somestring** could be retained. For a search of the form **\(foo\)bar** and a replacement of **\1barr** would replace **foobar** with **foobarr**.
\~	Not the next character. For example, **c\~ad** would match **cod** but not **cad**.
\{char\!char}	Matches any one of the characters between the range specified. For example, **\{a\!b}** would match any combination of a and b, such as aa, ab, ba, bb, and so on. This option is often called or.

*	Matchs 0 or more of the preceding character(s). **Fo*bar** matches **fbar**, **fobar**, **foobar**, **fooobar**, and so on.
+	The same as asterisk, but requires one or more matches. **Fo+bar** matches **fobar** but not **fbar**.
{\somechars\}	Matches any sequence of **somechars**. For example, {\foo\}bar matches **foobar**, **foofoobar** and so on.

In addition, there are a group of special expressions having the following meanings:

\:a	Matches any single alpha character. Equivalent to [a-zA-Z0-9].
\:b	Matches white space.
\:c	Matches any single alpha character. Equivalent to [a-zA-Z].
\:d	Matches any single number character. Equivalent to [0-9].
\:n	Matches any unsigned number. Equivalent to \{[0-9]+\.[0-9]*\![0-9]*\.[0-9]+\![0-9]+\}.
\:z	Any unsigned integer.
\:h	Any hex character. Equivalent to [0-9a-fA-F].
\:i	Any C/C++ identifier. Equivalent to [a-zA-Z_$][a-zA-Z0-9_$]+.
\:w	Any English word. Equivalent to [a-zA-Z].
\:q	Any quoted string. Equivalent to \{"[^"]*"\!'[^`]*'\}.

TIP

Regular Expressions in Epsilon and BRIEF

The Epsilon and BRIEF emulations also support regular expressions, but using a different set for pattern matches. See the Visual J++ online documentation for more information.

We've learned a little about regular expressions. Let's now see how we can put that knowledge to use.

Searching   There are three ways for a search to be conducted. First and simplest is simply string matching, where you enter a search string and the editor finds instances of that string. The second is incremental search. Using incremental search you enter text, and as the text is entered matches are displayed. The third method is using regular expressions. Visual J++ supports all three of these methods of finding strings as well as more advanced techniques such as searches through multiple files and tagged expressions.

Simple and Regular Expression Searches   To search in a file using a text search string, click the mouse pointer somewhere in the text window. The place where you clicked, often called the *insertion point*, is where the search will begin. Select **Find** from the **Edit** menu. The find dialog, shown in Figure 25.3 will be displayed.

The fields in the Find dialog are:

Find what

Enter the search string or a regular expression. You can use the arrow to the right of the **Find What** field to select a regular expression template. Once a template is selected, you can then enter into the regular expression the exact strings you are interested in. If you use a regular expression, make sure you set the **Regular expression** check box. In addition, you can use the dropdown list to select from any one of the last sixteen searches.

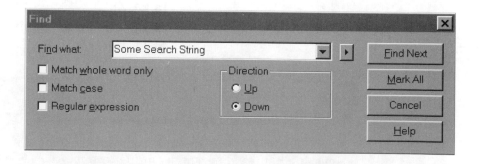

Figure 25.3   Sample find dialog.

Match whole word only	Only exact whole word matches will be highlighted. Words embedded in other words will not match.
Match case	Only those strings that match exactly (if checked) will be selected.
Regular expression	Set this check box if you have entered a regular expression in the **Find what** field.
Direction	Search either backward in the file (up, toward the beginning of file) or forward in the file (down, toward the end of file).
Find next	Repeat the last search.
Mark All	Set a bookmark on each of the lines that matches the search.

Searching with regular expressions is almost as easy as searching for normal text strings. Simply enter a regular expression in the **Find what** field of the **Find** dialog, check the **Regular expression** check box, and then hit OK.

Finding Strings across Files   You can do searches across files as easily as in a single file by selecting **Find in Files** from the **Edit** menu. The **Find in Files** dialog, shown below in Figure 25.4, will be displayed.

The fields in the find in files dialog are:

Find what	Enter the search string or a regular expression. You can use the arrow to the right of the **Find what** field to select a regular expression template. Once selected, you can then enter into the regular expression the exact strings you are interested in. If you use a regular expression, make sure you set the **Regular expression** check box. In addition you can use the dropdown list to select from any one of the last sixteen searches.
In files of type	Enter the file extension of the files type(s) you wish to search. Separate different types with a semicolon or select from the dropdown list.

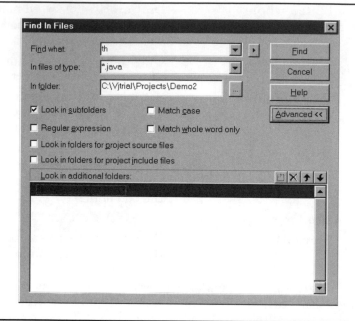

Figure 25.4   Find in Files dialog after pressing the Advanced button.

In folder	Select the top of the search tree. Use the browse button to view the current device and directory path.
Look in subfolders	Set this check box if you wish your search to examine subdirectories as well.
Match case	Only those strings that match exactly (if checked) will be selected.
Regular expression	Set this check box if you have entered a regular expression in the Find What field.
Match whole word only	Only exact whole word matches will be highlighted. Words embedded in other words will not match.
Advanced	Choose the **Advanced** button if you wish to select specific subdirectories to search rather then all subdirectories.

Look in Project Folders for Source Files	Set this option to look in project subdirectories as well. These directories are control by the **Project Settings** directories. See the **Directories** tab of the options dialog from the tools menu for a list o f source and include file directories.
Look in Project Folders for Include Files	Does not apply to Visual J++.
Look in Additional Folders	Displayed when the advance button is pressed. Add specific folders to the search list. Choose the browse button to browse up and down the directory tree.

Incremental Search   Incremental Search is a powerful tool for finding the text or section of a file you want. With Incremental Search, as you type, the next string that matches what you have typed is displayed. As you enter more text, you can further and further refine the search until the exact text you are looking for can be found. See the note box below to see how to enter your own special keyboard sequence for the Incremental Search command.

NOTE

Incremental Search Is Now Bound to a Shortcut in Advanced Edit menu

Visual J++ did not previously bind Incremental Search to either a menu or a toolbar. You can select your own keyboard bindings by selecting **Toolbars** from the **View** menu. From the **Toolbars** menu, click **customize** and then select the **keyboard** tab. Select the name of the editor where you want to add the keyboard sequence to represent (main or text would be the most logical) and then choose an appropriate command from the commands list. Finally enter a shortcut key in the **Press New Short Cut** field and select **Assign**. You can now hit your custom key sequence to execute the command. Try adding a sequence such as **[ctrl+shift+I]** for incremental search backward.

Once you have bound the Backward Incremental Search command to a keyboard sequence, you can use it. Hit your keyboard sequence and the command will be displayed in the status bar. Enter text until you find the desired string. Hit the **[esc]** key to end the search.

Replacing Text   Well, now we know how to find text. It's often just as important to replace text as well. The **Replace** dialog, shown in Figure 25.5, is used for this and brought up by selecting **Replace** from the **Edit** menu.

The fields in the replace dialog are:

Find what	Enter the search string or a regular expression. You can use the arrow to the right of the **Find what** field to select a regular expression template. Once this is selected, you can then enter into the regular expression the exact strings you are interested in. If you use a regular expression, make sure you set the **Regular expression** check box. In addition, you can use the dropdown list to select from any one of the last sixteen searches.
Replace with	Replacement text. You cannot use regular expressions in the **Replace with** field.

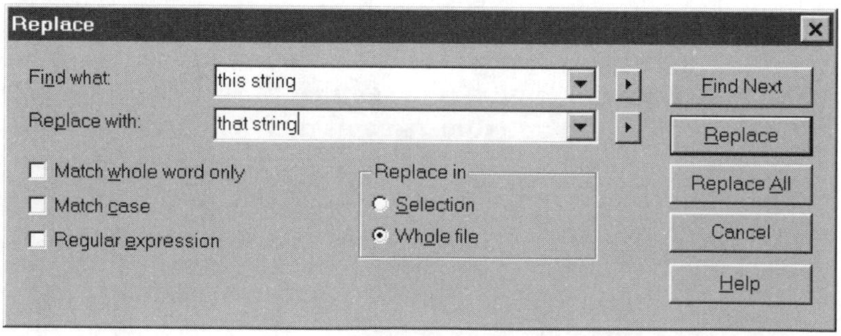

Figure 25.5   The Replace dialog.

Match whole word only	Only exact whole word matches will be highlighted. Words embedded in other words will not match.
Match case	Only those strings that match exactly (if checked) will be selected.
Regular expression	Set this check box if you have entered a regular expression in the **Find what** field.
Replace in	Replace in either the whole file or the selected section.
Find next	Redo the most recent find.
Replace	Replace the single found instances with the **Replace with** text.
Replace All	Replace all strings found, without asking.

TIP

Search and Replace Regular Expressions

If you plan on using search and replace with regular expressions, be careful. Try out your regular expression, first using find only. Regular expressions have a habit of matching things you don't expect. And you can only undo the LAST regular expression replace. Not an entire set.

USING MULTIPLE SOURCE WINDOWS

If you have opened more then one file, or edited a project's resource while having source code open, then you have already used multiple windows. In this section will examine briefly how multiple windows operate and operations that can be performed on them.

Everyone has seen the basic operations that can be performed on windows. Let's just list them for the record, all available from the **Windows** menu item.

New Window	Create a new empty window.
Split	Split the current window.
Hide	Hide a hideable window (such as the output window).

Cascade	Cascade the currently open windows.
Tile Horizontally	Tile the current set of windows horizontally.
Tile Vertically	Tile the current set of windows vertically.
Close All	Close all the current opening windows, prompting to save changed buffers.

In addition to the previous commands, the **Windows** command in the Windows menu displays a dialog, similar to the one shown in Figure 25.6, that can be used to select and manipulate windows and buffers.

Each of the current windows is shown, whether displayed or not. Windows listed with an asterisk to the right of the name denote buffers that have been changed but not saved.

If you have many windows open, it's convenient to be able to display the list and activate windows without having to search for them. You can select windows to save or perform other actions on by either clicking, shift-clicking, or control-clicking. Once one or more windows

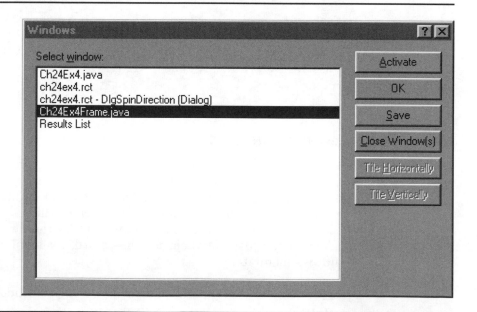

Figure 25.6   The Windows dialog.

have been selected, you can then either activate, save, or close the windows by selecting the appropriate button.

TIPS AND TRICKS

There are so many additional topics that we might discuss with respect to the Developers Studio editor. Several of the most useful topics have been chosen and documented here. Enjoy!

Using Bookmarks

Bookmarks are a way to note where you were in a particular file you left off. You can set named or unnamed bookmarks and then reference them quickly. Named bookmarks are saved between editing sessions. Unnamed bookmarks are temporary and are lost when the file they are in is closed.

Unnamed bookmarks Unnamed bookmarks are by far the most useful of the two types. They are quick and easy to use. To set an unnamed bookmark, set the cursor on the line where you wish the bookmark to be placed and hit **[Alt +F2]**. A blue round cornered square will appear as a visual indicator of the bookmark. Select **[Alt +F2]** again to remove a previously set bookmark. To move between unnamed bookmarks, hit the **[F2]** key.

Named bookmarks You can also set named bookmarks in your code. Named bookmarks are different from unnamed bookmarks for more the just the obvious reason that they have a named assigned to them. Named bookmarks are permanent until removed. That is, they survive file opens and closes. In addition, you can jump to a named bookmark whether the file it is in is open or not. Even if you delete the line where a named bookmark is set, the bookmark remains. An unnamed bookmark is lost if the line it is set on is deleted.

You set a named bookmark by selecting **Bookmark** from the **Edit** menu. The bookmark dialog is displayed. You can enter a new bookmark by entering a name in the **Name** dropdown and then pressing the **add** button. You can delete a named bookmark by selecting it from the list of known bookmarks beneath the name dropdown and then pressing the **delete** button. And you can go to a named bookmark by selecting it from the list of known bookmarks and then pressing the **go to** button.

> **TIP**
>
> ### Deleting Multiple Named Bookmarks
>
> You can delete several named bookmarks at once by selecting them from the bookmark's dialog by clicking, shift-clicking, or control-clicking and then pressing the delete button. The selected bookmarks will then be deleted.

Syntax Coloring

Developers Studio provides an interesting feature known as syntax coloring. Syntax coloring displays different parts of your code in different colors, offering visual clues as to what something is. Syntax coloring is on by default and can be turned off on a file-by-file basis. Right click in a window or choose **Properties** from the **View** menu. Using the language dropdown, select none for no coloring or select the appropriate language.

Changing the Default Syntax Coloring Scheme   You can change the colors, fonts, and other attributes of a file type with Visual J++. See the online documentation under the topic *Setting Syntax Coloring* if you wish to enhance the coloring schemes to support user-defined types.

If you wish to change the default coloring for Java or HTML defined language elements, choose **Options** from the **Tools** menu and select the **Format** tab. From the **Category** window choose **Source Windows**. The **Colors** list box will then be updated to display the known language elements. Choose an element and then its foreground and background color. Select OK to make the change.

Editor Emulations

Developers Studio supports two of the more popular editors via the **Compatibility** tab in the **Options** dialog. The currently supported editor emulations are:

- Visual C++ 2.0
- BRIEF
- Epsilon

To select an editor emulation choose **Options** from the **Tools** menu and select the **Compatibility** tab. From the **Recommended Options For** dropdown, select your emulation of choice.

> **NOTE**
>
> ### Not All Features Are Supported
>
> Developers Studio does not support all the features of the BRIEF and Epsilon editors, specifically, those that support macros and shelling to the OS. See the online Visual J++ documentation for an exact list of supported versus unsupported features.

Recording and Playing Back Keystrokes

Developers Studio allows you to record and play back keystrokes. This makes the task of entering repetitive or otherwise tedious commands a little easier. Recorded keystrokes are called Macros and may be named and run as required.

Macros are recorded, deleted and selected for playback by choosing **Macro** from the **Tools** menu selection. You will be presented with the Macro dialog. Select an existing macro to edit or enter a name and choose **Record**. You may now enter keystrokes etc. Choose either stop or pause from the **Record** dialog to complete your macro. Macros are recorded in VBScript and you have the full power of VBScript at your fingertips! You can edit and change your macro to your hearts content!

In addition to creating and editing macros, you can use the **Macro** dialog to assign your macros to toolbar entries or bind them to keys. Press the **Options** button to expand the Macro dialog and then choose **Toolbars** to add a macro to a toolbar. Or choose **Keystrokes** to bind a keyboard sequence to a new or existing macro.

In addition to the macros you create Visual J++ comes complete with an extensive set of sample macros which you can use, view and edit.

And of course, if you are ever struck, you can always use the **Macro Help** button to display the help and learn more about macros in general and the VBScript macro language.

Customizing Print Jobs

You can customize the way a file prints by changing the header, footer, file name, and margins. From the **File** menu choose **Page Setup**. The **Page setup** dialog is displayed. The following keywords are recognized as having special meaning when entered in a header or footer.

Command	*Action*
&f	Insert File Name into header/footer.
&p	Insert page number.
&t	Insert current System Time.
&d	Insert current System Date.
&l	Left align the date, time, or page number.
&r	Right align the date, time, or page number.
&c	Center align the date, time, or page number.

Set the margins are required and then choose OK.

Editor Settings

The last topic we will look at in out tips and tricks section is that of editor settings. Many editor settings are maintained by the **Options** dialog. We've seen the supported emulations under the **Compatibility** tab of the **Options** dialog as well as **Syntax Coloring**. But there are many other bells and whistles that can be set. For instance, the **tabs** tab sets default tab behavior; the **editor** tab supports various save options; the **debug** tab supports various debug settings.

There are eight options tabs in all, supporting a wide variety of editor settings. Look closely at the **Options** dialog. I'm sure you'll find something there that will make your editing easier and more productive.

EXERCISES

25-1 Bind some keyboard sequence to incremental search forward and a different sequence to incremental search backward. What keyboard shortcuts did you choose and why?

25-2 Write out the meaning of the following regular expressions in English and give examples of strings matched.

```
fo*bar
fo+bar
[a-zA-Z_$][a-zA-Z0-9_$]+
[^abcd][e-zA-Z]+
```

25-3   Find all instances of the word **Thread** in the your projects
        directory. Can you change them all to **MyThread**? Can you
        write a regular expression search to replace some import state-
        ment with one that includes not only the original statement but
        also one that includes your own thread class definition?

25-4   How you would customize your print jobs to print the file name
        in the upper left corner and the current system date and time in
        the right corner? Add the page number, centered at the bottom.

25-5   Set the color of comments to black on gray using Syntax color-
        ing. Are there any other coloring schemes that you like?

CHAPTER 26

Additional Visual
J++ Tools

In this chapter we cover the following topics:

- Jview.exe **reference**
- JVC.exe **reference**
- Windiff.exe **reference**
- Zoomin.exe **reference**

In this, the final chapter of Section II, we will take a look at several miscellaneous topics that have not been covered in prior chapters. Covered in depth are the **JView.exe** interpreter; **JVC.exe**, the Java compiler; **Windiff.exe**, a program for showing files differences graphically; and **Zoomin.exe**, a tool for examining portions of the screen.

Jview.exe **REFERENCE**

Jview.exe is a tool for running Java applications that supports both retail and debug versions of applications. **Jview.exe** does not currently support running pure Java applets, but rather only can run Java applications that contain a **main** function.

Command Syntax

In its simplest form **Jview.exe** is run from the command line and takes the name of a class file containing a **main** function and begins execution there. For example,

```
Jview someclass[.class]
```

The class extension is optional.

The application defined in **someclass** will then start up and run to completion.

The complete syntax of the **Jview.exe** command is

```
JView [options] Someclass [application arguments]
```

where **options** is zero or more of the following

1. **/cp:a** *path*
   - Append *path* to the path specified by the **CLASSPATH** variable, that is, add it to the end of the **CLASSPATH**.
   - If you enter more then one **/cp:a** path, then the paths are concatenated together.
2. **/cp:p** *path*
   - Prepend *path* to the path specified by the CLASSPATH variable, that is, add *path* to the beginning of the CLASSPATH.
   - If you enter more then one **/cp:p** path then the paths are prepended right to left, with the left most being entered in the **CLASSPATH** first.

Someclass is the class file containing the main method, and *application arguments* are the arguments to be passed to the main method.

NOTE

Jview **Is Heavily Influenced by the** CLASSPATH

The way **Jview** runs and where it ultimately finds the classes required to run is heavily influenced by the CLASSPATH. See the section DialogLayout.java Class and User Classes in Chapter 24 for a detailed description of how the **CLASSPATH** variable is used.

Examples

Example 1

```
JView /cp:a apath someclass
```

would execute **someclass** using the current CLASSPATH variable but appending to the end of the search path the path **apath**. The resulting class path would look something like

```
${CLASSPATH};apath
```

If several **/cp:a** options were entered, they would be added to existing CLASSPATH left to right. For example,

```
JView /cp:a apath1 /cp:a apath2 someclass
```

would result in

```
${CLASSPATH};apath1;apath2
```

Example 2

```
JView /cp:p ppath someclass
```

would execute **someclass** using the current **CLASSPATH** variable but prepending to the start of the search path the path **ppath**. The resulting class path would look something like

```
apath;${CLASSPATH}
```

If several **/cp:p** options were entered, they would be added to existing **CLASSPATH** right to left. For example,

```
JView /cp:p ppath1 /cp:p path2 someclass
```

would result in

```
ppath2;ppath1;${CLASSPATH}
```

NOTE

JVC.exe **is Heavily Influenced by the CLASSPATH**

The way **JVC.exe** runs and the resulting code it produces is heavily influenced by the **CLASSPATH**. See the section DialogLayout .java Class and User Classes in Chapter 24 for a detailed description of how the **CLASSPATH** variable is used.

JVC.exe **REFERENCE**

> **JVC.exe** is the Miscrosoft Java compiler. **JVC.exe** produces a compiled **.class** file that may or may not contain debugging information based on compilation switches.

Command Syntax

> In its simplest form **JVC.exe** takes a .java file and produces a **.class** file. The complete syntax of the **JVC.exe** command is
>
> ```
> JVC [options] somefile.java
> ```
>
> **somefile.java** can be any valid operating system file name. The file name can be relative or defined by an exact path and may omit the **.java** extention.
>
> **Command Options** You may use any combination of options. JVC will use the last option encountered (rightmost) if conflicting options are entered. The following options are available in alphabetical order by function.
>
> ***Displaying Options***   The **/?** option causes JVC to display all the supported options. When run, it produces output similar to that shown below.
>
> ```
> Microsoft (R) Visual J++ Compiler Version 1.00.6229
> Copyright (C) Microsoft Corp 1996. All rights reserved.
>
> Usage: JVC [options] <filename>
>
> /cp <classpath>    set class path for compilation
> /cp:p <path>       prepend path to class path
> /cp:o[-]           print classpath
> /d <directory>     root directory for class file output
> /g[-]              full debug information (g:l, g:d)
>    /g:l[-]         generate line numbers <default=none>
>    /g:t[-]         generate debug tables <default=none>
> /nowarn            turn off warnings <default=warn>
> /nowrite           compile only - do not generate class files
> /O[-]              full optimization (O:I,O:J)
>    /O:I[-]         optimize by inlining <default=no opt>
>    /O:J[-]         optimize bytecode jumps <default=no opt>
> /verbose           print messages about compilation progress
> /w{0-4}            set warning level <default=2>
> /x[-]              disable extensions <default=enabled>
> ```

Generating Debugging Information   **/g[-]** generates debugging information.

For example,

```
JVC /g somefile.java
```

In addition, the **/g** option has two suboptions:

/g:i   Generate line number information

/g:t   Generate debug tables.

The default is to generate both. Prepend either **i** or **g** with a minus sign to turn off that option.

Language Extensions   The **/x** option disables any Visual J++ extensions to the Java language. Language extensions are available by default.

No Output   **/nowrite** tells JVC to not generate an output **.class** file. Use this option when you are still developing to help find syntax errors in your **.java** files.

For example,

```
JVC /nowrite somefile.java
```

would only compile **somefile** and would not produce a **.class** file but would output all errors and warnings.

Optimize Output   The **/o** switch tells JVC to produce the fastest code possible. **/o** has two suboptions.

/o:i   Optimize by inlining functions where possible.

/o:j   Optimize bytecode jumps.

The **/o** switch alone defaults to both inlining and bytecode jump optimization. Turn off either option by appending a minus sign after the option. For example, **/o:j-** would turn off bytecode jump optimization.

Overriding CLASSPATH

Use **/cp** option to completely override the CLASSPATH variable.

For example,

```
JVC /cp somedevice:\somedir;. somefile.java
```

uses **somedevice:\somedir** as the class path; in addition, look in the current directory when searching for system or other classes. You may enter several subdirectories by separating them with semicolons.

Printing **CLASSPATH**   The **/cp:o** option prints the class path to the screen.
For example,

```
JVC /cp:o
```

might produce

```
Microsoft (R) Visual J++ Compiler Version 1.00.6229
Copyright (C) Microsoft Corp 1996. All rights reserved.

Using classpath:
    c:\windows.95\java\trustlib\tclasses.zip;c:\windows.95\java\trustl
ib;c:\windows.95\java\classes\classes.zip;c:\windows.95\java\classes;.;c
:\windows.95\java\lib
```

Prepending to **CLASSPATH**   This option prepends the entered path to the current value of **CLASSPATH**.

```
JVC /cp:a path
```

Append *path* to the path specified by the **CLASSPATH** variable, that is, add it to the end of the CLASSPATH. If you enter more then one **/cp:a** path, then the paths are concatenated together.

Setting Output Directory   This option sets the output directory for the resultant class file.

```
JVC /d directory someinput.java
```

tells **JVC.exe** to use **directory** for the output class file. The name of the output class with be the same as the input **.java.exe** file. **directory** will be created if it does not exist.

Verbose Output   The **/verbose** switch tells **JVC.exe** to produce verbose output detailing each compile phase.

For example,

```
JVC /verbose somefile.java
```

might produce something like (some text omitted)

```
Microsoft (R) Visual J++ Compiler Version 1.00.6229
Copyright (C) Microsoft Corp 1996. All rights reserved.

Parsing somefile.java:
    Loading class: .\somefileFrame.class (referenced in somefile.java)
    Loading class: .\NewDialog.class (referenced in somefile.java)
    Loading class: .\AMenu.class (referenced in somefile.java)
    Loading class:
[c:\windows.95\java\classes\classes.zip]\java\applet\Applet.class
    (referenced in somefile.java)
Loading class: [c:\windows.95\java\classes\classes.zip]\java\awt\Panel.class
    (referenced in somefile.java)
  Loading class:
[c:\windows.95\java\classes\classes.zip]\java\awt\Container.class
    (referenced in somefile.java)
...
  Loading class:
[c:\windows.95\java\classes\classes.zip]\java\lang\Runnable.class
    (referenced in somefile.java)
  Loading class:
[c:\windows.95\java\classes\classes.zip]\java\lang\Thread.class
    (referenced in somefile.java)
Compiling somefile.java:
  Loading class:
[c:\windows.95\java\classes\classes.zip]\java\lang\ThreadGroup.class
    (referenced in somefile.java)
...
Generating file 'somefile.class'
```

Warning Levels   The **/w[level]** option controls how JVC produces warning messages.

The options work as follows:

/w	Turns off all warnings.
/w1	Shows severe errors.
/w2	Default. Shows severe and less severe warnings.

| /w3 | Shows all w1 and w2 level errors. In addition, flag methods without defined return types, methods without return statements where required, and casts and conversions which might result in loss of data. |
| /w4 | Displays all warnings no matter how minor. |

Windiff.exe **REFERENCE**

Windiff is a tool for graphically comparing two files and showing their differences. **Windiff.exe** also allows you to change the contents of one or both of the files. It is run at the command prompt as follows:

```
Windiff path1 [path2] [-s [options] savefilename]
```

where options are

path1	Compares **path1** file with the files in the current directory.
path1 path2	Compares the file specified with **path1** to the file specified with **path2**.
/s	Compares files that contain the same name in both paths.
/t	Compare only files in **path1**.
/r	Compares only files in **path2**.
/d	Compares two different files in both paths.
-s savefile	Saves the result of the compare in file savefile.

The Windiff Interface

The windiff interface is composed of an expand/outline button, several menus, and a differences window.

The Expand/Outline Button The expand/outline button either contracts or expands the Differences window to show differences. When the display is outlined only the file names and some text describing whether there are differences is displayed. When expanded, the differences are shown graphically as follows:

White	Lines that are the same.
Red	Lines in the first file that differ from the second.
Yellow	Lines in the second file that differ from the first.

The File Menu Use the file menu to select files or directories to compare, abort a compare operation, or perform other operations. The list below shows the file menu commands and what each does.

File Menu Commands

Compare files	Prompts the users for the names of two files to compare.
Compare directories	Prompts the user to enter two directories to compare.
Abort	Aborts a difference in progress.
Save file list	Prompts the user to enter a file to save the compare results to.
Copy files	Presents the user with a copy files dialog that can be used to copy files from one place to another.
Print	Prints the differences result.
Exit	Exits Windiff.

The Edit Menu The edit menu allows you to specify and edit a file being used in a difference operation. The list below shows the edit menu commands and what each does.

Edit Menu Commands

Edit Left File	Opens an editor on the left or the first file in the difference operation.
Edit Right File	Opens an editor on the right or the second file in the difference operation.
Edit Composite File	Opens a composite of both files.
Set editor	Allows you to select a editor to use in editor operations. The default is notepad.

The View Menu The view menu allows you view either expanded or contracted versions of files as they move from change to change within a differences report. The list below shows the view menu commands and what each one does.

View Menu Commands

Outline	Switches from expanded output to outline.
Expand	Switches from outline to expanded output.
Picture	Displays a graphical picture of the differences report.
Previous change	Moves the cursor to the previous difference.
Next change	Moves the cursor to the next difference.

TIP

Moving from Difference to Difference

The easiest way to move from difference to difference is with the **[F7]** and **[F8]** functions keys, which move you to previous and next differences, respectively.

The Expand Menu The expand menu allows you to view an expanded version of either the first or second file, with or without line numbers. The list below shows the expand menu commands and what each one does.

Expand Menu Commands

Left file only	Expand the left file only, showing changes colored as required.
Right file only	Expand the right file only, showing changes colored as required.
Expand both files	Expand both files, showing changes colored as required.
Left line number	Toggle line numbers in the left file.

Right line numbers	Toggle line numbers in the right file.
No line numbers	Toggle line numbers in both files.

The Options Menu The Options Menu allows you to control how differences are reported, whether white space is considered a difference or not, and so on. The list below shows the options menu commands and what each one does.

Options Menu Commands

Ignore blanks	Do not consider differences only resulting from blanks as different.
Mono colors	Display differences in black and white.
Show identical files	When in outline view show files that are identical.
Show left-only files	When in outline view display only left files.
Show right-only files	When in outline view display only right files.
Show different files	When in outline view show files that are in both paths, but only if different.

The Mark Menu The Mark Menu allows you to mark the results of a difference. The list below shows the Mark Menu commands.

Mark Menu Commands

Mark file	Marks only selected comparison results.
Mark pattern	Shows the Mark Files dialog and prompts the user to enter a marking pattern.
Hide marked files	Hides all files that have been marked.
Toggle marked files	Inverts the status of marked files. Files marked are no longer marked and unmarked files are marked.

Zoomin.exe REFERENCE

The last tool we will examine is the **Zoomin** tool. The **Zoomin** tool allows you to select an area of the screen and *zoom in* on it, displaying it larger than normal.

To run **Zoomin**, either type **zoomin** from the command line or run it directly from the **msdev\bin** directory. Select the area to zoom by positioning the mouse in the **Zoomin** window and pressing the mouse button. While holding the mouse button, move the **Zoomin** bounding rectangle over the section of the screen you wish to view. You may then use the scroll bar to zoom in or out the selected region.

Zoomin has several menu commands that control its behavior. Selecting **C**opy from the **E**dit menu copies the current **Zoomin** window to the clipboard. Selecting **R**efresh from the **E**dit menu refreshes the screen image. Selecting **R**efresh **R**ate from the **O**ptions menu displays the **Refresh** dialog, which allows you to set a refresh interval.

PART III

Advanced Topics

CHAPTER 27

Techniques for Animation

In this chapter we cover the following topics:

- **An Overview of Animation**
- **Creating a Minimal Animation with the Applet Wizard**
- **Issues Pertaining to Performance**
- **Double Buffering**
- **Use of the ClipRect method**
- **Eliminating Flicker**
- **Arrays of Pixels**

AN OVERVIEW OF ANIMATION

Does the word **animation** conjure up images of a round-eared mouse wearing baggy suspended shorts? Perhaps it makes you think of *Johnny Quest*, *Sailor Moon*, or MTV's *Liquid Television*. More likely you have computer leanings, and you imagine it as morphing, or the view from some flight simulator. Hopefully, however, you are exposed to what the net offers, and your image of animation is something very simple, like moving text, a bouncing ball, or that spinning globe in the upper righthand corner of Internet Explorer 3.

It is that last category that is covered here. It is rather ambitious to try to get real-time animation (synthesized, or from a downloaded gif stream) to look great in a platform-independent environment. We will stick to what can be quickly downloaded. To that end, we will be covering the topics listed above.

Animation was the first thing that got Java noticed by the masses. It is also something that would not be intuitive without a further bit of explanation as to the roles of threads, image buffers, and other tricks of the trade. Once you have mastered the brief look supplied here, you will learn more by examining at the source code of whatever examples you can find. Animation is a fairly broad topic, rife with rapidly evolving tricks and techniques. Do you actually own a copy of Visual J++? The book that comes with it, *Learn Java Now*, is a little weak on several fronts, but it has two reasonable chapters on animation.

CREATING A MINIMAL ANIMATION WITH THE APPLET WIZARD

In Part II we saw how to create a minimal applet that does animation. If we follow these steps, and have the comment generation turned on, we get a source file with several **to do** sections in it. It is pretty long, and we are presuming that you have Visual J++ and can generate the code yourself, so we won't give the whole six-page (of mostly comments) listing here. It is available on the CD-ROM. Let's look at some key features.

Just for Starters

Any animation applet must have a thread that handles the animation. This is not just a good idea, it's the law. So, as we see below, an animation applet must implement the **Runnable** interface.

```
public class Anim1 extends Applet implements Runnable
{
    //      m_Anim1 is the Thread object for the applet
    Thread  m_Anim1 = null;
```

Animation Object Fields

The animation applet generated by Visual J++ has several fields that are necessary for one kind of applet animation—that is, the kind in which several **gif** or **jpeg** images are loaded and then displayed in sequence.

```
// ANIMATION SUPPORT:
//    m_Graphics        used for storing the applet's Graphics context
//    m_Images[]        the array of Image objects for the animation
//    m_nCurrImage      the index of the next image to be displayed
//    m_ImgWidth        width of each image
//    m_ImgHeight       height of each image
```

```
//    m_fAllLoaded    indicates whether all images have been loaded
//    NUM_IMAGES      number of images used in the animation
// -------------------------------------------------------------
private Graphics m_Graphics;
private Image      m_Images[];
private int        m_nCurrImage;
private int        m_nImgWidth = 0;
private int        m_nImgHeight = 0;
private boolean    m_fAllLoaded = false;
private final int NUM_IMAGES = 18;
```

Of course, the comments provided by the Wizard tell all.

The Constructor

You don't normally need a constructor for an applet. This is a vestigial artifact from other kinds of code that can be automatically generated.

```
public Anim1()
{
    // TODO: Add constructor code here
}
```

The init Method

The **init** method is critical to an animation applet. It is where you populate any fields in the applet that need initializing. You may have used the resource wizard to create some widgets (in the parlance of Visual Basic, these are called controls). If this is so, you want to follow the directions given in the comments about calling the **CreateControls( )** method and commenting out the **resize( )** method.

```
// The init() method is called by the AWT when an applet is 1st loaded or
// reloaded. Override this method to perform whatever initialization your
// applet needs, such as initializing data structures, loading images or
// fonts, creating frame windows, setting the layout manager, or adding UI
// components.
//————————————————————————————-
public void init()
{
    // If you use a ResourceWizard-generated "control creator" class to
    // arrange controls in your applet, you may want to call its
    // CreateControls() method from within this method. Remove the
    // following
    // call to resize() before adding the call to CreateControls();
    // CreateControls() does its own resizing.
```

It begins with some initialization. The first **for** loop is used to load the images from the **gif** files. It is this code that constructs the image file name *strImage*, which limits us to 100 images. It draws the images off screen to force them to load entirely. There is a **TO DO** here that will almost never be used. It is an opportunity to do something special if another thread interrupts while this thread is sleeping. In this situation, there really is nothing that you need to do.

The second loop (a while loop) waits until all the images are really loaded. It also has a **TO DO**, which will never be fleshed out. The wizard just throws these things in every time a there is a call to the **sleep** method. Both of these first two loops are only executed once on our way to the real ongoing work of the applet.

Finally, we get to the main run loop (*while(true)*). This code updates the variable *m_nCurrImage*, which keeps track of the current image, sleeps, and calls **repaint**. There is another one of those **TO DO** comments after the sleep invocation. Don't worry about it; there is nothing very useful that you can put there, unless you are logging on when your thread gets interrupted.

One last **TO DO** is provided at the very end of the file. This is for any additional code you want to add to your Applet. There are numerous things that you might consider putting here including, but not limited to:

- Methods which JavaScript may call to affect the Applet based on user inputs to the Browser
- Methods to add user inputs to the applet
- Methods to render images in the background
- Methods to move foreground objects over your animation
- Methods to do input and output to the Server to update image data during execution.

If you are adding code to control a second animation or control the moving position of some special feature, you must add it within the *while(true)* loop. In normal animation type applets, you would simply include the control of applet fields that are used by the **paint** or **update** methods. These would include indexes like *m_nCurrImage*, or perhaps arrays of objects to be drawn. Bet you already have some ideas; take a few minutes and give them a try.

```
//     The run() method is called when the applet's thread is started. If
// your applet performs any ongoing activities without waiting for user
// input, the code for implementing that behavior typically goes here. For
// example, for an applet that performs animation, the run() method
// controls the display of images.
// ----------------------------------------------------------------
```

```java
public void run()
{
    repaint();

    m_Graphics = getGraphics();
    m_nCurrImage = 0;
    m_Images = new Image[NUM_IMAGES];

    // Load in all the images
    // ----------------------------------------------------------------
    String strImage;

    // For each image in the animation, this method first constructs a
    // str containing the path to the image file; then it begins loading
    // the image into the m_Images array. Note that the call to getImage
    // will return before the image is completely loaded.
    // ----------------------------------------------------------------
    for (int i = 1; i <= NUM_IMAGES; i++)
    {

        // Build path to next image
        // ----------------------------------------------------------
        strImage = "images/img00" + ((i < 10) ? "0" : "") + i + ".gif";
        m_Images[i-1] = getImage(getDocumentBase(), strImage);

        // Get width and height of one image.
        // Assuming all images are same width and height
        // ----------------------------------------------------------
        if (m_nImgWidth == 0)
        {
            try
            {
                // getWidth() and getHeight() methods of the Image class
                // return -1 if the dimensions are not yet known. The
                // following code keeps calling getWidth() and getHeight()
                // until they return actual values.
                // NOTE: This is only executed once in this loop, since we
                //       are assuming all images are the same width and
                //       height. However, since we do not want to dup
                //       the above image load code, the code resides in
                //       the loop.
                // -------------------------------------------------
                while ((m_nImgWidth = m_Images[i-1].getWidth(null)) < 0)
                    Thread.sleep(1);

                while ((m_nImgHeight = m_Images[i-1].getHeight(null)) < 0)
                    Thread.sleep(1);
            }
```

```
            catch (InterruptedException e)
            {
                // TODO: Place exception-handling code here in case an
                //       InterruptedException is thrown by Thread.sleep(),
                //       meaning that another thread has interrupted this one
            }
        }

        // Force image to fully load
        // ------------------------------------------------------------
        m_Graphics.drawImage(m_Images[i-1], -1000, -1000, this);
    }

    // Wait until all images are fully loaded
    // ------------------------------------------------------------
    while (!m_fAllLoaded)
    {
        try
        {
            Thread.sleep(10);
        }
        catch (InterruptedException e)
        {
            // TODO: Place exception-handling code here in case an
            //       InterruptedException is thrown by Thread.sleep(),
            //       meaning that another thread has interrupted this one
        }
    }

    repaint();

    while (true)
    {
        try
        {
            // Draw next image in animation
            // --------------------------------------------------------
            displayImage(m_Graphics);
            m_nCurrImage++;
            if (m_nCurrImage == NUM_IMAGES)
                m_nCurrImage = 0;

            // TODO: Add additional thread-specific code here
            Thread.sleep(50);
        }
        catch (InterruptedException e)
        {
```

```
        // TODO: Place exception-handling code here in case an
        //     InterruptedException is thrown by Thread.sleep(),
        //     meaning that another thread has interrupted this one
        stop();
    }
  }
}
// TODO: Place additional applet code here
}
```

That's it for the simple animation applet generated by the applet wizard. This is the starting point for the discussions that follow. Since this is the simplest animation, some discussion of where to go from here might be of use.

ISSUES PERTAINING TO PERFORMANCE

Visual J++ works with the Windows API. This has some nice benefits in terms of standardization and reliability, but it sometimes has some drawbacks when it comes to speed of execution. If you are used to game software, and the speed at which backgrounds can be redrawn and many moving objects can be maintained, you will find that the most straightforward approaches to animation here will be a disappointment.

In an ideal world, you would like the screens in your animation applet to be completely redrawn 72 time a second (or whatever the refresh rate on your monitor is). You would also like to have a way to know when that brief moment occurs in which you may make that redraw without interfering with a live display. In reality, you don't have the resources to do all of this directly, but you can make good approximations to these ideals.

In the case of the simple animation given above, we have a series of images that are loaded into the applet's memory resources and swapped sequentially into the display buffer. These pictures are well defined before the applet is loaded and do not change based on any user interaction. You will also note that they are a bit slow to load, which may tax the patience of the person waiting to view your applet.

You can achieve the movement of animation without resorting to the downloading of **.gif** files. You can, for example, create an applet that appears to move easily reproduced images, such as geometric figures or typographic characters. Such applets require no storage or download time for the animation frames and can be made with fairly few Java byte codes. This would normally be done by putting the animation code into the **update** method, so that the screen is not cleared and completely with each **repaint( )**. The result is that with some extra effort on the programming end, you can minimize the number of pixels that need redrawing.

Minimally, to accomplish something like this, you need new and old position fields in the applet, which all of the methods can reference. These fields are initialized in **init( )**, updated in a loop in the **run( )** method, and is referenced by the methods that actually paint the screen (usually **update( )** or **paint( )**).

The following example creates a rectangular box inside the border of the applet that, by being redrawn, appears to move in and out periodically. In reality, each iteration of the loop redraws the rectangle with the background color, and then draws the new rectangle in the new position.

```java
import java.awt.';
import java,applet.*;

public class PulsingRect extends Applet implements Runnable (
    // These variables are available to every method of the Class.
    Thread runner;
    int MaxX;          // The max X value for the applet's graphics
    int MaxY;          // The max Y value for the applet's graphics
    int Disp;          // pixels the moving box is from the edge
    int oldDisp;       // previous displacement;
    int MaxDisp;       // when to turn around.
    int Delay;         // how long to wait between repaints.
    Color appBack;     // App's background color;
    Color appFore;     // App's forground color;

    // the init method runs when an Applet is first loaded.
    public void init() {
    MaxX = this.size().width;
    MaxY = this.size().height;
    Disp = 5;
    oldDisp = 0;
    MaxDisp = 25;
    Delay = 30;
    appBack = new Color(0, 0, 68);
    appFore = new Color(128, 255, 255);
    }

    // start is called by init, and also whenever you return to the page.
    public void start() {
    if (runner == null) {
        runner = new Thread(this);
        runner.start();
    }
    }
```

```
// stop is called whenever you exit the page.
public void stop() {
if (runner != null) {
    runner.stop();
    runner = null;
}
}


// the run method for this class is called by the start method of
// the thread (in this case, runner.start()).
// This is the active body of the thread.
public void run() {

setBackground(appBack);
while (runner != null) {
    for (Disp 1 = 2; Disp<MaxDisp; Disp++) {
    repaint();
    try { Thread.sleep(Delay); }
    catch (InterruptedException e) { }    // catch interrupts that
                        // come while sleeping.
    }
    for (Disp = MaxDisp; Disp > 2; Disp—) {
    repaint();
    try { Thread.sleep(Delay); }
    catch (InterruptedException e) { }   // same as above.
    }
}
}


// the repaint method (in run, above) normally calls update(),
// which normally calls paint. Here we have modified update, to
// reduce flicker.
public void update(Graphics g) {
int D2;

// paint the text initially, and once in a while.
if ((oidDisp == o) II (oldDisp == MaxDisp)) {
    // fix for Win95 version
    g.setCoLor(appBack);
    g.fillRect(0, 0, this.size() .width, this.size() .height) ;
    // end of Win95 fix

    g. setColor(Color. red);
    g.drawString("Your Message Here", MaxDisp+5, 60);
    g.drawString("-Middletown Billboard Company", MaxDisp+25, 90);
}
// cover the previous box with the background color.
D2 = oldDisp * 2;
```

```
    g.setColor(appBack);
    g.drawRect(oldDisp, oldDisp, MaxX-D2, MaxY-D2);

    // draw the new box with the foreground color.
    g.setColor(appFore);
    D2 = Disp * 2;
    oldDisp = Disp;
    g.drawRect(Disp, Disp, MaxX-D2, MaxY-D2);
    }
}
```

DOUBLE BUFFERING

Double buffering is displaying one screen image while building the next one off-screen, and then using the fastest possible method of getting the new one into place. Some windows systems are a little slow, and this is one way to avoid distracting the viewers of your animation by letting them see the process of building up each image one item at a time.

In the following code fragment, we can see how double buffering is accomplished. This very simple example is part of an applet that appears to move a filled rectangle back and forth across the screen. Note that no effort has been made to eliminate flicker; we will see more about that later.

```
import java.awt.*;
import java.applet.*;

public class SlidingRect extends Applet
    implements Runnable
    {   Thread myThread;
        int x;

        public void start()
        (   if  (myThread==null)
            {   myThread = new Thread(this);
                myThread.start();
            }
        }
        public void stop()
        {   if  (myThread !=null)
            {   myThread.stop();
                myThread = null;
            }
        }
        public void run()
        (   setBackground(Color.blue);    // try white
            while (true)
```

```
    {       for (x=5; x<=205; x+=4)
            (    repaint();
                 try
                 {Thread.sleep(100);
                 }
                 catch (InterruptedException e) {}
            }
            for (x=205; x>5; x-=4)
            {    repaint();
                 try
                 {Thread.sleep(100);
                 }
                 catch (interruptedException e) {}
            }
    }
}
public void paint(Graphics g)
{   g.setColor(Color.black); //draw the night
    g.fillRect(0, 0, 200, 200) ; // from 0 + 200
    g.setColor(Color.white); //draw the day
    g.fillRect(200, 0, 200, 200); // from 200 + 399

    g.setColor(Color.red);
    g.fillRect(x, 20, 160, 160);
}
}
```

USE OF THE CLIPRECT METHOD

The Java AWT provides methods for **Graphics** objects that let you specify a small region of the graphics image to work on. This is called the **clipRect** method. **clipRect** is especially handy for situations in which only a small portion of the screen is changing. It is usually used in conjunction with double buffering or with moving a simple figure across a complex background. It is also useful for distorting the size or aspect ratio of an image.

There are some constraints with the **clipRect** method; for example, you cannot clip one region, and then on the same **Graphics** object clip another region outside the first within the same **repaint( )** invocation. Still, it is invaluable for limiting the number of pixels that need redrawing in mostly static complex images. We can imagine moving a small circle across an image that has been downloaded. It does this by keeping a frame of the image stored off-screen. Whenever the circle is going to move, a matching rectangle from the off-screen image is copied to cover the old circle. Then the circle is drawn in its new position.

ELIMINATING FLICKER

Have you built an animation applet yet? Do you think maybe you've seen a little bit of flicker here or there? If you haven't seen any flicker, you have either been given nonflickering applets to modify, or your applets are very simple and are cleverly designed to not flicker.

Any time that your applet goes through the **repaint( )** → **update ( )** → **paint( )** process **update** (if you haven't overridden it), it calls **clear( )** before calling **paint**. The result is that if your applet is drawing any sizable number of pixels in something other than the background color, there is every likelihood that the screen will be displayed while the applet's pants are down (so to speak), and the viewer will see a flash of incompleteness.

There are some things you can do to avoid this unpleasant and annoying situation. These things include minimizing the number of pixels being redrawn at any one time. If you have a complex image, this probably includes overriding the **update( )** method and eliminating the call to **clear( )**. Not using clear means that you must manually build into the applet the logic to overwrite those pixels that are changing. This may seem tedious to you, but don't let it overwhelm you. Just remember that it is your ability to deal with this monotony that separates you from nonprogrammers.

You may find that even using every trick mentioned above, you still are getting some flicker. In such situation, you may resort to putting the code that does the copy from the off-screen buffer into a very short method that is **synchronized**. Be judicious in your use of the **synchronized** keyword. Too many methods being **synchronized** can (with some careless programming) lead to a situation called deadlock. Deadlock sounds bad, even if you don't know what it is. It has been described in more detail in Part I of this book, but just remind yourself, deadlock is bad.

ARRAYS OF PIXELS

Any animator at one time or another wants to build an image up from individual pixels, computed on the fly. It may also be that you have a need to build such an image. In most windowing systems, Java is a bit slow doing this sort of thing, but it can be done, and experimenting with it can demonstrate a lot of things you can only guess at without such tests.

The following code fragment shows how we can build an image up as an array of integers, and then convert it to an off-screen image, and then put it on the screen of your applet.

```java
import java.awt.*;
import java.awt.image.*;
import java.applet.*;

public class Pyramid extends Applet {
    int[] light = new int[256];
    int[] dark = new int[256];
    int[] backImage = new int[4096];
    Image diamond;

    public void init() {
        Color lightColor = new Color(0, 0, 0);
        Color darkColor = new Color(0, 0, 0);

        for (int i=0; i<192; i++) {
            lightColor = new Color(64, i+64, i+64);
            light[i] = lightColor.getRGB();
            darkColor = new Color(32, i+32, i+32);
            dark[il = darkColor.getRGB();
        }
        for (int i=0, j=0, n=0; i<64; j++, n++) {
            if (j==64) {
                j=0;
                i++;
            }
            if (i==64) break;
            if (i<32) {
                if (i>j) backImage[n] = light[j];
                else if (i>64-j) backImage[n] = dark[64-j];
                else backImage[n] = light[i];\
            }
            else {
                if (64-i>j) backImage[n] = light[j];
                else if (i<j) backImage[n] = dark[64-j];
                else backImage[n] = dark[64-i];
            }
        }
        diamond = createImage(new MemoryImageSource(64, 64, backImage, 0, 64));
    }    // end of init()
    public void paint(Graphics g) {
        g.drawImage(diamond, 0, 0, 64, 64, this);
    }
} // end of applet.
```

As we can see, there are many subtle things to learn about Java and animation. Whole books can be written on the subject, but better class libraries, and better development tools are coming so quickly that such books will be obsolete very quickly. It will be interesting to see how the animation Wizard improves with future versions of Visual J++.

EXERCISES

27-1   Build the pulsing rectangle example above.

27-2   Modify your result from exercise 27-1 and include a parameter for the applet that is a line of text that will be displayed inside the rectangle (in a different color).

27-3   Modify it some more by including a square, a circle, and a triangle (use fillPolygon) bouncing around inside the rectangle, behind the text.

27-4   Modify it some more by making the letters in the text string move.

27-5   Generate a pattern using individual pixels. Copy that pattern on the background of the applet. What do you have to do to make the pulsing rectangle work now?

27-6   Make an off-screen image with the background pattern, and use it to facilitate all of the moving patterns. Try building the rectangle from four individual lines.

27-7   Build a new applet with a large green triangle sliding across a background of one blue and one white rectangle.

27-8   Use **synchronized** to eliminate the flicker on the green triangle.

27-9   Is there another way to eliminate the flicker? Try it.

CHAPTER 28

Java, COM and ActiveX

In this chapter we cover the following topics:

- **Basics of the Component Object Model (C.O.M.), OLE and ActiveX**
- **Connecting ActiveX and Java**
- **The Java Type Library Wizard**
- **The OLE Object Viewer**
- **Java and COM data types**
- **Java and Scripting**

INTRODUCTION

Java, COM and ActiveX are huge topics. This chapter will not even attempt an in-depth review of ActiveX, but rather gives the reader a gentle introduction. The basics elements of the Component Object model will be introduced and then we will transition those to ActiveX and finally show how a ActiveX control can be used in Java. And, conversely, how a Java applet can act as an ActiveX control.

OK, but what does that mean? ActiveX extends Java in many different ways. ActiveX allows a software engineer to take advantage of the many existing OLE objects. Using ActiveX and Java you can place directly into your Java applet that spreadsheet control you have been so happily using for ages. Or use Visual Basic as the scripting language to control how your Java applet works. Or, conversely, you can use your

Java applet within an ActiveX control and make it available to Visual Basic, Borland Delphi etc. Amongst other things, ActiveX allows you, the developer, to develop in the language your are most comfortable with and still integrate that development effort into your Java applet!

THE COMPONENT OBJECT MODEL

The Component Object Model is a vast topic, but the underlying theme throughout is the *Windows Object*. A Windows Object is different from a C++ object in subtle and not so subtle ways. For example a Windows Object will never grant you access to its data. While Windows objects can and often are implemented in C++, it is by no means a requirement. Each and every Windows Object has an **interface** and its associated code and data. Beneath it all, an **interface** is just a way for two objects to communicate.

NOTE

ActiveX Interfaces and Java Interfaces Are Not the Same Things

ActiveX, and COM objects in general, are referenced through one or more **interfaces**. These are not the same interfaces the Java developers are familiar with. As you will remember, Java interfaces contain no code and describe how an object implements a definition. On the other hand ActiveX interfaces contain both the definition of the interface and the actual code and data which implement it.

But what exactly is COM anyway? Well, COM is really the underlying protocol that connects two processes. Once connected, COM drops out of the picture. But how does this work? Each and every COM object supports a simple interface called **IUnknown** (and usually at least one additional interface). When an application wishes to use a COM object the application queries the **IUnknown** interface to determine if an interface exists that both sides can agree on. Each of these interfaces typically supports a given way that an object may be used. Interfaces, and pointers to interfaces, are normally just pointers to arrays of functions which make up how an object acts. Under COM, an objects data is *never* visible and can only be manipulated via its provided interface functions. In many ways, COM objects are used much like Java objects: an instance of an object is created, that object is queried to determine what interfaces it supports; and an appropriate interface is selected. At this point your application, or ActiveX control for that matter, can use the COM object for whatever it was intended for.

> ### NOTE
>
> #### OLE, OLE2 and COM
>
> When OLE hit the streets it was known as Object Linking and Embedding (hence OLE). As OLE's popularity and functionality grew it became known as OLE2. OLE2 was a major improvement over OLE, leaving behind the dependency on dynamic data exchange, commonly called D.D.E, and the cumbersome interfaces of OLE1. Finally arrived COM, a unification of these concepts into a comprehensive object-oriented model that supports a variety of standards such as: language-independent 32bit DLL's; standardized interprocess communications model(DDE replacement); and a Visual Basic control extension called OCX, as well as other functionality. So, here we are again, expanding COM to become ActiveX. Who knows what tomorrow will bring!

Note that throughout this chapter you will see the terms COM and OLE used almost interchangeably. While they are not strictly the same thing, the concepts are close enough for this discussion to use one term for the other.

Figure 28.1 shows pictorially how an application might use COM

THE BASICS OF ACTIVEX

Just what is ActiveX? Many people are under the impression that ActiveX is just another name for OLE. While this is true in that ActiveX and OLE are both based on the COM specification, in the stricter sense they are very different. ActiveX is very much a slimmed down version of OLE, specifically optimized for speed and size. OLE, on the other hand, is optimized for integration with applications and general usability.

ActiveX Elements

There are five major area's where ActiveX plays. They are,

- Controls: ActiveX controls are just like other controls expect that they typically are much more interactive.

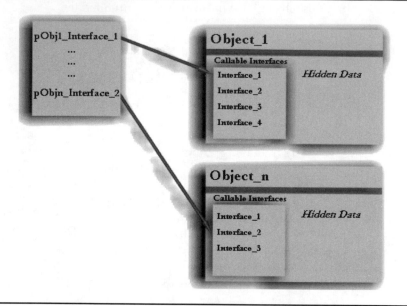

Figure 28.1   COM object(s) being used from an application.

- Documents: ActiveX documents are the feature most people are familiar with. ActiveX documents allow the web site developer to embed Miscosoft Word, Excel, or other OLE-aware documents into a Web page.
- Scripting: ActiveX scripting is that feature of ActiveX which allows either a Java applet or an ActiveX control to be controlled by an outside source. Visual J++ is the first, and currently only, development environment which allows two Java applications to be scripted together. This is provided thru the Java Virtual Machine in the Microsoft Internet Explorer 3.0.
- Automation: Automation allows your Java application to control the way an ActiveX control functions.
- Server Framework: The ActiveX server framework is a new technology which allows Web servers to add specific functionality such as security via ActiveX.

The remainder of this chapter will look at how an ActiveX control or component can be called from Java and touch briefly on how a Java applet can be used as an ActiveX control!

Java Applets as Seen from COM

We have covered just the tip of COM/ActiveX as seen from Java. What about Java as seen by COM? The Java virtual machine shipped with Internet Explorer 3.0 is completely OLE-aware. What that means is that Java classes are available as ActiveX controls while Internet Explorer is running (actually **Jview.exe** is enough). So you can use Visual Basic or Visual C++ to control your Java application as if it were a native DLL.

ActiveX and Other Platforms

One of the concerns of programmers everywhere is portability. Java was built from the ground up to be portable. One of the first thoughts which came to mind when I first encountered ActiveX was that it's proprietary. However, on October 1, 1996, the Cambridge, MA based group Open Group took control of the ActiveX technologies from a willing Microsoft effectively placing ActiveX into the open! The Open Group, together with Microsoft, then released the list of ActiveX core technologies which are expected to form the framework of the ActiveX of tomorrow. These technologies are:

- Component Object Model (COM) and DCOM: The underlying distributed object model for ActiveX.
- Microsoft remote procedure call (MS-RPC): A compatible implementation of DCE/RPC. Provides scalability, marshaling, and privacy support.
- NTLM Standard Security Provider Interface (SSPI): Allows secure invocation of components.
- Structured Storage: Rich, transaction-based, hierarchical file format. Enables applications to share files across applications and platforms.
- Registry: Provides a database of COM components and their configuration information.
- Monikers: Provides for persistent, intelligent names.
- Automation: Allows objects to expose functionality to high-level programming languages and scripting environments.

Several companies have committed to bringing these technologies, or at least a subset of them, to other platforms. Metrowerks (a provider of Macintosh development tools) and Macromedia have both stated there intent to bring ActiveX to the Mac. Other companies, such as Bristol Technologies and Mainsoft have expressed an interest in bringing ActiveX to UNIX.

So while ActiveX is only available under Microsoft operating systems today, you can certainly expect to see it on other operating systems tomorrow!

> **NOTE**
>
> ### For More Information
>
> For more information on ActiveX and its core technologies, see the ActiveX working group page, which can be found at **http://www. activex.org/**.

USING ACTIVEX FROM JAVA

Enough talk and background. Let's look at how we can actually use an ActiveX component from within a Java applet. Using ActiveX from Java is quite simple—ActiveX classes look almost exactly like Java classes. So much so that Java treats then exactly like Java imports. Visual J++ provides a very simple example of using ActiveX with its **javabeep** project.

> **NOTE**
>
> ### Javabeep Project
>
> The following sample comes complete on the Microsoft CD-ROM. To work with the project you will need to copy it to your hard drive. The following steps describe that process. From the Info Viewer tab select **Samples** (if you have more then one set of books online make sure you select Visual J++ books online from the Infoview toolbar). Select **Microsoft Samples** and then **Javabeep**. Follow the instructions in the help page from there to copy the sample and open its project file **javabeep.mpd**.

The javabeep.java file has has some sections removed.
See the original Microsoft sample for the complete listing.

```
//********************************************************************
// javabeep.java: Applet
//      Most of the code of interest can be found in the
//      javabeep.mouseDown() method
//********************************************************************
```

```java
import java.applet.*;
import java.awt.*;

// Import the class files that JavaTLB generates from beeper.dll
import beeper.*;

//=====================================================================
// Main Class for applet javabeep
//=====================================================================
public class javabeep extends Applet implements Runnable
{
    // Beeper COM Interface variable
    IBeeper m_Beeper=null;
...
    // MOUSE SUPPORT:
    //     The mouseDown() method is called if the mouse button is
    // pressed while the mouse cursor is over the applet's portion
    // of the screen.
    // -------------------------------------------------------------
    public boolean mouseDown(Event evt, int x, int y)
    {
        String BeeperString = new String();
        // Check if the Beeper object exists, and create it if necessary
        if(m_Beeper==null)
            m_Beeper = (IBeeper) new Beeper();

        // Call Beeper object 'Beep' method. Note that the Beep object
        // has been written such that on the sixth call to Beep(), the
        // Beep object will return an OLE error code which gets thrown
        // as a Java exception.
        // This sample catches the exception, Releases the Beeper
        // object, creates a new Beeper object, and continues
        try
        {
            m_Beeper.Beep();
        }
        catch(com.ms.com.ComException e)
        {
            // Release the Beeper object by setting m_Beeper=null
            m_Beeper=null;
            // Create a new Beeper object
            m_Beeper = (IBeeper) new Beeper();
            m_Beeper.Beep();
        }
    ...
    }
}
```

Examining Javabeep.java

As you can see, calling the beeper object from Java is a very straightforward process. The code looks identical to that of a 'regular' Java application. Let's look at each of the lines so that we understand what is actually going on.

First we have the import statement **import beeper.***; This looks just like your average import, and in fact it is. Under normal circumstances the import statement causes the compiler to look for a **.java** or a **.class** file. Visual J++ does exactly that. In addition, if it does not find one it begins searching for an ActiveX control (such as OCX's, ActiveX aware DLL's, etc.) and runs The Java Type Library Wizard internally to produce a **.class** file, seamlessly integrating ActiveX into your application.

> **NOTE**
>
> ### ActiveX Imports
>
> Visual J++ contains a tool known as the Java Type Library Wizard or **JavaTLB**. **JavaTLB** reads an ActiveX aware DLL, OCX, TLB, EXE or similar 'thing' and creates an import **.class** file which Visual J++ can handle. This seamlessly integrates ActiveX and Java. We shall look at JavaTLB and its syntax in detail in the following sections.

Right at the top of the javabeep class definition is the following statement. **IBeeper m_Beeper=null**; Basically the import beeper class, shown below as defines two objects.

The beeper Object and Interface as Copied from C:\WINNT40\java\trustlib\beeper\summary.txt after Running the Java Type Library Wizard and Selecting the beeper Object

```
public interface beeper/IBeeper extends com.ms.com.IUnknown
{
    public abstract int getCount();
    public abstract void Beep();
    public abstract com.ms.com.IUnknown get_NewEnum();
    public abstract java.lang.String getItem(int);
}
public class beeper/Beeper extends java.lang.Object
{
}
```

ActiveX objects typically have two definitions. The first is the actual interface which defines how you use the object. This interface name normally starts with an I to show that it is an interface. The second object is the actual object itself. Since we reference the object from its interface, we define **m_Beeper** to be of type **IBeeper**.

The remainder of the code for working with the beeper class is in the mouseDown method. The javabeep application places a string into the frame each time you press the mouse and causes the system speaker to beep. The first lines of code of interest in this method are:

```
if(m_Beeper==null)
    m_Beeper = (IBeeper) new Beeper();
```

If you have not yet created a beeper object, then create one. Notice that **we do not new the interface IBeeper** but rather the actual beeper object. While we reference a beeper object through its interface, we are actually referencing is the actual beeper object.

TIP

Choosing the Right Interface

When you run the Java Type Library Wizard you will always be presented with a text file, shown in the output window, which describes the interface(s) of the ActiveX control you are working on. Always look at this file to determine which object is the 'real' object and which are just the interfaces to that object. In most cases the actual object will be shown as having super class **java.lang.Object** and the interfaces super class **com.ms.com.IUnknown**.

Finally the code **m_Beeper.Beep()**; actually causes the beeper to beep. As we shall see in a moment, the beeper has a built in bug which causes it to stop working after the fifth beep. However, for purposes of this explanation, this is OK and allows us to introduce COM Exceptions.

Handing COM Exceptions

ActiveX objects, and COM components in general, can cause exceptions just like any other object. And, as always, it makes sense to check for them. The **beeper.dll** has a built-in bug such that it will only beep five times and on the sixth time raise an exception. We would like our application to beep every time the user hits the mouse button so that when a **ComException** occurs we discard our old object, create a new one, and continue on our merry way. All of this is summed up in the code found in the catch block and shown below:

```
// Release the Beeper object by setting m_Beeper=null
m_Beeper=null;
// Create a new Beeper object
m_Beeper = (IBeeper) new Beeper();
m_Beeper.Beep();
```

We simply free the resources associated with the current beeper by assigning it to the null pointer. Create a new beeper object and then cause it to beep!

> **TIP**
>
> **Capturing** ComExceptions
>
> **ComExceptions** are used to wrap the **HRESULT** normally returned by an COM or ActiveX object. **ComExceptions** are derived from **RunTimeExceptions** ands so it is the responsibility of the developer to catch and deal with COM errors. Since **Com Exceptions** extends **RunTimeExceptions** you may use all the normal exception methods to determine what happened.

Java Type Library Wizard

Well, at this point we have examined a single example of how to access an ActiveX control. But how can we determine exactly what controls we have access to and how to use them? The Java Type Library Wizard in the answer! You can run the Java Type Library Wizard by choosing **Java Type Library Wizard** from the **Tools** menu. Figure 28.2 shows the Java Type Library Wizard Dialog.

Select one or more or the squares on the left and press the **OKButton** or **CANCEL** to cancel. If you select **OK** then the Java Type Library Wizard will generate **.class** files for the control you have selected and will show any warnings or errors in the Java Type Library Wizard tab of the output window. Note that all classes generated by Java Type Library Wizard are placed into a 'trusted' directory. (More on trusted vs untrusted applets later.)

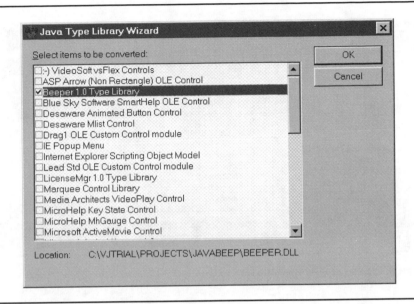

Figure 28.2   The Java Type Library Wizard Dialog.

> **NOTE**
>
> ### Not All Controls Are Created Equal
>
> Just because you can see a control in the Java Type Library Wizard, and then produce a **.class** file from it, doesn't automatically guarantee that you can use the class. Many COM controls were created before the existence of Java and as a result use data types which are foreign to Java. These classes will produce warnings as you generate **.class** files from them and those function calls will not have prototypes generated for them. So look carefully at what you get.

OLE Object View

In addition to the Java Type Library Wizard, whose job is primarily to convert COM objects into Java **.class** files, Visual J++ includes an tool known as OLE Object View. OLE Object View, shown as Figure 28.3, allows you to look into a COM object and see in advance what interfaces

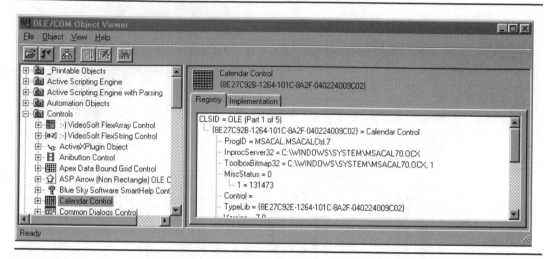

Figure 28.3   The OLE/COM Object Viewer.

it supports and how the functions for a selected interface actually work. Run OLE/COM Object View by selecting **OLE Object View** from the **Tools** menu.

You can select and view most any object, however only those objects which are shown with the ![icon] symbol are ActiveX controls which can be used with Java. Select the beeper control and double right click it. Select View Type Information from the popup menu and you will be presented with the ITypeLib viewer, shown as Figure 28.4.

Figure 28.4 shows the Beeper ActiveX control and its *Typeinfos*. Typeinfos are so much like Java classes that Visual J++ treats them as such. Lets look closely at the dialog so we can understand what it is we are being show.

The ITypeLib viewer provides a simple and straightforward display of types which can be used by a Java application. The left pane shows the open type library name and the class it implements (in our case Beeper 1.0). The right page shows whatever aspect of the type library has been selected.

Selecting the highest level interface causes the associated Interface Description to be displayed. The simplest classes will have a *coclass* entry, in our case Beeper, one or more *disinterface* entries and zero or more *interface* entries. In addition any enumeration's supported by the object are displayed.

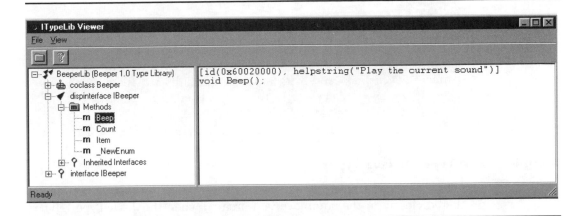

Figure 28.4   The **IBeeper TypeTypeinfo**.

As we have seen from our Javabeep example, the coclass entry describes actual beeper object, along with its class uuid and a list of its interfaces.

Opening it shows its underlying associated interfaces. Each of the interfaces is then shown with its own entry.

For each *interface* we can drill down and show the methods that interface supports and how the calls are formatted as well as *constants* and *properties* of the control. Selecting the beep method from the IBeeper dispinterface shows that has id 0x60020000 and is defined a void Beep () using a 'C' like conventions. Also shown is the help string associated with the call, if defined.

Typelibs are very much like standard Java classes and have most of the same attributes. One of those attributes is *properties*. The properties of a typelib can be thought of as externally visible variables for the class. Each has a type and a name. For example, if we agumented the Beeper class to beep a number of times we might have controlled the number of beeps by adding a property such as short beepcount. A application could then update the beep count through this external variable.

An extensive set of variable types exists for class properties. See the IDL language guide for an in-depth description of the IDL type and language as a whole.

So as you can see the COM classes are quite extensive, but look almost identical to Java classes. Providing a natural way to hook one to the other.

> **NOTE**
>
> ### Coclass and Interfaces
>
> As was previously mentioned the actual object you want to **new** is normally coclass. And interfaces are normally started with the letter I. However this is a style and not a strict requirement. As usual, your mileage may vary.

Mapping COM Types to Java Types

The classes and methods exposed by the ActiveX and COM objects are listed clearly in the summary text created when the Java Type Library Wizard is run on a given class. However, it's often helpful to understand the conversion between COM types and their associated native Java types. And, as COM has a class concept, it's important to understand how COM classes and associated concepts map to there Java counterparts.

Mapping COM Classes to Java Equivalents The object description language of the COM model supports five class or library-specific constructs. The following library elements and the associated constructs are described in the table on the following page.

Note that when developing Java applications which use COM objects its always important to look at the **summary.txt** file generated by the Java Type Library Wizard to see exactly what was generated. Not all constructs supported by COM are supported by Java.

> **NOTE**
>
> ### For More Information on IDL
>
> The Object Definition Language can be compiled by the Microsoft Interface Definition Language compiler or the **MkTypLib** utility. For more information on either of these tools or a complete description of the IDL syntax and language, refer to the MIDL Programmer's Guide and reference available through the WIN32 SDK or see the Visual J++ books-on-line book *Java and COM*, and search for MIDL.

Mapping COM Data Types to Java Equivalents As with COM libraries and classes, most COM data types have Java equivalents. The following table lists the Java equivalents for COM data types.

Table 28.1 COM to Java Class Mappings.

COM	Java Equivalent	Description
Coclass	public class	A 'normal' everyday class.
interface	public interface	The methods which can be applied to a given class. Normally the keyword interface is applied to a set of functions which an act on a given object.
		Note that generated methods do not include those inherited from the **IUnknown** or **Idispatch.** You can access these methods by strategic casts of your class object
dispinterface	public interface	A special kind of COM interface known as a *Dispatch* interface. Dispatch interfaces are used to get and set properties of a object. Normally these properties can also be accessed via the **Idispatch::Invoke** method of the object.
typedef (struct, enum or union only)	public final class	Normal typedef. Works almost identically to a C or C++ typdef.
module	public final class containing static final members	A specific class construct under COM which defines a final class with externally visible member variables. Modules typically describe a set of function calls which are normally packaged together in a DLL rather then a class.

Any ODL type not listed is currently unsupported in Java and will generate an error when the class using the type is run through the **Java Type Library Wizard**. Note that you can still use the class, just not any methods which do not have a Java equivalent for the various parameters.

> **TIP**
>
> ### More Information on the Variant Class
>
> For more information on the Variant class, see the Class variant section in the Visual J++ Books on-line, and search for package, **com.ms.com**.

Table 28.2 COM to Java Type Mappings.

ODL/COM Type	Java Type
boolean	boolean
char	char
double	double
int	int
int64	long
float	float
long	int
short	short
unsigned char	byte
BSTR	class **java.lang.String**
CURRENCY/CY	long (divide by 10,000 to get the original value as a fixed-point number)
DATE	double
SCODE/HRESULT	int, See the section titled **Handing COM Exceptions**
VARIANT	class com.ms.com.Variant More on variants in a moment.
IUnknown *	interface **com.ms.com.Iunknown**
IDispatch *	class **java.lang.Object**
SAFEARRAY(**typename**)	class com.ms.com.SafeArray
typename *	single-element array of **typename**
void	void

Often COM classes will take arguments of type **variant**. The variant class is really a wrapper around a variant structure which allows a single object to contain values of many types. For all practical purposes you can think of the variant class as a large union which can store most, if not all, the Java data types. Variants are primarily used to pass variables to interfaces which are derived from **IUknown** where the exact data type of the parameters is either unknown at compile time or may change.

Java Applications and Scripting

Another interesting feature of ActiveX support is scripting. Scripting is the action of manipulating an applet or ActiveX control via some external interface. Microsoft Internet Explorer allows all the public methods and variables of an applet to be available to an external scripting language like VBScript or any other language supporting ActiveX scripting.

If we wished we could extend our javabeep example to insert a button onto the javabeep page and use it to play a beep when pressed as follows: add a public method, **DoBeep** to the javabeep applet and from the **mouseDown** method copy the appropriate commands to perform a 'beep'. (You may wish to simply cause mouseDown to call DoBeep instead of cutting and pasting the actual code statements.)

TIP

Adding a New Method or Variable

Remember way back when we discussed classes and adding new methods to them? Well don't forget that you can add a new method or variable to a class by selecting the class, in the class view pane, right clicking, and then selecting **add method**.

Once you have added the method it will be available when Microsoft Internet Explorer 3.0 is running. Next we need a button which the user can push to cause a beep—add a button to the HTML page with the following statement:

```
<INPUT TYPE=BUTTON VALUE="Beep!" NAME="BtnBeep" OnClick="MakeABeep()">
```

And of course you need the correct script code to supports the button. Microsoft Internet Explorer support JavaScript as do other browsers; it is the scripting language of choice. The follow code snippet actual calls the **DoBeep** method:

```
<SCRIPT LANGUAGE="JavaScript">
<!-
function MakeABeep()
{
    document.javabeep.DoBeep();
}
//-->
</SCRIPT>
```

A few things to note. We access the Java applet by adding **document** to the name used in the applet ID tag: in our example, **document.javabeep**. You can reference variables in the same way. If **java**

beep supported a volume variable, you could reference the volume variable with a statement like:

```
document.javabeep.volume = 1;
```

NOTE

Microsoft Internet Explorer 3.0 Also Supports VBScript

While we glossed over it, Microsoft Internet Explore 3.0 also support VBScript as a scripting language. Now you have two choices for writing scripting code into your web page. In the next chapter we will explore scripting in more detail. You can also learn more about **JavaScript** and **VBScript** and their support in Microsoft Internet Explorer through the web pages **http://www.microsoft.com/jscript/** and **http://www.microsoft.com/vbscript/** respectively.

Wow! That was really simple! The last thing you might want to do is call methods which came from the parent class of the applet. Only those methods in the derived applet are available for use through scripting. If you wish to call a method which is from a parent class, you need to define a public method in the child applet class.

CONCLUSION

We have only just begun to touch on the power of integrating COM objects and Java. Many excellent books exist on the subject of COM including books by Kraig Brockschmidt and David Kruglinski. COM objects open up an entire new world to Java applets allowing them to do anything any other Windows application can do and more. You can expect to see many exciting things from ActiveX-enabled Web pages in the future.

And on a final note. You should always make sure that the any pages which are available to the outside world and use COM can only be run on a page which supports COM integration. You can do this by inserting the following HTML tag into your page.

```
<OBJECT
CLASSID="clsid:08B0E5C0-4FCB-11CF-AAA5-00401C608500"
CODEBASE="http://www.microsoft.com/java/IE30Java.cab#Version=1,0,0,1">
</OBJECT>
```

The purpose of this tag is the check the version of Microsoft Internet Explorer or that the current browser supports ActiveX and COM. Under Internet Explorer, if the version is not current an attempt is made to download the current version from **http://www.microsoft.com**.

EXERCISES

28-1   What are the five areas ActiveX 'play's in?

28-2   What are the seven 'core' technologies defined by Open Group and Microsoft?

28-3   Run OLE Object View and store the object definition for some object to a file. What can you tell about the object?

28-4   Run OLE Object View and store the object definition for some object which contains externally visible variables. What can you tell about the variables?

28-5   Run the OLE Object viewer on a class. Describe briefly each of the interfaces found. What each is for and what methods exist in each. What object would you create vs what interface to access it?

28-6   Implement the enhancements to javabeep discussed in the scripting section. What if any problems did you encounter?

28-7   Add a public variable to the javabeep class of exercise 28-6 and call it beepcount. Update javabeep to default the variable to 1 and DoBeep to do beepcount beeps. Add then new buttons to javabeep which set beepcount to 1, 3, and 5 respectively.

CHAPTER 29

Advanced Topics in COM and Scripting

In this chapter we cover the following topics:

- **Scripting using JavaScript and VBScript**
- **Data Access Objects**
- **Remote Access Objects**
- **Trusted Versus Untrusted classes**
- **Creating and Signing Cabinet Files**

INTRODUCTION

In the last chapter we introduced ActiveX, COM and Scripting. One of the greatest features of ActiveX and Internet Explorer is their combined ability to be controlled by scripting. Now you can actually control your Java applet from a Visual Basic program! In this chapter we will learn a little more about Java and scripting using both VBScript and JavaScript. We shall also touch on a few other packaged ActiveX controls which ship with Visual J++, Data Access Objects, and Remote Access Objects. We will complete our discussion of ActiveX and COM with a description of **Trusted** and **Untrusted** classes and Cabinet files.

SCRIPTING IN DEPTH

In Chapter 28 we saw a very simple applet which exposed several of its methods and then we used these exposed methods to control the applet using JavaScript. But what we didn't see was how full-featured JavaScript is and how Internet Explorer supports both JavaScript and VBScript. VBScript is yet another scripting language supported by Internet Explorer. In the next few sections we will examine both of these scripting languages and gain a better understand of how we might use them to create better Web pages and control our ActiveX and Java applets.

JavaScript

JavaScript was designed to be a compact, lightweight interpreted scripting language which can be embedded into an HTML page for developing full-featured client/server Web applications. As with other scripting languages, JavaScript provides support for most common Web page events like mouse clicks, input from forms, 'mouse over' and other page navigation. One of the best features of JavaScript is that it is executed at the remote browser, making it quick and easy to perform validation of user input without resorting to something as heavy weight as a Java applet.

JavaScript supports most of the control constructs and expression syntax of Java but with less strict type checking and a simpler object model. JavaScript contains only a limited number of data types including numeric, string, and Boolean types, (but none of the large classes which are supported by Java in general).

NOTE

JavaScript Only Supports Three Variable Types

Currently JavaScript only supports three variable types: numeric, Boolean and string. These types match their Java counterparts exactly. Note that the numeric type is somewhat like a VBScript variant in that numeric could be integer, float, double, as well as others.

The main differences between Java and JavaScript are described in Table 29.1.

Where do we start? Now that we have a little better understanding of the differences between Java and JavaScript, where do we start? The following is a simple HTML page with some embedded JavaScript code:

Table 29.1 Java and JavaScript Compared.

Java	JavaScript
Not Applicable	Can control a Java Applet
Compiled into byte codes on server	Interpreted by client
Strong Typing	Loose Typing.
Methods declared and typed	Variable types not required in functions
Large number of build in types	Only three built in types. Numeric, string and boolean.
Class based	Classes not supported
Supports Inheritance	Can use other objects but not define new ones.
Separate applet	Embedded into a page
Static Binding. Checked at compile time	Dynamic Binding, checked at run time.

```
<html>
<head>
Some Very Simple JavaScript!
</head>
<body>
<br>
This is regular everyday text!
<br>
<script language="JavaScript">
document.write("Wow I did it!")
</script>
<br>
</body>
</html>
```

> **NOTE**
>
> This section gives you a basic flavor of JavaScript. Most of the code you will see will be snippets or fragments, not complete programs. If you wish to find more information about JavaScript **visit http://www.microsoft.com/jscript/** or the Netscape home page. Or alternatively buy and read one of the many excellent books available from John Wiley & Sons about JavaScript.

This example is simple and straightforward, but not very interesting. Lets look at something a little more useful. Often JavaScript statements are associated with some sort of external event such as pressing a button or a mouse click. As we saw in Chapter 28, we can connect a button press with a Java Script method as follows.

```
<INPUT TYPE=BUTTON VALUE="Beep!" NAME="BtnBeep" OnClick="MakeABeep()">
```

This simple statement creates a button labeled 'Beep!' and associates it with a function **MakeABeep**, which should be executed when the button is clicked.

Table 29.2 gives a short list of the events which are handled by JavaScript with a explanation of when they occur.

> **NOTE**
>
> ### Statements in an Event Handler
>
> The **OnClick** tag within the HTML statement above is an example of an event handler. While **MakeABeep()** calls the JavaScript-defined function, you are not constrained to such simple statements. You can place whatever JavaScript statements you wish in the **OnClick** handler, separated with semi-colons. But adding the statements to a **<SCRIPT>** block makes your code easier to read and reuse.

Table 29.2   JavaScript Events.

Event	Occurs when	Handler
blur or lose focus	User removes focus from a form element	**OnBlur**
mouse click	Use clocks on a form element, link or button	**OnClick**
change	User changes a value of some text area	**OnChange**
gain focus	User gives focus to an new element	**OnFocus**
load	A page is loaded	**OnLoad**
mouseover	User moves a mouse over a link or anchor	**OnMouseOver**
select	User selects one of a form element's fields	**OnSelect**
submit	User submits a form	**OnSubmit**
unload	User closes or unload's a page	**OnUnload**

We then add the function call with the following code:

```
<SCRIPT LANGUAGE="JavaScript">
<!—
function MakeABeep()
{
    document.javabeep.DoBeep();
}
//—>
</SCRIPT>
```

> **TIP**
>
> ### HTML, Comments and Old Browsers
>
> Most older browsers are smart enough to ignore HTML tags they don't understand, but not smart enough to ignore the text in between them! When you are writing JavaScript you can fool an old browser into ignoring your script by **hiding** it in comments. By placing the **<!—** start comment and **//—>** end comment delimiter, an old browser will ignore the script code because it thinks its a comment!

Let's take a few moments and look at just a little bit more of JavaScript.

Statements, Control Structures, and Looping Constructs Statements are the basic element of any language. Control structures allow for the conditional execution of statements; looping structures for repeating commands; and other constructs such as **new** and **this** for working with objects. JavaScript provides all of these and Table 29.3 gives a short, but not complete, list of Key JavaScript constructs and what each is for.

Anyone who has programmed with C or C++ will feel right at home with JavaScript!

Referring to Java Applets in JavaScript Of course this is a book on Java and not JavaScript, and we would like a better understanding of how to connect our Java applets with JavaScript.

For non-frame-based HTML pages, it's easy to reference applets. You simply reference them through the default document using the name provided in the Applet ID tag. As we saw in Chapter 28, you ref-

Table 29.3   JavaScript Constructs

Construct	Usage
if.. else	'C' Style if statement.
for	'C' Style for statement.
While	'C' Style while statement.
break	Terminate the current for loop or while statement.
continue	Terminate the current loop and continue execution at next iteration.
for... in	Iterate through a set of properties of some object.
new	Create a new instance of an object.
with	Pascal styles with statement. Specify and object and the interpreter assumes references relative to the object.
Function call	Supports function calls with returns. Supports function calls without returns via void.
//	Single line comment.
/* */	Multi-line comment.

erence an applet whose ID is **foo** and where **foo** exposes a public variable SomeNumber within JavaScript as:

```
document.foo.Somenumber = 5
```

Simple and straightforward. If your applet exposed some method which took as a parameter a number you would simply reference it as follows.

```
document.foo.MethodTakingNumber(5);
```

For frame-based HTML, you reference the variable applet in a similar fashion. Only now we differentiate via the frame. For example, given a frame titled **someframe** we would reference our Java applet within it as follows:

```
someframe.document.foo.Somenumber = 5
```

For more information about windows, frames, documents and JavaScript objects, see your favorite JavaScript book!

VBScript

For those more comfortable with Visual Basic, the Microsoft Internet Explorer also supports VBScript. VBScript is a lightweight version of Visual Basic which Microsoft plans to license to other companies free of charge. Visual Basic also comes in two other flavors. Visual Basic for Applications, for those who need a lightweight programming language which supports scripting and comes complete with a development environment. And Visual Basic Version 5; for those individuals who want a complete programming environment suitable for developing corporate mission-critical applications.

In a nutshell, VBScript allows you to embed Visual Basic functions within your Web page. VBScript supports controlling ActiveX controls, Visual Basic and Java applets, all within your Web pages and executed on the client!

Where do we start? We've seen some simple JavaScript, but how can we do the same thing in VBScript that we did in the first sample JavaScript program in this chapter. Here's the same example, this time using VBScript:

```
<html>
<head>
Some Very Simple VBScript!
</head>
<body>
<br>
This is regular everyday text!
<br>
<script language="VBScript">
document.write("Wow I did it!")
</script>
<br>
</body>
</html>
```

Certainly no rocket science there! The primary difference was that we stated that the scripting language we wished to use was VBScript. Let's look at the another sample. This one creating a button and then adding a handler for it.

First create the button, notice the lack of the OnClick keyword.

```
<INPUT TYPE=BUTTON VALUE="VBBeep!" NAME="BtnVBBeep">
```

Then the scripting code for beeping:

```
<SCRIPT language = "VBScript">
<!-
Sub BtnVBBeep_OnClick
    document.javabeep.DoBeep
End Sub
->
</SCRIPT>
```

> **TIP**
>
> ### Mixing VBScript and JavaScript
>
> There's nothing that says you can't mix VBScript and JavaScript in the same page. Nothing but readability that is. If you have been following along with the examples you should be able to add the VBScript button above and cause our sample applet to beep just like the JavaScript examples.

There are other ways to capture events than the one shown. The following code does the same thing as the button and event handler above, although the connection is not as clear:

```
<SCRIPT language = "VBScript" Event="OnClick" For="BtnVBBeep">
<!-
    document.javabeep.DoBeep
->
</SCRIPT>
```

Variables in VBScript Variables are handled differently in VBScript versus JavaScript. Under most languages you have a selection of variables, each strongly typed. For example 'C' has longs, shorts, floats, strings and a host of others. VBScript has one 'super' type called a **Variant**. A variant is a special type of variable which takes on its type when it is used. Variants behave like strings when treated likes strings, and numbers when treated likes numbers, etc. In addition a whole set of conversion functions exist which allow you to convert from one type to another.

Statements, Control Structures, and Looping Constructs As with JavaScript, VBScript contains a rich set of control and looping structures. Table 29.4 shows a list of some of these constructs.

Table 29.4   VBScript Constructs

if..then..else	Standard 'basic' if then else.
Do..loop	Loop while or until a condition is true
While..wend	Loop while a condition is true.
For..Next	Loop via counter.
Sub	Create a sub routine without a return
function	Create a sub routine which returns a value
REM	Single line comment

While not as extensive as JavaScript, VBScript certainly contains an adequate set of looping and control structures for program development.

Referring to Java Applets in VBScript The object reference model for VBScript is identical to that of JavaScript—no differences worth noting exist. Even the syntax is the same! Simply reference the Java applet through the document that contains it.

> **NOTE**
>
> ### The JavaScript and VBScript Object Models
>
> You can download an excellent document on JavaScript and VBScript object models from the Microsoft page **http://www. microsoft.com/intdev/sdk/docs/scriptom/**. Select download **omscript.zip** or simply read about the object model right on the page.

JavaScript and VBScript Compared

JavaScript and VBScript are both capable languages. Both support a variety of looping constructs, conditionals, and other attributes. Table 29.5 shows a short list of some of the similarities and differences between the languages.

As with most things, both languages have advantages and disadvantages. VBScript supports a much wider range of data types, but only within a **Variant**. JavaScript supports a larger number of looping constructs, but nothing that can't be simulated with VBScript. VBScript is stable, whereas JavaScript is still evolving. All in all it comes down to personal preference and the fact that JavaScript is supported by browsers other than Microsoft Internet Explorer!

Table 29.5   Java and VBScript Compared

JavaScript	VBScript
[] used for array references	() used for array references.
Case Sensitive	CasE iNsEnsiTivE
Supports three variable types, numeric, string and boolean (Numeric is somewhat like varient)	Supports only the special variant type
Supports both call by value and call by reference (only supports call by reference for objects)	Currently only call by value supported
Support functions with returns.	Supports subprocedures (Like 'C' void) and functions.
Supports if else	Support if then else
Supports looping with while, do, for and for In. Also break and continue.	Supports looping with do..loop, while..wend and for next.
	Supports exit do which is similar to break.
Can be embedded in HTML statements **Ie <a href="JavaScript:alert(document.title)">Show Document Title.</a>**	Cannot be embedded as shown
Evolving language	Well defined stable language

DATA ACCESS OBJECTS

Database access under Windows was originally a difficult task. Each and every database came with its own set of API calls and with each a new learning curve. Then **O**pen **DataB**ase **C**onnectivity (ODBC) entered the scene. Instead of a proprietary API, each database provider provides an ODBC-compliant driver. Using the ODBC interface, you can now access data from different databases using a uniform API set. Having learned one interface, you're done!

Data Access Objects, or DAO as they are more commonly called, brings ODBC to Java. DAO is an OLE2 object which allows you to connect your Java applet with ODBC, and consequently to any database which supports OBBC, or the Jet engine database.

Visual J++ ships with a simple DAO sample. The DAOSample creates a simple form which allows you to step backwards and forwards in a database. Basically the calls of interest are:

- Opening the database (**_DBEngine and OpenDatabase()**)
- Moving from record to record (Using recordsets, **MoveFirst**, **MoveLast**, **MoveNext**, **MovePrevious**)
- Gathering and displaying data using fields.

> **NOTE**
>
> ### Additional Information About ODBC
>
> ODBC is a vast topic which complete books have been published on. For more information on ODBC see the Microsoft Web page **http://www.microsoft.com/kb/faq/backoffc/** and select ODBC or search for ODBC in the back office SDK available to subscribers of the Microsoft Developers Network Level II.

> **NOTE**
>
> ### DAO Sample
>
> If you haven't already, now would be a good time to load the DAO sample application. Simply select **DAOSample** from the Microsoft Samples section of the Visual J++ book on-line and follow the direction to create a copy of the sample.

Let's look at each of these areas so we can get a better understanding of how DAO objects work and how we might use them to create powerful database-enabled applets.

> **TIP**
>
> ### Data Access Objects Definitions
>
> Before you jump right in you might find it handy to have a copy of the class definitions which go with the DAO calls. The Java Type Library Wizard will produce a summary file for you which contains these class definitions. If you haven't run Java Type Library Wizard before, it's quite simple: choose **Java Type Library Wizard** from the **Tools** menu. Find Microsoft DAO in the list and select it and then hit the OK button. From the Java Type Library tab of the Results window, check the name and location of the summary file and open it.

Opening the database

Before you can access any sort of database you must first establish a connection to it. You connect to a data source by first creating a license to use it (DAO is a licensed COM object) and then using the **OpenDatabase** call to open the database.

> **NOTE**
>
> ### Using the LicenseMgr **COM Object**
>
> The **LicenseMsg** interface implements the **ILicenseMsg** interface which allows you to use controls or COM objects which require licenses. You use this object by creating an instance of it and then calling the **createWithLic** method to grant a license. You must know the license key for the object you wish to gain access to before you can make this call. See the **dao_dbengine** class in the DAO sample for an example of how to use this interface.

The **_DBEngine** class grants and controls access to databases. Using the **_DBEngine** class, you can open existing databases (**Open Database** method); create new databases(**CreateDatabase** method); and manipulate **workspaces**. Workspaces allow the developer to manage sessions. Sessions provide security and transaction control mechanisms such as **Begin Transaction**, **Rollback**, and **Commit**. For our simple read-only application, a workspaces is not required.

Let's look at how the database is opened. In the **start** method of the class **simpledao**, we see the following code:

```
_DBEngine idbengine = dao_dbengine.create();
Database database;

// Create Variants for optional parameters
Variant v1 = new Variant();
Variant v2 = new Variant();
Variant v3 = new Variant();

v1.putBoolean(false);
v2.putBoolean(false);
v3.putString("");

// Open the database for non-exclusive access
database = idbengine.OpenDatabase(filename, v1, v2, v3);
```

This code first creates a license to use the DAO COM object and then allocates a DOA Database object to store the database. The **Open Database** method has the following syntax:

```
Database somedatabase=[workspace.]OpenDatabase(dbname[,exclusive[,read-only[, source]]])
```

Where:

workspace	If you are using a workspace then you may open the database within the context of that workspace and have all the mechanisms associated with workspaces available for use.
database	The **OpenDatabase** method returns a instance of a Database object data type that refers to the dbname you are opening.
dbname	A string that is the name of an existing database file. Note that an error will occur if you attempt to open a database which is already open for exclusive access by another user.

In addition to required arguments you may also specify the following optional arguments.

exclusive	A Boolean which represents whether the database should be opened for exclusive access (exclusive = true).
read-only	A Boolean which represents whether the database should be opened for read-only access or not(readonly = true).
source	A string representing the source of the database. A blank string is used for the Microsoft Jet Engine. You may specify other sources based on the databases installed on your machine.

NOTE

Always Close What You Open

Don't forget to close the database before your application exits! The **stop** method closes the record set associated with the database opened in the **start** method.

Using Record Sets

After you have opened a database, you will want to access it. You access the actual data by creating one or more record sets which represent logical sets of records which you may wish to access. The following creates a record set:

```
v4.putShort(Constants.dbOpenDynaset);
v5.putShort(Constants.dbReadOnly);
recordset = database.OpenRecordset(m_Recordset, v4, v5);
```

The syntax of the **OpenRecordset** class is:

```
Recordset rs = database.OpenRecordset([type[, options]])
```

Where:

database	The database object created in the prior step.
Type	You can create three types of record sets. The default, **dbOpenTable**, opens a flat table type record set. **dbOpenDynaset**, creates a **Dynaset** type database record set—that is one which is kept in sync with the database. And the type. **DbOpen Snapshot** creates a snapshot of the current database. New records are not shown, nor are deletes or changes.
source	A string specifying the source of the records for the new **Recordset**. The source can be a table name, a query name, or an SQL statement that returns records. For table-type Recordset objects, the source can only be a table name.

In addition, an entire set of options exist, such as **SQlPassThrough** for passing SQL statements to the underlying database driver. **Read Only**, **DenyWrite** and a host of others.

Once you have created a record set you can call one of the many record set methods to manipulate it. The following table shows just some of the more interesting record set methods as well as a variety of methods for determining fields, indexes and making SQL based queries.

Table 29.6   More Recordset methods.

MoveFirst	Move to the first record in the record set.
MoveLast	Move to the last record in the record set.
MoveNext	Move to the next record in the record set.
MovePrevious	Move to the previous record in the record set.
Delete	Delete the selected record.
Update	Update the selected record.
AddNew	Add a new record.

Since we wish to look at the entire set of records, we ignore doing any special SQL queries to reduce or change the set of records we were looking at.

> **TIP**
>
> ### Visual J++ and Visual C++ Books Online
>
> Much ODBC and DAO access is done from Visual C++. As such Visual C++ has a vast set of documentation for using DAO. For those developers lucky enough to also have Visual C++ installed, select the Visual C++ set of books online and look into the various recordset and database definitions found there. The information is presented well, is easy to use, and goes into much greater depth then the Visual J++ books online!

Reading Data

After creating a record set, you normally want to query and display data from it. The **SimpleForm** class does this for us by creating a form with a set of fields on it and then displaying the data. Using a Fields object get the list of fields the record set supports using the getFields method:

```
Fields fields = m_recordset.getFields();
```

We could then cycle thru the fields list, creating a list of available fields and displaying them all, but we know which fields we want so using the **getItem** method we extract each field one by one and store the data in the appropriate display field. The following code snippet, from the showData method of the simpleForm class, shows an example of using both the **Fields** class and individual field entries:

```
_Field f;
f = fields.getItem(name1);
// Get its value
value = f.getValue();
// Set the field in the form
field1.setText(value.toString());
```

We have only touched on the very beginnings of what can be done with ODBC and DAO. There is nothing to prevent you from mixing data from many sources, using sophisticated SQL queries to create temporary tables and then displaying the results! Most likely if you can do it with embedded SQL you can do it with DAO!

TRUSTED VERSUS UNTRUSTED CLASSES

The last topic requiring discussion is security and ActiveX. Since ActiveX controls, and COM in general, can be implemented in any language, they normally are not covered by the standard Java security model. Internet Explorer attempts to cover this by using the concept of **Trusted vs Untrusted** classes:

- *Untrusted classes* run within the browser and cannot normally use COM. Any downloaded class or class not loaded via the CLASS-PATH are considered untrustworthy. Classes which are packaged as signed cabinet files (.CAB) are considered trusted. (More on cabinet files in a moment.)
- *Trusted classes* are the only ones which are allowed to normally use COM services. Trusted classes include those which were loaded locally from the class path and those classes which were extracted from digitally signed cab files. Trusted classes are freed from the constraints of the Java security model and are allowed to perform actions which normally might violate system integrity. (Such as file I/O.)

When developing using ActiveX controls its important to understand how Microsoft Internet Explorer behaves with respect to classes and the **CLASSPATH**. There are four registry variables which control the variables values used by Microsoft Internet Export, all of which are normally found under:

```
HKEY_LOCAL_MACHINE\Software\Microsoft\Java VM.
```

They are:

ClassPath	Classes available to all applets.
LibsDirectory	Libraries available to all applets.
TrustedClassPath	Classes available to trusted applets.
TrustedLibsDirectory	Libraries available to trusted applets.

The primary difference between these four paths is the order in which they are searched when a trusted or untrusted applet is run. For a trusted applet, the four paths are searched in the following order: the **TrustedClassPath**; and then the **TrustedLibsDirectory**. Additionally the **ClassPath** and **LibsDirectory** paths are searched.

For untrusted applets, the **ClassPath** and **LibsDirectory** paths are the only paths searched.

Internet Explorer takes security one step further in that even COM classes which are wrapped in Java classes found in either the **ClassPath** or **LibsDirectory** cannot be run by an untrusted applet.

> **NOTE**
>
> ### Path Searching During Development
>
> When you run an application from within Visual J++ your application is considered trusted and the trusted applet rules. In addition, if the applet was run from the command line using **JView.exe** then the **CLASSPATH** environment variable is also searched. If the applet was run from within Visual J++, then any directory specified in the **Directories** tab of the **Options** dialog is searched.

Basically, a trusted applet can access any class, trusted or otherwise. Where as an untrusted applet can only access those classes found in the **ClassPath** or **LibsDirectory** directory.

CREATING SIGNED CABINET FILES

Cabinet files benefit the Java developer and person browsing the net in several ways. First and foremost cabinet files are compressed collections of files which are decompressed and saved on the host machine. If created correctly, download time can be saved when Microsoft Internet Explorer discovers that a cabinet has already been downloaded and need not download it again. Cabinet files provide a second major benefit, that of security. When you combine cabinet files and digital signing you get a more robust security model which the user can trust.

NOTE

Complete Updates on Cabinet Files and Signing

For a complete description of Cabinet files and digital signing, see the **readme.txt** and **overview.html** for the cabinet developers kit (**CabDevKit.exe**) and the various html files provided with the code signing kit (**CodeSignKit.exe**). Both are available in the **Cab&Sign** directory of the Visual J++ developers kit. The code signing and cabinet developers kits update often. Get the most recent version of the cabinet developers kit from from the site **http://www.microsoft.com/workshop/java/cab-f.htm**. Additional information about code signing can be obtained from the site **http://www.microsoft.com/workshop/**.

To use the Cabinet Developers Kit, you must first find and install the kit. Under Visual J++ version 1.1, the kit can be found in the directory **Cab&Sign\CabDevKit.exe**. You can copy the Cabinet Development Kit to a directory and install it from there or simply run **CabDevKit.exe** from the **cd** directly. Run the executable and then follow the directions.

TIP

Directories for the Cabinet Developers Kit and Code Signing Kit

A simple and easy place to install the Cabinet Developers Kit and Code Signing Kits is beneath the **MSDEV** directory where you installed Visual J++. I prefer to use directories **msdev\cabdev** and **msdev\codesign**. By placing the kits under the **msdev** tree, you will not have trouble remembering where they are installed later.

You can install the Code Signing Kit by running **Cab&Sign\ CodeSignKit.exe** and following the instructions.

Creating Cabinet Files

You can create Cabinet files simply and easily using the **CABARC** utility packaged with the CabDevKit. In its most simple form **CABARC** is run as follows:

```
CABARC n somecab.cab somedevice:\somedirectory\*.class
```

This command says create a new cabinet (n) named **somecab.cab** from the class files found in **somedevice:\somedirectory**.

The syntax of **CABARC** is:

```
CABARC [<options>] <command> <cabfile> [<filelist...>] [dest_dir]
```

Where commands are:

L	List contents of cabinet (for example **CABARC** l test.cab)
N	Create new cabinet (for example **CABARC** n test.cab *.c app.mak *.h)
X	Extract file(s) from cabinet (for example **CABARC** x test.cab foo*.c)

The various options are:

-c	Confirm files to be operated on
-o	When extracting, overwrite without asking for confirmation
-m	Set compression type [MSZIP | NONE] (default is MSZIP)
-p	Preserve path names (relative paths only)
-P	Strip specified prefix from files when added
-r	Recurse into subdirectories when adding files
-s	Reserve space in cabinet for signing (for example -s 6144 reserves 6K bytes)
-i	Set cabinet set ID when creating cabinets (default is 0)
—	Stop option parsing (can be used when an file name contains a dash)

Another common use of **CABARC** is to create Cabinet files which recreate an existing directory structure. You can do this by combining the **-p** and **-r** arguments. For example, the following command creates a new cabinet, **recurse.cab**, which replicates the directory structure under **somedir**.

```
CABARC -p -r n recurse.cab somedir\*.class
```

Another interesting command option is the **-s** option. In the next section we will discuss code signing. But before you sign code, you need to reserve space for the signature. The **-s** parameter defines how much additional space should be allocated in the cabinet file for the digital signature.

For example, to create cab file from a set of Class files stored under **myclassdir** which contains extra space for a **1k** signature you would run **CABARC** as follows:

```
CABARC -p -r -s 1024 n myclasses.cab myclassdir\*.class
```

HTML for Cabinets Once you have created a cabinet file, you need to incorporate it into your Web page. This is done easily with the following simple HTML code. For applets you enter:

```
<APPLET CODE ="MainClass.class" CODEBASE="/java/classes"
WIDTH=x HEIGHT=y>
<PARAM NAME="cabbase" value="mycab.cab">
</APPLET>
```

In this example, **mycab.cab** is the cabinet file name and **/java/classes** is the path to the classes directory used to store the unpacked cabinet. You can ignore the **CODEBASE** parameter if the code is in the same directory as the Web page.

For libraries the object tag would be as follows:

```
<OBJECT CLASSID="clsid:123456789-abcf-efghijklmnop"
CODEBASE="somecab.cab:Version=1,0,0,0">
</OBJECT>
```

In this example, **clsid** is the ID generated for the library by the ActiveX toolkit **uuidgen.exe** tool. Note that the version number is optional but always a good idea.

> **NOTE**
>
> ### Creating Downloadable Library Files
>
> If you intend, or even think you might, create downloadable libraries it is in your best interest to read and understand the sections from the Cabinet Developers Kit **readme.txt** file which deal with libraries. Libraries are much more complex then simple cabinets and require a much deeper understanding of how they are used from both a user and developers standpoint.

Signing Cabinet Files

In the previous section we discussed how to create cabinet files and how you might allocate empty space for a digital signature. Let's take a few moments and look at how you would actually create and apply a digital signature to a cabinet file and the HTML required to use that signature.

Why you Want to Sign Files Before the Internet, software was released prepackaged and through reliable trusted sales outlets. Originally Web pages contained only static data for display. With the advent of Java and scripting languages, code can be delivered directly to your machine off the net—with or without your knowledge. With anyone and everyone creating Web pages, how do you tell the good guys from the bad? In cyberspace, it's pretty hard to tell the black hats and the white hats apart.

Two real issues exist. How can we be sure where the code we are executing came from? And how can we be sure that the code we are running hasn't be changed or tampered with?

Enter digital code signing. Code signing doesn't certify that code is good or correct. But it does state categorically who it came from and that it wasn't tampered with during transit. Microsoft distributes with Visual J++ a set of tools known collectively as **Authenticode** which allow the software developer to create and assign digital signatures to cabinet files.

Digital Signing and Public Key Signatures Digital signatures are created using algorithms typically called RSA public key/private key ciphers. Public key/private key encryption is designed such that one key (the private key) is used for encryption and the second (public key) is used for decryption. The private key is known only by the signer of the code where as the public key is known by everyone. The two keys are designed such that having one does not mean you can generate the other.

Public key/private key signatures work as follows:

1. A hash code is created from a document.
2. The hash code is encrypted with a private key and used as a digital signature.
3. The file and its signature are both transferred to the recipient.
4. The recipient recreates the hash code from the document.
5. Using the public key, the receiver decodes the hash code and compares the two; if the hash coded match, then the document is intact and unchanged.

> **NOTE**
>
> ### Public Key/Private Key Encryption and Cabinet Signing
>
> The entire concept of Public Key/Private key Encryption and Cabinet signing is way beyond the scope of this document. An in-depth description of the entire process can be found in the documents which come with the code signing kit distributed with Visual J++.

Note that several agencies exist for assigning **certificates** to both individuals and corporations. Certificates are just that, certification that you are who you say you are. They are issued by someone who is generally trusted by all. These certificates follow a very strict specification known as X.509 and can then be used to digitally sign files. The remainder of this section describes the Authenticode package shipped with Visual J++.

Authenticode Authenticode is actually a set of five tools which allow you to create signatures, assign them to files, test those files, and generally determine that the process of signing worked.

Developing signed Cabinet files is a simple five-step process.

1. Run **MakeCert** to create a test certificate which can be used to sign a file. For example:

   ```
   MakeCert -u:somekey -n:CI=AnIndividual MyCert.cer
   ```

2. Run **Cert2SPC** to generate a *Software Publishing Certificate* from the result of Step 1. For example:

```
Cert2Spc MyCert.cer MyCert.spc
```

3. Run **SignCode** to apply the certificate created in Step 2 to sign a piece of code or Cabinet files. For example:

```
SignCode -prog MyCabinet.cab -spc MyCert.spc -pvk MyKey.pvt -i individual
```

Note that the private key was also generated by Step 1. At this point you would normally be able to distribute your cabinet to the outside world.

4. Run **PeSignMgr** to make sure that the addition of the certificate was successful. For example:

```
PeSignMgr -l MyCabinet.cab
```

5. Run **ChkTrust** the check the validity of the file normally. For example:

```
CkhTrust MyCabinet.cab
```

> **NOTE**
>
> ### Obtaining a Certificate from a Certification Authority
>
> Both individuals and corporations can obtain certificates for signing software. The certification process for corporations is much more rigorous then that for individuals. Certification Authorities are currently being created and are expected to be available when this book publishes. See the Microsoft Web Site at **http://www .microsoft.com** and also the Web page, **http://www.microsoft. com/corpinfo/press/1996/mar96/digsinpr.htm**, which contains information about current certification authorities. Or see VeriSign at **http://www.verisign.com** for more information.

Using digital signatures is a straightforward and important process. For a complete description of Microsoft Authenticode and its associated utilities, see the HTML pages which come with the Code&Sign kits shipped with Visual J++.

CONCLUSION

Security is a thorny problem and the Internet only makes it worse. Visual J++ and the *Authenticode* tool set goes a long way to solving the Internet security problems. Data Access Object and Remote Access objects are just one powerful way to let the strength of databases shine through into Web pages. While these technologies are not for the faint-of-heart it is clear that they are the wave of the future! And when combined with scripting provide a powerful and robust Web development environment.

EXERCISES

30-1　Name 3 differences between VBScript and JavaScript.

30-2　Choose VBScript or JavaScript for developing scripted Web pages. Backup your choice.

30-3　Update the JavaBeep example to contain both VBScript and JavaScript buttons which control the javabeep applet. Make sure that if you do something in JavaScript you also show how to do it in VBScript.

30-4　Describe some of the more important features of Data Access Objects.

30-5　Select and build the DAO sample from the Visual J++ CDROM. Update the sample to show the count of records in the recordset. What method in the recordset class did you use?

30-6　Create a cabinet file from a set of class files. Describe two uses for cabinets.

30-7　Describe the basics of signing a cabinet file. What reasons are there for digital signatures.

30-8　How might you go about listing all the fields in a record set rather then selected ones. Could you modify the SimpleForm class of the DAO example to be driven from the database rather then be hard coded?

CHAPTER 30

The Visual J++
Database Wizard

In this chapter we cover the following topics:

- An Overview of the Database Wizard
- A Sample Database
- Creating a Database Applet with DAO
- Understanding the Generated Code
- Modifying the Code
- Building an RDO Applet

AN OVERVIEW OF THE DATABASE WIZARD

When I begin trying to build a new application, I try to build it up from parts that work. When I try to learn something a bit new, I look at a simple working example, and try to modify it, to see if my grasp of the concepts are good. With some allowance for variation in the details, it seems likely that this is how we all approach any new issue pertaining to computers.

Visual J++ offers the Database Wizard, when you are creating a new project (See Figure 30.1). This Wizard uses four short pages of dialog to walk you through creation of a database viewing or manipulating applet/application. You have no control of the form of the applet, except to define which database items will appear in your Graphic User Interface.

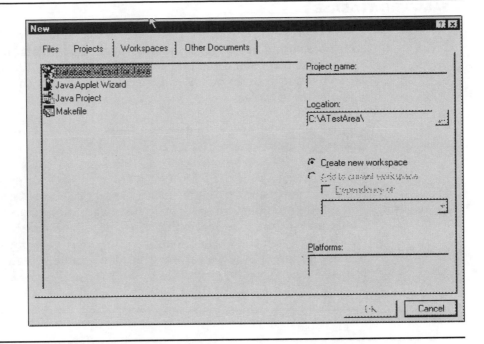

Figure 30.1   Notice the Database Wizard at the top left of the New Project dialog.

> ### TIP
>
> ### You Need a Database to Use the Wizard
>
> Before you begin using the Database Wizard, you should already have a database created. It can be a Microsoft Access database, or one available through Access, or it can be any database for which there is an ODBC driver, including text files. Our point is that the Database Wizard examines the database, and asks you to select items from it to make visible in your applet.

The resulting code from the database wizard is a well designed applet that views one database table. Such an applet is unlikely to serve as a final product, unless all of your data is in one table (usually a sign of poor database design). However, that resulting code should serve as an example to imitate, and a basis for modifying to your needs.

A SAMPLE DATABASE

Using Microsoft Access, I have created a small database called *ArchFoes.mdb*. (See Figures 30.2 through 30.4). This database has three small interconnected tables in it. The Database Wizard will only let us use one of these tables, but we can later modify the applet to see a join of these tables.

> **NOTE**
>
> This is not any former President's 'enemies' list, nor of mine. The names mentioned are not meant to be real people. It is simply a list of fictitious names and fictitious places. Younger readers may want to note that in older, less enlightened days, not everyone had the best interest of the world's population foremost in their minds, and some people abused power, or even used criminal and unethical means to achieve their ends. An Arch Foes list is a relic of that dark and gothic bygone era.

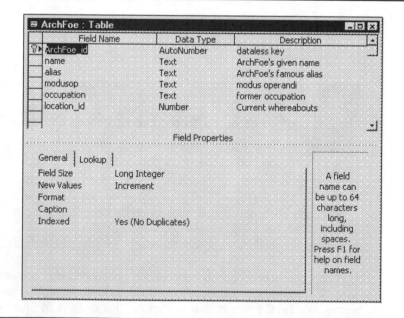

Figure 30.2   ArchFoe table definition.

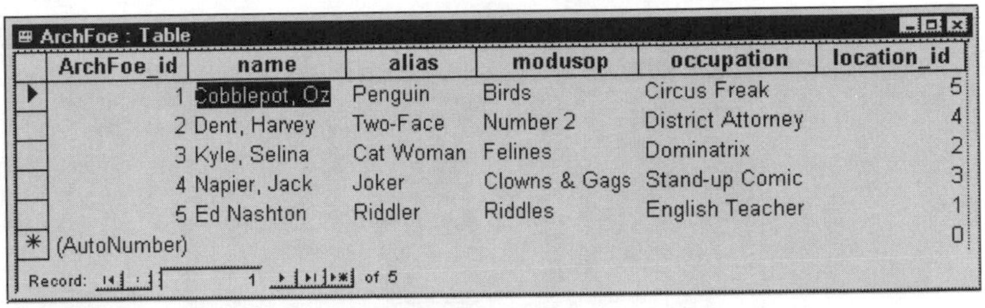

ArchFoe : Table

ArchFoe_id	name	alias	modusop	occupation	location_id
1	Cobblepot, Oz	Penguin	Birds	Circus Freak	5
2	Dent, Harvey	Two-Face	Number 2	District Attorney	4
3	Kyle, Selina	Cat Woman	Felines	Dominatrix	2
4	Napier, Jack	Joker	Clowns & Gags	Stand-up Comic	3
5	Ed Nashton	Riddler	Riddles	English Teacher	1
(AutoNumber)					0

Record: 1 of 5

Figure 30.2a The ArchFoe table contents.

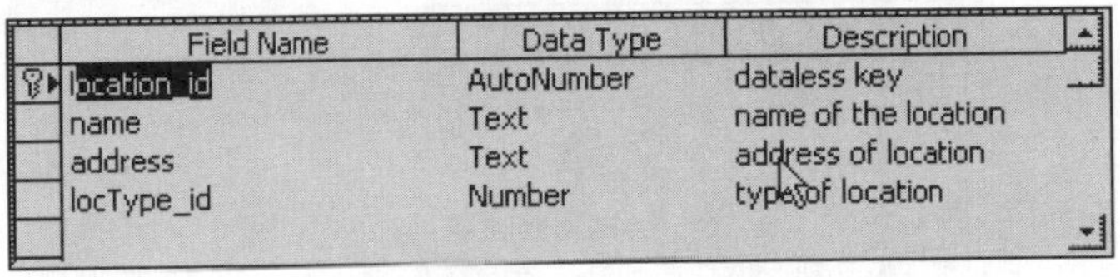

Field Name	Data Type	Description
location_id	AutoNumber	dataless key
name	Text	name of the location
address	Text	address of location
locType_id	Number	type of location

Figure 30.3 The location table definition.

We put this database in the directory *C:\ATestArea\BatDB\Arch Foes.mdb.* This expression will appear in our figures and steps listed below. Naturally you should use your own directory structure.

CREATING A DATABASE APPLET WITH DAO

Creating our database Applet with DAO (for Microsoft Access) is a very simple job. As noted above, it is dependent on the pre-existence of the database and table that it will use.

Start the Process

We begin this endeavor by making certain launching Visual J++ (Visual Studio) and making certain that the current workarea(s) are closed. (This is not a necessary step, but one that makes this description less crowded with if-else constructs.)

- Select **New** from the **File** menu (on the top bar all the way to the left). The resulting dialog box should look like Figure 30.1.

location : Table

location_id	name	address	locType_id
1	unknown	unknown	1
2	Gotham State Penatentury	Faust Island	2
3	Belle Reeve	Withering Heights	2
4	City Lockup	Police HQ	2
5	Arkham Asylum for the Criminally Insane	West Arkham	3
(AutoNumber)			0

Record: 1 of 5

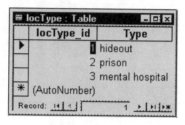

Figure 30.4 The locType table definition.

locType : Table

locType_id	Type
1	hideout
2	prison
3	mental hospital
(AutoNumber)	

Record: 1

Figure 30.4a The locType table contents.

- The default project type is the Database Wizard (see large box on left).
- Give the project a name. We called ours *BatBase*.
- Make sure the Location box's value meets your approval.
- Make sure the **Create new workspace** checkbox is checked.
- Click OK

You have now started the process. You will soon be presented with a four page series, which will navigate you through constructing this customized sample applet.

Fill Out Step One of Four

Step one of four has a page with three items to fill out. The first item is that you must select whether you are getting an Access database from your machine or the local network it is connected to, or whether you are going to a remote data source. In this example, we are selecting a DAO object.

Now we must enter (or browse for) our database, namely the ArchFoes.mdb file in the ATestArea\BatDB directory. Remember that it is not sufficient to find your database, you must select it.

Finally, we must indicate whether this is a read only view of the database, or one that permits inserts, updates, and deletes. For our example, we will not make it read only. There are situations in which you'd like to build up from a read only applet.

> ### TIP
>
> ### Selecting *Read Only* Will Not Change Applet Much
>
> When you create this applet, it supplies all of the underlying code, no matter what you select. Choosing to make it read only sets one variable. The Wizard does not simplify things by selectively leaving out the code required to support database Updates, Inserts, and Deletes.

Let's not dawdle. Your page should look like Figure 30.5. Click **Next** and go to step two.

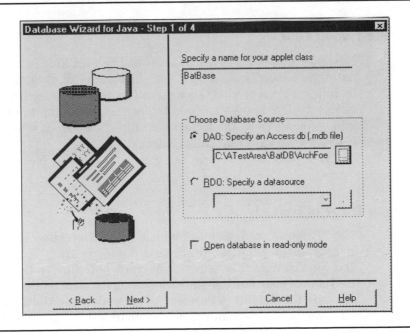

Figure 30.5   Step one. When filled out correctly should look like this.

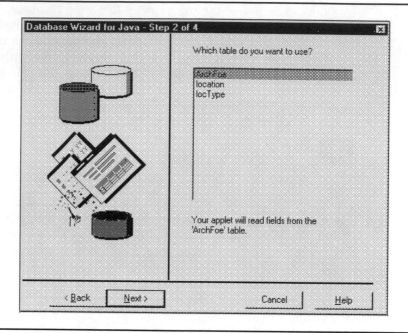

Figure 30.6   Step two. So many tables, so little . . . Hey that's not so many.

Fill Out Page Two of Four

Now you must choose which table will be available in this Applet. The database wizard will only let you select individual table. This does not include result sets from Queries, unless they are specifically stored into visible tables. It does include tables that are links to external ODBC tables. In our case, the table we want is listed first, so it is the default. If you want a different table, select it.

Your page should look like Figure 30.6. Click **Next** and go to step three.

Fill Out Page Three of Four

Step Three is to determine which fields from the table you want to include in your applet. Notice that the fields are listed alphabetically. You can't change this using the Wizard, but you can change the generated source code to alter the order of appearance on the Applet GUI. In this case the default is to select all of the fields in the table, and that is what we have done. Your page should look like Figure 30.7. Click **Next** and go to step four.

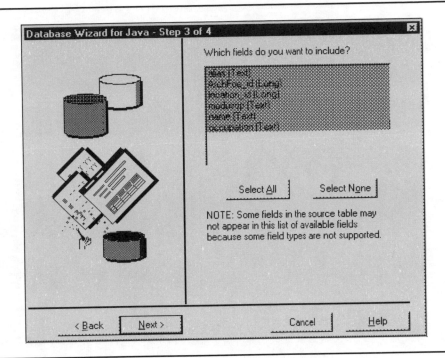

Figure 30.7   Step three. Go ahead, just take them all.

Fill Out Page Four of Four

Do you want comments. Of course you do. The output generated is about 860 lines, including 300 lines of comments. Many of these comments tell you what is being done in the code, and why. Perhaps in a terse fashion, but you would only use this powerful but inflexible tool if you are looking for clues. Why not go for every clue you can get?

You also have the opportunity to get some helpful "**TO DO**" comments. These may or may not be so big a help, but what are you saving by not including them? When it is filled out, you page should look like Figure 30.8. Click **Finish** and see what you get.

Build It

We will take a look at the code that the wizard generated in a few minutes. For now, lets treat this as a gift with the wrapping still on it. We need to build it and run it. This takes two steps:

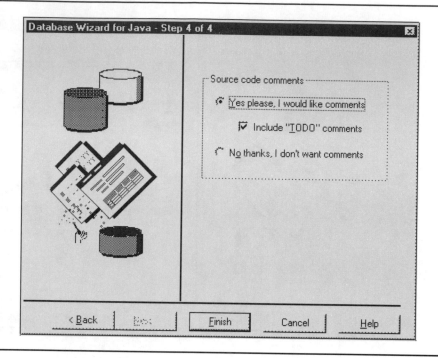

Figure 30.8   Step four. Do you have time for unsolicited free advice? In this case we think you should take it.

- Go to the build menu (see Figure 30.9) and select **Build All**. The computer will chug away for up to a few seconds, and then report *0 errors and 0 warnings*.
- The second step is to select **! Execute**. This time it will take a bit longer, as your computer loads Internet Explorer, loads the web page that the wizard made for you, and then loads and runs your new applet.

Finally, after tens of seconds (depending on your system and memory situation) up it comes.

Execute It

If all goes well, it should look like Figure 30.10. Try it out. This applet has will permit you to scroll through the rows in the ArchFoe table of the ArchFoes database. It will also permit you to add and delete rows! If you want your changes to be persistent, you must also save them.

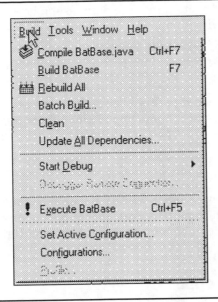

Figure 30.9   The Build drop down. If you've been doing the exercises, we don't need to
point this out.

Database: C:\ATestArea\BatDB\ArchFoes.mdb

Table: ArchFoe

Record: 1 of 5

alias (Text) :	Penguin
ArchFoe_id (Long) (Auto) :	1
location_id (Long) :	5
modusop (Text) :	Birds
name (Text) :	Cobblepot, Oz
occupation (Text) :	Circus Freak

First | < Prev | Next > | Last >> | Save! | Add! | Delete! | Re-read

Figure 30.10   The result: one very nicely built applet to see one database table.

This is a full blown connection into the database, much the same as you could have achieved with Visual Basic, Visual C++, or any of the other ActiveX compatible tools that Microsoft sells.

Run It Under jview

All this time, we've referred to this as an Applet, but as it turns out, you can also run this as a stand alone application. To do so, try opening a **DOS** window, and type *cd \ATestArea\BatBase*. At the C: prompt, type:

```
jview BatBase
```

This will bring up a new window with that same database front end on it. It is not usually the case that Applets can also run as stand alone applications, but they can be built that way, and the Database Wizard did that for us.

UNDERSTANDING THE GENERATED CODE

Depending on your database table, the wizard produces about 860 lines of code, of which about 300 are comments. What do the other 560 lines do? They demonstrate a very civilized database applet using DAO.

Imports

The applet imports **applet, awt,** and **util**, in the usual way. It make the following additional imports:

```
import dao350.*;
import com.ms.com.*;
import Alert;
```

DAO350 provides support Java classes for Data Access Objects DAO 3.5. The next line makes a lot of COM support available. The final one is Alert. It is a dialog box created especially for you by the Wizard itself. You can find the source code in the **fileview** window.

Support Classes

The main file (*BatBase.java*) contains definitions of three classes:

DBField   This is a unit which keeps the information about a database field tied together with the tools needed to display it, such as the name, contents, attributes, and the actual Label and textField widget used to display it on the screen.

DBFrame This is a frame which gets created to hold and display the Applet, if the main method is invoked (i. e. the Applet is run as an application and launched from the command line.)

BatBase We will look at this in the section below

The Applet, an Overview

The Applet has quite a number of attributes and methods, some of which are empty, and some of which are quite complex. We list general categories of the attributes, and assume you'll understand what they do. For the methods, we list them all, with a brief look at what they do below:

Attributes	*Code*
| **DAO supporting objects.** | ```
protected boolean readOnly = false;
protected String strDatabase =
   "C:\\ATestArea\\BatDB\\ArchFoes.mdb";
protected String strRecordset = "ArchFoe";
protected int recordCount;
protected static Variant varEmpty;
// DAO Objects
protected _DBEngine m_IEngine;
protected Database database;
protected Recordset recordset;
``` |
| **Screen objects from table. These are put in a hash table for easy reference.** | ```
static DBField[] field = {
  new DBField( "alias", "Long", Variant.VariantInt ),
  etc...
``` |
| **COM support** | ```
Variant vName;
Variant vValue;
etc . . .
``` |
| **GUI Objects, Lots of them. (See Chapter 10)** | ```
  // Containers of database components
protected Panel db = new Panel();
protected Panel dbcolumn[] = new Panel[columns * 2];
// Toolbar with "Next", "Prev", "First" and "Last"
protected Panel tools = new Panel();
protected Panel toolbar = new Panel();
protected Button buttonFirst = new Button("<< First");
etc...
``` |

Method	*Description*
MakeFrame( )	Create the frame used when this is a stand alone application
main(String[] args)	main method called when run as a stand alone application.
getAppletInfo( )	Provides browser with text information about the applet, such as who wrote it.
init( )	This does many things including:
	• set up COM connection to the DAO object.
	• open the Database
	• create a recordset
	• count the records
	• initialize the GUI components (including several panels)
	• load the current record
destroy( )	Standard Applet equipment, called when browser exits. This one does nothing
start( )	Standard Applet equipment, called after init( ). This one does nothing
stop( )	Standard Applet equipment, if called from a frame object (only during a stand-alone application), it exits back to the operating system. Otherwise it does nothing.
action(Event e, Object o)	Handles the button clicks. This is where a lot of the database actions are requested.
exit( )	Close the recordset and then call the **stop( )** method (see above). This is the action of clicking the "*exit*" button.
updateTextField (DBField f)	Update the contents of a particular field on the screen with its corresponding recordset field contents.
updateDatabase Field (DB Field f)	Update the database recordset field based on the contents of the corresponding field on the screen.
getException Message( )	For a few database exceptions, provide a more human readable message.
updateDatabase (int nMode)	Call updateDatabaseField( ) for all the fields.
updateUI( )	Call updateTextField( ) for every Field.

MODIFYING THE CODE

There are a number of good and useful constructs in the example created by the Wizard. You should not use the strategy of modifying this code slightly to make it into what you really want. Odds are that what you want involves having information from several tables on the screen at once. For example in our *ArchFoes* database, we would probably prefer to show the user data from the *location* table, rather than see the *location_id* field; and when changing that field, they should probably choose from the values in the location table.

To affect such a change, we would need to get down to the roots of the display mechanism, and put a list or choice box into the GUI in one case. We would need to add some support code to load the *location* data into an array, and use it.

We should also add another frame that can come up and permit the user to modify the *location* table in much the same way as the *BatBase* Applet permits alteration of the *ArchFoe* table. Needless to say, that from needs to get the data from the *locType* table.

There are some simple changes you can make:

- You can change the display order of the *DBFields* array.
- You can add a **Textarea** component to display diagnostic messages, and you can play with opening different record sets, to see what the field names look like.
- You can make trivial decorative changes, such as setting the background color to something more cheerful than *Seattle Sky Gray*.

BUILDING AN RDO APPLET

Creating an RDO Applet is just as simple as the DAO applet, except that specifying your remote data source requires a bit more understanding of databases and networks. It is not within the scope of this document to teach you this material.

One other difference is that you will have to run the **Java Type Library Wizard** on the RDO object. This Wizard is available from the **Tools** menu.

SUMMARY

Almost nothing that you do in the world of programming could be as easy as using the Visual J++ Database Wizard to create an Applet to manipulate an existing Microsoft Access table. The code it produces is a fine example of how Java 1.02 code should look and work. A necessary corollary to it being easy to use is that there are very few choices to make, and it therefore is only good at producing one narrow variety of Applets. You will be happiest with this fine tool if you consider it a teaching device, and not a general utility for making database related Applets with Java.

CHAPTER 31

Using the Java ActiveX Wizard

In this chapter we cover the following topics:

- Running the Java ActiveX Wizard
- Generated IDL

INTRODUCTION

In Chapter 28 we saw how we might use COM classes from inside Java. Well, Visual J++ 1.1 supports the inverse as well, calling a Java class from COM. This opens the entire world of Java to Visual Basic, Visual C++ and other COM enabled applications. In this chapter we will explore how to convert a Java .class file to something COM callable and all the steps in between.

Running the Java ActiveX Wizard

The Java Active X Wizard is run by selecting **ActiveX Wizard for Java** from the **Tools** menu. You will be presented with a screen which looks something like Figure 31.1, shown below.

Step 1—Entering a Name and specifying IDL. The first step in running the ActiveX wizard for Java is to enter the name of a valid java class. Enter the name of a Java class or use the browse button to select an appropriate .class file. Note that by default the wizard will fill in the name of the current class you are working on.

> **NOTE**
>
> ### ActiveX Wizard Assumes Some Things
>
> When running the ActiveX Wizard for Java be aware that it assumes the name of your .class file matches that of your .java file. For example Javabeep.class corresponds to Javabeep.java. Also note that the wizard will not expose methods of the base class that your class extends. If you wish to expose these methods you need to define them yourself in your class and then connect then to the underlying methods yourself. Also note that the java to IDL conversion will skip methods with Java types which cannot be converted to IDL types.

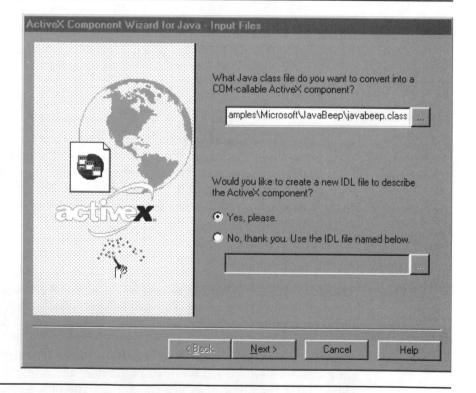

Figure 31.1   ActiveX Component Wizard for Java—Input files.

In addition to specifying the name of the input Java class you can specify the name of an IDL file to associate with the class. For our example we will let the wizard create the file. But there are very good reasons for giving your own. Some of which are:

- You have already run the wizard once and a version of the IDL already exists;
- You've previously created the IDL and have removed some public methods which you would rather not expose.
- For some other reason you already have an IDL file which you would like to use.

If you are specifying your own IDL file enter its name or use the browse button to find it.

If you did supply your own IDL file the wizard would then compile it into a type library directly.

Once you filled out the dialog select the next button to move on.

Step Two—Specifying a Class ID. COM classes are normally selected via there class id. In this step we will either enter an existing class ID or generate a new one.

NOTE

How COM Automation Files You Java Class

For COM automation to find your Java class it must know where to look. This is normally done by entering information into the registry. The wizard do this all for you. In fact it will suggest you use an existing ID if one is found that matches your class!

Figure 31.2, shown below, shows the CLSID dialog.

By default the wizard will attempt to create a new CLSID for your java class. As with the prior step, you can enter your own CLSID if your already have one. Remember that the wizard will suggest you reuse an existing CLSID if it finds one which appears to match your class.

This dialog also allow you to register your new class. The default is yes, please register my class. When you select register the wizard will create a file name *class*.REG with the appropriate commands to register your class.

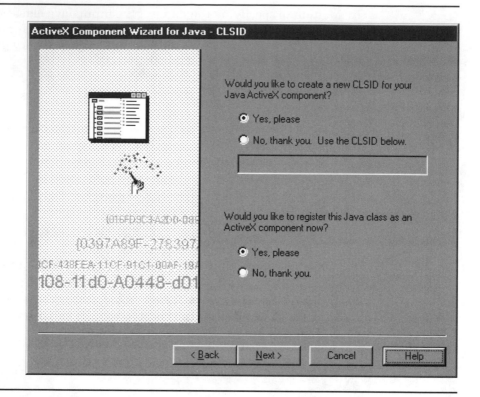

Figure 31.2   The ActiveX Component Wizard for Java CLSID dialog.

NOTE

Visual Basic Users Beware

If you are running Visual Basic you are better off to generate a new class id each time. The wizard does not guaranteed binary compatibility from one run to the next. If you change your class often regenerate the CLSID as well.

Entering Your Own CLSID Into Your Java Class

If you had previously run the ActiveX Wizard for Java you will be prompted to perform some additional work. This work is required to make your class COM accessible. This additional work involves simply adding a private static string to your class which contains the class id. For example if you had previously generated a class id with value "12345678-1234-4321-123412340000" then you would simple add a variable to your class as follows,

```
private static final String = CLSID("12345678-1234-
   4321-123412340000");
   And your done!
```

Select Next to move to the next screen.

Step Three—Define Your Interfaces. COM classes can have many forms. This set allows you to define how the IDL for your class will be created. Figure 31.3, shown below prompts you to define your COM interfaces.

The default choice is *dispinterface* and currently required by the Microsoft Java Virtual Machine and Visual Basic. If either of these is your target the use the default. *Dual* interfaces are more flexible in that they create both an IDispatch interface and a virtual function table.

Incompatibilities in the Current Java Virtual Machine

An incompatibility exists in the current Java Virtual machine which prevents it use from Visual Basic or MFC. Enter the following <OBJECT> into your HTML to automatically download the new version.

```
<OBJECT CLSID="clsid:08B0E5C0-4FCB-11CF-AAA5-
   00401C608500"
CODEBASE ="http://www.microsoft.com/Java/IE30Java.cab
   #Version=1,0,0,1">
   </OBJECT>
```

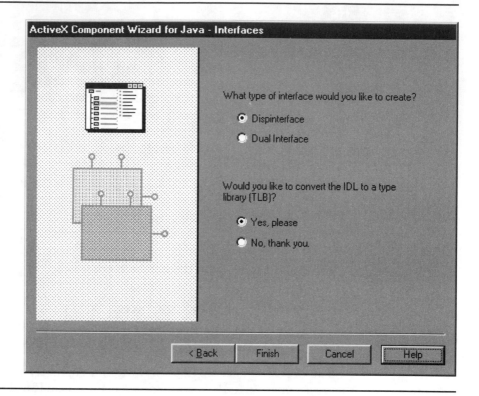

Figure 31.3   The ActiveX Component Wizard for Java—Interfaces dialog.

Lastly this dialog allows you to automatically generate a .TLB file from the generated IDL description. Select the default. If you select **no** then you will need to convert the IDL to a .TBL file later by hand.

Click Finish to move on.

Step Four-Final Modifications to Your Java Class to Make it COM Callable. Once you have completed the prior four steps your almost there! All you need to now is add the class id to your Java class and compile it into the correct directory.

Figure 31.4, shown below, is a visual reminder of these additional steps.

The most important step we've already covered. Adding the CLSID to your java class. But for the sake of completeness lets review the steps now.

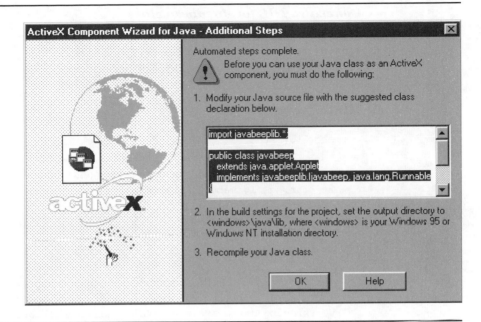

Figure 31.4   The ActiveX Component Wizard for Java—Additional Steps.

Additional Step 1: Add the generated class ID to your Java class. In our example this involved adding the private variable shown below:

```
private static final String = CLSID("12345678-1234-4321-123412340000");
```

Additional Step 2: Set the output directory of your build to `<win­dows>\java\lib` where `<windows>` is the directory you installed windows too. If you would prefer not to change the output directory make sure that you copy your class file to the correct location after step 3 below.

Additional Step 3: Rebuild you application.

And that's it! You can now embedded your Java object into your Visual Basic application or call it from HTML using the `<OBJECT>` tag!

Conclusion

To complete this simple chapter we show the end result IDL generated by running our Javabeep class thru the ActiveX Wizard for Java.

Generated IDL for Javabeep.class

```
[
  uuid(14288443-806b-11d0-a24d-08002b000063),
  helpstring("javabeepLib Type Library"),
  version(1.0)
]
library javabeepLib
{
  importlib("stdole31.tlb");

  [
    uuid(14288442-806b-11d0-a24d-08002b000063),
    helpstring("Ijavabeep Interface")
  ]
  dispinterface Ijavabeep
  {
    properties:
    methods:
    [ helpstring("stop Method"), id(1) ]
    void stop();

    // skipping method paint—contains non-translatable types

    [ helpstring("destroy Method"), id(3) ]
    void destroy();

    [ helpstring("start Method"), id(4) ]
    void start();

    [ helpstring("getAppletInfo Method"), id(5) ]
    BSTR getAppletInfo();

    // skipping method mouseDown—contains non-translatable types

    [ helpstring("run Method"), id(7) ]
    void run();

    [ helpstring("init Method"), id(8) ]
    void init();
  }
  [
    uuid(14288441-806b-11d0-a24d-08002b000063),
    helpstring("Cjavabeep Object")
  ]
  coclass Cjavabeep
  {
    [ default ]
    dispinterface Ijavabeep;
  };

};
```

NOTE

For More Information

For more information on using COM Classes from Visual Basic, Visual C++ or other products see one of the excellent publications on the topic of ActiveX and COM published by John Wiley and Sons. For example ActiveX Web Programming by BLUM or the ActiveX SOURCEBOOK by Coombs,Coombs and Brewer.

Tips of the Day

Microsoft's Development Studio has a feature that presents you with a new tip about using Visual J++ every time you bring it up (until you uncheck the box at the bottom of the Tip of the Day dialog box labeled "Show tips at startup"). These tips are handy, but for your convenience we list them all here, so that you may turn off this slightly time-consuming feature as soon as possible. Future releases of this product will doubtless contain more and improved tips. They can be found in files in the IDE folder under your Visual J++ installation. These files have the **.TIP** extension (currently **MSDEV.TIP** and **VJTOOLS.TIP**). The are stored as text files with a three-letter code for the tip category prepended and comma separated.

For your convenience, we have sorted these tips by category.

NOTE

More Categories

The files that came with the early release version of Visual J++ had three categories of tips with no entries. These were: **brw=Browsing, shp=Advice** on **Shipping Software**, and **wks=Using Workspaces** and **Projects**.

Can we expect that tips will be added to these categories? Perhaps . . . but we can also expect new categories.

GRATUITOUS ADVICE (ADV)

Did you know . . .

- For critical subsystems, you can use an alternate algorithm to validate results in debug builds.
- ASSERT helps you catch bugs early.

ALL TIPS (ALL)

Did you know . . .

- Welcome to Microsoft Visual J++!\n\nVisit http://www.microsoft.com/visualj for product release information, updates, and other cool stuff!
- You can convert your Visual C++ dialogs and menus directly to Java code. [new line] Use the Java Resource Wizard, found on the Tools menu.
- You can use custom tools to build non-Java files in your project. [new line] From the Build menu, choose Settings. Select your file in the lefthand pane and click on the Custom Build tab.
- The source editor is compliant with special tags for
  - HTML 2.0
  - Internet Explorer 2.0
  - Internet Explorer 3.0
  While editing an HTML file, right click and select **Properties** from the popup menu. Use the **Language** list to make a selection.
- You can debug within the Internet Explorer 3.0 browser. From the **Build** menu, select **Settings** and choose the **Debug** tab. Set the **Category** to **General** and select **Debug** project under **Browser**.
- You can debug without the Internet Explorer 3.0 browser. From the **Build** menu, select **Settings** and choose the **Debug** tab. Set the **Category** to **General** and select **Debug** project under **Stand-alone interpreter**.
- Create a simple Java applet using the Java Applet Wizard. From the **File** menu, select **New** and choose **Project Workspace**. Select Java Applet Wizard, enter a name for your project, and select the **Create** button to start the applet wizard.
- It's easy to turn a **.java** file into a Visual J++ project. Just load the **.java** file without a project workspace and build the file. A default workspace will be created for you!

BUILDING APPLICATIONS (BLD)

Did you know . . .

- You can press {**RebuildAll**} to rebuild all of your project files.
- You can press {**Build**} to build the current target.
- You can press {**ToolStop**} to stop any running tool or a build in progress.

DEBUGGING (DBG)

Did you know . . .

- You can press {**DebugStopDebugging**} to stop debugging.
- You can press {**DebugRestart**} to restart debugging.
- The popup menu often has debugger commands specific to that window.
- When debugging, you can single-step into functions by pressing {**DebugStepInto**}.
- You can change how variables and expressions are displayed in the **Watch** or **QuickWatch** window by using format specifiers such as **,us** (Unicode string) and **,x** (hexadecimal integer).
- You can press {**DebugToggleBreakpoint**} to toggle a breakpoint at the cursor. The shortcut works in the **Call Stack**, too!
- In the **Variables** window and the **Watch** window, you can autosize a column to fit its contents by double clicking on the divider.
- The **Watch** window has several panes, but only the visible pane is evaluated. This behavior means you can quickly change variables by placing assignment statements in a **Watch** pane and activating it when you want to change the variables. For example, in Watch 2 enter "debug=1" and in Watch 3 enter "debug=0".
- Compile when including the Windows header files.
- When debugging, you can press {**ViewWatchWindow**} to display the **Watch** window.
- When debugging, you can press {**DebugRunToCursor**} to run the program to the cursor. This shortcut works in the **Call Stack**, too!
- You can easily add variables to the **Watch** window by selecting them in your code and dragging them into the **Watch** window.
- You should single-step new or changed code.
- When debugging, you can press {**DebugHexadecimalDisplay**} to toggle the hexadecimal-display option.
- When debugging, you can step over functions by pressing {**Debug-StepOver**}.

- When debugging, you can press {**DebugQuickWatch**} to open the **QuickWatch** window to evaluate an expression.
- When debugging, you can press {**ViewWatchWindow**} to display the **Watch** window.
- When debugging, you can press {**ViewDisassemblyWindow**} to display the **Disassembly** window.
- With **Data Tips**, you can place the mouse pointer on a variable when debugging and instantly see its value.
- When debugging, you press {**ViewCallStackWindow**} to display the **Call Stack** window.
- When debugging, you can press {**DebugToggleBreakpoint**} to set a breakpoint at the return address of a function in the **Call Stack** window. You can press {**DebugRunToCursor**} to execute to that frame.
- When debugging, you can find the cause of an assertion by using the **Call Stack** window to view the calling function frames.

MICROSOFT DEVELOPER (DEV)

Did you know . . .

- You can add buttons to any toolbar. From the **Tools** menu, choose **Customize**. Select the **Toolbars** tab. Drag any button or command onto a toolbar. If you drop the button or command outside an existing toolbar, a custom toolbar is automatically created.
- You can hide all screen elements to see more information. From the **View** menu, choose **Full Screen**. To restore the screen, click the **Full Screen** button or press Esc.
- You can resize the dropdown edit control on a toolbar. From the **Tools** menu, choose **Customize** and select the **Toolbars** tab. Click the control on the toolbar to display the selection box and then drag the right edge.
- You can move a toolbar button by holding down Alt and dragging it to a new position. You can drag it to a different toolbar or remove it by dragging it off the toolbar.
- You can get help on any dialog box or error message. Click the **Help** button in the dialog or message box or press **F1**.
- Many useful commands are accessible only from toolbar buttons. To discover the available toolbar buttons, choose the **Toolbar** tab on the **Customize** dialog box. To add a toolbar button to an open toolbar, drag the toolbar button from the tab to the toolbar. Dropping the toolbar button outside an existing toolbar creates a custom toolbar.

- To close and save multiple source files, you can choose the **Windows** command on the **Window** menu.
- You can display multiple toolbars. From the **View** menu, choose **Toolbars**, and then select the toolbars you want.
- You can undock a dockable window by double clicking its border. To see a list of dockable windows, choose the **Workspace** tab on the **Options** dialog box.
- You can cycle through panes in a tabbed window by pressing Ctrl+PageUp or Ctrl+PageDown. You can cycle through tabs in a tabbed dialog by pressing Ctrl+Tab or Ctrl+Shift+Tab.
- You can display a popup menu by clicking the right mouse button in a window. The popup menu contains commands specific to the window where you clicked.
- You can move the insertion point to the previous word by pressing {**WordLeft**}. To move to the next word, press {**WordRight**}.
- You can scroll text up one screen by pressing {**PageUp**}. Pressing {**PageDown**} scrolls text down one screen.
- You can close a dialog box by pressing Esc.
- Pressing {**EditProperties**} displays properties for the selected item or window.
- When editing, you can move selected items by dragging. To copy the selection, hold down Ctrl as you drag.
- {**WindowDockingView**} toggles a docking window's docked state.
- You can see all of the standard and custom keyboard bindings by choosing the **Keyboard** command on the **Help** menu.
- You can press Esc or Shift+Esc to hide a window in a dockable state. When focus is either in the output or topic window, pressing Esc returns focus to an open source window, without hiding the output or topic window. Pressing Esc again hides the output or topic window.
- You can learn about any command on a menu by highlighting the command and reading the text in the status bar at the bottom of the main window.
- You can quickly select a large block of text with the mouse. Click at the beginning of the text, press Shift, and then click at the end of the text.
- You can display a menu of toolbars by pointing to a toolbar and then clicking the right mouse button.
- You can move a toolbar by clicking between the toolbar buttons and dragging. Return the toolbar to its original position by double clicking its titlebar.
- You can drag toolbar buttons to a new position on a toolbar or to a different toolbar. Hold down Alt and drag the button. To copy buttons, press Alt+Ctrl.

USING THE INFORMATION SYSTEM (HLP)

Did you know . . .

- You can toggle an **InfoViewer Topic** window title by pressing {**InfoViewerToggleTopicTitle**}. You can toggle the **Topic** window toolbar by pressing {**InfoViewerToggleToolbar**}.
- You can define an **InfoViewer** subset to display a smaller set of books in the **InfoView** pane, to narrow the scope of a query, or to narrow the scope of an F1 search in a source file. To set the default subset for the **InfoView** pane, **Search Query**, or **F1** source-file search, choose the **Set Default Subsets** command on the **Help** menu.
- {**InfoViewerJumpNext**} moves to the next hotspot in the **InfoViewer Topic** window.
- Pressing F1 displays help for the keyword at the cursor in a source window or the **Output** window. This shortcut works in an **InfoViewer Topic** window, too! When you select text and then press **F1**, **InfoViewer** displays help for the selected text. You can select a word by double clicking it.
- When you click a hotlink in an **InfoViewer** topic, you go to a related topic. To return to the previous topic, press {**InfoViewerBack**}.
- When using **InfoViewer**, you can query for a search string in text or a search string "just in titles." Querying for a search string just in titles is a good technique to find a topic your have visited before.
- You can do a subsequent query on a list of topics from a previous **InfoViewer** query. This is a good method to cast a wide net and then pick out the catch. From the **InfoViewer Search** dialog, choose the **Last** topics found option from the "Where would you like to search?" step.
- You can pin the **InfoViewer Query Results** window to browse and display topics. When the window is unpinned, it hides when you open a topic. Press {**InfoViewerQueryResult**} to display it again.
- You can choose the **Keyboard** command on the **Help** menu to see the current keyboard shortcuts. The keyboard list is updated when you make a change to a shortcut assignment. Change assignments from the **Customize** command on the **Tools** menu.
- You can use your own **WinHelp** files to provide F1 help in source files. For information, see Microsoft Developer Studio Extension Help (**EXTHELP.HLP**) in the product **\Help** subdirectory.
- In an **InfoViewer Topic** window, {**InfoViewerSeeAlso**} displays the **See Also** list. This shortcut works even if you've hidden the toolbar with {**InfoViewerToggleToolbar**}.

- With the new **InfoViewer** glossary feature, you can easily find the definition of an unfamiliar term in an information title such as **Books Online**. Just click a term to see its definition in a popup window. If this tip were in **Books Online**, you could click the term "information title" to find out exactly what it is! (An information title is what **InfoViewer** displays.)

- When an **InfoViewer** topic is active, you can enter a keyword in the **Find** box on the **Standard** toolbar to begin a query. Press Enter to query within the current topic. Press Shift+Enter to query the current information title (your last settings on the **Query** tab are used as defaults).

- There are two default **InfoViewer** toolbars: **InfoViewer**, which contains buttons for common operations, and **InfoViewer Contents**, which lists available subsets for the **InfoView** pane.

- Pressing **F1** on a keyword in a source file displays help for that keyword.

- You can turn off title tips in any **Workspace Window** pane by toggling **Title Tips** on the popup menu for the pane.

- You can use Microsoft Development Library for **F1** help in source files rather than Visual C++ Books Online. If you are a subscriber to MSDN, just open the latest version from the **Open Information Title** dialog box. Until you open another title, Microsoft Development Library will remain current between sessions.

- Files in online sample programs are opened up directly in Developer Studio. See the Tutorials and Samples node in Books Online or the Samples node under Product Documentation in Microsoft Development Library for a list of samples.

- You can set the default size and position of the application help window. After pressing the **Help** button on a dialog, for instance, size and position the help window where you want it (perhaps at the bottom of the application frame). When you request help again from a dialog, window, or property page, the help window opens where you last placed it.

- You can dock the **InfoViewer Contents** toolbar at the top of the **Workspace** window by holding down the Shift key while dragging the **InfoViewer Contents** toolbar into position. The **InfoViewer Contents** toolbar allows you to change subsets in the **InfoView** pane. By default, the **InfoViewer Contents** toolbar is docked at the top of the **Workspace** window.

- When clicking glossary text in a Books Online topic, you see the popup definition for the term. Glossary text is dark gray by default.

- You can open Microsoft Development Library from within Microsoft Developer Studio.
- You can drag-and-drop text from the **InfoViewer** topic window to a source window.
- You can determine the scope of a full-text help query by using subsets. Create or choose a subset that includes only the books you want to search.
- You can change the color of the glossary popup text to any color. To change the default gray color, choose the **Format** tab on the **Options** dialog and then select the **InfoViewer** category.
- You can dock the **InfoViewer** topic window. Choose **Docking View** from the popup menu to switch the topic window to a floating state and then drag the topic window to the application frame to dock it.
- Dock your **InfoViewer** toolbar to either side of the application frame for easy access.
- You can apply **InfoViewer** subsets in three areas: content displays in the **InfoView** pane, full-text queries in the **InfoViewer Search** dialog, and F1 help searches in source files. Subsets are independently applied in each area. For example, changing an **InfoView** pane subset does not affect F1 source-file help.
- You can determine the scope of a **F1** source-file help by using subsets. Create or choose a subset that includes only the books you want to search. This technique helps you pinpoint the reference topics most relevant to your programming task.

USING THE RESOURCE EDITORS (RES)

Did you know . . .

- Holding down Shift as you draw constrains the shape of an object. For example, it constrains a rectangle to a square or an ellipse to a circle.
- You can align controls by clicking the **Snap-to-Grid** button on the **Layout** toolbar and then selecting the **Snap-to-Grid** check box.

MICROSOFT DEVELOPER TOOLS (TWL)

Did you know . . .
- You can open one of the last files you worked on by choosing it from the bottom of the **File** menu.
- You can move to the beginning of a line by pressing {**Home**}. You can move to the end of a line by pressing {**LineEnd**}.

- You can undo most actions by clicking the **Undo** button on the **Standard** toolbar.
- You can hide all screen elements to see more of your code. From the **View** menu, choose **Full Screen**. To restore the screen, click the **Full Screen** button or press Esc.
- You can use macros to insert the filename, date, page number, and other information into a header or footer.
- You can repeat your last action by clicking the **Redo** button on the **Standard** toolbar.
- You can press {**ViewOutputWindow**} to display the **Output** window.
- You can press {**ViewInfoViewerTopic**} to display the **InfoViewer Topic** window.
- In the United States or Canada, you can call the Microsoft Wish Line to make suggestions about features you would like to see in any Microsoft product or service. The number for the Wish Line is (206) 936-WISH.
- When editing, you can go to the beginning of a file by pressing {**DocumentStart**}. You can go to the end of a file by pressing {**DocumentEnd**}.
- You can move or copy selected text or graphics by dragging and dropping. To copy the item, hold down Ctrl as you drag.
- When editing, you can press {**GoTo**} to move to a line, address, or bookmark.
- You can select text by holding down Shift and then pressing an arrow key.
- Developer Studio has a wealth of cool features—more than can fit in the main menu. To see what's available, explore the toolbars, popup menus, window and item properties. Look at what's in the **Customize** and **Options** dialogs on the **Tools** menu, too.
- You can open a file by clicking the **Open** button on the **Standard** toolbar. To see the file in the list, you may need to select a different drive or directory or select **All Files** from the **List Files Of Type** box.

EDITING AND NAVIGATING TEXT (TXT)

Did you know . . .

- You can repeat the last **Find** command in the source editor by pressing {**FindNext**}.
- The source editor can emulate BRIEF and Epsilon.
- Esc moves the focus back to a source or topic window from the **Find** box on the toolbar.

- Before you can change text or graphics, you must first select the item you want to modify.
- You can press {**GoToNextErrorTag**}and {**GoToPrevErrorTag**} to move to the next and previous build error or **Find-in-Files** match.
- When editing, you can go to the next and previous find by pressing {**FindNext**} and {**FindPrev**}.
- You can undo your last edit by pressing {**Undo**}. To undo more than one change, press the key again.
- When editing, you can select a word by double clicking it. This shortcut works in the **InfoViewer Topic** window, too!
- When editing, you can press {**BookmarkToggle**} to toggle a book-mark at the cursor.
- When editing, you can replace text by selecting it and then typing.
- When editing, you can press {**IndentSelection**} to indent and {**UnindentSelection**} to unindent selected lines.
- You can press {**Find**} to display the **Find** dialog.
- When editing, you can press {**GoTo**} to move to a line in the file.
- When editing, you can use the selection bar to select text. In the space to the left of text, click once to select a line. Ctrl+Click to select the entire contents of the window.
- The status bar at the bottom of the application frame shows the current line number, column number, editor mode, current time, and other information.
- When editing, you can press {**LineCut**} to delete the current line.
- You can find a match for a parenthesis, square bracket, or angle bracket by placing the insertion point on it and pressing {**Go-ToMatchBrace**}.
- You can scroll through a file when using drag-and-drop editing. Drag the selected item beneath the horizontal ruler or above the horizontal scroll bar.
- Developer Studio displays the name of a toolbar button when you point to the button.
- You can assign a shortcut key to the **WindowCycle** command to cycle through the open source windows. To assign a shortcut key, choose the **Keyboard** command on the **Customize** dialog. The **WindowCycle** command is under the **Window** category.
- You can select a rectangular block of text by holding down Alt while you drag.
- You can record commands and other actions and then play them back when you need to perform the same series of tasks. To begin recording, press {**ToolsRecordKeystrokes**}. To stop recording,

press it again. To play back the recording, press {**ToolsPlayback-Recording**}.

- You can split the window into two panes and see two parts of a file simultaneously. Drag the split bar at the top of the scroll bar to split the window.
- When editing, you can press {**FindNextWord**} to find the next occurrence of the selected text. {**FindPrevWord**} finds the previous occurrence.
- You can press {**Compile**} to compile the current file.
- Many source code control packages, such as SourceSafe, can be seamlessly integrated into Visual J++.
- When editing or using Books Online, you can use a bookmark to mark your place. Choose **Bookmark** or **InfoViewer Bookmark** from the **Edit** menu and then type a name for the bookmark. Press {**GoTo**} to return to the bookmark.
- When editing, you can press {**GoToMatchBrace**} to find the matching brace, parenthesis, or angle bracket.

Appendix B

Compiler Errors

This appendix covers error and warning messages produced by **JVC.exe**. **JVC.exe** Error messages are always preceded by a J.

Note that you can see the complete version of any error message by placing the cursor on the error number and hitting the [F1] key.

0001   **INTERNAL COMPILER ERROR:** *'identifier'*
The compiler was unable to recover following detection of an error. If you receive this message, consult your technical support help file for information on how to address this problem.

0002   **Out of memory**
The compiler attempted to allocate some additional memory during processing, but was unable to do so. When this error occurs, check the location, size, and validity of your system swap file. Also, check that there is sufficient growth space available on the drive on which your swap file resides.

0003   **Invalid code:** *'string'*
The compiler may have detected invalid code being generated. Try dividing larger methods defined within your classes into smaller methods and compiling again.

0004   **Cannot open class file** *'filename'* **for reading**
The compiler could not open the program source file for reading. This error most likely occurs when another program has an exclusive lock on the source file. Try shutting down other processes that may be accessing the source file and compiling again.

0005   **Cannot open class file** *'filename'* **for writing**
The compiler failed to generate the output .CLASS file. This error most likely occurs when the compiler cannot get write or create per-

mission for the file. Make sure the file does not have its read-only attribute set, and that it is not currently in use by another a process.

0006   **Cannot read class file *'filename'***
The compiler failed to read the specified .CLASS file. This error most likely occurs when the compiler encounters an error reading the storage device, or when the compiler cannot otherwise get read permission for the file. Check to ensure the file is not currently in use by another process. Also, use whatever means available (i.e., SCANDISK) to ensure the validity of the storage device you are attempting to use.

0007   **Cannot write class file *'filename'***
The compiler failed while attempting to write the contents of a buffer to the specified .CLASS file. This error most likely occurs when space is exhausted on the targeted storage device. Try freeing up any available space on the storage device and compiling again.

0008   **Cannot locate class file *'filename'***
The compiler could not locate a core language class for the **java.lang** package. This error most likely occurs when the Java **CLASSPATH** variable is not properly set. Try correcting the CLASSPATH variable, and compiling again.

0009   Not currently used.

0010   **Syntax error**
The compiler could not determine the meaning of an expression or statement within the source program. This error most likely occurs when the line indicated in the error message is syntactically invalid. This error usually accompanies a more descriptive error. Try correcting any accompanying errors and compiling again.

0011   **Expected ' : '**
The compiler expected to find a colon following a **case** label or in a conditional expression that makes use of the ternary operator. This error most likely occurs when the colon is accidentally omitted.

0012   **Expected ' ; '**
The compiler expected to find a semicolon in the position indicated by the error message. This error most likely occurs when the semicolon is accidentally omitted from the end of a statement. This error can also occur when a conditional expression is not syntactically correct.

0013   **Expected ' ('**
The compiler expected to find a left parenthesis in the position indicated by the error message. This error most likely occurs when the left parenthesis is accidentally omitted in any of the following situations:
- type initializations
- **catch** statements
- parenthesized expressions
- **while** loops
- **for** loops
- **if-else** statements

0014   **Expected ') '**

The compiler expected to find a right parenthesis in the position indicated by the error message. This error most likely occurs when the right parenthesis is accidentally omitted in any of the following situations:
- type initializations
- type casts
- **catch** statements
- parenthesized expressions
- **while** loops
- **for** loops
- **if-else** statements

0015 **Expected '] '**

The compiler expected to find a right square bracket in the position indicated by the error message. This error most likely occurs when the right square bracket is accidentally omitted from an array declaration.

0016 **Expected ' { '**

The compiler expected to find a left brace in the position indicated by the error message. This error most likely occurs when the left brace is accidentally omitted from the beginning of a class declaration.

0017 **Expected ' } '**

The compiler expected to find a right brace in the position indicated by the error message. This error most likely occurs when a statement containing a right brace is not syntactically correct.

0018 **Expected 'while'**

The compiler expected to find the keyword **while** in the position indicated by the error message. This error most likely occurs when a **do/while** loop is not syntactically correct. The correct structure for a **do/while** loop is:

```
do {
// do something useful here
} while (condition);
```

0019 **Expected identifier**

The compiler expected to find an identifier toward the end of a class, interface, variable, or method declaration. This error most likely occurs when the type is accidentally omitted in a declaration.

0020 **Expected 'class' or 'interface'**

The compiler expected to find either **class** or **interface** used within the corresponding declaration. This error most likely occurs when the keywords are accidentally omitted from a **class** or **interface** declaration. Another possible cause of this error is unbalanced scoping braces.

0021 **Expected type specifier**

The compiler expected to find a type specifier in the position indicated by the error message.

0022 **Expected end of file**

The compiler expected to encounter an end of file character, but did not. This error most likely occurs when the source file has been corrupted in some way. Try visually checking the source file for obvious corruption, saving any changes, and compiling again.

0023 **Expected 'catch' or 'finally'**

The compiler expected to find a **catch** or **finally** block immediately following a corresponding **try** block.

0024 **Expected method body**

The compiler expected to find a method body immediately following a method declaration. This error most likely occurs when the braces surrounding the method body are not properly balanced. This error may also occur when the method was intended to be **abstract**, but the **abstract** keyword was mistakenly omitted from the method declaration.

0025 **Expected statement**

The compiler expected to find a statement before the end of the current scope. This error most likely occurs due to misplacing the end of the current scope.

0026 **Expected Unicode escape sequence**

The compiler expected to find a valid Unicode escape sequence. This error most likely occurs when a syntactical error is found in a Unicode escape sequence.

0027 **Identifier too long**

The compiler detected an identifier with a length greater than 1024 characters. Shorten the identifier and compile again.

0028 **Invalid number**

The compiler detected a numeric value that the Java language is not capable of supporting. This error most likely occurs when the number specified is an amount greater than any of Java's primitive types can accept.

0029 **Invalid character**

The compiler detected an ASCII character that could not be used in an identifier. This error most likely occurs when a class, interface, method, or variable identifier uses an invalid character.

0030 **Invalid character constant**

The compiler detected an attempt to assign an invalid character or character escape sequence to a variable of type **char**.

0031 **Invalid escape character**

The compiler detected the use of an invalid escape character. This error most likely occurs when a syntactical error is found in a Unicode escape sequence.

0032 **Unterminated string constant**

The compiler did not detect a terminating double-quote character at the end of a string constant. This error most likely occurs when the string terminator is accidentally omitted, or when the string constant is divided onto multiple lines.

0033 **Unterminated comment**

The compiler detected the beginning of a block comment, but did not detect a valid ending for it. This error most likely occurs when the comment terminator is accidentally omitted.

0034 Not currently used.

0035 **Initializer block must be declared 'static'**

The compiler detected a static initializer block, but did not detect the keyword **static** immediately preceding it. This error most likely occurs when the keyword **static** is accidentally omitted. This error may also occur when some other syntactical error exists.

0036   **A data member cannot be 'native', 'abstract', or 'synchronized'**
The compiler detected one of the modifiers shown above used in the declaration of a variable. The modifiers **synchronized** and **native** can only be applied to method declarations. The **abstract** modifier can be applied to methods, classes, and interfaces.

0037   **A method cannot be 'transient' or 'volatile'**
The compiler detected one of the modifiers shown above used in the declaration of a method. The modifiers **transient** and **volatile** can only be applied to variable declarations.

0038   **'final' members must be initialized**
The compiler detected an uninitialized **final** variable. Variables declared as **final** must have their value set at declaration. Once set, the value cannot be programmatically changed. Note that variables declared within interfaces are implicitly defined as **final** or **static**. As such, this error occurs when their initial values are not set.

0039   Not currently used.

0040   **Cannot define body for abstract/native methods**
The compiler detected a method body defined immediately following the corresponding declaration of an **abstract** or **native** method. Note that methods declared as members of an interface are implicitly **abstract**. As such, this error will occur when you attempt to define its body in the interface.

0041   **Duplicate modifier**
The compiler detected a modifier used twice within a declaration. This error most likely occurs when the same modifier is used more than once within a declaration.

0042   **Only classes can implement interfaces**
The compiler detected an interface declaration using the **implements** keyword. Interfaces cannot implement other interfaces. Rather, interfaces may only be implemented by classes.

0043   **Redeclaration of member *'identifier'***
The compiler detected the same identifier name being declared more than once within the same scope. This error most likely occurs when a variable is mistakenly declared more than once.

0044   **Cannot find definition for class *'identifier'***
The compiler could not locate the definition for the specified class. This error is most likely caused by a typographical error. It may also occur when the package containing the specified class cannot be found.

0045   ***'identifier'* is not a class name**
The compiler detected one of the following conditions:
- A class name provided as part of an **import** statement could not be found or, the import statement was not syntactically valid.
- The class attempted to extend an interface.

0046   ***'identifier'* is not an interface name**
The compiler detected that the identifier referred to by the keyword **implements** is not an interface.

0047   *'identifier'* **is not a package name**
The compiler detected an invalid package name. This error most likely occurs when a syntactical error exists in an import statement, or when the package name does not otherwise exist.

0048   **Cannot extend final class** *'identifier'*
The compiler detected an attempt to subclass a class declared with the keyword **final**. Classes declared as **final** cannot be subclassed.

0049   **Undefined name** *'identifer'*
The compiler detected an unknown class name while reading an **import** statement. This error most likely occurs when the identifier is misspelled or does not exist. This error may also occur if the CLASS-PATH variable is not set correctly.

0050   *'identifier'* **is not a member of** *'identifier'*
The compiler detected a reference to an identifier that is not a member of the specified package. This error most likely occurs when the identifier is misspelled or does not exist.

0051   **Undefined package** *'identifier'*
The compiler detected a package name, but was unable to locate the package definition. This error most likely occurs when a syntactical error exists in an import statement. This error may also occur when the package cannot be found.

0052   Not currently used.

0053   **Ambiguous name:** *'identifier'* **and** *'identifier'*
The compiler could not resolve an ambiguity between the two identifiers shown. Try correcting the ambiguity between the type specifiers and compile again.

0054   **Methods** *'identifier'* **and** *'identifier'* **differ only in return type**
The compiler detected two or more method overloads having identical parameters. In Java, overloaded methods must be distinguished by unique signatures. A unique signature consists of the method name, the number, type and positions of its parameters, and the return type.

0055   **A constructor may not specify a return type**
The compiler detected a constructor declaration specifying a return type. Constructors must implicitly return an instance of the declared class. As such, their return type may not be specified.

0056   **Missing return type specification**
The compiler detected a method declaration without a return type specified. All method declarations must specify a return type. If the method is not meant to return a value, use the **void** keyword.

0057   **Class file** *'identifier'* **doesn't contain class** *'identifier'*
The compiler did not detect the class name shown above within the specified file. This error most likely occurs when the class name is either misspelled or does not exist. This error may also occur when a .CLASS file has been renamed after successful compilation.

0058   **Cannot have a variable of type 'void'**
The compiler detected a variable declared as type void. The keyword void is not allowed in variable declarations. Rather, void can only be

used in a method declarations return type to note the method does not return a value.

0059 **Cannot reference member *'identifier'* without an object**
The compiler detected an attempt to reference a variable without a known object association. This error most likely occurs when an instance variable (a variable declared without the keyword **static**) is referenced from within a class (or static) method.

0060 **Invalid forward reference to member *'identifier'***
The compiler detected an attempt to initialize a variable with another variable that had not yet been defined.

0061 **The members *'identifier'* and *'identifier'* differ in return type only**
The compiler detected a subclass attempting to overload a base class method, but the methods differed only in return type. In Java, overloaded methods must be distinguished by unique signatures. A unique signature consists of the method name, the number, the type and the positions of its parameters, and the return type.

0062 **Attempt to reduce the access level of member *'identifier'***
The compiler detected an overload method in the class being compiled that reduces the access level of a base class method.

0063 **Declare the class abstract, or implement abstract member *'identifier'***
The compiler detected the declaration of an abstract method within a class, but the class was not declared to be abstract.

0064 **Local variable *'identifier'* shadows another local variable**
The compiler detected two variables with the same identifier defined within the same scope of a method.

0065 **Cannot assign to this expression**
The compiler detected an expression in the position normally held by an lvalue for assignment.

0066 **'this' can only be used in non-static methods**
The compiler detected use of the keyword **this** within a class (or static) method. Class methods are not passed implicit **this** references. As such, they cannot reference instance (non-static) variables or methods.

0067 **Cannot convert *'identifier'* to *'identifier'***
The compiler detected a variable type used out of its correct context. As such, the compiler could not implicitly convert the result to anything meaningful.

0068 **Cannot implicitly convert *'identifier'* to *'identifier'***
The compiler could not convert the specified variable without an explicit type cast.

0069 **Cannot apply '.' operator to an operand of type *'identifier'***
The compiler detected the '.' operator applied to an invalid type. This error most likely occurs when the .length method is applied to an invalid type.

0070 **Need argument list for call to member *'identifier'***
The compiler detected syntax for a known method call, but did not detect an associated argument list. This error most likely occurs when a syntactical error exists in the call.

0071   **Cannot use argument list with *'identifier'***
The compiler detected syntax for a method call, but the identifier used is not a method. This error most likely occurs when a method name is misspelled and matches a variable name.

0072   ***'identifier'* is not a member of class *'identifier'***
The compiler detected a method call, but the method remains undefined. This error most likely occurs when a class member is either misspelled, or cannot be found within proper scope. This error may also occur when the method does not exist.

0073   ***'identifier'* cannot access member *'identifier'***
The compiler detected an invalid attempt to access a class member within a different package. Correct the visibility of the member being accessed, and compile again.

0074   **Operator cannot be applied to *'identifier'* and *'identifier'* values**
The compiler detected an operator that cannot be applied to the identifiers shown in the error message.

0075   **Invalid call**
The compiler detected a method call, but the identifier does not represent a valid method name. This error most likely occurs when a method name is misspelled or contains characters that are not recognized as valid in Java naming conventions.

0076   **Too many arguments for method *'identifier'***
The compiler detected a method call, but the call contained more arguments than needed.

0077   **Not enough arguments for method *'identifier'***
The compiler detected a method call, but the call contained fewer arguments than needed. This error most likely occurs when one or more arguments are accidentally omitted from the call.

0078   **Class *'identifier'* doesn't have a method that matches *'identifier'***
The compiler identified a call to an overloaded method within another class, but was unable to find a matching method with the correct number of arguments.

0079   **Ambiguity between 'identifier' and *'identifier'***
The compiler could not distinguish the correct method to execute. This error most likely occurs when the method parameters specified in a call do not exactly match any of those defined within the called methods declaration or any of its base classes.

0080   **Value for argument *'identifier'* cannot be converted from *'identifier'* in call to *'identifier'***
The compiler detected a method argument that does not match the parameters specified in the method declaration.

0081   **Value for argument *'identifier'* cannot be converted from *'identifier'* in call to *'identifier'***
The compiler detected a method call, but was unable to convert one of the arguments from the supplied type to the type supplied in the method declaration. This error most likely occurs when either a method is called with the arguments in the wrong order, or the wrong method was called.

0082 **Class 'identifier' doesn't have a constructor that matches 'identifier'**
The compiler did not detect a constructor matching the call identified in the error. This error most likely occurs when a constructor is called with the wrong number of arguments.

0083 **'super( )' may only be called within a constructor**
The compiler detected use of the keyword **super** within a method. This keyword can only be used within a constructor.

0084 **Can't return a value from a 'void' method**
The compiler detected a **return** statement within the body of a method declared with a return type of **void**.

0085 **Expected return value of type 'identifier'**
The compiler detected the keyword **return** within the body of a method which was declared to **return** a specific type, but the return had no associated value.

0086 **'[ ]' cannot be applied to a value of type 'identifier'**
The compiler detected array brackets used with a non-array variable type.

0087 **The 'goto' statement is not currently supported by Java**
The keyword **goto**, while defined as a keyword, has not yet been implemented in the Java language.

0088 Not currently used.

0089 **Already had case: 'identifier'**
The compiler identified two or more **case** statements having the same identifier or value occurring within the same **switch** statement.

0090 **Already had 'default'**
The compiler identified two or more instances of the keyword **default** occuring within the same switch statement.

0091 **'case' outside of switch statement**
The compiler identified the keyword **case** used outside the scope of a **switch** statement.

0092 **Constant expression expected**
The keyword **const**, while defined as a keyword, has not yet been implemented in the Java language.

0093 **'break' only allowed in loops and switch statements**
The compiler detected the keyword **break** occuring outside the scope of a loop or **switch** statement.

0094 **Label 'identifier' not found**
The compiler detected a label name associated with one of the keywords **continue** or **break**, but could not find the label.

0095 **'continue' only allowed in loop**
The compiler detected attempted use of the keyword **continue** outside the scope of a loop.

0096 **Class value expected**
The compiler detected a synchronization block, but the **synchronized** modifier was applied to an invalid type.

0097 **Class or array expected**
The compiler detected the **instanceof** operator applied to a type that did not resolve to a class or array.

0098 **Attempt to access nonexistent member of *'identifier'***
The compiler detected an array member specified, but could not identify it.

0099 Not currently used.

0100 **Cannot throw *'identifier'*—the type doesn't inherit from 'Throwable'**
The compiler detected an object in a **throw** statement that was not derived from the class Throwable.

0101 **The type *'identifier'* does not inherit from *'Throwable'***
The compiler detected an invalid class argument used as an argument in a **catch** declaration.

0102 **Handler for *'identifier'* hidden by earlier handler for *'identifier'***
The compiler detected an exception handler that will never be executed because an earlier handler would have already caught the exception. This error is most likely caused by putting catch statements in the wrong order.

0103 **Cannot override final method *'identifier'***
The compiler detected a class method attempting to override one of its base class methods, but the base class method was declared with the keyword **final**.

0104 **Unreachable statement or declaration**
The compiler detected a statement or declaration that cannot be reached under any circumstances.

0105 **Method *'identifier'* must return a value**
The compiler detected a method declaration which included a return type other than **void**, but the keyword **return** was not found in the method body.

0106 **Class *'identifier'* has a circular dependency**
The compiler detected two or more classes directly or indirectly attempting to subclass each other.

0107 **Missing array dimension**
The compiler detected the initialization of an array, but failed to detect a valid array dimension.

0108 **Cannot 'new' an instance of type *'identifier'***
The compiler detected an attempt to instantiate a data type that does not require use of the keyword **new.**

0109 **Cannot 'new' an instance of abstract class *'identifier'***
The compiler detected an attempt to instantiate a class object declared as **abstract**.

0110 **Cannot 'new' an interface *'identifier'***
The compiler detected an attempt to instantiate an interface object declared as **abstract**. Note that interfaces are abstract by default, regardless whether the keyword **abstract** is used in their declaration.

0111 **Invalid use of array initializer**
The compiler detected an attempt to initialize an array, but the initialization statement was not syntactically correct.

0112 **Cannot assign final variable *'identifier'***
The compiler detected an attempt to change the value of a variable declared as **final**.

0113   **Call to constructor must be first in constructor**
The compiler detected a constructor called from within the body of a second constructor, but the constructor call was not placed at the beginning of the second constructor body.

0114   **Cannot reference 'this' in constructor call**
The compiler detected a reference to **this** in a constructor. As the object has not been fully created while in the constructor, references to **this** are illegal in constructors.

0115   **Cannot call constructor recursively**
The compiler detected a recursive constructor call.

0116   **Variable *'identifier'* may be used before initialization**
The compiler detected an attempt to use a variable before it was properly initialized.

0117   **Cannot declare a class to be 'private'**
The compiler detected use of the modifier **private** in a class declaration. This modifier may only be used with variables and methods.

0118   **Too many local variables in method—must be ≤ 256**
The compiler detected more than 256 local variables defined within a method. Try reducing the number of variables local to the method and compile again.

0119   **Too much code in method**
The compiler could not support the number of instructions local to a particular method. Try reducing the code in your larger methods by dividing them into smaller, more general purpose methods, and compile again.

0120   The compiler detected a division by zero error in code.

0121   **Unable to recover from previous error(s)**
The compiler encountered a serious error and could not continue processing the file reliably. Try fixing whatever errors are already flagged and compile again.

0122   **Exception *'identifier'* not caught or declared by *'identifier'***
The compiler detected an exception that was thrown but never caught within the exception class.

0123   **Multiple inheritance of classes is not supported**
The compiler detected a class attempting to apply the keyword extends to more than one base class. The Java language does not support multiple inheritance.

0124   **Operator cannot be applied to 'identifier' values**
The compiler detected an operator being applied to an invalid type.

0125   **'finally' without 'try'**
The compiler detected the keyword **finally** but did not find a corresponding **try** statement.

0126   **'catch' without 'try'**
The compiler detected the keyword **catch** but did not find a corresponding **try** statement.

0127   **'else' without 'if'**
The compiler detected the keyword **else** but did not find a corresponding **if** statement.

0128 **Cannot declare an interface to be 'final'**
The compiler detected an interface declared with the keyword final.

0129 **Cannot declare a class to be 'abstract' and 'final'**
The compiler detected a class declared with the keywords **abstract** and **final**.

0130 **Cannot declare an interface method to be 'native', 'static', 'synchronized', or 'final'**
The compiler detected one of the keywords shown above used in the declaration of an interface method.

0131 **Cannot declare a method to be *'identifier'* and *'identifier'***
The compiler detected the use of two or more incompatible modifiers in the declaration of a method.

0132 **Cannot declare a field to be *'identifier'* and *'identifier'***
The compiler detected the use of two or more incompatible modifiers in the declaration of a variable.

0133 **Constructors cannot be declared 'native', 'abstract', 'static', 'synchronized', or 'final'**
The compiler detected the use of one of the modifiers shown above in the declaration of a constructor.

0134 **Interfaces cannot have constructors**
The compiler detected an interface containing a constructor declaration.

0135 **Interface data members cannot be declared 'transient' or 'volatile'**
The compiler detected one of the modifiers shown above used in the declaration of a interface member variable.

0136 **Public class *'identifier'* should not be defined in *'identifier'***
The compiler detected more than class declared with the keyword **public** in a source file.

0137 **Code page *'identifier'* not supported**
The compiler detected an unsupported system code page. Refer to your Operating System help for instructions on changing the system code page.

0138 **Interface cannot have static initializer**
The compiler detected a **static** initializer within an interface.

0139 **Invalid label**
The compiler detected an invalid label.

0140 **Cannot override static method *'identifier'***
The compiler detected an attempt to override a **static** method from within a subclass.

0141 **Argument cannot have type void**
The compiler detected a method argument defined as type **void**.

0142 **Cannot make direct (nonvirtual) call to abstract method *'identifier'***
The compiler detected an attempt to directly call an abstract method.

0143 **Cannot throw exception *'identifier'* from initializer *'identifier'***
The compiler detected an attempt to throw an exception from within a static initializer.

0144   **Cannot find definition for interface *'identifier'***
The compiler could not locate a definition for the named interface.

0145   **Output directory too long: *'identifier'***
The output directory exceeded 228 characters in length. Try shortening the length of the output directory path and compile again.

0146   **Cannot create output directory *'identifier'***
The output directory could not be created. This error most likely occurs when you do not have write permission on the specified drive.

0147   **Cannot access private member *'identifier'* in class *'identifier'* from *'identifier'***
The compiler detected an invalid attempt to access a private member contained within another class.

0148   **Cannot reference instance method *'identifier'* before super-class constructor has been called**
The compiler detected an attempt to reference an instance method before the superclass constructor was called.

0149   **The value *'identifier'* cannot be represented by type *'identifier'***
The compiler detected an invalid conversion during an assignment.

0150   **Cannot have repeated interface *'identifier'***
The compiler detected an interface name being repeated within a class declaration.

0151   **Variable *'identifier'* is already defined in this method**
The compiler detected two variables with the same name defined twice within the same scope of a method.

0152   **Ambiguous reference to *'identifier'* in interfaces *'identifier'* and *'identifier'***
The compiler detected an ambiguous reference to an identifier. The identifier may have been declared in two or more interfaces, and the compiler could not determine which reference to use.

0153   **Could not load type library *'identifier'*—LoadTypeLib( ) failed**
The compiler failed to load the specified type library. This error may occur in any of the following situations:
- The system is low on available memory.
- Adequate write permissions do not exist.
- Adequate read permissions do not exist.
- The library has an unsupported format.
- The LCID could not be found in the OLE support DLLs.
- The type library or DLL could not be loaded.

0154   **Could not get library attribute**
The compiler failed to retrieve the library's attributes. This error may occur in any of the following situations:
- The system is low on available memory.
- Adequate write permissions do not exist.
- Adequate read permissions do not exist.
- The library has an unsupported format.
- The library could not be opened.

0155   **Could not get library name**

The compiler failed to retrieve the type library's name. This error may occur in any of the following situations:
- The system is low on available memory.
- Adequate write permissions do not exist.
- Adequate read permissions do not exist.
- The library has an unsupported format.
- The library could not be opened.

0156 **Could not load library *'identifier'* looking for *'identifier'***
The compiler could not load the library. This error may occur in any of the following situations:
- The system is low on available memory.
- Adequate write permissions do not exist.
- Adequate read permissions do not exist.
- The library has an unsupported format.
- The library could not be opened.

0157 **Could not load type *'identifier'* from library *'identifier'***
The compiler could not load the specified type. This error may occur in any of the following situations:
- The system is low on available memory.
- Adequate write permissions do not exist.
- Adequate read permissions do not exist.
- The library has an unsupported format.
- The library could not be opened.

0158 **Class *'identifier'* already defined**
The compiler detected two or more classes defined with the same name.

0159 **'@' must be followed by the response file name**
The compiler did not detect a response file following the character @. Supply the response file name and compile again.

0160 **Response file *'identifier'* could not be opened**
The compiler could not open the response file for reading. This error most likely occurs when the response file does not exist or cannot be found.

0161 **Cannot open source file: *'identifier'***
The source file shown could not be opened. This error most likely occurs when the file name specified does not exist or cannot be found.

0162 **Failed to initialize compiler—maybe you didn't set the class path?**

0163 **Array *'identifier'* missing array index**
The compiler detected access to an array type, but the index value was missing.

0164 **Ambiguous import of class *'identifier'* from more than one package**

0165 **Cannot throw exception *'identifier'* from method *'identifier'*— it is not a subclass of any exceptions thrown from overloaded method *'identifier'*.**

0166 **Cannot access member *'identifier'* in class *'identifier'* from *'identifier'*—it is in a different package**

0167   **Nonstatic methods can't be overridden by a static method**

0168   **The declaration of an abstract method must appear within an abstract class**

The compiler detected a method declared with the modifier abstract within a class that was not defined as abstract.

0169   **Cannot access *'identifier'*—only public classes and interfaces in other packages can be accessed.**

5001   **Local variable *'identifier'* is initialized but never used**

The compiler detected an initialized variable that was never referenced in any class code. This message occurs at warning level 3 or greater.

5002   **Compiler option *'identifier'* is not supported**

5003   **Ignoring unknown compiler option *'identifier'***

The command line option provided was not found. This warning is most likely caused by a typographical error.

5004   **Missing argument for compiler option *'identifier'***

5005   **Package *'identifier'* was already implicitly imported.**

5006   **'private protected' not supported, using 'protected'.**

5007   **Nonstandard conversion from *'identifier'* to *'identifier'*.**

Glossary of Terms

.AU file   A standardized file format containing audio data. Currently the only natively supported sound data format in Java.

.CLASS file   See also *.JAVA* file. The compiled byte code result file of an input *.JAVA* class.

.DLL file   Dynamic Link Library. A code library which may be called dynamically as require rather then statically linked to an application.

.EXE file   Executable format file.

.GIF file   Graphics Interchange format file. A .GIF file normally contains some sort of graphical image.

.HTML file   Hypertext markup language file. A .HTML file normally contains commands for creating and displaying a Web page.

.JAVA file   Java language file. A .Java file normally contains code and commands written in the Java language.

.JPEG file   See *.JPG*.

.JPG file   Joint Photographic Group format. A .JPG file normally contains some sort of graphical image.

.MAK file   See also *.MDP* file. Pronounced *make*. A file that contains commands for building an application. Under Visual J++ a .MAK file has the same name as its corresponding .MDP file.

.MDP file   Visual workspace configuration file. A configuration file contains all the settings and options associated with a Visual J++ project.

.RES file   Resource file. A file containing resources such as dialogs, menus and strings which can be bound into a program at link time.

.WAV file   A standardized file format for storing waveform audio data.

ActiveX   See also *OLE* and *COM*. common term used to describe a set of technologies based on Microsoft COM, but excluding OLE.

Append   To add to the back of a string or list of objects.

Applet   A small program that is not intended to be run on its own, but to be embedded inside another application and which is derived from the Java **Applet** superclass.

Application   An application may be run stand-alone, see *applet*, and must contain a class which defines a main method.

Asynchronous function   A type of function which returns immediately, even though the function may still be executing. Asynchronous functions enable an application to continue with other processing work and check for completion of the function later.

Asynchronous   Not synchronous.

Attribute   A variable contained within a *class* which may or may not be externally visible.

Breakpoint   A location in a program from which execution can be stopped or controlled. *Breakpoints* allow developers to examine program state, change variables and resume or cancel program execution.

Call Stack   A list of functions, normally ordered from most recent to least, which have been called but have not yet returned.

Class   A definition of the interface, variables and methods of a particular object is called a *class*. A class can be thought of as describing a template for creating instances of objects.

COM   Common Object Model. COM defines a standard for development of cross-platform applications.

Compiler   A tool for turning raw code into an executable or *compiled* image.

Configuration   Within projects you normally have one or more *configurations* which contains settings and control the way the end result is built. Projects start with both a debug and a release *configuration* and you can add additional *configurations* and change the settings associated with a *configuration* as required.

Constructor   A special method called by compiler when an object is first created or *constructed*. Normally contains initialization code.

Debugger   A tool for manipulating and examining the state of variables etc. in executing code.

Destructor   A special method called by the compiler when an object is *destroyed*. Normally contains clean up code.

Dithered   The process of arranging adjacent pixels (See *Pixel*) to contain different color values such that when view from a distance they seem to represent a third color which is a combination of the original two.

Embedding   The process of placing an instance of an OLE object into a container object is called *embedding*.

Encapsulation   The process of hiding the internals of a object is often called *encapsulation*.

Event   See *Message.*

Exception   An event which occurs outside the normal process of an application is often called an *exception.* Division by zero is an example of an arithmetic *exception.*

Field   See *Attribute.*

Framework   A group of one or more classes which implement basic functionality required by all applications is often called a *framework.* MFC and the Java AWT are examples of frameworks.

HTML   See *HTML* files.

Inheritance   When a sub class is created from a parent class we say the sub class *inherits* the public attributes and method of the parent class. These methods and variables may then be available to the child class.

Instantiation   The process of construction of an object is often referred to as *instantiation.* When an actual instance of a class is created, that class is said to be *instantiated.*

Interface   An *interface* is a specification of how one class may interact with another.

JVM   The Java Virtual Machine. The Java Virtual Machine interprets or runs the byte code files downloaded to a browser.

Light Weight Process   See *Thread.*

Marshal   To assemble and dispatch. Marshalling is the process of collecting variables and then transferring them to an underlying function often across process boundaries.

Member function   See *Method.*

Member variable   See *Attribute.*

Message   Some externally or internally generated event which is delivered to an application. The application may then act on this *message* or ignore it.

Method   A function contained within a class which may or may not be externally callable.

Mnemonic   Letters which are underlined in a menu or dialog and which are called *mnemonics.* For an active menu or dialog, pressing the key which corresponds to the mnemonic causes the associated function to be executed.

Multiple Inheritance   When a class has two or more parents that class is said to be defined as having *multiple inheritance.* Java does not support multiple inheritance.

Multiprocessing   The process of running more then one application of thread within a application or operating system at one time is often called *multiprocessing.*

Multi-Threaded   When an application which contains two or more concurrent and independent threads of execution, any of which may be active at one time, is called *multi-threaded.*

Object Linking and Embedding A definition and support libraries for sharing information between applications.

OLE Pronounce Oh-lay. See *Object Linking and Embedding*.

OOP Object Oriented Programming.

Package A group of classes declared with the *package* keyword. Classes which logically go together are often collected into a *package*.

Palette, color A group of colors available to an application or specific to a device.

Pixel Picture Element. Normally the smallest addressable unit of a display device.

Platform The underlying software and hardware which support a programming language.

Polymorphic From the greek poly meaning many and morph meaning forms. Taking many forms. In standard OOP many classes will have methods with the same names (**print** for example). These like named methods are said to be *polymorphic* to each other.

Prepend To add to the front of a string or list of objects.

Project A *project* is a set of some number of source files and at least one configuration. The project itself specifies what will build. That is a **.class** file or an **.EXE** or something else.

RCT file **R**esour**C**e **T**emplate file. Also see *.RES*. A resource template file contains resources such as dialogs, menus and strings. However, unlike a .RES file a resource template may be used as the starting point for developing other resources

Register A small special purpose piece of memory on a board which is used for a very specific purpose such as tracking the current program instruction or adding two integers.

Resource A *resource* is a particular piece of code or data which may be used by one or more applications. Windows resources are typically the strings, dialogs, menus and similar items which make up the applications user interface.

Static A method, variable or instance of an object which cannot be changed or manipulated is called *static*.

Stream Java provides a standard set of input, output and error functions normally called *streams* within **java.lang.System** and called **in**, **out**, and **err**.

Synchronous 1. Happening, existing, or arising at the same time 2: recurring or operating at exactly the same periods.

Tab Order The order in which the cursor moves from field to field when the tab key is pressed is called *tab order*.

Thread A unit of granularity within a program or application which may be run consecutively with other *threads*.

Try/Catch/Throw A structured method for handling unexpected programming events or executions. You *try* a function, *catch* any errors that the underlying function may have *thrown*.

WYSIWYG What you see is what you get.

Index

abstract method, 83, 84
Abstract modifier, 74
Access, 477
ActiveX
  basics, 435–438
    ActiveX elements, 435–436
    ActiveX and other platforms,
      437–438
    Java applets as seen from
      COM, 437
  using ActiveX from Java,
    438–442
    examining javabeep.java,
      440–441
    handling COM exceptions,
      441–442
  Wizard, using, 491–499
Ada95, 28
ad hoc cast, 57
Animation, 246, 249–251,
  415–432
  arrays of pixels, 430–432
  creating a minimal animation
    with the applet wizard,
    416–425
    animation object fields,
      416–417
    constructor, 417
    destroy method, 418
    general animation support
      methods, 418–419
    getting started, 416

    init method, 417–418
    paint and update methods,
      419–420
    run method, 421–425
    start and stop methods, 421
  double buffering, 428–429
  eliminating flicker, 430
  issues pertaining to
    performance, 425–428
  overview of animation, 415–416
  use of clipRect method, 429
Applet class, 125–127
AppletContext interface,
  130–131
Applet Wizard, 50. *See also* Java
  Applet Wizard; Java
  AppWizard
ArithmeticException, 71
Array declarations, 62, 63
Arrays, 53
Arrays of pixels, 430–432
AudioClip interface, 131
Authenticode, 472, 473–474
AWT. *See* Java Abstract Window
  Toolkit

Bitmap, converting to an image
  file, 342
BitSet, 192
Bitwise arithmetic, 48
Blocks of statements, 59
Bookmarks, 395–396

  named, 395–396
  unnamed, 395
Booleans, 36, 52, 53, 57
Boolean wrapper class, 106
BorderLayout, 164–165
Breakpoints, and debugging,
  295–301
  managing breakpoints with
    the Breakpoints dialog,
    297–299
  setting conditional
    breakpoints, 300–301
  setting simple breakpoints,
    296–297
break statements, 68
Build menu, 18
Button, 145–146
Byte, 73
Byte arrays, 181–182
Byte code verifier, 27

C, 210–215, 456, 459
C++, 3, 4, 210–215, 434, 456
Cabinet files, 468–474
  creating, 469–472
    HTML for cabinets, 471
  signing, 472–474
    Authenticode, 473–474
    digital signing and public
      key signatures, 472–473
    reason for signing, 472
Canvas, 146

CardLayout, 165–166
Cascading menus, 361–362
Casting, 47, 56–57
Certification Authority, 474
Character wrapper class, 106–107
charAt method, 6
Checkbox, 146–147
CheckboxMenuItem, 161
Child class, 11
Choice, 147–148
Class, 5, 73
  extending, 75–76
  implementing an interface, 77
  modifiers, 74
  running as a thread, 77–78
Class class, 103
Class declaration, 60, 61
  modifiers, 74
    abstract, 74
    final, 74
    public, 74
CLASSPATH, 25
  and JVC.exe, 402, 404–405
ClassView pane, 273–279
  manipulating class
    information, 274
    adding classes to existing
      application, 274–276
    adding methods and
      variables to existing class,
      276–278
    setting breakpoints from
      within the ClassView, 279
clipRect method, 429
CLSID dialogue, 493–497
Color class, 139
Color palette, 333–336
  custom colors, 334–335
  saving and restoring color
    palettes, 335–336
  selecting foreground and
    background colors, 335
COM. *See* Component Object
  Model
Comments, 50–51
Compiler, Visual J++, 226
Compiler class, 103
Component Object Model (COM),
  434–435
  handling COM exceptions,
    441–442

Java applets as seen from
  COM, 437
  mapping COM types to Java
    types, 446–448
Component superclass, 144–145
Configurations, 281
  projects and, 287–288
Constructor, 5, 6
continue statements, 68
Copy, 384
Creating new files, 378–379
Custom brushes, 339
Custom colors, 334–335
Customizing print jobs, 397–398
Cut, 384

DAO. *See* Data Access Objects
Data Access Objects (DAO),
  461–467, 479
  opening the database, 462–464
  reading data, 466–467
  using record sets, 465–466
Datagrams, 202–205
  DatagramPacket, 202–203
  DatagramSocket, 203–205
Dates, 189–190
Deadlock, 94
Debug configuration, 281, 287
Debugger. *See* Visual J++
  debugger
Debugging techniques, 309–321
  advanced debugger features,
    312–319
    Call Stack window, 313–315
    debugging exceptions,
      317–319
    debugging threads, 315–317
  debugging a sample
    application, 310–312
  debugging compiler errors,
    309–310
  disassembly window, 320–321
Declaration statements, 60
  array declarations, 62, 63
  class declarations, 60, 61
  interface declarations, 60–61
  method declarations, 62
  object declarations, 63, 64
  primitive type declarations, 63,
    64
Delete, 384

Dialog, 153–154
  as debugger element, 291
Dialog editor, Visual J++,
  264–265
  interface, 344–357
    adding and positioning
      controls, 345–355
    control properties, 357
    defining mnemonic keys,
      355–356
    testing a dialog box, 357
DialogLayout.java class, 375–377
Dictionary class, 190
Disassembly window, 320–321
DLL. *See* Dynamically linked
  library
DoBeep method, 449
Double buffering, 428–429
Double wrapper class, 107–108
do-while statements, 66–67
Dynamically linked library
  (DLL), 212

Editing operations, 384–393
  copy, 384
  cut, 384
  delete, 384
  editing with drag-and-drop,
    385
  paste, 384
  search and replace, 385–393
Editor emulations, 396
Editor settings, 398
Empty statements, 59–60
Encapsulation, 5, 12–13
Enumerations, 187–188
Error classes in Java, 118, 120
Exceptions in Java, 113–121
  debugging, 317–319
    associating actions with
      exceptions, 319
  standard exceptions, 118, 119
  Throwable class, 114, 116
  throw and throws keywords,
    116–118
  try-catch-finally, 115–116
Expression evaluation order,
  55–56
Extending a class, 75–76
Event class, 159–160
Event-driven applications, 8

Fields, 78–80
  modifiers, 78–80
    final, 78, 79
    private, 78, 79
    protected, 78, 79
    public, 78
    static, 78, 79, 80
    transient, 78, 79
    volatile, 78, 79
File class, 177–180
FileDialog, 154–155
File operations, 378
  creating new files, 378–379
  opening existing files, 379–
    382
  opening multiple files, 382
  printing files, 383–384
    complete source file, 383
    selected text, 383
  saving files, 382–383
File pane, 262
File-Save, 23
FileView pane, 279–280
Filters, 183–184
finalize( ) method, 82–83
final method, 83, 84
Final modifier, 74
Flicker, eliminating, 430
Float wrapper class, 107–108
FlowLayout, 166
Focus events, 158
Font class, 139–140
FontMetrics class, 140
for statements, 67
Frame, 155
Frame class, 255–257

Garbage Collection, 82–83
Global Java Exception, 319
Gosling, James, 14
Graphics, 142–144
Graphics editor, Visual J++,
    226–227, 228, 259–263,
    322–342
  color palette, 333–336
  graphics editor interface,
    322–324
    viewing an image, 323–324
  graphics toolbar, 324–333
    closed figure drawing tools,
      327–328

freehand drawing and
    erasing tools, 325–326
  other tools, 328–331
  toolbar options, 332–333
Image menu, 336–338
status bar, 338
tips and tricks
  applying actions to selected
    images, 341–342
  converting a bitmap to an
    image file, 342
  custom brushes, 339
  image properties, 339–340
  pixel grid, 338–339
  resizing images, 340–341
Graphics User Interfaces (GUIs),
    7
GridBagLayout, 167–168
GridLayout, 168–169
Guarding statements, 70–71

Hash tables, 190–191
Help system, 230–231
HTML APPLET tag, 127–128

Identifiers, 40–41
IDL file, 491–493, 495–498
if statements, 65
if-else statements, 65
Image menu, 336–338
Image properties, 339–340
Images, 169–170
  displaying, 419
  loading, 418–419
Imports, 486
Incremental search, 391–392
Indenting schemes, 22
InetAddress, 199–200
InfoView pane, 272
Inheritance, 5, 11–12
init( ) method, 246, 247–248
Input, standard, 176–177
InputStream, 174–176
instanceof, 39, 44
Integer wrapper class, 108
Integrated Development
    Environment (IDE), 18
Interface, 77, 86–87
  implementing, 77
Interface declarations, 60–61
Interthread communication, 93

IOException, 178, 205
Iteration statements, 66–67
  do-while, 66–67
  for, 67
  while, 66

Jamba, 28
java (interpreter), 17
Java
  applications, 32, 72, 73
  classes, objects, and interfaces,
    72–88
  connecting to native code,
    210–216
  exceptions in, 113–121
  expressions and statements,
    52–71
  Java Abstract Window Toolkit
    (java.awt), 133–173
  Java applets and the
    java.applet package,
    122–132
  Java, COM and ActiveX,
    433–451
  java.io package, 174–185
  java.lang package, 99–112
  java.net package, 197–209
  java.util package, 186–196
  and Java Virtual Machine,
    14–31
  keywords and other tokens,
    32–51
  threads in, 89–98
Java Abstract Window Toolkit
    (java.awt), 133–173
  containers, panels, and
    components, 144–156
    Button, 145–146
    Canvas, 146
    Checkbox, 146–147
    Choice, 147–148
    Component, 144–145
    creating a new Component,
      155–156
    Label, 148–149
    List, 149
    Panel, 149–150
    Scrollbar, 150–151
    TextArea, 151–152
    Textfield, 152
    Window, 152–155

Java Abstract Window Toolkit (java.awt)
  containers, panels, and components (*cont.*)
  events and observables, 156–160
    Event class, 159–160
    focus events, 158
    key events, 158
    mouse events, 157
    Observables, 160
    other events, 158
    special event methods, 158–159
  graphics, fonts, and colors, 139–144
    Color, 139
    Font, 139–140
    FontMetrics, 140
    Graphics, 142–144
    Point, 140–141
    Polygon, 141
    Rectangle, 141–142
  Image, 169–172
  java.awt.peer package, 172
  layout managers, 163–169
    BorderLayout, 164–165
    CardLayout, 165–166
    FlowLayout, 166
    GridBagLayout, 167–168
    GridLayout, 168–169
  Menus, 160–163
    CheckboxMenuItem, 161
    Menu, 161
    MenuBar, 161
    MenuComponent, 160
    MenuContainer, 160–161
    MenuItem, 161
Java ActiveX Wizard, using, 491–499
Java applets, 32
  and java.applet package, 122–132
    Applet class, 125–127
    AppletContext interface, 130–131
    AudioClip interface, 131
    constructing an applet in an application, 128–129
    differences between applet and application, 124–125

HTML APPLET tag, 127–128
Java Applet Wizard, creating a project with, 232–242. See *also* Java AppWizard
Java AppWizard, 243–257
  Ch17Ex1.html, 244–245
  Ch17Ex1.java, 245
  class generated by AppWizard, 246
  init and paint methods, 247–249
  mouse event support, 254–255
  start, stop and run methods, 249–253
  threads within skeleton applet, 247
  standalone application support, 255–257
    main method, 256–257
  what it does, 243–244
java.awt. See Java Abstract Window Toolkit
java.awt.peer package, 172
javabeep.java, 440–441
javabeep project, 438
javac (compiler), 17
Java, COM and ActiveX, 433–451
  basics of ActiveX, 435–438
    ActiveX elements, 435–436
    ActiveX and other platforms, 436–437
    Java applets as seen from COM, 437
  Component Object Model, 434–435
  Java applications and scripting, 448–450
  Java Type Library Wizard, 442–443, 447
  mapping COM types to Java types, 446–448
  OLE Object View, 443–446
  using ActiveX from Java, 438–443
    examining javabeep.java, 440–441
    handling COM exceptions, 441–443
Java Developers Kit (JDK), 17
Java expressions, 54–58

constructing, 54–55
  examples, 57–58
  expression evaluation order, 55–56
  type conversion and casting, 56–57
javah utility, 212, 213–216
java.io package, 174–185
  byte arrays, 181–182
  files and file descriptors, 177–180
  filters, 183–184
  pipes, 183–184
  random access files, 180–181
  standard input and standard output, 176–177
  StreamTokenizer, 184
  string buffers, 181–182
  using with java.net, 206–208
Java keywords and other tokens, 32–51
  tokens, 36
    comments, 50–51
    identifiers, 40–41
    keywords, 36–39
    literals, 40–42, 43
    operators, 44–49
    separators, 42–43
    white space, 49
    unicode characters, 33–35
java.lang package, 99–112
  Math class, 108–109
  Object class, 102–103
    Class class, 103
    compiler class, 103
    String classes, 103–105
      methods, 104–105
  system-related classes, 109–111
    Process, 109
    Runtime, 109–110
    SecurityManager, 110
    System, 110–111
  wrapper classes, 105–108
    Boolean, 106
    Character, 106–107
    Double and Float, 107–108
    Integer and Long, 108
Java language, 32–33
java.net package, 197–209
  Datagrams, 202–205

DatagramPacket, 202–203
DatagramSocket, 203–205
InetAddresses, 199–200
Sockets and ServerSockets,
    205–206
URL utilities, 200–202
    URLConnection objects,
        200–202
    URLEncoder objects, 202
    URL objects, 200
using java.net and java.io
    together, 206–208
Java packages, 32, 33
java.applet, 122–132
java.awt.peer, 172
java.io, 174–185
java.lang, 99–112
java.net, 197–209
java.util, 186–196
Java programming model,
    222–224
compared with Windows
    model, 219–224
event/message processing
    model, 222–223
memory management, 224
resource-based programming,
    224
threads and multiprocessing,
    223–224
Java Resource Wizard, Visual
    J++, 364–377
DialogLayout.java class and
    user classes, 375–377
integrating a generated dialog,
    367–369
    accessing dialog controls
        data, 369
    add new class to project,
        368–369, 373
    import new class, 367
integrating a generated menu,
    369–373
    adding the menu to a frame,
        371–373
    creating a simple frame,
        370–371
simulating mnemonic keys,
    374–375
supporting mnemonic keys,
    374–375

JavaScript, 453–457
compared with Java, 454
compared with VBScript,
    460–461
events, 455
referring to Java applets in
    JavaScript, 456–457
statements, control structures,
    and looping constructs,
    456, 457
Java statements, 58–71
blocks of statements, 59
declaration statements,
    60–63
empty statements, 59–60
expression statements,
    63–64
guarding statements, 70–71
iteration statements, 66–67
jump statements, 67–69
labeled statements, 60
selection statements, 64–66
statement construction, 59
synchronization statements,
    69
unreachable statements, 60
Java Type Library Wizard,
    442–443, 447
java.util package, 186–196
BitSet, 192
dates, 189–190
enumerations, 187–188
hash tables, 190–191
observables, 194–195
random numbers, 193–194
StringTokenizer, 192–193
vectors and stacks, 191–192
Java Virtual Machine, Java and,
    14–31
Java is compiled, 18–24
Java is interpreted, 25–27
Java verifies code before
    running it, 27–28
Java checks pointers at run-
    time, 28–29
Java eliminates memory leak,
    30
Jump statements, 67–69
break, 68
continue, 68
return, 68

throw, 68–69
JVC.exe, 403–407
command syntax, 403–404
overriding CLASSPATH,
    404–405
Jview.exe, 400–402
command syntax, 400–401
examples, 401–402

Key events, 158
Keystrokes, recording and
    playing back, 397
Keywords, 36–39

Label, 148–149
Labeled statements, 60
Layout managers, 163–169
BorderLayout, 164–165
CardLayout, 165–166
FlowLayout, 166
GridBagLayout, 167–168
GridLayout, 168–169
Lea, Doug, 40
List, 149
Literals, 41–42, 43
Long wrapper class, 108

main method, 256–257
Maintainability, 7–8
make file, 225
Memory leak, 30
MenuBar, 161
Menu class, 161
MenuComponent class, 160
MenuContainer interface,
    160–161
Menu debugger, 293–295
Menu editor, Visual J++,
    265–266
interface, 358–362
    cascading menus, 361–362
    creating and manipulating
        menu entries, 358–361
    moving and manipulating
        menu items, 362
MenuItem, 161
Menus, 160–163
Methods, 5, 6, 72, 73, 80–86
constuctors, 81–82
finalize, 82–83
main method, 82

Methods (*cont.*)
  modifiers, 83–84
    abstract, 83, 84
    final, 83, 84
    native, 83, 84
    private, 83
    protected, 83
    public, 83
    static, 83, 84
    synchronized, 83, 84
  parameters, 85–86
  return values, 84–85
Method declarations, 62
Microsoft Access database, 477, 478
Microsoft Developers Studio, 221, 261
Mnemonic keys, simulating, 374–375
mode parameter, 180
Modifiers, 74, 83–84
Mouse events, 157
Mouse event support, 254–255
Multiple source windows, 393–395

Native code, connecting to, 210–216
  better alternatives to native methods, 212–213
  Java's javah utility, 213–216
  native methods, 212
native modifier, 83, 84
notify( ) method, 95

Object, 5, 72, 73
Object-based programming, 9–10
Object class, 11
Object declarations, 63, 64
Object-oriented programming concepts, 3–13
  encapsulation, 12–13
  inheritance, 11–12
  object-based programming, 9–10
  object-oriented programming, 3–7
  polymorphism, 13
  properties of object-oriented programming, 7–9
    event-driven, 8
    maintainability, 7–8

reusability, 7
scalability, 8, 9
Observables, 160, 194–195
Observer class, 195
ODBC. *See* Open Database Connectivity
OLE Object View, 443–446
On line help, 230–231
OOP. *See* Object-oriented programming
Open Database Connectivity (ODBC), 461, 462, 477
Opening existing files, 379–382
Opening multiple files, 382
Operations on selected images, 341–342
Operators, 44–49
Output, standard, 176–177
OutputStream, 174, 175, 176
Overloading, 80

Packages, 87. *See also* Java packages
paint( ) method, 246, 247–249
Panel, 149–150
Parameters, of methods, 85–86
Parent class, 11
Paste, 341, 384
Pipes, 183–184
Pixel grid, 338–339
Pixels, arrays of, 430–432
Platform Neutral, 15
Point class, 140–141
Pointers, 28–29
Polygon class, 141
Polymorphism, 5, 13
Popups, as debugger element, 292–293
POSIX threads, 97
Primitive type declarations, 63, 64
Primitive types, 37, 41, 52, 78
Printing files, 383–384
Process class, 109
Projects
  and configurations, 287–288
  and subprojects, 280–287
Project Workspace, 19–20
Properties class, 191
Property sheet. *See* Resource property sheets
Public modifier, 74
Push button properties, 265

QuickWatch, 290, 303–305
Quick zoom, 324

RandomAccessFile, 180–181
Random numbers, 193–194
RDO Applet, building, 489
Record sets, using, 465–466
Rectangle, 141–142
Redo, 385
Reference, 29, 53
Regular expressions, 385–388
Release configuration, 281, 287–288
repaint( ), 419–420
Replace, 385, 386
  replacing text, 392–393
resize method, 247
Resizing images, 340–341
  extending or cropping an entire image, 341
  shrinking or expanding an entire image, 340
  shrinking or expanding a selection, 341
Resource editor. *See* Visual J++ resource editors
Resource property sheets, 267–268
Resources, Visual J++
  creating from Insert Resource menu selection, 270–271
  creating from resource toolbar, 269–270
Resource templates, 268–269
  creating a new resource from a template, 269
  creating a new template, 268–269
  saving, 362–363
Resource Wizard, and Visual J++, 230
return statements, 68
Return values, 84–85
Reusability, 7
run( ) method, 246, 249–253
Runnable interface, 91, 92
Runtime class, 109–110
RuntimeException, 71

Saving files, 382–383
Scalability, 8, 9

Scripting, 448–450, 452–461
JavaScript, 453–457
compared with Java, 454
events, 455
JavaScript and VBScript
compared, 460–461
VBScript, 458–460
Scrollbar, 150–151
Search, 231, 385–392
finding strings across files,
389–391
incremental search, 391–392
simple and regular expression
searches, 388–389
SecurityManager, 110
Selection statements, 64–66
if, 65
if-else, 65
switch, 65–66
Separators, 42–43
ServerSockets, 205–206
Setting breakpoints, 279
in Call Stack window, 314
Settings tabs, 286–287
Single-threaded applications, 238
Sockets, 205–206
Source browser/editor, Visual
J++, 227–229
Source code control, and Visual
J++, 230
Source editor, Visual J++,
227–229, 378–399
basic editing operations,
384–393
cut, paste, copy, and delete,
384
editing with drag-and-drop,
385
search and replace, 385–393
basic file operations, 378–384
creating new files, 378–379
opening existing files,
379–382
opening multiple files, 382
printing files, 383–384
saving files, 382–383
tips and tricks
customizing print jobs,
397–398
editor emulations, 396
editor settings, 398

recording and playing back
keystrokes, 397
syntax coloring, 396
using bookmarks, 395–396
using multiple source
windows, 393–395
Special event methods, 158–159
SQL queries, 465–466, 467
Stacks, 191–192
Standalone application support,
255–257
Standalone interpreter, 287
used in debugging, 290
start( ) method, 246, 247,
249–250
Static method, 84
Status bar, graphics editor, 338
Step functions, 301–302
stop( ) method, 246, 249, 250
StreamTokenizer, 184
StringBuffer class, 104
methods, 105
String buffers, 181–182
String classes, 103–105
String object, 6
Strings, 103
String tables, 267
StringTokenizer, 192–193
Subclass, 11
Subprojects
building, 284
and projects, 280–287
Superclass, 11
Support classes, 486–487
switch statements, 65–66
Synchronization statements, 69
synchronized method, 84
Syntax coloring, 396
changing the default syntax
coloring scheme, 396
System class, 110–111

telnet, 207–208
TextArea, 151–152
Textfield, 152
ThreadGroups, 97
Threads, 77
debugging, 315–317
in Java, 89–98
interthread communication,
93
POSIX threads, 97

Runnable interface, 92
Thread class, 91–92
ThreadGroups, 97
using synchronized, 93–94
using wait and notify, 95
within skeleton applet, 247
Throwable class, 114, 116
throw keyword, 116–118
throws keyword, 116–117
throw statements, 68–69
Tip of the Day dialog box, 19
Tokens, 36. *See also* Java
keywords and other
tokens
Toolbar
debugger, 294, 295
dialog editor, 264
graphics editor, 263, 324–333
Project Workspace, 281
Tools, Visual J++, 400–411
JVC.exe, 403–407
command syntax, 403–404
overriding CLASSPATH,
404–405
Jview.exe, 400–402
command syntax, 400–401
examples, 401–402
Windiff.exe, 407–410
Windiff interface, 407–410
Zoomin.exe, 410–411
Top-level project, building, 284
Trusted vs Untrusted classes,
467–468
try-catch-finally, 115–116
statement, 70
Type conversion, 56
Typeinfos, 444, 445

Undo, 385
Unicode characters, 33–35
Unreachable statements, 60
update method, 419–420
URL utilities, 200–202
URLConnection objects,
200–202
URLEncoder objects, 202
URL objects, 200
Utilities, 186–187

valueOf methods, 6
Variables window, 305, 308
VBScript, 458–461

VBScript (*cont.*)
  compared with JavaScript,
    460–461
  referring to Java applets in
    VBScript, 460
  statements, control structures,
    and looping constructs,
    459–460
  variables in VBScript, 459
Vectors, 191–192
Visibility modifiers, 78, 83
Visual C++, 466
Visual J++
  Database Wizard, 476–490
  debugger, 289–308
  debugging technique, 309–321
  Developers Studio and the
    build process, 219–231
  dialog editor, 264–265, 344–357
  graphics editor, 259–263,
    322–342
  Java AppWizard, 232–257
  Java Resource Wizard, 364–377
  menu editor, 265–266,
    358–362
  resource editors, 258–259
  source editor, 378–399
  tools, 400–411
  workspace, 272–288
Visual J++ Database Wizard,
    476–490
  building an RDO Applet, 489
  creating a database applet
    with DAO, 479–486
  modifying the code, 489
  overview of, 476–486
  sample database, 478–479
  understanding the generated
    code, 486–488
    Applet, an overview,
      487–488
    imports, 486
    support classes, 486–487
Visual J++ debugger, 226, 227,
    289–308
  debugger basics, 289–290
    setting up applet or
      application for debugging,
      290
  debugger interface, 290–308
    breakpoints and watches,
      295–308

controlling execution in
    other ways, 301–302
  elements of, 291–293
  menu, 293–295
Visual J++ Developers Studio
  and the build process,
    219–231
  comparison of Windows and
    Java programming
    models, 219–224
  Java programming model,
    222–224
  Windows programming
    model, 219–222
  creating a project with Java
    AppWizard, 232–242
  features of Visual J++
    Developers Studio,
    226–231
  compiler, 226
  debugger, 226, 227
  graphics editor, 226–227, 228
  on line help (InfoView),
    230–231
  resource editor, 229–230
  source browser/editor,
    227–229
  Visual J++ and the Resource
    Wizard, 230
  Visual J++ and source code
    control, 230
  Visual J++ Workbench, 224–225
Visual J++ resource editors,
    229–230, 258–271
  creating resources, 269–271
  dialog editor, 264–265
  graphics editor, 259–263
  menu editor, 265–266
  resource editors, 258–259
  resource property sheets,
    267–268
  resource templates, 268–269
  string tables, 267
Visual J++ workspace, 272–288
  ClassView pane, 273–279
  FileView pane, 279–280
  projects and configurations,
    287–288
  projects and subprojects,
    280–287
  building projects and
    subprojects, 284–285

creating a project workspace
    with subprojects, 282–284
  creating a simple project
    workspace, 281
  project and subproject
    settings, 285–287
  simplest configuration, 281

wait( ) method, 95
Watch window, 290, 302–303,
    305–307
while statements, 66
White space, 49
  used in expressions, 55
Windiff.exe, 407–410
  Windiff interface, 407–410
    edit menu, 408
    expand menu, 409–410
    expand/outline button,
      407–408
    file menu, 408
    mark menu, 410
    options menu, 410
    view menu, 409
Window, 152–155
  Dialog, 153–154
  FileDialog, 154–155
  Frame, 155
Windows, as debugger element,
    291–292
Windows programming model,
    219–222
  compared with Java model,
    219–224
  event/message processing
    model, 220–221
  memory management, 222
  other interesting features, 222
  resource-based programming,
    221–222
  threads and multiprocessing,
    221
Workspace. *See* Visual J++
    workspace
Wrapper classes, 105–108
  Boolean, 106
  Character, 106–107
  Double and Float, 107–108
  Integer and Long, 108

Zoomin.exe, 410–411

What's on the CD-ROM

The Microsoft Visual J++ SOURCEBOOK companion CD contains the following:

Directory	Content
Appendix\	Additional Visual J++ SOURCEBOOK Appendicies.
Exercses\	Selected Visual J++ SOURCEBOOK exercises completed.
Images\	Misc images of rockets and satellites.
JDKV102\	The SunSoft Java SDK Version 1.02
MindQBas\	A demo from MindQ,
AimTech\	Jamba Trial from AimTech.
Samples\	Installable version of the Visual J++ SOURCEBOOK Examples.
SampExpd\	Expanded version of the Visual J++ SOURCEBOOK Examples.

Hardware Requirements

- **Processor:** Personal computer with a 486 or higher processor running Microsoft Windows 95 or Windows NT Workstation 4.0.
- **RAM Memory:** 8MB of memory (16MB suggested)
- **Hard-disk space:** The entire install requires less then 50mb of disk space.
- **CR-ROM drive:**
- **Monitor:** The autoplay program will run at any monitor resolution but may look slightly off. 800x600 or better with 256 colors is recommended.
- Mouse or other pointing device.

Using the Software

The Java SDK V1.02(JDKV102\) is provided free of charge from SUN Microsystems. See the accompanying readme for information about installing the Java SDK.

The appendix(Appendix\) directory contains additional appendices which were not included in the text of the book. Each of these appendices is stored as rich text format file. You may view them on-line using write or any word processor which supports RTF files.

The exercises (Exercses\) directory contains answers to selected exercises. View the view Answers.rtf directly from the cdrom application or using any word processor which supports RTF files.

In addition to exercises all the book examples are included. You may install the samples to your hard drive by running the setup.exe application from the Samples\ directory or by clicking install samples from the autoplay application. Additionally all the samples are store uncompressed on the CDROM under the SampExpd\ directory. You may view and run most of the samples directly.

The images (Images\) contains miscellaneous JPG and GIF images for your enjoyment.

The CD-ROM also contains a demo from MindQ(MindQBas\) software and a Trial version of Jamba from AimTech(Aimtech\). Install either by simply clicking the appropriate button from the Autorun application or by running setup.exe in the MindQBas directory or jambatrl.exe from the Aimtech directory.

From the MindQ literature:
MindQ an introduction to Java Applets.
MindQ Publishing Inc. is a company dedicated to using multimedia technology to simplify and improve an individualís experience in using computer and communications technology.

For more information contact MindQ at:

MindQ Publishing Inc   800-646-3008
450 Springpark Place, Suite 1200.   703-708-9381
Herndon, VA 22070   www.mindq.com

From the Jamba literature:
Jamba enables webmasters, Internet developers and creative professionals to increase the business benefits of corporate websites by enlivening static pages with rich multimedia and interactivity. Jamba developers can now leverage the ubiquity of Java web browsers and operating systems, eliminating the need for browser ëplug-insí. The end result is Java for programmers and non-programmers alike.

For more information contact Aimtech at

Aimtech Corporation 603-883-0220
20 Trafalgar Square 603-883-5582 (fax)
Nashua, NH 03063-1987 www.aimtech.com

User Assistance and Information

The software accompanying this book is being provided as is without warranty or support of any kind. Should you require basic installation assistance, or if your media is defective, please call our product support number at (212) 850-6194 weekdays between 9 am and 4 pm Eastern Standard Time. Or, we can be reached via e-mail at: **wprtusw@wiley.com.**

To place additional orders or to request information about other Wiley products, please call (800) 879-4539.